VIOLENCE AND THE STATE IN LANGUEDOC, 1250–1400

Although it is often assumed that resurgent royal government eliminated so-called 'private warfare', the French judicial archives reveal nearly one hundred such wars waged in Languedoc and the Auvergne between the mid-thirteenth and the end of the fourteenth century. Royal administrators often intervened in these wars, but not always in order to suppress 'private violence' in favour of 'public justice'. They frequently recognized elites' own power and legitimate prerogatives, and elites were often fully complicit with royal intervention. Much of the engagement between royal officers and local elites came through informal processes of negotiation and settlement, rather than through the imposition of official justice. The expansion of royal authority was due as much to local cooperation as to conflict, a fact that ensured its survival during the fourteenth-century crises. This book thus provides a new narrative of the rise of the French state and a fresh perspective on aristocratic violence.

JUSTINE FIRNHABER-BAKER is a lecturer in Medieval History at the University of St Andrews.

Cambridge Studies in Medieval Life and Thought
Fourth Series

General Editor
ROSAMOND McKITTERICK
Professor of Medieval History, University of Cambridge, and Fellow of Sidney Sussex College

Advisory Editors:
CHRISTINE CARPENTER
Professor of Medieval English History, University of Cambridge

JONATHAN SHEPARD

The series *Cambridge Studies in Medieval Life and Thought* was inaugurated by G. G. Coulton in 1921; Professor Rosamond McKitterick now acts as General Editor of the Fourth Series, with Professor Christine Carpenter and Dr Jonathan Shepard as Advisory Editors. The series brings together outstanding work by medieval scholars over a wide range of human endeavour extending from political economy to the history of ideas.

This is book 95 in the series, and a full list of titles in the series can be found at: www.cambridge.org/medievallifeandthought

VIOLENCE AND THE STATE
IN LANGUEDOC, 1250–1400

JUSTINE FIRNHABER-BAKER

CAMBRIDGE
UNIVERSITY PRESS

CAMBRIDGE
UNIVERSITY PRESS

University Printing House, Cambridge CB2 8BS, United Kingdom

Cambridge University Press is part of the University of Cambridge.

It furthers the University's mission by disseminating knowledge in the pursuit of education, learning and research at the highest international levels of excellence.

www.cambridge.org
Information on this title: www.cambridge.org/9781316635056

© Justine Firnhaber-Baker 2014

This publication is in copyright. Subject to statutory exception and to the provisions of relevant collective licensing agreements, no reproduction of any part may take place without the written permission of Cambridge University Press.

First published 2014
First paperback edition 2016

A catalogue record for this publication is available from the British Library

Library of Congress Cataloguing in Publication data
Firnhaber-Baker, Justine.
Violence and the state in Languedoc, 1250–1400 / Justine Firnhaber-Baker.
pages cm. – (Cambridge studies in medieval life and thought. Fourth series)
Includes bibliographical references.
ISBN 978-1-107-03955-1 (hardback)
1. Languedoc (France) – History, Military. 2. Languedoc (France) – Social conditions. 3. Languedoc (France) – Politics and government. 4. Aristocracy (Social class) – France – Languedoc – History – To 1500. 5. Elite (Social sciences) – France – Languedoc – History – To 1500. 6. Violence – France – Languedoc – History – To 1500. 7. Social conflict – France – Languedoc – History – To 1500. 8. State, The – History – To 1500. 9. France – Politics and government – 987–1328. 10. France – Politics and government – 1328–1589. I. Title.
DC611.L298F57 2014
944'.8025–dc23
2014002991

ISBN 978-1-107-03955-1 Hardback
ISBN 978-1-316-63505-6 Paperback

Cambridge University Press has no responsibility for the persistence or accuracy of URLs for external or third-party internet websites referred to in this publication, and does not guarantee that any content on such websites is, or will remain, accurate or appropriate.

For Audrey and Sophie and in memory of Sylvia

CONTENTS

Contents

ILLUSTRATIONS

ACKNOWLEDGEMENTS

Many people, in France, Britain, and the USA, have contributed time, knowledge, and support to this project. I cannot thank them all, and I cannot thank them enough. At Harvard, Tom Bisson taught me that lordship was fundamental to the experience of power in the Middle Ages and then gave me the time and space to figure out the rest for my own stubborn self. Katy Park and Charlie Donahue were careful readers of the dissertation that has become this book and asked pertinent questions at the right time. I am especially grateful to Katy for mentorship that reaches back to my undergraduate days at Wellesley. I am also very grateful to Fred Cheyette and to Peggy Brown, who both went out of their way in my early days in Paris to help me outline the contours of the project. I am especially grateful to Peggy for her on-going friendship, not to mention her incredible generosity in running over to the archives to check something for me every once in a while.

In France, I owe everything to the staffs of the Archives nationales and the Bibliothèque nationale, as well as to archivists in Montauban, Toulouse, Albi, Narbonne, and Montpellier. At the Archives nationales, the scholars at the Centre d'étude d'histoire juridique working on the Parlement and Françoise Hildesheimer herself made their various data-bases and card catalogues available to me. Without them, I simply could not have navigated series X. I also benefited from the hospitality of Hélène Débax and Mireille Mousnier in Toulouse, and back again in Paris, the International Medieval Society/Société internationale des médiévistes gave me a community of young scholars, many of whom continue to be close friends and intellectual partners. Meredith Cohen, Mark O'Tool, and Elma Brenner have my particular thanks.

In Britain, Chris Wickham and Paul Brand gave insightful feedback and formal mentorship, though talks over meals are probably where I learned most from them. Indeed, I am very grateful to all the fellows of All Souls College for the intellectual stimulation that their company provided

Acknowledgements

during my post-doctoral years. Finally, at St Andrews, where this project was finished, Chris Given-Wilson, John Hudson, and James Palmer read and commented on the whole manuscript or parts of it, for which I thank them kindly.

I have been the lucky beneficiary of a number of grants and fellowships without which I could not have spent the time or afforded the travel to go and look at so many crumbling bits of parchment. A Bourse Chateaubriand supported my first year in France, and the second year was made possible by a Sheldon fellowship from Harvard and a Thomas Jefferson fellowship from Wellesley. A Whiting dissertation completion fellowship allowed me to complete my dissertation, and a post-doctoral research fellowship from All Souls College, Oxford gave me the time to turn that text into what I hope is a proper book. I am thankful to all of these funders and hope that I have repaid their generosity.

The most important support over the past decade has been the love and patience of my family. I am particularly grateful to Mathew and Audrey Schwartz, to the Schwartz family, and to the Palmers. My parents, step-mother, brother-in-law, and my sisters Vanessa and Kate have all been wonderful to come home to, even if they can't understand why I have to live so bloody far away. Finally, thanks again to James, this time for coffee, cake, and all the rest of it.

ABBREVIATIONS

AD	Archives départementales
AHR	*American Historical Review*
AM	Archives municipales
AN	Paris, Archives nationales de France
BEC	*Bibliothèque de l'École des chartes*
BN	Bibliothèque nationale de France, Paris
CTSEEH	Collections de textes pour servir à l'étude et à d'enseignement de l'histoire
DI	Collection de documents inédits sur l'histoire de France
EHR	*English Historical Review*
Gallia regia	*Gallia regia, ou état des officiers royaux des bailliages et des sénéchaussées de 1328 à 1515*, ed. G. Dupont-Ferrier, 6 vols. Paris, 1942–61.
HF	*Recueil des historiens des Gaules et de la France*, ed. M. Bouquet *et al.*, 24 vols. in 25. Paris, 1738–1904.
HL	C. Devic and J.-J. Vaissete, *Histoire générale de Languedoc avec des notes et les pièces justificatives*, new ed. by A. Molinier *et al.*, 16 vols. Toulouse, 1872–1904.
l.t.	*livres tournois*
LTC	*Layettes du Trèsor des chartes*, ed. A. Teulet *et al.*, 5 vols. Paris, 1863–1909.
Mansi	*Sacrorum conciliorum nova et amplissima collectio*, ed. J. D. Mansi, 31 vols. Florence and Venice, 1759–98.
MGH	Monumenta Germaniae Historica
Olim	*Les Olim ou registres des arrêts rendu par la cour du roi...*, ed. A. Beugnot, 3 vols. in 4. Paris, 1839–48.
Ord.	*Les ordonnances des rois de France de la troisième race...*, ed. E. de Laurière *et al.*, 21 vols. and supplement. Paris, 1723–1849.

List of abbreviations

RH	*Revue historique*
RHDFE	*Revue historique de droit français et étranger*
SHF	Société de l'histoire de France
X	*Liber extra (= Decretales Gregorii IX)*. . ., ed. E. Friedberg in *Decretalium collectiones*, Leipzig, 1881; ed. with glosses, Lyon, 1553.

MAP

Languedoc and the Auvergne in 1360

INTRODUCTION

History, historians, and seigneurial war

In the spring of 1348 a war (*guerra*) broke out in southern France between
Géraud de la Barthe (or la Barre), lord of Aure, and Hugh, lord of Arpajon,
over the marital fate of an heiress named Hélène de Castelnau.[1] Hélène's
late father had specified in his will that the girl could only be married with
the agreement of her 'paternal friends and that of his barony's people',
but Hélène's widowed mother, herself having married Hugh d'Arpajon,
married the girl to her new step-son, Jean d'Arpajon.[2] Disappointed in
his hopes that these paternal friends would hand the girl and her lands to
him, Géraud de la Barthe assembled his troops and attacked the Arpajons.
According to royal pardons and other documents issued later, Géraud
gathered '200 armed and horsed men and 300 foot-soldiers', and 'with
arms and banner displayed ... on his own authority and against royal
prohibitions', he invaded Arpajon's lands. As it was reported:

They forcefully attacked the castle of Brousse and did all they could to kill the
Arpajons' people and those with them inside the castle, and they overran
Arpajons' land and that of their vassals and subjects, destroying, robbing and
damaging them ... they destroyed Brousse, the castle Caumont ... and other
places, castles, and towns, and many houses, mills, and manors, and shelters, and
they set many on fire and killed many of their men and wounded others ... and
they took many animals, foodstuffs, and other moveable goods in the Arpajon
lands and those of their vassals and subjects ...[3]

---

[1] The sources for this war include *Lettres closes, Lettres 'de par le roy' de Philippe de Valois*, ed. R. Cazelles
(Paris, 1958), no. 198; AN x2a 5, fols. 109v, 118r, 119r, 147v, 152r, 176v, 177v–178r; AN JJ 77, no.
402, fol. 247; AN JJ 78, no. 250, fol. 139; AN JJ 80, no. 60, fols. 33v–34r.

[2] AN x2a 5, fol. 118r.

[3] AN JJ 77, no. 402, fol. 247. There is a confirmation of this grant at AN JJ 80, no. 60, fols. 33v–34r. A
royal mandate issued a year later (AN x2a 5, fol. 177v–178r) provides substantially the same
narrative. The detail about the number of troops is taken from the latter document. Further
discussion can be found below, pp. 10–11, and in Chapter 3, below.

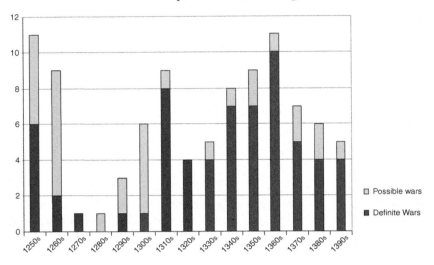

Figure 1   Seigneurial wars, 1250–1400

By such violence, Géraud succeeded in driving the Arpajons out of Hélène's lands and taking the barony (though not the girl) for himself.

The sort of war fought between Arpajon and la Barthe was not a unique occurrence. From about 1250 to about 1400, somewhere between sixty-four and ninety-five such conflicts took place in southern France alone (see Figure 1), and royal court registers, which contain dozens of cases against those making war in other parts of the kingdom, show that they were also frequent north of the River Loire.[4] Modern historians usually call such conflicts 'private wars' or 'feuds', but such terms (which never appear in the sources) belie the fact that these were substantial, organized hostilities waged between important people with significant economic and political interests at stake.[5] Indeed, when the sources use an umbrella term for them, it is usually *guerra* (war), the same term employed for the wars of the king.[6] Like that of Arpajon and la Barthe, such 'seigneurial

---

[4] See the list of southern wars in Appendix B. The definition of war and the quantification of violence are discussed below. The second section of each chapter is devoted to narrative descriptions of each war with documentary citations. Comparative cases from other parts of the kingdom are cited throughout this book, and see J. Firnhaber-Baker, 'Seigneurial War and Royal Power in Later Medieval Southern France', *Past & Present* 208 (2010): 55, nn. 48 and 50, and pp. 58–60.

[5] According to J.-P. Juchs, the first instance of *guerre privée* dates from the early seventeenth century: 'Vengeance et guerre seigneuriale au XIVe siècle (royaume de France–principauté de Liège)', Ph.D. thesis, 2 vols., Université Paris 1 Panthéon–Sorbonne, 2012, I: 53.

[6] See below, pp. 18–19.

wars' (as I will call them) normally involved castles and several hundred men, many of whom were on horseback and some of whom, especially in the mid-fourteenth century, were mercenaries.[7] They generally lasted at least several months, though some endured for years, and many affected a sizable geographic area. That of Arpajon and la Barthe, for example, involved places and fortifications in the districts of Toulouse, Beaucaire, and Cahors. Such wars were fought by lords, here meaning not only hereditary nobles holding fiscal and jurisdictional rights over a barony, but also prelates, and even town consulates, whose powers sometimes approximated those of ecclesiastical and hereditary lords. The point of these wars was nearly always to claim or exercise lordship.[8] They were fought for reasons such as conflicts over the inheritance of a barony or possession of a castle; over the right to exercise justice or to collect taxes; or, as in the la Barthe/Arpajon case, over the right to marry an heiress to a barony. Sometimes they were fought to discipline recalcitrant vassals or to assert independence from an overlord.

Such wars are historically significant in their own right as they obviously damaged local property and rearranged local power relations and land holdings. But they are also important because they speak to the relationship between lordship, violence, and justice during a key period in the development of French political history. It was in the thirteenth and early fourteenth century that the French crown consolidated and further developed the territorial, administrative, and ideological advances begun under Kings Louis VI, Louis VII, and especially Philip II Augustus. Part of this development entailed channelling disputes into judicial courts and away from the sort of violent 'self-help' of the sort that wars like that of Arpajon and la Barthe exemplified. In the process, the crown asserted royal prerogatives over a seigneurial class accustomed to independence as a result of centuries of weak centralized power. But the fourteenth century, particularly in its later decades, was one of many challenges as the plague and the Hundred Years War took their toll on the country and the crown's ability to rule. Moreover, as has been recently emphasized, monarchy was not the only type of political power undergoing change at the end of the Middle Ages. Political, military, and economic developments meant that

---

[7] For a comparison of the military aspects of seigneurial and royal conflicts, see J. Firnhaber-Baker, 'Techniques of Seigneurial War in the Fourteenth Century', *Journal of Medieval History* 36 (2010): 90–103, mercenaries at 99–101, and Chapter 4, below.

[8] Although perhaps surprising, there is almost no evidence that motives such as vengeance for slights to honour or long-standing family feuds incited seigneurial wars in southern France from 1250 to 1400. In the few cases in which such a motive seems supportable from the evidence, I have noted this, but even in these cases, there was always also *casus belli* involving money, land, or power. See pp. 42, 139–40.

3

lordship and municipal government may have changed just as much, if not more than, that of the crown, which, as recent work has argued, was more in dialogue with these other sorts of power than in opposition to them.[9] The wars of the lords, and similar conflicts fought by municipalities, thus provide an important window on to the role of violence and government in the development of political power at both the central and local levels during a critical, if tumultuous, period.

This book draws on data from the entire realm of France, but it focuses primarily on the South, here meaning the three southern seneschalsies (or administrative districts) of Languedoc seated at Toulouse, Carcassonne, and Beaucaire/Nîmes, as well as the two bailliages of the Auvergne and the Mountains of Auvergne. These areas constituted about a quarter of the kingdom of France, and much more during the decade after the Treaty of Brétigny (1360), which made huge territorial concessions to the English. This part of the kingdom is not unproblematically representative of the whole, but it is certainly not any *more* exceptional in its regional variations than, say, Normandy or Champagne, or even the Île-de-France itself. Southern society experienced the same sorts of large-scale changes underway in the rest of France, both in rural contexts, where demographic and military developments undermined traditional lord/peasant relationships, and in municipal ones, as commercial, military, and political developments made urban centres increasingly complex and important.

In fact, for the study of the development of royal power in relation to seigneurial society, the South's particularities offer considerable advantages. The region had only recently come into French royal possession following the Albigensian Crusade (1209–29), which meant that, unlike in regions closer to Paris, where the crown had to contend with long-established jurisdictional boundaries and customary rights, many of the great established powers, like the counts of Toulouse and the viscounts of Carcassonne, had been eliminated. This allowed the crown to establish its own administrative organization and even some new lordships, such as that of the Lévis in Mirepoix, in a large area that mainly consisted of royal domain land. There were still great barons – Foix, Armagnac, Comminges, and Albret – on the borders of these lands whose activities and rights impinged upon the crown in ways that those of lesser lords did not, and whom the crown had to approach based on political rather than legal and governmental considerations. But in most

---

[9] J. Watts, *The Making of Polities: Europe, 1300–1500* (Cambridge, 2009); G. Small, *Late Medieval France* (Basingstoke, 2009).

of Languedoc, the crown had the opportunity to institute structures and practices reflecting its philosophy of rule rather than the political accretions of history.

By focusing on seigneurial wars in this part of the kingdom, this book aims to understand how royal/seigneurial engagement was influenced by and in turn contributed to changes in royal government. The answers that follow may sometimes appear contradictory. At certain times and in particular contexts, the king and his officers sought to prohibit seigneurial war and to divert such conflicts into royal courts, thus asserting the superiority of coercive royal justice to violent seigneurial self-help. Yet such impulses ran contrary to other, robust tendencies, like respect for seigneurial rights and an approach to law and justice that favoured negotiation, clemency, and settlement over coercive enforcement. My central contention is that the authority of the French royal state over seigneurial violence expanded substantially in the thirteenth and fourteenth centuries, but that this occurred as much through cooperation as through coercion. Much of this development was unplanned and unintentional: the result of ad hoc administrative and bureaucratic adaptation, often in the face of challenging circumstances, in ways that sometimes competed with and sometimes complemented institutional, normative justice, and in which the lords were frequently fully complicit. There was no single trajectory of development, and many of the judicial and bureaucratic elements that became integral to later political organization coexisted with features that appear antithetical to them. While the crown did become stronger in some ways over the course of the later thirteenth and the fourteenth century, this happened differently, less intentionally, and in a less linear fashion than has been previously shown.

APPROACHES TO SEIGNEURIAL WAR

In arguing for the simultaneous growth of royal government based on coercive justice and the persistence of seigneurial self-help, I am drawing upon two historiographical approaches to medieval violence that have often appeared incompatible or even antagonistic. One emphasizes the growth of royal justice and government, paying particular attention to the development of institutions and ideology, while the second focuses on the ways that processes of disputing could create social order, even when pursued violently and/or outside institutional channels.

The first camp often depicts later medieval government as the fruit of a struggle between the crown and the lords, seeing seigneurial war as a stumbling block on the road to state-building: a relic of the violent seigneurial privilege that re-emergent royal power was well on the way to eliminating.[10] This tradition has a long pedigree, dating to at least the seventeenth century, but it remains a durable argument: thus, while at the end of the seventeenth century Charles du Cange characterized royal efforts against seigneurial war as a battle against 'a detestable custom' and a 'breach of royal authority', in 2007 Louis de Carbonnières argued that the royal court sought to suppress seigneurial war 'in order to ensure the monopoly (*monopole*) of the king's sovereign authority against the nobility's customs'.[11] This perspective is particularly characteristic of French scholarship, owing to the later experience of absolutism and to the importance of the modern *État*, but the idea of seigneurial war as primarily an impediment to the consolidation of royal power also appears in some Anglophone scholarship on France.[12] As Richard Kaeuper put it, 'When lords at all levels, and townsmen as well, sallied forth in arms to settle their own grievances, a long tradition of private rights . . . ran headlong against a developing theory of public authority vested in kingship . . .'[13] A more recent book goes even further, asserting that in France by the end of the fourteenth century, 'The private urge to violence was well on its way towards being co-opted by the institutions of public justice.'[14]

Part of the purpose of this book is to complicate this narrative of the nascent state's triumph over private violence, but that does not mean that I find it wholly unconvincing: lordship and royal government looked very different in the sixteenth century from the way that they did in the twelfth, and these changes had a great deal to do with legal, ideological, and especially administrative developments that began in the thirteenth and fourteenth centuries.[15] A preference for non-violent judicial redress over violent self-help was part of these developments. There could be no question of the crown successfully defending the sort of Weberian 'monopoly on legitimate violence' that is an integral feature of most modern

---

[10] Firnhaber-Baker, 'Seigneurial War', 38–43; H. Kaminsky, 'The Noble Feud in the Later Middle Ages', *Past & Present* 177 (2002): 55–83.

[11] C. du Fresne du Cange, 'Des guerres privées, et du droit de guerre par coutume', in *Glossarium mediae et infimae latinitatis*, new edn, 10 vols. in 5 (Niort, 1883–7), x: 100, 106; L. de Carbonnières, 'Le pouvoir royal face aux mécanismes de la guerre privée à la fin du moyen âge. L'exemple du Parlement de Paris', *Droits. Revue française de théorie, de philosophie et de culture juridiques* 46 (2007): 4.

[12] It is also characteristic of an older school of thought on later medieval English history. See n. 32, below.

[13] *War, Justice, and Public Order: England and France in the Later Middle Ages* (Oxford, 1988), 226.

[14] W. C. Brown, *Violence in Medieval Europe* (Harlow, 2011), 283.

[15] Among many others: A. Rigaudière, *Penser et construire l'état dans la France du moyen âge (XIIIe–XVe siècle)* (Paris, 2003); A. Harding, *Medieval Law and the Foundations of the State* (Oxford, 2002); J. Krynen, *L'empire du roi: Idées et croyances politiques en France, XIIIe–XVe siècle* (Paris, 1993); A. Gouron and A. Rigaudière, eds., *Renaissance du pouvoir législatif et genèse de l'état moderne* (Montpellier, 1988).

states,[16] but by the later thirteenth century, and perhaps even before, the coexistence of royal and seigneurial authority backed up by force was running into difficulty as the growth of royal government confronted long-standing seigneurial rights, privileges, and habits, including that of going to war. As this book shows, the crown did prosecute – and eventually criminally prosecute – lords who went to war against one another, and it very early on developed the administrative networks necessary to execute its judgments.

But the perdurance of seigneurial war suggests that focusing exclusively or primarily on such developments must leave out a great deal of the experience of power, violence, and government in this critical period. As this book will help to demonstrate, lords were governmental entities in their own right with the same sort of responsibilities for doing justice and maintaining peace that confronted the king. Although this could create tension, it also meant that the crown and the lords were engaged in the same project of governance and that most of the time they worked together rather well.[17] Lords' legitimate judicial and fiscal responsibilities meant that they were themselves public entities, and it is difficult to see how they could execute justice or enforce the collection of taxes without recourse to violence. Indeed, the crown recognized the forcible correction of seigneurial subjects and vassals as a legitimate cause for even large-scale violence, sometimes to an extent that resembled warfare.[18] Of course, lords themselves, not to mention their lawyers, frequently argued that their wars were licit, even if the royal courts disagreed.[19] If viewed from the perspective of lordship, rather than the royalist state, seigneurial war resembles the role that Otto Brunner identified for feud in his seminal work published in 1939, which argued that the socio-political order of medieval Austria and Bavaria was structured around lordship, an

---

[16] Max Weber's famous characterization of the state is that its 'administrative staff successfully upholds a claim to the *monopoly* of the *legitimate* use of physical force in the enforcement of its order': *The Theory of Social and Economic Organization*, ed. and trans. A. M. Henderson and T. Parsons (New York, 1947), 154, emphasis in original.

[17] There is very little scholarship on the governmental role of ordinary lords in France in the later Middle Ages. A major exception is P. Charbonnier, *Une autre France: la seigneurie rurale en Basse Auvergne du XIVe au XVIe siècle*, 2 vols. (Clermont-Ferrand, 1980), and now also see I. Mathieu, *Les justices seigneuriales en Anjou et dans le Maine à la fin du moyen âge* (Rennes, 2011). For the governmental role of the English nobility and gentry, see G. Harriss, 'Political Society and the Growth of Government in Late Medieval England', *Past & Present* 138 (1993): 28–57, esp. 31–4 and discussion below, p. 10. For the 'nobility as an intrinsic part of the public sphere' in Flemish government, see F. Buylaert, W. de Clercq, and J. Dumolyn, 'Sumptuary Legislation, Material Culture, and the Semiotics of 'Vivre Noblement' in the County of Flanders (14th–16th Centuries)', *Social History* 36 (2011): 393–417, quote at 399.

[18] Firnhaber-Baker, 'Seigneurial War', 62–7, and below, pp. 51–2, 78, 100.

[19] De Carbonnières, 'Pouvoir royal'.

expression of power whose constitutive element was the assertion and protection of rights through the exercise of violence.[20]

Though it is now recognized that he overstated the case for a seigneurial right to feud unimpeded by legal restrictions of sovereign authority, Brunner's idea that seigneurial violence might be legitimate and even socially and politically constructive has been a fruitful point of departure for a second historiographical camp focused on the pursuit and resolution of disputes.[21] Drawing upon anthropological studies of conflict in 'traditional' societies, a primarily Anglophone and particularly American strand of scholarship has argued that 'self-help', meaning organized, premeditated violence committed (usually by social elites) for the redress of wrong outside institutional judicial channels, should be seen as one aspect of disputing processes that, while violent, were governed by social norms and therefore legitimate in their own way.[22] Such disputes were not inimical to social order but actually constructive of it. The goal of disputes and their resolution was not adherence to the law, but rather the maintenance of rights and the satisfaction of the parties. Settlement of disputes was processual, entailing on-going processes of negotiation, exchange, and settlement of which violence between the disputants was one aspect. The arbitration and resolution of conflict came through the intervention of friends and local notables, without recourse to judicial courts.

While many of this second camp's seminal works focus on France in the immediate post-millennial centuries, this approach has had considerably

---

[20] O. Brunner, *Land und Herrschaft: Grundfragen der territorialen Verfassungsgeschichte Südostdeutschlands im Mittelalter* (Baden bei Wien, 1939); O. Brunner, *Land and Lordship: Structures of Governance in Medieval Austria*, trans. (of the 4th German edn) H. Kaminsky and J. Van Horn Melton (Philadelphia, 1992).

[21] Brunner's Nazi sympathies obviously influenced his views in this regard. For criticism, see C. Terharn, *Die Herforder Fehden im späten Mittelalter: Ein Beitrag zum Fehderecht* (Berlin, 1994), 14–18; H. Zmora, *State and Nobility in Early Modern Germany: the Knightly Feud in Franconia, 1440–1567* (Cambridge, 1997), 7–10; G. Algazi, 'The Social Use of Private War: Some Late Medieval Views Reviewed', *Tel Aviver Jahrbuch für deutsche Geschichte* 22 (1993): 254–6; A. Patchovsky, 'Fehde im Recht: Eine Problemskizze', in *Recht und Reich im Zeitalter der Reformation. Festschrift für Horst Rabe* ed. C. Roll (Frankfurt am Main, 1996), 145–78, esp. 147.

[22] P. Geary, 'Living with Conflicts in Stateless France: a Typology of Conflict Management Mechanisms, 1050–1200', in *Living with the Dead in the Middle Ages* (Ithaca, 1994 [1986]), 125–60. See also F. L. Cheyette, '"Feudalism": a Memoir and an Assessment', in *Feud, Violence, and Practice: Essays in Medieval Studies in Honor of Stephen D. White*, ed. B. S. Tuten and T. L. Billado (Farnham, 2010), 119–33; F. L. Cheyette, 'Suum cuique tribuere', *French Historical Studies* 6 (1970): 287–99; S. D. White, 'Feuding and Peace-Making in the Touraine around the Year 1100', *Traditio* 42 (1986): 195–263; G. Althoff, 'Satisfaction: Peculiarities of the Amicable Settlement of Conflicts in the Middle Ages', *Ordering Medieval Society: Perspectives on Intellectual and Practical Modes of Shaping Social Relations*, ed. B. Jussen, trans. P. Selwyn (Philadelphia, 2001), 270–84. The idea of 'dispute processing' has also been important to Scandinavian historians, for example, W. I. Miller, *Bloodtaking and Peacemaking: Feud, Law, and Society in Saga Iceland* (Chicago, 1990).

less traction in the historiography on France in later centuries.[23] Historians have tended to assume that such disputing processes were eliminated by the advent of official royal justice from Louis IX on. With the exception of Claude Gauvard, who has highlighted the ways in which clemency and negotiation affirmed the idea of royal sovereignty even in the tumultuous reign of Charles VI,[24] there has been virtually no work on seigneurial conflict in France after 1250. This is understandable given the unabashedly statist tilt of most historiography on France and the related perception that royal government was but a prelude to the absolutist state of early modern France.[25] But it is not necessary to abandon the insights granted by a focus on the crown in order to pay more attention to local society. Historiography focused elsewhere has shown that informal disputing (including violence) and official, institutional justice could coexist in fruitful ways. Daniel Lord Smail, for example, has argued that centralized justice in Marseilles grew because people used it as another avenue in which to pursue their enmity, while Paul Hyams has advocated studying 'feud alongside the law courts and within a single system of conflict resolution and social control'.[26]

If we look to German and English historiography, historians have emphasized the role that this sort of dispute processing played in the socio-political landscape well into the later Middle Ages and the early modern period. For Germany, Christine Reinle has shown that politically important discourses about right, violence, and authority could also operate in non-noble contexts.[27] Gadi Algazi has demonstrated that it was not just a question of power in the narrow sense of politics and government, but also one of social organization, affective relationships, and economic domination.[28] And Hillay Zmora has argued that seigneurial conflicts in fifteenth-century Franconia were closely related to German princes' efforts at state-building, being both a result of rivalries among

---

[23] J. Firnhaber-Baker, '*Jura in medio*: the Settlement of Seigneurial Disputes in Later Medieval Languedoc', *French History* 26 (2012): 441–4.

[24] See particularly C. Gauvard, '*De grace especial*': *Crime, état, et société en France à la fin du moyen âge*, 2 vols. (Paris, 1991) and essays collected in his *Violence et ordre public au moyen âge* (Paris, 2005). One of Gauvard's students recently finished a doctorate on seigneurial war (Juchs, 'Vengeance et guerre'). I am grateful to Dr Juchs for sending me his work.

[25] As noted in the Conclusion to this book, however, the royalist character of 'absolutism' has undergone significant revision in recent decades.

[26] D. L. Smail, *The Consumption of Justice: Emotions, Publicity, and Legal Culture in Marseille, 1264–1423* (Ithaca, NY, 2003); P. R. Hyams, *Rancor and Reconciliation in Medieval England* (Ithaca, NY, 2003), 8.

[27] *Bauernfehden. Studien zur Fehdeführung Nichtadliger im spätmittelalterlichen römisch–deutschen Reich, besonders in den bayerischen Herzogtümern* (Stuttgart, 2003).

[28] *Herrengewalt und Gewalt der Herren im späten Mittelalter: Herrschaft, Gegenseitigkeit und Sprachgebrauch* (Frankfurt am Main, 1996) and 'Social Use of Private War'.

would-be sovereign princes and an incitement to further princely wars.[29] England is normally regarded as a more centralized and royalist polity than the fractured Empire, but in it, too, recent historiography has emphasized the constructive role that aristocrats played in government, including through their disputes.[30] Decentralized by nature as well as necessity, royal government had to rely upon local powers to carry out the essential functions of taxation, justice, and peace-keeping. Obviously, this left open the possibility of the use of violence and justice for private ends, and much aristocratic conflict – primarily provoked by land disputes – was pursued not only through judicial litigation, but also by forcible seizure and informal arbitration by the disputants' friends, family, and lords.[31] This was once seen as a reflection of royal weakness, corruption, tolerance towards aristocratic excesses, and an easy acceptance of violence alien to modern sensibilities.[32] More recent scholarship, though, has understood violence in aristocratic disputes not as a less 'civilized' alternative to public justice, but as a complementary means of pursuing conflict, often in conjunction with centralized governmental structures.[33]

Later medieval France had very different political circumstances from either the Empire or England, but the evidence suggests that in France, too, both violence and 'old-style' arbitration remained key to conflicts and were combined with, rather than eliminated by, royal justice.[34] To turn again to the Arpajon/la Barthe case, when news of Hélène's marriage first came to the king's ears in February 1348, it was feared that the situation might lead to war, and royal commissioners were sent out to put the girl and her lands under royal protection until the matter could be worked

---

[29] Zmora, *State and Nobility*, ch. 5, esp. p. 100.

[30] K. B. McFarlane, '"Bastard Feudalism"', *Bulletin of the Institute of Historical Research* 20 (1943–5): 161–80; McFarlane, *The Nobility of Later Medieval England: the Ford Lectures for 1953 and Related Studies* (Oxford, 1973), esp. 102–21; G. Harriss, *Shaping the Nation: England, 1360–1461* (Oxford, 2005); Harriss, 'Political Society'; C. Carpenter, *The War of the Roses: Politics and the Constitution in England, c. 1437–1509* (Cambridge, 1997), chs. 1–3.

[31] J. G. Bellamy, *Bastard Feudalism and the Law* (London, 1989). For the nobility's and gentry's governmental violence, see Carpenter, *Wars of the Roses*, esp. 35, and discussion in P. C. Maddern, *Violence and Social Order: East Anglia, 1422–1442* (Oxford, 1992), esp. 1–5, and chs. 3–4. There is an impressive number of works on the arbitration of aristocratic disputes. Among others, see E. Powell, 'The Settlement of Disputes by Arbitration in Fifteenth-Century England', *Law and History Review* 2 (1984): 21–43; Maddern, *Violence and Social Order*, ch. 2, esp. 33–44; and discussion in Harriss, 'Political Society', 50–2 and n. 60.

[32] S. J. Payling, 'Murder, Motive, and Punishment in Fifteenth-Century England: Two Gentry Case Studies', *EHR* 113 (1998): 1–17; P. R. Coss, 'Bastard Feudalism Revised', *Past & Present* 125 (1989): 55–62; B. A. Hanawalt, 'Fur-Collar Crime: the Pattern of Crime among the Fourteenth-Century English Nobility', *Journal of Social History* 8 (1975): 1–17.

[33] E.g. Harriss, *Shaping the Nation*, 197–202; Maddern, *Violence and Social Order*, chs. 3–4.

[34] An argument developed throughout this book but also in Firnhaber-Baker, '*Jura in medio*'.

out.[35] The commissioners failed in their duties, and Géraud de la Barthe went to war later that year, conquering castles, ravaging lands, and killing people as detailed above. On account of this violence, the seneschal (royal governor) of the province of Rouergue began investigations against Géraud and his accomplices, seizing them and their property, and by December 1348, at least one of these accomplices was being criminally prosecuted in the Parlement de Paris.[36] But in January 1349, Géraud and his accomplices were granted a royal pardon for all the crimes they had committed in this war.[37] Such a pardon was explicitly not meant to cut off any civil pursuit by wronged parties, but the Arpajons evidently found it difficult to recover anything from Géraud. In February 1350, Jean d'Arpajon successfully requested that the seneschal of Beaucaire investigate the war and cite Géraud and his accomplices before the next session of Parlement.[38] Géraud's remission would likely have short-circuited Jean's efforts despite the attempted change in jurisdiction from the district of Rouergue to that of Beaucaire, but the threat that the case would be reopened may have increased the pressure on Géraud to make some sort of restitution for his conquest of the barony. Five months later, in July 1350, the king confirmed an accord brokered by the parties' friends 'for the good of peace and agreement between the parties'.[39] By this accord, Géraud retained everything he had conquered and Hélène accepted her disinheritance in exchange for an annual rent of 1,000 *livres tournois* (l.t.).

The pursuit and resolution of this conflict combined coercive royal justice with less formal methods. Clearly, Géraud's violence did not delegitimize his claim to Hélène's lands; rather his success seems to have proved his case. While royal officials and their courts worked first to prevent the conflict and then to punish its perpetrators, Géraud's remission and the settlement negotiated between the parties *pour bien de pais et d'accort* (the good of peace and accord) evince the importance placed on such time-honoured values as reconciliation, satisfaction, and peace. The use (and, as will be seen, growth and development) of such extra- and quasi-judicial methods of conflict resolution well into the fourteenth century might be taken as a sign of royal weakness. It is true that such methods appear more frequently in the disorderly second half of that century than in the earlier period. But just because the crown's role became less coercive over the course of the century does not necessarily

---

[35] '[P]ropter que Guerre & pericula quampluria in partibus evenerunt et graviora evenire sperantur' (AN x2a 5, fol. 118r, and see fol. 119r and *Lettres closes*, ed. Cazelles, no. 198).

[36] '[P]luseurs informationes, proces & enquestes ont este faiz ... encontre le dit Geraut & ses complices par nostre Seneschal de Roergue ... Et yceulz Geraut & complices a estre prins avent [*sic*] tous leurs biens pour cause des diz crimes' (AN JJ 77, no. 402, fol. 247); AN x2a 5, fol. 147v.

[37] AN JJ 77, no. 402, fol. 247.   [38] AN x2a 5, fols. 177v–178r.   [39] AN JJ 78, no. 250, fol. 139.

mean that its role in seigneurial conflict was becoming less important. That someone like Géraud might seek a royal pardon, that Jean d'Arpajon would appeal to the seneschal of Beaucaire, and that their accord would be sent to Paris for royal approval all speak to how deeply the crown had penetrated the kinds of relationships of power that had once been outside its purview. This was not a development that necessarily occurred to seigneurial detriment or with seigneurial protest. As the Arpajon/la Barthe case shows, having the crown involved in one's conflicts could be very useful for pursuing the issues further, as well as for resolving them. The ability to participate in less formal methods of dispute resolution also meant that when the crown's coercive faculties waned, as they did after the mid-fourteenth century, royal agents could nonetheless exert influence over seigneurial conflict and maintain a role for the crown in provincial politics.

That the royalist state could coexist with seigneurial violence and non-institutional methods of disputing thus challenges but also affirms both the historiography that insists on the development of royal authority in this period and that which argues for the possibility of social order outside coercive state control. Exploring the ways in which royal justice engaged with violent seigneurial disputes (and vice versa) over a century and a half demonstrates both the synchronic stability of conflict negotiation and its diachronic (if multidirectional) shifts in relation to the changing circumstances of the later Middle Ages, including the development of royal government. Seigneurial war was *both* a challenge to and an opportunity for the crown and its agents. Similarly, the judicial and administrative advances made by the crown offered lords new tools with which to resolve or pursue disputes in old ways, even as some of them chafed against royalist ambitions.

PROSECUTIONS AND PARDONS: THE SOURCES FOR SEIGNEURIAL WARFARE

The starting point for investigations of seigneurial war in France has traditionally been the edicts or *ordonnances* that French kings issued to limit or prohibit non-royal wars.[40] Often issued as general prohibitions applicable to the entire kingdom,[41] these acts are the most explicit surviving

---

[40] Du Cange, 'Des guerres privées'; E. de Laurière and D.-F. Secousse, Prefaces to *Ord.*, I: xxv–xxxiii, II: v–viii, and III: xvi–xvii; L. Buisson, *König Ludwig IX., der Heilige, und das Recht: Studie zur Gestaltung der Lebensordnung Frankreichs im hohen Mittelalter* (Freiburg, 1954), ch. 5; R. Cazelles, 'La réglementation royale de la guerre privée de Saint Louis à Charles V et la précarité des ordonnances', *RHDFE*, 4th ser., 38 (1960): 530–48; J. Firnhaber-Baker, 'From God's Peace to the King's Order: Late Medieval Limitations on Non-Royal Warfare', *Essays in Medieval Studies* 23 (2006): 19–30.
[41] See pp. 27, 62–3, 87–8, 119 for evidence for their general applicability. Cf. Cazelles, 'La réglementation', esp. 539–40, 546.

statement about the crown's conception of its own power in relation to this type of violence. From the reign of Louis IX through to that of Charles V, several dozen such *ordonnances* were issued, all of which are published, though the editions are old and recourse to the manuscripts is advisable.[42] These acts were once read as making a single coherent statement about seigneurial war. Yet, as Raymond Cazelles pointed out, they are not a uniform corpus with a consistent message, and, as this book emphasizes, the crown's courts and officers rarely used the *ordonnances* as laws that provided a basis for their decision to pursue or penalize someone waging war.[43] As a reflection of royal ideology and legal thinking, though, they evince the crown's ambitions and show how the changing circumstances of the period affected them.

Because the emphasis of this book is on what actually happened in practice, the majority of the sources are documents produced by the daily workings of royal justice and administration in response to seigneurial conflicts. For Languedoc and the Auvergne, I have examined more than 550 such documents, about two-thirds of which are instructions and sentences emanating from the high royal court known as the Parlement de Paris, most of which are only available in manuscript. Another quarter of the documents consist of royal pardons for crimes (*lettres de rémission*), copies of which were generally entered into the chancery's registers. Most of these pardons have been published. The rest of the documentary base is made up of sources of various genres and provenances, including the correspondence of royal provincial officials, accords between warring parties, and the occasional financial account. This is a rich source base upon which to draw, but it does present some particular problems of interpretation, particularly as the disposition of the documents changes a great deal over the century and a half covered here.

To begin with the sources from the Parlement de Paris, unofficial compilations and official registers of the court's business are available for the entire period under consideration here. The earliest compilation begins in 1254.[44] This compilation and the next three collections (AN x1a 1–4), which together span the years 1254–1319, are known as the *Olim* (so named

---

[42] Most of these are published in *Ord.*, I–V and XI. This collection is to be used in preference to the later but greatly inferior *Recueil général des anciennes lois françaises, depuis l'an 420 jusqu'à la révolution de 1789*, ed. F. A. Isambert *et al.*, 29 vols. (Paris, 1821–33).

[43] Cazelles, 'La réglementation': Firnhaber-Baker, 'Seigneurial War', esp. 54–60.

[44] There are indications that the king was holding some sort of assembly called Parlement as early as 1239: 'quando rex ivit ad pallamentum Parisius' (*HF*, XXII: 605, also excerpted in *Textes relatifs à l'histoire du Parlement depuis les origines jusqu'en 1314*, ed. C.-V. Langlois (Paris, 1888), no. 22). See discussion in C.-V. Langlois, 'Les origines du Parlement de Paris', *RH* 42 (1890): 88–90.

for the first word of the first folio of the second register).[45] For the most part, the *Olim* consists of judicial decisions, though a number of notes and mandates are also included, reflecting Parlement's identity in this early period as a venue for administrative and political matters, as well as judicial business.[46]

After the *Olim*, the documents' disposition reflects the civil and criminal division of Parlement that took place at some point during the first decade of the fourteenth century.[47] The first explicitly criminal register dates from 1312,[48] and there are twelve others in more or less unbroken chronological succession covering the rest of the fourteenth century (x2a 1–13). Along with these criminal registers, Parlement also kept registers for its civil division, which clearly saw a great deal more business than its criminal side, producing forty-three registers from 1319 to 1400 (x1a 5–47). Both civil and criminal registers comprise a mix of procedural matters, decisions (*arrêts* and *jugements*), and mandates. The first eleven folios of the second criminal register (x2a 2) contained letters from 1338–9, though the rest of the register dates from the reigns of the last Capetians.[49] The fourth criminal register also contains transcriptions of confessions,[50] and beginning in 1375, every other criminal register (x2a 10 and 12) comprises records of testimony and argument (*procès-verbaux*). In addition to these main registers, there are records for the later fourteenth century known as *plaidoiries* (x1a 1469–77, 4784, and 8300), as well as internal procedural notes in registers called *registres du greffe* for most of the fourteenth century (x1a 8844–9). Most of the information on local war is to be found in the criminal registers, probably because civil parties could pursue redress much more cheaply in conjunction with a criminal suit,[51] but there are sometimes related documents in the civil registers or mentioned in the *greffe*.

---

[45] See A. Grün, 'Notice sur les archives du Parlement de Paris', *Actes du Parlement de Paris*, ed. E. Boutaric, 2 vols. (Paris, 1863–7), I: ch. 6. In addition to these four registers, there were once three others, which have disappeared.

[46] For the 'less restricted concept of justice' at work in thirteenth- and early fourteenth-century Parlement (or parlements), see T. N. Bisson, 'Consultative Functions in the King's Parlements (1250–1314)', *Speculum* 44 (1969): 353–73, quote at 372.

[47] M. Langlois, 'Les archives criminelles du Parlement de Paris', in *La faute, la répression et le pardon, vol. I of Actes du 107ème Congrès national des sociétés savantes (Brest, 1982)* (Paris, 1984), 7–8. A. Grün noted evidence in the earliest extant registers, which date from 1312, that suggests a *terminus post quem* of 1306 ('Notice sur les archives', CCXXII).

[48] Though this first register is a much later compilation: C. Bloch and J.-M. Carbasse, 'Aux origines de la série criminelle du Parlement: Le registre x2a 1', *Histoire et archives* 12 (2002): 8–12.

[49] Because the foliation starts over, I refer to documents from these first eleven folios as coming from x2abis and those from the rest of the register as x2a.

[50] The entirety of this portion of the register has been published as *Confessions et jugements de criminels au Parlement de Paris (1319–1350)*, ed. M. Langlois and Y. Lanhers (Paris, 1971).

[51] Y. Bongert, 'Rétribution et réparation dans l'ancien droit français', *Mémoires de la Société pour l'histoire du droit et des institutions des anciens pays bourguignons, comtois et romands* 45 (1988): 67–8.

Most of Parlement's judgments contain an epitome of the testimony, investigation, and legal arguments involved in each case, but Parlement's records become better and more plentiful as time goes on. For the thirteenth century, I have supplemented them with records from the *enquêtes* (administrative investigations) undertaken by Louis IX and his brother Alphonse de Poitiers in Languedoc following the Albigensian Crusade.[52] For the period between Louis IX's death and the turn of the fourteenth century, however, there are relatively few documents.[53] The situation for the fourteenth century is much better. By the mid-fourteenth century, an *arrêt* typically covered at least two folios and some records are much longer, running in excess of five thousand words. As time went on, wars also began to generate multiple Parlement documents, sometimes for both sides of the affair. Multiple sources for the same event allow the construction of a fuller picture. But even these records are not entirely complete, and because Parlement's records are only partly catalogued and organized by date, rather than by case, even after an exhaustive search, it often still occurs that the case seems simply to disappear.

Such disappearing acts are not only a reflection of the likely losses suffered by the sources, though. The court records' apparent incompleteness also has to do with how people approached their legal business. As emphasized throughout this book, formal, judicial processes were only one avenue through which the crown and its subjects approached the resolution of their conflicts. Even when it pronounced a sentence, Parlement did not always have the last word because parties might pursue extra-legal negotiations with one another and with royal officials. Thus what the documents show is frequently an open-ended process rather than a teleological progression, and what happened in Parlement rarely constitutes the whole story. This situation is exacerbated by the frequent contumacy of defendants in the mid- and later fourteenth century, which renders the sources partial in another sense, for when defendants failed to show up, their side of the story is lost. This is, however, less problematic than it may seem since the details of each case are less important than what was considered believable and how royal officials reacted to it.

---

[52] Louis's *enquêtes* and related business in the South are found in *HF*, xxiv: 296–695, but are more focused on heresy. More of interest here is to be found in *Enquêtes administratives d'Alfonse de Poitiers, arrêts de son Parlement tenu à Toulouse, et textes annexes, 1249–1271*, ed. P.-F. Fournier and P. Guébin (Paris, 1959), and *Correspondance administrative d'Alfonse de Poitiers*, ed. A. Molinier, 2 vols. (Paris, 1894–1900).

[53] This probably reflects the fact that most royal judicial business for the South would have been handled by the short-lived Parlement de Toulouse, which functioned only in the last quarter of the thirteenth century, the records from which have apparently disappeared.

In addition to Parlement's records, significant weight has been given to *lettres de rémission* or royal pardons granted upon the recipient's request for crimes committed or alleged. The practice of granting such letters originated in the latter half of Philip IV's reign,[54] but the bulk of the remissions for southern local war dates from the reign of Philip VI (1328–50) and later, when the royal chancery issued these pardons with greater and greater frequency.[55] Although the vast majority of the tens of thousands of remissions issued relate to offences unconnected with seigneurial warfare,[56] several dozen bear on the wars of the South and provide a counterpoint to the records of Parlement. They are particularly useful because a narrative portion describing the recipient's offences and their circumstances makes up the bulk of each letter. This narrative often provides valuable details about the conflict such as time and place, alliances brokered, and motives for going to war. Since remissions were frequently sought to avoid prosecution or to annul a sentence, they also often bear witness to the functioning of royal administration and the legal rationales invoked to justify judicial pursuit of war-makers.

In contrast to Parlement judgments, which were usually issued after an inquest, testimony, and sometimes interrogation, remissions were based on the petition requesting forgiveness, and this petition was naturally a document biased in the recipient's favour. As Natalie Zemon Davis's work on the pardons of a later date has demonstrated, the narrative techniques employed by the genre serve more to arouse the audience's sympathy and to win forgiveness than to convey the truth of the matter.[57] Nevertheless, a pardon's account can often be compared with other sources for the same war since wars that generated a *lettre de rémission* usually produced other evidence as well, including Parlement records and remissions for other parties implicated in the dispute.[58] Moreover, letters of remission had to maintain reasonable fidelity to reality because excessive fabrication risked obviating the letter's benefits: a judge had to confirm the letter in order for

---

[54] The first letter of remission conserved in the chancery registers dates from May 1304: P. Texier, 'La rémission au XIVème siècle: significations et fonctions', in *La faute, la répression et la pardon, vol. I of Actes du 107ème Congrès national des sociétés savantes* (Brest, 1982), *Section de philologie et histoire jusqu'à 1610* (Paris, 1984), 196, n. 15.

[55] M. François, 'Note sur les lettres de rémission transcrites dans les registres du Trésor des chartes', *BEC* 103 (1942): 317–24; Texier, 'La rémission', 200–2; and see below, Chapter 3, pp. 107–8.

[56] C. Gauvard's survey of the registers for the later fourteenth century indicates that only a relatively small number deal with war-related crimes, most of them primarily related to the war between France and England (*'De grace especial'*, II: 528–64).

[57] N. Z. Davis, *Fiction in the Archives: Pardon Tales and their Tellers in Sixteenth-Century France* (Stanford, 1987).

[58] P. Braun, 'La valeur documentaire des lettres de rémission', in *Actes du 107ème Congrès national des sociétés savantes (Brest, 1982), Section de philologie et histoire jusqu'à 1610* (Paris, 1984), 207–21.

it to take effect, which involved cross-examination of the recipient, and there are instances in which confirmation was refused.[59] Indeed, the alleged victim of the crime could contest the letter him- or herself, and sometimes did so successfully.[60] Like Parlement's decisions, remissions were usually just one part of a process.

The rest of the sources are drawn from various genres and provenances, collected as opportunity afforded. I have incorporated the rare mentions of southern seigneurial wars found in narrative sources. Municipal documents from the consulates of Toulouse and Albi and seigneurial documents from the count of Armagnac gathered during sustained research at archives in the South provide some local perspective. In addition, I have frequently come across related documents either in isolated manuscript copies or printed as *pièces justificatives* in local, antiquarian histories. Obviously, this accretion of evidence is haphazard, and I have only used it to supplement what I gleaned from the sources that I approached more systematically. Where possible, though, they provide some colour and the occasional flash of insight into local processes that are otherwise inaccessible.

THE DEFINITION AND QUANTIFICATION OF WARFARE

Making sense of this mass of documentation requires careful categories of analysis, particularly when it comes to the delicate matter of defining warfare and quantifying the violence.[61] There is an argument to be made that quantification is useless given the unevenness of the sources, the small size of the samples, and the semantic slipperiness of 'violence'.[62] Certainly, in and of itself, announcing that 'x number of wars were fought in Languedoc in the 1340s' says more about the survival of the sources and my definition of war (given below) than it does about levels of violence. Yet, I think it is vital to do some counting and comparison of numbers across time for two reasons. First, I do actually believe that there exists

---

[59] E.g. in 1339, a seneschal refused to honour a pardon because the inquest turned up crimes not mentioned in the remission (AN x1a 8, fols. 19v–21r). On challenges to remissions and the perils of false information for the recipient, see also Gauvard, *'De grace especial'*, I: 67; Braun, 'La valeur documentaire', 218; Y.-B. Brissaud, 'Le droit de grâce à la fin du moyen-âge (XIVe–XVe siècles): Contribution a l'étude de la restauration de la souveraineté monarchique', doctoral thesis, Université de Poitiers, Faculté de droit et des sciences sociales, 1971, 233–7, 465–7.

[60] E.g. AN x1a 9, fol. 388r; AN x2a 4, fols. 104r, 107r; AN x2a 5, fol. 14r; AN x2a 6, fols. 299v–304r; AN x2a 8, fols. 24v–29r.

[61] For two different efforts to do so for other types of violence, see S. K. Cohn, *Lust for Liberty: the Politics of Social Revolt in Medieval Europe, 1200–1425: Italy, France, and Flanders* (Cambridge, MA, 2006), 2–13, and S. Carroll, *Blood and Violence in Early Modern France* (Oxford, 2006), 257–63.

[62] An argument made cogently in Maddern, *Violence and Social Order*, 7–17.

some relationship between historical reality and the sources' reportage. Second, numbers give a point of departure for investigation as to reasons why those numbers change, reasons which certainly encompass changes in sources, patterns of enforcement, and rhetorical expression, as well as changes in the actual incidence of violence. Thus, while I think it is essential to count, and even to represent the numbers graphically, I caution that interpretation of the numbers must be done in relation to archival, legal, military, and stylistic considerations, for which one must turn to the text, rather than the graphs.

My definition of 'war' is thus a central analytic decision, one that I made primarily through close observation of the variable semantics of the sources. Although the records often speak of wars as *guerra/guerre*,[63] a term that consistently describes large-scale, armed conflict involving fortifications and territorial/rights disputes, it would not be defensible to limit the corpus to only those conflicts always described as such. *Guerra* was not the only term used, and until the first quarter of the fourteenth century it was not even used frequently in royal judicial sources.[64] Even later in the period, it is rare for a conflict to be called a *guerra* in every one of its documents. Rather, the conflict may sometimes be presented as a series of discrete offences committed in prosecution of war, like homicide, rapine, arson, and so forth.[65] It could also or alternatively be called by other terms such as 'cavalcade' (*cavalcata/chevauchée*), 'peace-breaking' (*fractio pacis/bris de paix*), 'bearing (illicit) arms' (*portatio armorum/port d'armes*), the 'way of force' (*voie de fait*), and/or acts done 'in the manner of an army' (*ad modum exercitus*), many of which had fields of meaning extending beyond war to indicate lesser acts or states of aggression.[66] The Arpajon/la Barthe war, for example, is called a *guerra* in the royal commissions of 1348, in the remission granted

---

[63] The classical word for war, *bellum*, was used in fourteenth-century royal sources to mean battle, and the term *guerra* was also used for royal wars. For example, in 1368, the proctor for some men accused of warfare argued for leniency, claiming that they 'had very faithfully and strongly served in our wars in the battle of Poitiers, as well as elsewhere' (*bello quod fuit prope Pictavis quod alibi in guerris nostris bene fideliter & potenter servierant*) (AN X2a 8, fols. 24v–29r, and see *HL*, VIII: 1455–63 and *Ord.*, I: 390 for other examples). Cf. F. H. Russell, *The Just War in the Middle Ages* (Cambridge, 1975), 49, where (following Accursius's gloss to Dig. 49.15.5.2, v. 'hospitium' and to Dig. 49.15.24, v. 'hostes') *bellum* is taken to mean a 'public war' as opposed to the *guerrae* fought by bandits and other private individuals. See also discussion in G. Duby, *Le dimanche de Bouvines, 27 juillet 1214* (Paris, 1973), 145–59.

[64] *Guerra* was used consistently to describe the rebellions of the Trencavels and the count of Toulouse against Louis IX in the early 1240s (e.g. *HF*, XXIV: 301, 682, etc.), but the use of the term to describe an intra-seigneurial war in Parlement was rare until the 1310s. For a quantitative approach to the semantics, see Juchs, 'Vengeance et guerre', ch. 3.

[65] Comparatively, see Terharn, *Herforder Fehden*, 29–31.

[66] In addition to war, peace-breaking included factional struggles and attacks on public highways (*HL*, X: 132; *Ord.*, I: 344–5; and see discussion below on pp. 28, 61). *Portatio armorum* could simply mean the possession of arms. For example, carriage of illicit arms was alleged against a group of men

to Géraud, and in the accord, but not in the mandate to the seneschal of Beaucaire, which just narrates the conflict's violence.[67] When only one or two documents survive from a conflict, as is often the case in the earlier part of the period, one may have to discern the existence of a war without semantic assurance.

With this in mind, I have categorized as wars all those conflicts termed *guerrae* in the sources, and I have also included those that involved a siege (*obsidio*) and those in which banners (*vexilla*) were openly carried, the latter being a well-known, legal indicator of declared war.[68] But in cases where none of these definite indications are present, I have used the characteristics of conflicts explicitly described as *guerrae* to formulate a definition of seigneurial war based on three criteria:

1 The violence was committed under the authority of someone who held a lordship, be it a hereditary noble, an ecclesiastic, or a town consulate.[69] Except for Chapter 1, which deals with a period in which political boundaries were more fluid, I only include wars between lords who had no pretensions to sovereign independence, and while I include some trans-Rhonian conflicts, I generally restrict discussion to the wars of those who recognized the king of France as their overlord. This means, for example, that I do not deal with hostile actions between border lords and the English troops during the Hundred Years War, and I also only incidentally mention the great, on-going conflict between the counts of Foix and Armagnac that began in the late thirteenth century and lasted for most of the fourteenth.

2 The sources assert (truthfully or otherwise) that about a hundred armed men or more, some of whom were on horseback, participated in the conflict.

---

whose violence was limited to the unauthorized harvesting of grapes: AN x2a 2, fol. 49v. *Voie de fait* seems to have meant any type of violent self-help in the pursuit of one's perceived rights, including acts of narrower impact than war such as duels and assassinations, and was generally contrasted with the *voie de justice*, or the adjudication of disputes by judicial authority (e.g. AN JJ 98, no. 395, fols. 127–8 and AN x2a 12, fol. 283r).

[67] AN x2a 5, fols. 177v–178r.

[68] The only exception to my classification of every conflict termed *guerra* as a war is the conflict between the bastard of Comminges and the Lantar brothers in the mid-1390s, for which the single use of *guerra* (in recorded testimony) seems to connote a smaller-scale, more interpersonal conflict (p. 165, below). For banners, see M. Keen, 'Treason Trials under the Law of Arms: the Alexander Prize Essay', *Transactions of the Royal Historical Society*, 5th ser., 12 (1962): 93–5.

[69] Commoners were involved in every aspect of local warfare, and a few conflicts termed *guerrae* were fought by people without any claim to governmental authority. However, at least by the fourteenth century, such *guerrae* were unquestionably illegal. See P. Contamine, 'Les compagnies d'aventure en France pendant la Guerre de Cent Ans', *Mélanges de l'École français de Rome. Moyen-âge, temps modernes* 87 (1975), 371–3. Even the smallest of municipalities involved in my seigneurial wars had a consulate (e.g. *Olim*, III: 887–9). Cf., Reinle, *Bauernfehden*.

3 The conflict involved at least one castle or other stronghold, often one of the newly established fortified towns called *bastides*.

These are the characteristics that are common to those conflicts explicitly called *guerrae* in the fourteenth-century sources, and they serve to ensure that those conflicts discussed here are similar enough in scope and type to be collated and compared.

The purpose of counting wars is not to arrive at a final number, but rather to estimate (and to estimate conservatively) the relative incidence of a type of violence that has been carefully enough defined to allow comparison over time. It is clear from my sources and those of other studies that medieval people did not distinguish as sharply between war and other types of violence as do modern people, and that as a result, the terminology used in medieval texts for warfare has a certain fluidity.[70] I have therefore used these criteria as guidelines, rather than as rigid rules, in order not to exclude some borderline cases that seem likely to have been wars. In these cases, however, I have indicated my hesitations in the text, and have marked them as questionable in the list of wars that constitutes Appendix B. As a result, I always speak of both 'definite wars' and 'possible wars', which gives a range rather than an exact figure, and helps to avoid any impression of a false precision.

THE PLAN OF THE BOOK

Most works on violence, seigneurial or otherwise, take a thematic approach, which enables the exploration of the social meaning of violence, but can obscure change over time.[71] The question of chronological change is, however, central to this book in part because the historiography on the cumulative rise of the French state requires a congruently structured investigation, and in part because the changes that took place in the royal/seigneurial engagement over warfare did not take place in a progressive arc of development, but rather occurred fitfully and for various, sometimes conflicting reasons. I have thus elected a chronological treatment intended to highlight the disjunctive and frequently

---

[70] For semantics and characteristics in other contexts, see J. B. Netterstrøm, 'Introduction: the Study of Feud in Medieval and Early Modern History', in *Feud in Medieval and Early Modern Europe*, ed. J. B. Netterstrøm and B. Poulsen (Aarhus, 2007), 37–64; P. R. Hyams, 'Was There Really Such a Thing as Feud in the High Middle Ages?', in *Vengeance in the Middle Ages: Emotion, Religion, and Feud*, ed. S. Throop and P. Hyams (Farnham, 2010), 151–75; White, 'Feuding', 195–200; Terharn, *Herforder Fehden*, 20–8; Kaminsky, 'Feud', 55–6; Miller, *Bloodtaking*, ch. 6.

[71] Hyam's *Rancor and Reconciliation* is an important exception.

contingent nature of these changes and to demonstrate that while the crown was not acting on a purely ad hoc basis, both royal and individual seigneurial intentions were of fairly limited scope. If royal administrations in a later period capitalized on the developments of the later Middle Ages in order to build something that looks like a modern state with claims to monopolize justice and legitimate violence – and it is not at all clear that they did – this was an unintended consequence of arrangements that had a different meaning in a different historical context.

The division of chapters corresponds roughly to regnal breaks because such transitions frequently signalled a change in royal policy, both towards seigneurial war and to larger legal or military issues with implications for seigneurial war. Each chapter follows roughly the same plan: an introduction to the major events of the reign or reigns is succeeded by a discussion of royal *ordonnances* bearing on seigneurial war to trace the development of ideology and normative thought about seigneurial violence. The second section of each chapter contrasts the abstractions of the *ordonnances* with events in local society, narrating the occurrences of seigneurial war in the South during that period. The rest of each chapter is devoted to the engagement between royal and seigneurial interests and their arguments and manoeuvres both in and out of court. By looking at judicial and administrative proceedings, this part of each chapter (frequently broken into two sections) explores how the crown balanced the king's justice and the lords' prerogatives in practice, and what judicial and administrative efforts to resolve the conflict tell us about the royal government's penetration of local power relations. In sum, each chapter outlines the crown's ideal and the lords' experience and then discusses how these were reconciled (or not) by the king's courts and officers working both with and against the lords and their representatives.

Chapter 1, beginning in 1250, focuses on the first two decades of Capetian administration in the South following the Albigensian Crusade. It discusses the understanding of Louis IX and Alphonse de Poitiers (and their officers) of the responsibility to maintain peace and their use of peace-keeping in the government of their new lands and new vassals. As there are few sources for the period from 1270 to 1285, Chapter 2 is mainly devoted to the reign of Philip IV (the Fair), whose councillors and administrators made significant innovations in royal normative and judicial treatment of seigneurial war, redefining the problem in terms of royal prerogatives over justice and violence. Chapter 3 discusses the reaction to these changes, as well as the challenges to royal administration and seigneurial society presented by the coming of the Hundred

Years War and the plague. This chapter argues that while the crown's coercive powers clearly waned, its officers increasingly used methods of negotiation and pardon to settle conflicts and reintegrate offenders into the political community, in effect strengthening royal involvement in seigneurial society. The fourth chapter covers the brief reign of John II (1350–64), which was a turning point for royal government in relation to violence generally, as well as seigneurial war specifically. As control of the kingdom in general and violence in particular spun out of royal hands following the Battle of Poitiers in 1356, initiative and responsibility for the maintenance of order and the settlement of dispute increasingly devolved to individuals and communities. Yet, the consequent renaissance in 'self-help' did not wholly eclipse royal judicial and/or administrative functions because people tended to use the crown's courts and officers in their conflicts and settlements, albeit sometimes in novel ways. Chapter 5 demonstrates that this hybrid of self-help and royal justice continued to be the favoured model for the resolution of seigneurial war through to the end of the century, reflecting and contributing to a new stress on the delegation of royal authority in the face of actual royal enervation. A short conclusion discusses the early fifteenth century and the legacy of medieval developments with reference to recent work on violence, justice, and government in early modern France.

Seigneurial war is obviously not the only vantage point from which to view the story of royal government at the end of the Middle Ages. Fiscal and military developments, the growth of royal ceremonies and rituals, the evolution of national sentiment, and many other topics offer other insights, some no doubt contradictory to those suggested here. What this book does show, however, is that the conversation taking place between the crown and the seigneurs regarding warfare was an open-ended dialogue in which neither party was able – or usually willing – to dictate the terms unilaterally. Lords were rarely happy to be summoned to court to answer for criminal offences committed during (what they perceived as) a wholly justifiable effort to protect their rights, but they were perfectly pleased to see their enemies so treated. And frequently, it was not so much the summons to court that was important to people as how one could use that summons, and the institutions and people involved, to pursue the processes of disputing and dispute resolution to one's own best advantage. Yet, this processural approach to law and justice enabled and indeed required royal courts and officers to become embedded in local political society as arbiters of conflict and enforcers of settlement. As a result, even when the crown lost (or even lost interest in) the ability to enforce justice coercively for the maintenance of order, its authority over seigneurial conflict and thus over local society in general was maintained, and could even grow. If this tells us anything about what Joseph Strayer rightly called the 'medieval origins of the modern state',[72] it is simply how medieval – and how far from our own experience of the state – those origins were.

---

[72] J. R. Strayer, *On the Medieval Origins of the Modern State* (Princeton, 1970); J. R. Strayer, 'The Promise of the Fourteenth Century', in *Medieval Statecraft and the Perspectives of History* (Princeton, 1971 [1961]), ch. 20, esp. pp. 318–20.

Chapter 1

WAR AND PEACE IN POST-ALBIGENSIAN LANGUEDOC, 1250–1270

In 1250, Languedoc was at a turning point. After four decades of war, the Albigensian Crusade had finally begun to fade into the past. Montségur, last of the Cathar strongholds, had fallen in 1244, and the last Raymondine count of Toulouse, died in September 1249. The vast county of Toulouse passed to his daughter, Jeanne, and her husband, Alphonse de Poitiers, brother of King Louis IX. Upon their deaths in 1271, the county would become part of the royal domain. Along with the Auvergne – ruled by Alphonse as an appanage – and other Occitan lands subdued and absorbed during the Cathar war, the Capetians now directly controlled (at least in theory) almost the entirety of southern France west of the Rhône.[1] When Louis returned in 1254 from crusading in Palestine, he and Alphonse worked closely together to shape the governance of this land. They established a network of administrative officials, instituted taxes, and promulgated reforms, including those outlined in Louis's celebrated ordinance of 1254.[2] The long-recalcitrant South had become part of the Capetian world.

---

[1] For the annexation of the Auvergne to the royal domain in the early thirteenth century, see J. W. Baldwin, *The Government of Philip Augustus: Foundations of French Royal Power in the Middle Ages* (Berkeley, 1986), 199–200. For Alphonse's appanage, see W. C. Jordan, *Louis IX and the Challenge of the Crusade: a Study in Rulership* (Princeton, 1979), 39, and the outline of Alphonse's lands in *Enquêtes administratives d'Alfonse de Poitiers, arrêts de son Parlement tenu à Toulouse, et textes annexes, 1249–1271*, ed. P.-F. Fournier and P. Guébin (Paris, 1959), xiii–xviii.

[2] É. Boutaric, *Saint Louis et Alfonse de Poitiers. Étude sur la réunion des provinces du Midi et de l'ouest à la couronne* (Paris, 1870); A. Molinier's essay in *HL*, VII: 462–570; R. Michel, *L'administration royale dans la sénéchaussée de Beaucaire au temps de Saint Louis* (Paris, 1910); T. N. Bisson, *Assemblies and Representation in Languedoc in the Thirteenth Century* (Princeton, 1964), ch. 4; J. R. Strayer, *The Albigensian Crusades* (New York, 1971), ch. 10; J. H. Mundy, *Society and Government at Toulouse in the Age of the Cathars* (Toronto, 1997), 244–9. For Louis's reform ordinance: *HF*, XX: 392–9; *Ord.*, I: 65–75; *HL*, VIII: 1345–52; L. Carolus-Barré, 'La grande ordonnance de 1254 sur la réforme de l'administration et la police du royaume', in *Septième centenaire de la mort de Saint Louis: Actes des colloques de Royaumont et de Paris (21–27 mai 1970)* (Paris, 1976), 85–96. Alphonse issued a similar but lesser-known promulgation around the same time (*Enquêtes administratives*, ed. Fournier and Guébin, no. 5 and *HL*, VIII: 1352–6).

Like its new lands, the Capetian crown itself was also at an important juncture. After Louis VIII's brief reign and Blanche of Castile's successful but contentious regency, the long and prosperous years of Louis IX's majority gave the crown the opportunity to revitalize practices begun under Philip Augustus and to make their own innovations.[3] The new projects begun under Louis included the evolution of the Parlement de Paris, which eventually became the realm's court of final appeal, as well as a main venue for all matters involving royal jurisdiction. As much as the governmental novelties of Louis's reign changed the crown's administrative structure, though, the king's personal piety also established an important royal legacy of Christian prestige. Louis demonstrated his sanctity through his crusading, his foundation of the Sainte Chapelle, his devotional habits, and his many charitable works. As Louis was fully aware, his religious activities had positive implications for the crown's political machinations: his piety created an aura of sanctity that would cling to the throne long after his death in 1270 and his eventual canonization in 1297, his memory serving the political aims of disparate players for centuries.[4]

Above all, Louis's posthumous reputation would be that of a peace-maker: *rex pacificus magnificatus est*, as Boniface VIII sermonized in 1297.[5] Louis's regulations relating to seigneurial warfare confirm this reputation, demonstrating an innovative effort to curb violence within the realm for the moral good of peace. But this pacific aura belies another reality of his reign: Languedoc, like other parts of the realm, experienced significant internal disorder, including at least nine and possibly as many as twenty seigneurial wars waged after the Capetian takeover. Many of these wars were related to the Capetian presence in Languedoc, and some were directly waged against Louis's and Alphonse's representatives. Indeed, it is clear that to some extent Capetian government in the South caused more large-scale violence than it eliminated. The Capetian officers' reactions to

---

[3] Baldwin, *Government of Philip Augustus*; É. Berger, *Histoire de Blanche de Castille: Reine de France* (Paris, 1895).

[4] H. Kämpf, *Pierre Dubois und die geistigen Grundlagen des französischen Nationalbewusstseins um 1300* (Leipzig and Berlin, 1935); J. R. Strayer, 'France: the Holy Land, the Chosen People, and the Most Christian King', in *Medieval Statecraft and the Perspectives of History* (Princeton, 1971 [1969]), 300–14; E. A. R. Brown, 'Persona et Gesta: the Image and Deeds of the Thirteenth-Century Capetians, the Case of Philip the Fair', *Viator* 19 (1988): 219–46; Brown, 'Philippe le Bel and the Remains of Saint Louis', *Gazette des beaux-arts* 95 (1980): 175–82; C. Beaune, *The Birth of an Ideology: Myths and Symbols of Nation in Late-Medieval France*, trans. S. R. Huston, ed. F. L. Cheyette (Berkeley, 1991), ch. 3; M. C. Gaposchkin, 'Boniface VIII, Philip the Fair, and the Sanctity of Louis IX', *Journal of Medieval History* 29 (2003): 1–26; M. C. Gaposchkin, *The Making of Saint Louis: Kingship, Sanctity, and Crusade in the Later Middle Ages* (Ithaca, NY, 2008).

[5] Jordan, *Louis IX*, 195–205; Jean de Joinville, *Vie de Saint Louis*, chs. 59–60, ed. J. Monfrin (Paris, 1995), 179–81. Boniface's sermon: Gaposchkin, *Making of Saint Louis*, 53–7.

these wars were complex: while they were engaged in creating a workable, centralized administrative apparatus, they also had to take into account pre-existing local structures in a land devastated by decades of brutal war, most of which had been waged under royal aegis. In addition, the Church had played a role equal to that of the crown in the Languedocian conquest, and its interests, particularly as represented by inquisitions into heresy, continued to be in interplay with those of the crown. Although Louis's reign produced profound ideological developments, much of the engagement between seigneurial warfare and royal administration in Languedoc during this period was a consequence, and in some ways a continuation, of the Albigensian Crusade, rather than a struggle over the enforcement of royal policy.

GOD'S PEACE: THE IDEOLOGY OF CAPETIAN PEACE-KEEPING TO 1270

Louis's reign has often been understood by historians as a turning point in royal efforts to curb seigneurial violence,[6] and indeed that seems to be how many people understood it in the later Middle Ages. When later royal administrations sought to justify their own limitations or prohibitions against seigneurial warfare, they frequently pointed to Louis as the originator of their policies.[7] So strong was the association that by the mid-fourteenth century a tradition had grown up crediting Louis with peace-keeping measures that had probably pre-dated him.[8] The eagerness to claim Saint Louis's endorsement is an understandable affection, and one that is common to royal decrees on other matters, as well.[9] But in this case, a certain truth lay behind the legend. Although royal policy drew upon earlier ecclesiastical precedents, under Louis significant conceptual and logistical innovations took place that influenced the royal approach to seigneurial warfare for about a century.

---

[6] C. du Fresne du Cange, 'Des guerres privées, et du droit de guerre par coutume', in *Glossarium mediae et infimae latinitatis*, new edn, 10 vols. in 5 (Niort, 1883–7), X: 100–8. *Ord.*, I: xxv–xxxiii; L. Buisson, *König Ludwig IX., der Heilige, und das Recht. Studie zur Gestaltung der Lebensordnung Frankreichs im hohen Mittelalter* (Freiburg, 1954); R. Cazelles, 'La réglementation royale de la guerre privée de Saint Louis à Charles V et la précarité des ordonnances', *RHDFE*, 4th ser., 38 (1960): 530–48; A. Grabois, 'De la trêve de Dieu à la paix du roi: Étude sur les transformations du mouvement de la paix au XIIe siècle', in *Mélanges offerts à René Crozet*, ed. P. Gallais and Y.-J. Riou, 2 vols. (Poitiers, 1966), I: 585–96; J. Krynen, *L'empire du roi: Idées et croyances politiques en France XIIIe–XVe siècle* (Paris, 1993), 36–42; J. Firnhaber–Baker, 'From God's Peace to the King's Order: Late Medieval Limitations on Non-Royal Warfare', *Essays in Medieval Studies* 23 (2006): 19–30.

[7] E.g. *HL*, X: 131–2; *Ord.*, I: 390. [8] The so-called *quarantaine du roi*, see below, pp. 29, 120.

[9] See Beaune, *Birth of an Ideology*, esp. 92, 106, 114; Gaposchkin, *Making of Saint Louis*, 237–9.

The key document in this development is an *ordonnance* in the form of a mandate that Louis issued in 1258. Addressed to all the *fideles* of the realm in the diocese of le Puy-en-Velay and those in the fief of the church of le Puy, it constitutes the first known royal edict to prohibit war in France. The text advised its readers and auditors as follows:

> Know that, having taken advice, we have prohibited all wars in the realm (*guerras omnes inhibuisse in regno*), and arson and the disruption of carts. Wherefore we order you, with a stern warning, neither to make wars or arson against our prohibition, nor to disturb farmers (*agricolas*) who work with ploughs. Regarding which, if you dare to do otherwise, we order our seneschal [of Beaucaire], faithfully and attentively to help our faithful and beloved G. [bishop-]elect of le Puy to hold his land in peace, and to expel peace-breakers, who ought to be punished, according to their guilt.[10]

There has been some debate as to how broadly this prohibition was intended, particularly given the limited constituency of its address,[11] but there is evidence that its import was general. The text certainly lends itself to that interpretation, as Louis observes that he had prohibited wars 'in the realm' (*in regno*), not just in le Puy. That it is addressed specifically to le Puy may merely reflect that the text we have is a mandate for the prohibition's execution, sent, as mandates were, to local administrators and justiciars so that they could carry out general policy in their own areas. A general interpretation is also suggested by the only manuscript copy of this *ordonnance* that I have been able to locate, where this text is included in a late thirteenth- or early fourteenth-century compilation of Norman customary law and royal statutes.[12] Not only was the *ordonnance* considered relevant to Normandy, the redactor also explicitly indicated his understanding that it was valid for the entire realm, rubricking it 'the prohibition of wars, arson and assaulting ploughs in the realm' (*la defense des guerres des arsons & de destorber les charues el reaume*). Like the printed edition, edited from now lost sources, this manuscript copy is also addressed to le Puy.[13] It is possible that Louis promulgated the measure in response to something taking place in le Puy, but intended it to have general effect, an approach that he did take in other contexts.[14]

---

[10] *Ord.*, 1: 84. The text of this measure in BN Latin 4651, fol. 74v specifies that the seneschal in question is that of Beaucaire, which accords with the administrative geography of le Puy-en-Velay.

[11] Cazelles, 'La réglementation', 539. Prior to Cazelles's revisionist piece, it had been understood as generally applicable: e.g. Buisson, *König Ludwig IX*, 203.

[12] BN Lat. 4651, fol. 74v.

[13] The text in *Ord.*, 1: 84 was edited from 'Olim feuillet 28', but this must refer to one of the lost registers of the *Olim* since it is not to be found in AN x1a 1–4.

[14] Jordan, *Louis IX*, 37.

A broad interpretation is also suggested by the prohibition's apparently very specific allusion to G. *electum*, the bishop-elect of le Puy. 'G.' refers to Gui Foucois (later Pope Clement IV), who had recently begun a meteoric rise in the Church after an impressive stint as one of Louis's most able administrators.[15] Raymond Cazelles considered Foucois's involvement more proof of the prohibition's limited scope.[16] But as Jacques le Goff and Ernest Perrot both recognized, since Foucois had a hand in royal policy at the highest levels both as a lawyer and as one of Louis's *enquêteurs* in the South, the reference should probably be interpreted as evidence that this was a significant development in policy, rather than a matter of only local concern.[17]

Indeed, Foucois was responsible for at least one other measure on warfare that can be attributed to Louis IX: a mandate to the seneschal of Carcassonne sent by Louis's son, Philip III, to define the term 'peace-breaking' (an offence which included *guerra*). This mandate notes that the definition was based on the 'counsel that Pope Clement [IV] of happy memory is said to have given while serving our beloved lord and father of glorious memory, Louis king of France, in a lesser office'.[18] Foucois had told Louis that three situations constituted peace-breaking: (1) when one party attacked the other in arms during factional disputes in a castle or town, (2) when a town, castle or estate, or baron or lord of a castle made war (*guerram moverit*) on another, and (3) when (one of them) furtively occupied a castle or estate or fortification. Foucois's involvement in both of these peace-keeping efforts must be, as Ernest Perrot observed, *plus qu'une simple coïncidence*.[19] It suggests that Foucois played a consultative role in the self-conscious formation of royal policy against seigneurial war during Louis's reign.

The 1258 mandate and the evidence from Philip III's mandate are the two undoubted Ludovician statements on warfare. In addition, there are three other measures that possibly shed light on royal normative thought

---

[15] For the identification of G. as Gui Foucois, see *HL*, VI: 857–8; F. Lot and R. Fawtier, *Histoire des institutions françaises au moyen âge*, 3 vols. (Paris, 1957–62), II: 225–6. For Foucois's career, see Y. Dossat, 'Gui Foucois, enquêteur–réformateur, archevêque et pape (Clément IV)', and 'Patriotisme méridional du clergé au XIIIe siècle', both in *Les évêques, les clercs, et le roi (1250–1300)* (Toulouse, 1972), 23–57 and 437–45.

[16] 'La réglementation', 539.

[17] J. le Goff, *Saint Louis* (Paris, 1996), 266 and E. Perrot, *Les cas royaux: Origine et développement de la théorie aux XIIIe et XIVe siècles* (Paris, 1910), 150–1, n. 1.

[18] *HL*, X: 131–2; BN Latin 9988, fol. 117v; BN Latin 9989, p. 239. The address to the seneschal of Carcassonne is found only in BN Latin 9989, where this mandate is included among other correspondence of Philip III to this seneschal. Neither manuscript copy supplies a date, given as 16 October 1275 in the *HL*'s edition.

[19] Perrot, *Les cas royaux*, 150–1, n. 1. R. Kaeuper shares his suspicion (*War, Justice, and Public Order: England and France in the Later Middle Ages* (Oxford, 1988), 233).

during this period. First, there is the so-called *quarantaine du roi*, which implicitly allowed warfare, but required the challenging party to observe a forty-day delay before the onset of hostilities. (The challenged party could attack immediately.) No thirteenth-century text of the *quarantaine* exists, and there are questions about whether Louis was really its originator. Beaumanoir credited the measure to Philip II, and Philip himself may also have been co-opting a much earlier tradition, as Robert Bartlett notes a mid-eleventh-century example of the *quarantaine* practice among the Normans in southern Italy.[20] The forty-day restriction may have been in vigour in certain parts of the realm during Louis IX's reign, even if he was not its author, for it seems to be referenced in a Parlement case from 1260.[21] It must have been a geographically specific restriction, though, for while there is later evidence of its enforcement in the Île-de-France, Vermandois, and Flanders, there is no sign that either in Louis's reign or after it was ever applied in Languedoc.

In addition to the *quarantaine*, Louis reportedly ordered his bailiffs to force everyone in the kingdom to make a five-year truce in 1245 as preparation for crusade, though there is no surviving evidence for this measure.[22] A final prohibition that can be associated with Louis are the proscriptions against those who *movent guerram* in canons 28–35 of the 1229 Council of Toulouse, which the seneschal of Carcassonne attended as the king's representative.[23] The promulgations of this council, convened in the aftermath of the Albigensian Crusade, were intended to deal with remaining pockets of southern opposition to the crusade, but they had on-going relevance to the maintenance of order in the South: a 1239 accord speaks of the seneschal of Beaucaire's duty to uphold the peace according to the statutes promulgated at the Council of Toulouse,[24]

---

[20] Philippe de Beaumanoir, *Coutumes de Beauvaisis*, ch. 60, art. 1702, ed. A. Salmon, 2 vols. (Paris, 1899–1900), II: 371–2; see also *Ord.*, I: xxx. Parlement's records from the 1340s suggest that a tradition ascribing the *quarantaine* to Louis had developed by the middle decades of the fourteenth century: e.g. 'quarantenam per Beatum Ludovicum bone memorie francorum regem introductam' (AN x2a 5, fols. 75v–76r; see also AN x1a 8, fol. 143; Kaeuper, *War, Justice*, 232, n. 153). R. Bartlett, '"Mortal Enmities": the Legal Aspect of Hostility in the Middle Ages', in *Feud, Violence, and Practice: Essays in Medieval Studies in Honor of Stephen D. White*, ed. B. S. Tuten and T. L. Billado (Farnham, 2010), 201.

[21] *Olim*, I: 472–3.

[22] It is reported in du Cange, 'Des guerres privées', 104, who gives no reference to his source. If Louis did indeed decree these truces, precedent might be traced to Innocent III's *Ad liberandum*, which had required a four-year peace to be observed in Christendom.

[23] Mansi, XXIII: 191–204; Guillaume de Puylaurens, *Chronique (1145–1275): Chronica magistri Guillelmi de Podio Laurentii*, ch. 38, ed. and trans. (into French) J. Duvernoy (Paris, 1976), 142–9.

[24] '[S]enescallus ... pacem rogat et conservari faciat ... secundum statuta auctoritate domini pape et domini Regis Francorum in Tholosano consilio promulgata' (Michel, *L'administration royale*, no. 7); see also Perrot, *Les cas royaux*, 150–1, n. 1.

and an ordinance promulgated in 1270 by Alphonse de Poitiers (Louis's brother and effective co-ruler in Languedoc) may indicate the same thing. This measure ordered that those who engaged in *chevauchées* (*cavalcatae*, a frequently used synonym for *guerrae*) should be punished 'according to the statutes of the Peace of Paris' (*secundum statuta pacis Parisiensis a senescallo puniantur*).[25] But since neither the Peace of Paris agreed to by Louis IX and Henry III of England in 1259, nor the 1229 Peace of Paris that ended the Albigensian Crusade contains any apposite clauses,[26] it seems likely that Alphonse meant the Council of Toulouse, promulgated as a result of the 1229 peace agreement.

Although diverse and somewhat artificially assembled, this collection of Ludovician prescriptions bespeaks an effort to maintain public order through the absence of violence and thus to ensure the smooth running of the kingdom. The canons of the 1229 Council of Toulouse against those who made war were obviously intended in part to restore order in the war-torn South. And Louis's mandate of 1258 outlawing *guerras omnes . . . in regno* can clearly also be understood as an attempt to instate or perhaps reinstate a regime of order under royal authority. Complementary to this objective, some of the measures associated with Louis were meant to reserve fighting men and resources for Louis's crusades. This was the point of the forced truces of 1245 (if they did actually occur). Concern about crusade may also have been an unspoken aim of the 1258 mandate since little wars prevented fighting men from participating in royal wars and resulted in the wasteful deaths of men and horses, who might have been put to better use against the infidel, whenever Louis was able to turn his attention to them once more. As the 1258 mandate makes clear, such intramural conflicts also tended to damage peasants and agricultural resources, destroying the realm's wealth and limiting the king's resources.

Yet Louis's efforts against seigneurial violence had a pedigree that went beyond these mundane, short-term concerns about public order and military utility, deriving from ecclesiastical efforts at peace-keeping that had originated centuries earlier. This is visible, first of all, in terms of administrative infrastructure. In the thirteenth century, as Thomas Bisson has argued, the crown assumed direction of the peace structures that had been established – mainly by southern bishops – in late twelfth-century Languedoc.[27] In particular, post-Albigensian southern royal administration seems to have instituted (or perhaps co-opted) peace-keeping officers

---

[25] *Enquêtes administratives*, ed. Fournier and Guébin, no. 135, art. 30 (= *HL*, VIII: 1715–23).

[26] For the 1259 treaty, *LTC*, III: nos. 4416, 4554. For 1229, *LTC*, II: no. 1992.

[27] T. N. Bisson, 'The Organized Peace in Southern France and Catalonia (*c.* 1140–*c.* 1233)', *AHR* 82 (1977), esp. 309–11. See C. Brunel, 'Les juges de la paix en Gévaudan au milieu du XIe siècle', *BEC*

called *paciarii*. The thirty-first canon of the Council of Toulouse, dealing with peace-breaking by those who are supposed to be maintaining the peace, mentions the 'castles of the *paciarius' (castris paciariis)*.[28] Gui Foucois's definition of peace-breaking also stipulates that peace-breakers were to be handed over to either a (or perhaps, the) *paciarius* or his ordinary judge.[29]

This co-optation of the peace tradition is also evident in the ideas that shaped and appear in Louis's measures. Aryeh Graboïs argued in a classic article that the *ordonnance* of 1258 can be understood as the end point of a long arc extending from the millennial Peace of God movement whose ideas the Capetians gradually co-opted, transforming them from the sacred peace of God into the secular peace of the realm.[30] There would be continued development in royal thought on peace-keeping over the next century, but the 1258 *ordonnance* can be seen as a bridging measure from these older ecclesiastical traditions of peace-keeping. It exhibits the marked concern for the protection of peasants and their instruments – these *agricolae* who work with ploughs – that had characterized the Peace from its very inception, the second canon of the 998 Council of Charroux, for example, calling down anathema upon those who plunder the *res pauperum*.[31] As Graboïs points out, this focus on the protection of rural non-combatants and productive resources had a more recent French antecedent in councils that Louis VII had presided over in the 1150s where peace was guaranteed to 'all *agricolae*, as well as cattle and herds', and to 'herds, cattle, *agricolae*, and ploughs (*aratra*), as well as cultivators of vines, and merchants'.[32] But even more recent precedents can be found in the *Reichslandfrieden* promulgated in the Empire. The 1223 renewal of the

109 (1951): 32–41 for earlier precedent. Cognizance of peace infractions was among the disputed issues between the bishop of Albi, the consuls of Gaillac, and the seneschal of Carcassonne in the 1250s (*HL*, VIII: 1310–12 and below, p. 36).

[28] Mansi, XXIII: 202.

[29] '[S]ive ad manus paciarii sive ad sui ordinarii manus devenerint' (*HL*, X: 131–2).

[30] 'De la trêve'. See also H. Hoffmann, *Gottesfriede und Treuga Dei* (MGH, Schriften 20, Stuttgart, 1964), 207–16; and Y. Sassier, 'Les progrès de la paix et de la justice du roi sous le règne de Louis VII', in *Structures du pouvoir, royauté, et res publica (France, IX–XIIe siècle)* (Rouen, 2004), 177–90. For royal involvement in earlier peace efforts, see T. Riches, 'The Peace of God, the "Weakness" of Robert the Pious, and the Struggle for the German Throne', *Early Medieval Europe* 18 (2010): 202–22. On the Peace of God, see D. Barthélemy, *The Serf, the Knight, and the Historian*, trans. G. R. Edwards (Ithaca, NY, 2009), ch. 8 and Barthélemy, D., *L'an mil et la paix de Dieu: La France chrétienne et féodale, 980–1060* (Paris, 1999). For present purposes, the language and ideas employed in the associated texts are more important than the socio-political structures that produced them.

[31] Mansi, XIX: 90. See H.-W. Goetz, 'Protection of the Church, Defense of the Law, and Reform: On the Purposes and Character of the Peace of God, 989–1038', in *The Peace of God: Social Violence and Religious Response in France around the Year 1000*, ed. T. Head and R. Landes (Ithaca, NY, 1992), 267–9; T. Head, 'Peace and Power in France around the Year 1000', *Essays in Medieval Studies* 23 (2006): 1–17. J. Richard, *Saint Louis: Roi d'une France féodale, soutien de la Terre sainte* (Paris, 1983), 326–7 notes the similarity between Louis's prohibition and the Peace canons.

[32] *HF*, XIV: 387–8; Mansi, XXI: 844.

'ancient peace of Saxony', for example, had decreed eternal peace for *agricolae* and *aratra* as well as monks, clerics, and women.[33]

It is important to note that the key concept behind these measures was not the monopolization of force incumbent on modern governments, but rather the venerable idea of protection owed to the weak. The influence of this old tradition meant that disorder was represented in these prohibitions not as a usurpation of royal prerogatives, but rather as a violation of the peace. The 1258 *ordonnance* decreed that offenders were to be treated as peace-breakers (*fractores pacis*), a term one also finds in the advice that Louis received from Gui Foucois about how royal administrators ought to keep order.[34] The meaning of *pax* here was broader than the modern understanding of peace as an essentially negative condition that prevails before or after violence. As H. E. J. Cowdrey and Roger Bonnaud-Delamare have argued, for supporters of the Peace of God *pax* meant not just the absence of physical violence, but also freedom from the other afflictions of the world, such as disease, famine, and heresy.[35] This idea of peace as a moral as well as a social or political state can be seen in canon 27 of the Third Lateran Council held in 1179, which equated the heresies of the Cathars and the Patarenes with the violence of foreign mercenaries, ordering that the latter desist from destroying everything 'the way that pagans do' (*more paganorum*) lest they suffer the same 'sentence and penalty as the foresaid heretics' (*sententia et poena cum praedictis haereticis*).[36]

This understanding of peace as both a spiritual and physical condition influenced the 1229 Council of Toulouse, promulgated for the 'purification of heresy, [and] for the conservation of peace' (*ad purgationem haereticae pravitatis, conservationem pacis*). Its canons call both those who practise heresy and those who make war *violatores pacis*.[37] This connection between peace and faith, on one hand, and war and heresy, on the other, was also at work

---

[33] MGH, Leges, Const., II, no. 280.   [34] Ord., I: 84; HL, X: 131–2.

[35] R. Bonnaud-Delamare, 'Fondement des institutions de paix au XI siècle', in *Mélanges d'histoire du moyen âge dédiés à la mémoire de Louis Halphen* (Paris, 1951), 19–26; H. E. J. Cowdrey, 'The Peace and Truce of God in the Eleventh Century', *Past & Present* 46 (1970): 42–67. See also F. S. Paxton, 'History, Historians, and the Peace of God', in *The Peace of God: Social Violence and Religious Response in France around the Year 1000*, ed. T. Head and R. Landes (Ithaca, NY, 1992), 27–34. A thorough reappraisal of the meaning and uses of peace in this period is Malegam, J. Y. *The Sleep of Behemoth: Disputing Peace and Violence in Medieval Europe, 1000–1200* (Ithaca, NY and London, 2013), which was published too late to be fully integrated here.

[36] Mansi, XXII: 232. See Bisson, 'Organized Peace', 298.

[37] Canon 35: 'Item statuimus ut aliquis amicitiam, familiaritatem, vel treugas non habeat cum fayditis [heretics], vel aliis qui guerram moverunt'; canon 37: 'quod quando aliquis guerram moverit, fiat contra eum sacramentum de novo: quod qui procurare noluerit, fractor pacis reputetur: modo etiam expresse fiat sacrametum contra inimicos fidei atque pacis' (Mansi, XXIII: 202, 203).

for the intellectual architects of the Albigensian Crusade, who referred to the wars as the *negotium pacis et fidei*.[38] It also had suggestive semantic consequences as the meaning of the word *faiditus* changed in the second quarter of the thirteenth century from someone involved in a feud to someone involved in heresy.[39] It is true that the equivalence between illicit warfare and heresy was due partly to short-term political contexts – the Albigensian Crusade's influence is evident and Lateran III's language reflects Frederick Barbarossa's conflicts with the papacy – but it is also indicative of a way of thinking that perceives political behaviour, including warfare, along a spectrum of morality, essentially as a question of good or evil.

Such moral characterizations obviously had political intentions and consequences. Louis IX approached peace-keeping as a method of political consolidation, just as his twelfth-century ancestors had used peace statutes, peace institutions, and finally peace councils to subdue the great barons in northern France.[40] Moreover, while the legacy of the Peace and Truce of God was evident, his reign also saw innovations in peace-keeping that stamped it more firmly with a French, regalian character. The regulations associated with Louis IX were much more ambitious than those found in earlier legislation: unlike the Peace canons, Louis's statutes actually attempted to prohibit warfare. The Council of Toulouse, the 1258 ordinance, and the definition of peace-breaking formulated by Gui Foucois all expressly forbid *guerra*.[41] Peace legislation had sought to ameliorate the effects of violence by limiting its targets and the times during which it could be practised, but it had not gone so far as to specifically forbid wars, as opposed to general violence, let alone to try to wholly suppress armed conflict.[42] By prohibiting *guerres omnes ... in regno* in 1258 and by defining peace-breaking as including wars and seizures of fortifications,[43] the regulations of Saint Louis's reign manifested

---

[38] M.-H. Vicaire, '"L'affaire de paix et de fois" du Midi de la France (1203–1215)', *Paix de Dieu et guerre sainte en Languedoc au XIIIe siècle* (Toulouse, 1969), 102–27. M. Zerner points out that the phrase 'negotium pacis et fidei' circulated in a limited milieu ('Le *negotium pacis et fidei* ou l'affaire de paix et de fois, une désignation de la croisade albigeoise à revoir', in *Prêcher la paix et discipliner la société: Italie, France, Angleterre (XIIIe–XVe siècle)*, ed. R. M. Dessì (Turnhout, 2005), 63–102), but it was certainly an influential one.

[39] Du Cange, *Glossarium*, v. *faida, faidiare*, and *faiditus*.   [40] Graboïs, 'De la trêve', esp. 590–5.

[41] 'Si aliquis pacem fregerit vel moverit guerram ... excommunicetur, & extra pacem sit ...' (Mansi, XXIII: 201); 1258: 'guerras omnes inibuisse in regno' (*Ord.*, I: 84); 1274: 'cum ... baro aut castri dominus aliis guerram moverit ... pax dici debeat violata' (*HL*, X: 131–2).

[42] See Bartlett, '"Mortal Enmities"' on this point and for the regulation of self-help more generally.

[43] From Philip III's 1274 mandate 'cum in castris aut civitatibus, facta seditione publica, pars partem ejecerit vel cum armis invaserit, vel civitas, castrum, aut villa, aut baro aut castri dominus aliis guerram moverit, aut furtive castrum aut villam aut munitionem substraxerit' (*HL*, X: 131–2).

a much more extensive vision than that of their antecedents, and because Louis's measures concerned warfare – the type of violence most significant for seigneurial (and seigneurial/royal) power relations – this vision was also much more political.

Measures to limit violence under Louis also developed away from the old model of joint action by the temporal and spiritual powers. While the crown had acted according to this older paradigm in the 1229 Council at Toulouse, by issuing the 1258 ordinance it claimed jurisdiction over transgressions of the peace for itself, a continuation of a trend that can already be observed in the twelfth century. While excommunication had been the characteristic sanction threatened by earlier peace statutes, the resolution promulgated by the Council of Soissons presided over by Louis VII in 1155 enjoined no spiritual sanctions whatsoever, only vague promises that the king, great barons, and clerics would share responsibility for the punishment of violators.[44] The Council of Reims held two years later also prescribed secular judicial prosecution rather than spiritual sanctions for people who engaged in physical violence.[45] The movement away from shared ecclesiastical/royal surveillance of violence was not fully realized in Louis's reign. The 1258 ordinance did not mandate the seneschal to act alone in the preventions of misdeeds, but rather to help the bishop of le Puy with enforcement. Common sense suggests that the bishop used excommunication as a deterrent to transgressors, though as a prince-bishop, he also probably had significant secular measures at his disposal.[46] Unlike all prior statutes about violence, though, the 1258 ordinance did not issue from an extraordinary meeting of prelates and barons. It was an act of wholly royal provenance, simply issued after a consultation with Louis's council (if that is the way we should construe *deliberato consilio*). To be sure, this council was made up of prelates and barons, but it was an ordinary royal practice, not an extraordinary meeting.

Thus, although it incorporated many of the qualities of older, ecclesiastical peace-keeping efforts, as well as perhaps some of their administrative features, the regulation of local warfare under Louis was becoming a primarily royal prerogative. It is interesting to note that the bulk of the evidence for this development relates to Languedoc.[47] With the dubious exceptions of the *quarantaine du roi* and the forced truces of 1245, all of the normative texts related to the limitation of violence under Saint Louis are

---

[44] *HF*, XIV: 387–8; cf. Lot and Fawtier, *Histoire des institutions*, II: 290; Sassier, 'Les progrès de la paix' and 'Louis VII et la pénétration de la paix royale en Nivernais et Auxerrois', *Bulletin de la Société des sciences historiques et naturelles de l'Yonne* 113 (1981): 53–72.

[45] Mansi, XXI: 844.   [46] My thanks to Charles Donahue for pointing this out.

[47] Lot and Fawtier noted this without commenting upon it (*Histoire des institutions*, II: 426).

addressed to southern jurisdictions.[48] This may simply be coincidence or an impression created by the uneven survival of sources. Or it may be an indication of the opportunity that the conquest of Languedoc provided to the crown. Unlike the situation north of the Loire, where the crown was confronted with entrenched lordships governed by enshrined customary law, the Albigensian Crusade swept the board clean of most of the important local powers. The crown may have tried to assert itself in Languedoc in ways that it could not in lands where its authority was more encumbered.

AN ON-GOING BATTLE: SEIGNEURIAL WARS AFTER THE ALBIGENSIAN CRUSADE

Yet, whatever the considerable ideological developments detectable in royal prescriptions, these prohibitions did not result in an end to seigneurial warfare. During the twenty-one years of Alphonse de Poitiers's and Louis's southern administrative regimes, their officers and associates dealt with between eight and twenty wars in the South, as well as many other violent conflicts of a lesser nature. This violence reflected a society and a political structure in flux. The local powers of mid-thirteenth-century Languedoc warred against one another with regularity, as they had done for centuries and as they would continue to do for at least a century and a half longer. They also waged war over a geographic expanse and with adversaries that suggest the continuance of power struggles unconstrained by the Pyrenees or the Rhône, that is, by the new borders of French royal dominance. In addition, they waged wars against the Capetians and their representatives. This was in some ways a continuation of the wars between southern powers and Capetian interests that had constituted the Albigensian Crusade, as well as the rebellions of the great nobles that took place in the 1240s. But it also represented an intermediary stage in Capetian administrative growth in the South, whose rigour incited some of these wars and whose ultimate victory would mean the end of seigneurial warfare against the king's interests in the South by 1300.

The first evidence for seigneurial war in this period comes from the beginning of 1251, when Alphonse's constable of the Auvergne was implored to intervene in the war (*guerra*) being waged by Guillaume de Vendant, holder of several castles, against Chatard and Pierre, lords of

---

[48] Louis's 1258 ordinance addresses the seneschal of Beaucaire, as well as the inhabitants of le Puy. Philip III's 1274 mandate on peace-breaking is addressed to the seneschal of Carcassonne. That of Philip IV on the same subject was directed to the seneschals of Toulouse, Carcassonne, and Beaucaire.

Saint-Germain. Guillaume had attacked each of Chatard's and Pierre's holdings in turn, burning down their subjects' houses, taking their possessions, and kidnapping some of them, while Chatard and Pierre seem to have been guilty of some violence of their own.[49] The same year, Alphonse's representatives heard complaints that this constable had also failed to intervene in the *querela* between one Uldin Cholet and the lord of Thiers, allegedly involving arson in Thiers and the murder of some of the lord's subjects, though this violence may not have risen to the level of a war.[50] Around 1252, the bishop and inhabitants of Albi burned down a bastide and fortified their city against the seneschal of Carcassonne, who had led a great army (*magno exercitu*) against them, on account of disputed jurisdictional rights in the town, particularly as pertained to the confiscation of heretics' goods.[51] This conflict was only resolved because of a war (*calvacata et conflictus armorum*) involving important members of the local nobility that this bishop's successor pursued against the abbot of Gaillac at the end of the decade, and even so negotiations – particularly about rights to the fruits of heresy prosecutions – continued well into the 1260s.[52] At some point before Louis IX returned from crusade in 1254, men referred to as G. de Niort and B. Semon became involved in a dispute with one G. de Canet that may have been a war since it involved riding in arms, taking booty, and kidnapping.[53] In the spring and summer of 1256, the viscount of Béarn waged a war (*guerra*) against the count of Bigorre, whose succession he disputed.[54]

---

[49] *Enquêtes administratives*, ed. Fournier and Guébin, no. 4, arts. 98–111.

[50] Ibid., no. 3, arts. 2–6 and see no. 4, arts. 53–8.

[51] *HL*, VIII: 1301–5, 1305–10, 1310–12, 1358–60, 1364, quote at 1311; *LTC*, II: no. 3008, IV: nos. 4786, 4799, 4820, V: nos. 561–2, 594–605, 607–12, 614–30, 632 (bastide's combustion at no. 632). See J.-L. Biget, 'Un procès d'inquisition à Albi en 1300', in *Le credo, la morale et l'Inquisition* (Toulouse, 1971), 273–341, esp. 313–14.

[52] Quotes from *Correspondance administrative d'Alfonse de Poitiers*, ed. A. Molinier, 2 vols. (Paris, 1894–1900), no. 1892 (=*HL*, VIII: 1463–4). This war involved a battle (*bellum, bataille*): *HL*, VIII: 1455–63 and *Enquêtes administratives*, ed. Fournier and Guébin, no. 35, art. 1 (=*HL*, VIII: 1514). See also *Enquêtes administratives*, ed. Fournier and Guébin, no. 38; *LTC*, IV: nos. 4786, 4981 (=*HL*, VIII: 1518); *HL*, VIII: 1310–12, 1453; *Olim*, I: 460–1. The opinion that the war against Gaillac forced the bishop of Albi to negotiate with royal officials is that of Auguste Molinier (*HL*, VII: 292–4). See also Biget, 'Un procès', 313–15; M.-L. Desazars, 'Les évêques d'Albi aux XIIe et XIIIe siècles: Origines et progrès de leur puissance temporelle et de leurs revenus ecclésiastiques', *Mémoires de la Société archéologique du midi de la France* 12 (1880–2): 360–4. A seemingly final settlement was not reached until 1264 (BN Latin 9990, fols. 80r–82r).

[53] *HL*, VIII: 1357.

[54] An overview of this war and surrounding events is given in the introduction to *Le Cartulaire de Bigorre (XIe–XIIIe siècle)*, ed. X. Ravier and B. Cursente (Paris, 2005), xxxiv–v, with sources cited therein. See also G. Balencie, 'Procès de Bigorre, pièces justificatives', *Bulletin de la Société académique des Hautes-Pyrénées* 77 (1930): 1–128.

From 1255 to 1258, several southern lordships were involved in a war (or wars) waged by James the Conqueror, king of Aragon, as an extension of his conflicts with the king of Castile and in a failed effort to shore up his interests in Occitania and Provence.[55] This dispute, the exact contours of which are difficult to discern, arose out of James's policies in Catalonia as well as Occitania and seems to have begun with a war between James and his sons on one hand and the town of Montpellier, which was an Aragonese holding, on the other. In 1254, the inhabitants of Montpellier formed a military alliance with the viscount of Narbonne, who promised to make war (*guerra*) against any enemies of the town, aside from the king of France, his brothers, and the king of Castile.[56] Aragon was not explicitly mentioned in this agreement, but in 1255 the Aragonese king and his sons crossed the Pyrenees in arms, probably incensed by Montpellier's attempt to win French royal support by declaring that the bishop of Maguelone held the city from the king of France, and that the king of Aragon held part of the city from the bishop, but as a lord not a king (*non ut rex, set ut dominus*).[57] Whether Montpellier succeeded in holding the viscount of Narbonne to his promise to defend the city at this point is not clear, and Louis IX told his officers and subjects to remain on the sidelines of this *guerra*.[58] By 1257, the conflict had widened: although in February, Pope Alexander IV forbade anyone to attack Montpellier, in March the viscount of Narbonne challenged the Aragonese king to a *viva guerra* on behalf of the king of Castile,[59] and Louis IX dropped his neutral stance, characterizing Aragon's actions as an invasion against the crown (*occasione invasionis sibi facte*). Louis urgently sent commissioners down to the South, and the seneschal of Carcassonne raised troops to resist the incursion.[60] The Treaty of Corbeil in 1258 largely resolved the trans-Pyrenean component of James's conflicts, though jurisdictional rights in Montpellier remained subject to dispute.[61]

---

[55] For Aragon's trans-Pyrenean interests in this period, see T. N. Bisson, *The Medieval Crown of Aragon: a Short History* (Oxford, 1986), 68–9.

[56] *HL*, VIII: 1341–4.

[57] *LTC*, III: no. 4156. See also nos. 4160, 4247, 4285, 4312, 4325 for the business over the next two years; Jordan, *Louis IX*, 138–9.

[58] *HL*, VI: 847–9, VIII: 1362–3; see also VIII: 1393, 1393–4.

[59] Papal prohibition at *LTC*, III: no. 4323; *HL*, VI: 853–4, VIII: 1410–11.

[60] *HL*, VIII: 1411–12, 1506–9; *Olim*, I: 270–1.

[61] *HL*, VI: 858–62, 880–2, VIII: 1429–30, 1519–26. For the Treaty of Corbeil, through which James gave up his Occitan holdings apart from Montpellier and Louis gave up his trans-Pyrenean holdings, and related documents, see *LTC*, III: nos. 4399–400, 4411–12, 4433–5, 4457. See also Jordan, *Louis IX*, 199–200. There is almost no mention of these events in the collection *Documentos de Jaime I de Aragón*, ed. M. Desamparados Cabanes Pecourt and A. Huici Miranda, 5 vols. (Valencia and Zaragoza, 1976–88), but see III: nos. 864, 878 for a prohibition on Aragonese subjects going to Montpellier in 1257.

A penumbra of possibly related conflicts surrounded the Aragonese war. It seems likely that James's problems with Montpellier and Narbonne had some relation to wars that the count of Foix reportedly fought with James over Foix's Catalonian interests in 1251 and 1256, though so little is known about these wars that any relationship must be purely conjectural.[62] From 1255 to 1258, the viscount of Narbonne and the viscount of Lautrec were involved in a *controversia* with the lord of Castres over a castle and other holdings.[63] The timing of this conflict (which may not have actually entailed warfare) overlaps exactly with the period of Narbonne's alliance with Montpellier against Aragon, though it is difficult to tell if the two were linked. Similarly in the middle years of the 1250s, the merchants of Montpellier were engaged with those of Marseilles in a *guerra magna*, a dispute that seems to have arisen from events that took place in the Levant during Louis's crusade, but which must have affected Aragon's general interests in the Mediterranean, tangled as they were with Angevin rights in Provence, as well as Montpellier in particular.[64]

By the summer of 1262, a *guerra* had broken out between Gaston, viscount of Béarn, Géraud, count of Armagnac, and his mother on one hand, and the count of Comminges and the lord of Isle-Jourdain, on the other, in which Gaston was said to have invaded Comminges with a great army (*cum magno exercitu*).[65] In 1264, the count of Rodez's son and the nephews of one Gui de Séverac committed armed violence that included killing animals and setting fires, though laconic documentation makes the circumstances and extent of the violence unclear.[66] In 1267, the count of

---

[62] *HL*, VI: 886; *LTC*, V: no. 576. See also R. Viader, *L'Andorre du IXe au XIVe siècle: Montagne, féodalité, et communautés* (Toulouse, 2003), 127; P. de Marca, *Histoire de Béarn*, 2 vols. (Paris, 1640), bk. 7, ch. 25, II: 581–4. Trans-Pyrenean conflicts involving Foix are mentioned in the preamble to the Treaty of Corbeil, but are not actually settled by this agreement (*HL*, VI: 859).

[63] *HL*, VIII: 1361, 1363, 1434–5. Both Vaissete and A. Molinier characterized this conflict as a *guerre* (*HL*, VI: n. 1, 854–5), but because the sources do not contain any mention of specific violence, I have classified it as a possible war.

[64] *HL*, VI: 847–8, VIII: 1413–19; AD Hérault A 231, fols. 21–3. K. L. Reyerson notes the importance of this crusade for Montpellerian and Marseillian trade in the Levant (*The Art of the Deal: Intermediaries of Trade in Medieval Montpellier* (Leiden, 2002), 35–6).

[65] *HL*, VI: 874, n. 2; *Enquêtes administratives*, ed. Fournier and Guébin, no. 38, art. 14, no. 39 (includes *Correspondance administrative*, ed. Molinier, no. 1873), and nos. 40 and 56 (= *LTC*, IV: no. 4965); *Correspondance administrative*, ed. Molinier, nos. 1866, 1867, 1980–9, 2014; *LTC*, IV: no. 4981 (= French version in *HL*, VIII: 1517). A related episode was the war that Alphonse waged against the count of Armagnac in 1264 (*HL*, VI: 876–7).

[66] *Enquêtes administratives*, ed. Fournier and Guébin, no. 35, art. 7, see n. 13 for the participants (= *HL*, VIII: 1515–16 and Latin version at *LTC*, IV: no. 4981). These events may have been related to the violence of which the bishop of Rodez was accused in the county of Rodez, events complained about by the lord of Sévérac around 1260 (*LTC*, III: no. 4663), and possibly the cavalcades that this bishop and the abbot of Conques were then undertaking against one another (*Enquêtes administratives*, ed. Fournier and Guébin, no. 35, art. 3 [=*HL*, VIII: 1515 and Latin version in *LTC*, IV: no. 4981]; and *Correspondance administrative*, ed. Molinier, no. 1893).

Foix complained about invasions and pillage by the count of Comminges, though this violence may have just been incidental to the count's passage through the country on his way to Paris.[67] Another possible war took place that year when Philip de Montfort's bailiff burned the lands, killed the livestock, and mistreated the people of Sicard Alaman, one of Alphonse's lieutenants.[68] Around this time Jourdain, lord of Isle-Jourdain just west of Toulouse, found himself in a *guerra* with his cousin Isarn caused by a territorial dispute.[69] By March 1268, the people of Condom had complained that the count of Armagnac was committing violence against them, though the extent and duration of that violence is conjectural.[70] From 1268 to 1269, the marshal of Mirepoix and the inhabitants of Gaja-la-Selve and several other neighbouring settlements traded armed violence and undue seizures, which involved a coordinated attack upon Mirepoix's holdings by a coalition of villages, who 'entered the nobleman's land in arms with a rather large multitude of people' (*cum armis in non modica armatorum multitudine hostiliter intraverunt*), though *guerra* is not explicitly mentioned.[71] In 1269, the count of Foix seized the castle of Montégut, and was implicated in pillaging property belonging to the monastery of Lézat.[72] In 1270 we have indications of another possible war in that Anglise de Marestang (or de Ros) complained that the counts of Comminges, Astarac, and Armagnac had attacked her castle with arms and that the latter's men had killed her son.[73]

---

[67] *HL*, VIII: 1600–1.

[68] *Correspondance administrative*, ed. Molinier, nos. 307, 308 (=*HL*, VIII: 1606–7). For Sicard Alaman's career: *Enquêtes administratives*, ed. Fournier and Guébin, lxxxii–lxxxvi.

[69] *Correspondance administrative*, ed. Molinier, nos. 873, 942 (=*HL*, VIII: 1676–7), 1274. For this war, see also M. Mousnier, *La Gascogne toulousaine aux XIIe–XIIIe siècles: une dynamique sociale et spatiale* (Toulouse, 1997), 404; *Saisimentum comitatus Tholosani*, ed. Y. Dossat (Paris, 1966), 87, n. 3; AD Tarn-et-Garonne A 297, fol. 580r; *HL*, VI: 902, n. 5, 904–5, n. 5, VIII: 1602–3, 1647, 1676–7, 1687; *Enquêtes administratives*, ed. Fournier and Guébin, no. 128, art. 124. The war was preceded by almost a decade of litigation and accompanied by many emotive encounters and incitements to duel: J. H. Mundy, *Studies in the Ecclesiastical and Social History of Toulouse in the Age of the Cathars* (Aldershot, 2006), 123–6; Mundy, *Society and Government*, 114–16. See also 'Sentence d'arbitrage entre Jourdain et Isarn de l'Isle (30 avril 1265)', ed. F. Galabert, *Annales du Midi* 9 (1897): 97–106.

[70] Auguste Molinier described this conflict as 'une guerre assez vive' (*HL*, VI: 900, n. 1), but the sources for it do not clinch the characterization. I have classified it as possible rather than definite. See *Correspondance administrative*, ed. Molinier, no. 408 (= *HL*, VIII: 1635–6); *HL*, VIII: 1608–9.

[71] Quote at *Correspondance administrative*, ed. Molinier, no. 1336 (= *HL*, VIII: 1687–8); see also nos. 798 (= *HL*, VIII: 1639), 906 (= *HL*, VIII: 1644–5), 936 (= *HL*, VIII: 1648–9), 1270, 1272; *Enquêtes administratives*, ed. Fournier and Guébin, no. 128, art. 412.

[72] *Correspondance administrative*, ed. Molinier, no. 1394; see also nos. 1391–3 (= *HL*, VIII: 1709–10, 1710–11, 1711), 1403 (= *HL*, VIII: 1712); *Enquêtes administratives*, ed. Fournier and Guébin, no. 128, art. 122. See also *Correspondance administrative*, ed. Molinier, nos. 1255 (= *HL*, VIII: 1680), 1350 (= *HL*, VIII: 1690), which relate to damages done to Lézat, but may not be connected with Foix.

[73] *Enquêtes administratives*, ed. Fournier and Guébin, no. 128, arts. 414–15.

In total, at least eight and possibly as many as twenty wars took place in Languedoc from 1251 to 1270. Six of the eight definite wars took place in the 1250s, suggesting a decrease in violence over the period. But since the 1260s saw more 'possible wars' than the 1250s, the change should not be overstated, especially given the disposition of sources for this period.[74] Whether these numbers represent a shift in levels of violence as compared with earlier periods in southern history is impossible to determine with any confidence. The immediately preceding period was that of the Albigensian Crusade and the major baronial rebellions that followed it, and prior to the Albigensian Crusade, the landscape of power was quite different from that which would follow the war. But there is no doubt that lords waged war amongst themselves in pre-Capetian Languedoc. To take the example of Toulouse: the last Raymondine count waged a war (*guerra*) with the count of Astarac,[75] and the town's councillors (the *capitouls*) waged wars of conquest against their neighbours in the early thirteenth century, as John Hine Mundy has shown.[76] Beyond Toulouse, there is evidence of significant seigneurial warfare in Gascony, the Narbonnais, the Lauragais, the Auvergne, and elsewhere during the twelfth century.[77]

In terms of its geographic patterns, the bulk of seigneurial warfare reported from 1250 to 1270 took place in the county of Toulouse ruled by Alphonse de Poitiers, which probably reflects that he held the vast majority of Languedoc. Some wars were also fought in the royal seneschalsy of Carcassonne/Béziers controlled directly by Louis IX and his officers, though a number of these wars involved lands or people under the count of Toulouse's jurisdiction. Two conflicts, of which neither may have been a war, were fought in the Auvergne, both in the early 1250s. Except for Montpellier's wars with Aragon and Marseilles, there seems to have been no fighting in the royal seneschalsy of Beaucaire, though this may reflect the sources rather than reality.

The most striking geographic characteristic of these wars is how little they respected royal boundaries. Most obviously there were wars involving Spain, waged both on the southern side of the Pyrenees (in the case of Foix's possible wars) and to their north (in the case of Montpellier and Narbonne). Wars also took place that involved the imperial county of Provence, in the case of Montpellier and Marseilles, as well as Béarn, a viscounty that remained stubbornly beyond the French king's (and

---

[74] On my conservative classification of 'possible wars', especially in this earlier, less well-documented and more semantically varied period, see pp. 17–20, above.

[75] '[C]omes Raimondus, tempore quo habebat guerram cum comes Astaracensi, intulit ei dampna' (*Enquêtes administratives*, ed. Fournier and Guébin, no. 128, art. 534).

[76] *Society and Government in the Age of the Cathars*, 234.

[77] Mousnier, *Gascogne*, 250–8; see also A. Molinier's essay on 'guerres privées' in *HL*, VII: 142–4.

anyone else's) control for centuries.[78] The geographic extent of these wars perhaps seems unremarkable. Few would today argue that thirteenth-century France was a territorial state – let alone Aragon or the Empire – but the characteristic is worth noting because the seigneurial wars of later periods were much more territorially restricted.

A range of individuals and groups took part in these conflicts. Towns, most notably Montpellier, but also Albi, and even small villages like Gaja-la-Selve, went on the offensive, fighting not only against other munici-palities, but also against quite powerful lords. In the case of Montpellier against Aragon and Gaja-la-Selve's coalition against Mirepoix, they fought against their own lords. These wars perhaps reflect the wider struggle of towns for independence from seigneurial control, and they also suggest wider applicability for Christine Reinle's argument that *Fehden* were not restricted to the nobility, though these municipalities do still seem to have had an institutional communal identity.[79] The clergy, despite canonical prohibitions to the contrary, were also implicated in the violence. The monastery of Lézat appears to have been entirely on the receiving end of violence with Foix (or at least to have successfully portrayed events that way). But the abbey of Gaillac certainly had an offensive as well as defensive role in its conflict with Albi, and an abbot is among those mentioned as aiding the viscount of Béarn in his war in Bigorre.[80] Bishops also played a prominent role in the wars of this time. Two bishops of Albi waged wars, including one conflict that involved that rarest of medieval tactics, a battle (*bellum*). The bishop of Maguelone seems to have been a provocateur of the hostilities between Montpellier and Aragon. Within Alphonse's jur-isdiction, but outside the area considered here, there were also reports of cavalcades undertaken by the bishop of Rodez and the abbot of Conques against one another.[81]

But most of the wars and possible wars fought between 1250 and 1270 involved the hereditary nobility, including noblewomen in the case of

---

[78] Béarn in this period was technically held from the king of England, who exercised no real control there, and by the mid-fourteenth century, the count of Foix (at that point the celebrated Gaston Fébus) would claim that 'Bearn was held from God and not from any man on earth' (*Bearn, laquoau tee de Diu e no de nulh homi deu mont*). See P. Tucoo-Chala, *La vicomté de Béarn et le problème de sa souveraineté, des origines à 1620* (Bordeaux, 1961), esp. 59–93, quote from document no. 24.

[79] C. Reinle, *Bauernfehden. Studien zur Fehdeführung Nichtadliger im spätmittelalterlichen römisch–deutschen Reich, besonders in den bayerischen Herzogtümern* (Stuttgart, 2003).

[80] For the abbot (of Saint-Savin), see *LTC*, III: no. 4288.

[81] 'Cum illi qui ex parte abbatis de Conchiis fuerunt in calvacata et conflictu armorum habito inter ipsum abbatem ex una parte et venerabilem patrem episcopum Ruthenensem ex altera' (*Correspondance administrative*, ed. Molinier, no. 1893; see also *Enquêtes administratives*, ed. Fournier and Guébin, no. 35, art. 3 (= *HL*, VIII: 1515 and Latin version in *LTC*, IV: no. 4981). For the bishop of Rodez's 'arson and robbery' against the count of Rodez around this time, see *LTC*, III: no. 4663).

the dowager-countess of Armagnac and perhaps Anglise de Marestang. Eighteen of the twenty conflicts in total, and all but one of the definite wars, had at least one noble principal participant. More than half of the wars involving the nobility were fought by the greatest lords in the land, men like the count of Armagnac, the count of Foix, the count of Comminges, and the marshal of Mirepoix. The number of great lords is noteworthy because for most of the next century, the bulk of seigneurial warfare would be generated by those entitled *dominus* or *miles*: that is, men who hailed from the provincial elite, but not from its highest levels. The disproportionate number of great lords waging war in this period could be explained if Alphonse's and Louis's administrations simply did not penetrate very far down the social ladder, but this seems unlikely. They did deal with lesser lords' wars as well as those of magnates throughout the period, and there is no indication that they were delegating the adjudication of small lords' wars to other parties. Rather, warfare seems to have been something that great lords engaged in more regularly than did the petty lords. Most of those of viscomital status or higher who waged wars did so more than once, suggesting that war was not an exceptional event but rather a habitual option at this level of society.

The matters that provoked these conflicts are often hard to identify. For more than a third of the total conflicts, the cause is unspecified, though that proportion is slightly less for the definite wars.[82] Of those conflicts whose cause is known, most were about property rights: disputed possession of various territories and rights provoked wars between Castres and Lautrec, between Bigorre and Béarn, and between members of the house of Isle-Jourdain. Such disagreements were probably also at the heart of the participation of viscounts of Lautrec on both sides of the Albi/Gaillac war, and of the wars possibly waged by Foix against Aragon. One might also put in this category the war between Montpellier and Aragon, since it seems to have been fought over the bishop of Maguelone's claim that the king of Aragon was his vassal, as well as the violence committed by Gaja-la-Selve and affiliated villages against Mirepoix, a conflict set off by disputed forest rights. Vengeance was a possible motive in the conflict between Anglise de Marestang/Ros and Armagnac, Astarac, and Comminges, since the count of Armagnac was accused of killing Anglise's son,[83] but it is not clear whether this death caused the dispute or occurred incidental to it.

---

[82] Of the definite wars, only those between Guillaume de Vendat and Chatard de Saint-Germain, and between Armagnac, Béarn, Comminges, and Isle-Jourdain have unknown causes.

[83] For the accusation, see *Enquêtes administratives*, ed. Fournier and Guébin, no. 128, art. 415.

The preponderance of disputes over territorial rights would remain a stable feature of seigneurial warfare over the next century and a half; almost all wars with an identifiable cause can be traced to property rights connected with lordship. A particular feature of this period, though, is that these disputes were often also linked to the implantation of Capetian authority in the region. The clearest example of this is the bishop and town of Albi's war against the seneschal of Carcassonne and *viguier* of Albi in 1252, which was provoked by Albi's attempt to maintain the freedoms won after the Trencavels lost power in the early years of the Albigensian Crusade.[84] Montpellier's efforts to shake off the Aragonese yoke in favour of France must also have reflected the changed landscape of power in the post-Albigensian South, and it is difficult to imagine that Louis IX had forgotten Aragon's patronage of the Cathar and Trencavel cause.[85] There are also indications that the presence of Capetian representatives may have aggravated the amount of violence experienced by people in the South. Several of the wars fought during this period were waged by native southern powers against the new lords whose authority came courtesy of the Albigensian Crusade: the viscounts of Lautrec and Narbonne, both of southern families that survived the crusade, fought Philip de Montfort, lord of Castres, who was descended from Simon, Philip II's famous general. A municipal alliance attacked Gui de Lévis III, marshal of Mirepoix, whose grandfather, one of Simon de Montfort's lieutenants, was granted his lordship from the confiscated lands of heretics.[86] And the last truly undomesticated southern lord, the count of Foix, made war on Sicard de Montaut, who was apparently a favourite of Alphonse's officers, though not actually northern by origin.[87]

Alphonse's associates and the king's seneschals in Carcassonne/Béziers and Beaucaire/Nîmes also tended to engage in exactly the same actions as those they endeavoured to restrain: raising armies, seizing goods, and

---

[84] Biget, 'Un procès', 313–14.

[85] Raymond Trencavel had been raised in Aragon after his family's dispossession from the viscounty of Carcassonne and fought for James the Conqueror in Majorca and Valencia. He unsuccessfully attempted to retake his lands by force in 1240 but had to be satisfied with a small estate in Beaucaire and a small pension. There is no indication that James supported this expedition, but the Aragonese king's predecessor had fought against the French in previous episodes of the Albigensian Crusade (W. L. Wakefield, *Heresy, Crusade, and Inquisition in Southern France, 1100–1250* (Berkeley, 1974), 106–10; 153–5; see also *HL*, VII: 448–61). Nor did the Treaty of Corbeil solve all trans-Pyrenean problems between James and the Capetians, for in 1263 James's sons opened a *guerra* against Louis IX (*Correspondance administrative*, ed. Molinier, nos. 2007–8).

[86] *Cartulaire de Mirepoix*, ed. F. Pasquier, 2 vols. (Toulouse, 1921), I: 10–12.

[87] Sicard was a southerner, but he was strongly allied with Capetian government. He accompanied Alphonse for at least part of his attempted crusade in the East (*Correspondance administrative*, ed. Molinier, no. 1390), and on more than one occasion Capetian administrators were instructed to render him services (ibid., nos. 277, 344–5, 883–7).

destroying the resources of the lands they invaded.[88] As William Chester Jordan has noted, the post-Albigensian seneschals 'were little more than military governors',[89] and complaints about their violence were common. The count of Comminges, on whose lands the wrath of the administrators was unleashed following the count of Foix's accusations against him, protested in 1267 and 1268 that Alphonse's bailiffs had invaded his lands, seized goods, molested the inhabitants, cut down woods, and destroyed vegetation and pasturage.[90] Other lordships made similar representations about the behaviour of Capetian officers in their lands.[91] While some of these complaints were probably bogus, Louis's and Alphonse's reform ordinances show acute awareness that officers often abused their power.[92] Indeed, on more than one occasion Alphonse had to restrain his men from making unauthorized cavalcades, suggesting that the resentment was not groundless.[93]

PEACE-KEEPING AND THE NEW ORDER: THE ADMINISTRATION OF JUSTICE

Louis, Alphonse, and their representatives were not indifferent to these wars, even when the violence did not affect them directly. For most wars, there is evidence that the king or the count or both ordered intervention and generally sought to stop the conflict. They clearly saw a role for their authority in the regulation of violence and the settlement of dispute, though it is less clear that their actions were influenced by the ideas articulated in prescriptive measures like the *ordonnance* of 1258. Ideological reasoning and statements of policy are almost wholly absent from the sources in this period. Indeed, neither brother approached seigneurial

---

[88] For the composition and support of the officers' *exercitus*, see *Olim*, I: 270–1; *Correspondance administrative*, ed. Molinier, nos. 1394, 1463, 1499, 1500, 1531, among others. Among the expeditions of these armies was one against the count of Armagnac in 1264 ('convocando etiam exercitum et barones domini comitis ob culpam, rebellionem, et contumaciam ipsius domini Geraldi' (*LTC*, IV: no. 4965)).

[89] *Louis IX*, 47.

[90] '[A]liqui bajuli nostri hominess suos pignorant & alias molestias eisdem inferunt . . . nemora, herbas, pascua & alias res hominum suorum scindunt' (*HL*, VIII: 1638).

[91] In 1269, Jourdain, lord of Isle-Jourdain complained of violent seizures that one of Alphonse's men had carried out with an armed multitude of his enemies (*HL*, VIII: 1687).

[92] See n. 2, above.

[93] E.g. 'sine nostra licencia speciali aliquas calvacatas seu marcha[s] a vobis vel a vestris fieri permittatis, alioquin a vobis inde caperemus vindictam' (*Correspondance administrative*, ed. Molinier, no. 1879); 'Vos autem contra dictum comitem Fuxi . . . pendente ordinacione domini regis, guerram facere nullatenus presumatis vel aliud attemptare, quousque ab ipso domino comite aliud super hoc receperitis in mandatis' (*HL*, VIII: 1712).

warfare in a consistent manner or for consistent reasons, but rather treated each war as a separate problem. Capetian reactions to seigneurial warfare in the mid-thirteenth century, therefore, did not so much express a policy as reflect the Capetians' tenuous position in the South and their attempts to navigate its fraught political landscape.

The picture is complicated by the dual administration of the South, in which one brother ruled as a king and the other as a lord. One cannot simply speak of the crown's actions or those of royal officers in Languedoc, as would be the case after the royal absorption of Alphonse's lands in 1271. But the sources for Alphonse are illuminating precisely for what they do not say about royal – as opposed to comital – rights regarding violence and justice. Louis does not seem to have had any jurisdiction whatsoever over seigneurial warfare in Alphonse's lands. Of the nine definite wars, Alphonse dealt with three of them without royal involvement, while Louis's representatives were involved in only one war that did not also involve a comital response. Only one of the conflicts came before the royal court of Parlement, and this war, which was between Albi and Gaillac, also involved intervention by Alphonse and his officers.[94] In addition to the Albi/Gaillac war, one other war involved judicial or coercive action from both king and count or their officers, and another three wars, as discussed below, involved no enforcement activities from either party. As this indicates, during the mid-thirteenth century, seigneurial warfare was not considered what modern historians would call a *cas royal*, that is, a matter in which only the king was competent to judge.[95] In this regard, it is notable that although the reform *ordonnance* promulgated by Alphonse in the early 1250s envisages an appellate hierarchy, it offers no higher appeal than to the count.[96]

In addition to these jurisdictional limitations, coercive measures against warfare were also circumscribed because seigneurial warfare in mid-thirteenth-century Languedoc did not generally constitute a crime, if crime means an offence not only damaging a private party, but also injurious to the public interest or to the state (in this case meaning the king or the count). About a third of the conflicts seem to have entailed judicial intervention only in order to apportion damages to the aggrieved party, and this is equally true of cases that came under comital authority as

---

[94] *Olim*, I: 460–1; BN Doat 106, fol. 185. For Alphonse's judicial involvement, see *Enquêtes administratives*, ed. Fournier and Guébin, no. 35, art. 1. Cf. Jordan, *Louis IX*, 140.

[95] Perrot, *Les cas royaux*, 158–9, 172–8. Lot and Fawtier were more optimistic about the king's jurisdiction after 1260 (*Histoire des institutions*, II: 296, 318–23). See also Kaeuper, *War, Justice*, 233.

[96] *Enquêtes administratives*, ed. Fournier and Guébin, no. 5, arts. 8–15.

for those that pertained to the king.[97] In general (though not without exception), if the war had not damaged their domain lands or their direct vassals, neither comital nor royal authorities represented seigneurial warfare as prejudicial to the count's or the crown's interests. For example, when Louis IX ordered the seneschal of Carcassonne to deal with the damage done to Guillaume de Canet, he limited the action to be taken to reparations, with no penalties to be paid to the crown.[98] In other words, these wars were treated as purely civil matters.

There were also wars in which Capetian reaction took no judicial form whatsoever, but rather entailed a political approach and a diplomatic solution. Unsurprisingly, this was true of wars that involved a party who did not owe fealty to the French crown. The crown stayed out of the wars between Montpellier and Marseilles, and Béarn and Bigorre, allowing settlements to be brokered by the regions' great magnates, and it initially instructed its officers and subjects to stay out of the war between Aragon and Montpellier.[99] The war between Comminges and Béarn in 1263 entailed some judicial posturing on Alphonse's part, but it was largely treated in a manner consonant with the political and military issues that it raised.[100] In short, most wars in mid-thirteenth-century Languedoc did not offend the crown.

There were a few conflicts to which Louis and/or Alphonse reacted in a manner that suggests that these acts could be construed as offensive in ways beyond the material damage inflicted by opponents on one another. Particularly after the late 1250s, those who made war were often called upon to pay fines to the count or king, or to be punished in other ways. Of the eight definite wars, three – those of Albi and the Capetians'

---

[97] Those wars and possible wars in this category are Guillaume de Vendat and Chatard de Saint-Germain; Uldin Cholet and Chatard, lord of Thiers; Guillaume de Niort and Guillaume de Canet; Lautrec, Narbonne, and Castres; Comminges and Foix; Armagnac and Condom; and Anglise de Ros/Marestang and Armagnac, Astarac, and Comminges.

[98] '[P]lurima & gravia damna intulerunt G. de Caneto ... Quare vobis mandamus ... predicta damna & injurias emendari faciatis eidem' (*HL*, VIII: 1357).

[99] Montpellier/Marseilles was settled by Charles d'Anjou (*HL*, VIII: 1413–19) and Béarn/Bigorre by the count of Foix (*LTC*, III: no. 4286). Louis told his representatives not to intervene in the Bigorre affair, apparently as a favour to Béarn (*HL*, VIII: 1365). For Louis's initial orders to the seneschal of Carcassonne about Aragon, later retracted, see *HL*, VIII: 1362–3 ('vos non intromittatis, nec permittiatis quod homines terre nostre de ea se aliquatenus intromittant'). For the similarities between the king's reactions to Béarn/Bigorre and to Aragon/Montpellier, see Auguste Molinier's comments in *HL*, VI: 848–9, n. 3.

[100] See particularly Alphonse's correspondence with Queen Marguerite, Louis IX's wife, who asked that he broker an end to the war because Béarn's help was needed to aid the king and queen of England against their barons (*Correspondance administratives*, ed. Molinier, no. 2014). See also Alphonse's letter to Marguerite outlining his disinclination to interfere (ibid., no. 1988).

representatives; of Albi and Gaillac; and of Jourdain and Isarn d'Isle-Jourdain – involved penalties owed to the king or to Alphonse in addition to compensation owed to the aggrieved party. Four of the possible wars involved such penalties: those between the count of Rodez's son and Gui de Séverac's nephew; between Philip de Montfort and Sicard Alaman; between Foix and Sicard de Montaut and Lézat; and between Mirepoix and neighbouring villages. In the documents related to these wars, there is a sense that the violence involved injured royal or comital interests in some way that was distinct from the damages that the war-makers inflicted on one another. In 1269, for example, Alphonse ordered the seneschal of Toulouse to punish those involved in the Isle-Jourdain internecine war 'as it pertains to us' (*quantum ad nos pertinet, puniatis*), and distinguished these comital interests from the matter of the damages the parties had mutually inflicted (*de dampnis . . . a parte parti vicissim*).[101] Yet, while these cases may be said to have had a proto-criminal aspect, in many cases the language distinguishing between royal/comital interest and those of the aggrieved parties is less explicit, and it is not always clear that punishment was being inflicted for injury to king's or count's prerogatives rather than for actual material damage done to their lands or subjects.

These developments do not seem to have had much relation to Louis IX's prohibition of seigneurial war issued in 1258 or to the other norma-tive promulgations discouraging warfare. As noted above, the *quarantaine du roi* appears to have been enforced during Louis's reign because it is mentioned in Parlement, though, again, there are no indications that this limitation on warfare ever applied outside parts of northern France. There is evidence that the 'statutes of the Peace of Paris' on violence were being used during this period,[102] and mandates of Alphonse in response to the war among the Isle-Jourdains characterize the war as 'against the statutes of the peace' (*contra statuta pacis*).[103] Evidence for the 1258 *ordonnance*, on the other hand, is much sketchier. It is possible that the *statuta pacis* mentioned in Alphonse's mandate on Isle-Jourdain refers to Louis's *ordonnance* rather than the Peace of Paris or the Council of Toulouse. And there is also a mandate from Alphonse in 1270 that orders his men to

---

[101] Ibid., no. 1274; see also Alphonse's sanctions regarding Mirepoix/Gaja-la-Selve and others at no. 1336.

[102] *Enquêtes administratives*, ed. Fournier and Guébin, no. 135 (= *HL*, VIII: 1715–23). See above, pp. 20–30.

[103] *Correspondance administrative*, ed. Molinier, nos. 873, 1274. In another mandate, Alphonse ordered the seneschal of Toulouse to render his sentence 'secundum jus vel consuetudinem patrie seu statuta dudum edita in hac parte' (*HL*, VIII: 1676–7), but gives no further indications as to what these 'statuta' might be.

refrain from waging a *guerra* against the count of Foix 'during the king's ordinance',[104] a tantalizing but obscure reference.

In any case, no mandate or judgment from Louis or Alphonse suggests that *guerra* was cause for intervention in and of itself. Indeed, Louis gave special permission for his subjects to wage war on their own account for James of Aragon.[105] And there are statements from mid-thirteenth-century lords testifying to the legality of their wars, which seem to have gone unchallenged by higher authorities. The viscount of Narbonne's challenge to James of Aragon in 1257, for example, takes pain to explain his action as a vassalic duty, asserting that in issuing this *défi*, he was acting 'because vassals ought to obey ... their lords, to whom they swore fealty'.[106] And in the Limousin in the mid-1260s, a nobleman explained to Parlement that his violence had been done 'using his rights and through upright war' (*utendo jure suo et per rectam guerram*).[107] The case came to Parlement as a result of the disposition of some hostages, not because the war's legality was in question.

But if the Capetians' normative promulgations were of little apparent use for enforcement purposes, the idea of peace and its violation had greater currency. The bishop of Albi's war against the Capetians' representatives was said to have involved 'peace-breaking'. In 1253, the royal seneschal of Carcassonne called him to account for *pace fracta*, among other crimes,[108] and we also know that this offence was cause for citation to this seneschal's court based on Philip III's mandate using Gui Foucois's definition of a violation of the peace (*pax dici debeat violata*).[109] Peace and its divine sanction also had demonstrable influence on efforts to maintain order in Alphonse's county. The roll of his Parlement records the petition of his bailiff in Gascony regarding money spent 'harassing the violators and persecutors of peace' (*persequendo pacis violatores et persecutores*), which notes that he did this at the special mandate of the seneschal of Toulouse's lieutenant.[110] On one occasion, Alphonse himself also showed some

---

[104] 'Vos autem contra dictum comitem Fuxi ... pendente ordinacione domini Regis, guerram facere nulltatenus presumatis' (*Correspondance administrative*, ed. Molinier, no. 1403).

[105] For Louis's permission to his subjects prior to the crown's direct involvement in the war, see *HL*, VIII: 1394 ('licentiam concedamus ut quicumque ipsum regem juvare voluerit in hoc facto, hoc facere possit ... terre nostre vel subditis nostris ... nullam inferet violentiam sive dampnum').

[106] 'Cum vassali suis dominis, quibus fidelitatem juraverint, teneantur super promisis obedire ... de mandato predicti domini nostri regis Castelle tanquam vassallus ejusdem, diffidentes' (*HL*, VIII: 1410–11).

[107] *Olim*, I: 688–9.

[108] 'Carcassone compareatis coram nobis, parati super premisis procedere et facere prout de jure et usu curie nostre et secundum statuta patrie et usum curie domini regis fuerit faciendum' (*LTC*, V: no. 632).

[109] See above, p. 29.   [110] *Enquêtes administratives*, ed. Fournier and Guébin, no. 128, art. 321.

concern about seigneurial warfare's effect on the *pauperes* and expressed his duty to shelter them as a service to God, though the war in question – that waged between Béarn and Comminges – was largely dealt with on a political rather than legal basis.[111] Alphonsine sources also show some concern for the protection of clerics and their possessions from the violence of laypeople (*potencia laicorum*), another idea with ecclesiastical peace associations, though not one explicitly mentioned in royal peace promulgations from this period.[112] Capetian assertions about jurisdiction over peace-keeping did not go unchallenged by southern lords who considered this an infringement of their own rights, but the attention to peace-keeping would pay significant dividends in the decades to come, eventually replacing the old peace associations in the South with a general peace under royal aegis.[113]

The most common grounds for interfering in seigneurial warfare, though, was the charge of illegal carriage of arms (*portatio armorum*). All but one of the conflicts that involved criminal or proto-criminal penalties were said to have entailed this delict.[114] In 1259, the seneschal of Carcassone, acting for the king, argued that the bishop of Albi's war against Gaillac involved bearing arms illicitly (*arma portaverant illicite*) and fined his associates amounts ranging from 10 to 40 l.t. each,[115] and Alphonse de Poitier's representative condemned this bishop's men to a 500 l.t. fine for carriage of arms (*condampnati pro deportatione armorum*).[116] In 1264, the seneschal of Toulouse condemned the count of Rodez's son, the nephews of Gui de Séverac, and their accomplices to pay 400 *livres* for the *armes que porterent* in the count's lands.[117] For similar reasons, judgments were also ordered against Philip de Montfort's bailiff in 1267, and in 1269 against Jourdain de l'Isle, the monastery of Lézat's attackers, and Gaja-la-Selve and allied villages.[118]

The offence of bearing arms illicitly seems to have first appeared in a Parlement case from 1255 or 1256 regarding the bishop of Beauvais.[119] It had a future as one of the crown's major tools against seigneurial warfare,

---

[111] 'Deus offenditur ... pauperes destruuntur, unde principaliter propter servicium Dei' (*Correspondance administratives*, ed. Molinier, no. 1980, and see nos. 1981, 1988).

[112] Ibid., no. 1255; *Enquêtes administratives*, ed. Fournier and Guébin, no. 128, art. 428.

[113] Bisson, 'Organized Peace', 309–11; Bisson, *Assemblies and Representation*, 233; and see Chapter 2, below. For a (failed) seigneurial challenge to royal jurisdiction over peace-breaking and *portatio armorum*, see *HL*, VIII: 1705–6.

[114] The exception is the war of the early 1250s between Albi and Capetian representatives.

[115] *HL*, VIII: 1455–63. [116] *Enquêtes administratives*, ed. Fournier and Guébin, no. 38.

[117] Ibid., no. 35, art. 7.

[118] *Correspondance administrative*, ed. Molinier, nos. 308, 942, 1255, 1336.

[119] '[C]ontra inhibicionem domini Regis factam de armis non portandis' (*Olim*, I: 621). Perrot thought that the prohibition arose from the Council of Toulouse's peace-keeping clauses (*Les cas royaux*, 150–1, n. 1), but arms are not specifically mentioned in the Council's canons.

but this had not yet come to pass in the thirteenth century because, just as in other circumstances, the king or the count only dealt with carriage of arms when it occurred in his own domain or pertained to his own justiciables.[120] Thus, the charge against Albi and Gaillac included that there had been men in arms *en la terre mon segneur le conte*, but when Alphonse responded to the violence of Mirepoix against Gaja-la-Selve and other villages, he was only able to deal with the latter's violent response to Mirepoix, since they were under comital jurisdiction, while the marshal of Mirepoix was a royal vassal.[121] Indeed, not only was jurisdiction over *portatio armorum* in Languedoc divided between Louis and Alphonse, but even lesser lords like the bishop of Albi might claim cognizance of the crime in particular circumstances.[122]

The jurisdictional specificity of *portatio armorum* was typical of thirteenth-century offences, but the actual content of the crime also made it a difficult vehicle for the restriction of the authority to wage war. In the first place, it was vague. No ordinance on *portatio armorum* survives from the thirteenth century, and historians have consequently had a difficult time defining it.[123] Normative sources from the fourteenth century suggest that the crime's severity depended on the type of weapon carried, though they are contradictory about whether such everyday weapons as swords and knives were prohibited.[124] If one accepts Michel Toulet's definition that it involved the bearing of a prohibited weapon with malicious intent in the company of other people, which seems to accord with the sources, it indicated a much

---

[120] Kaeuper, *War, Justice*, 233.

[121] For Albi and Gaillac, see *Enquêtes administratives*, ed. Fournier and Guébin, no. 35, art. 1. For Mirepoix/Gaja-la-Selve and others, see Alphonse's sanctions against Gaja-la-Selve, and others at *Correspondance administrative*, ed. Molinier, no. 1336 ('culpabiles . . . de nostra jurisdictione in vestra senescallia existentes, ad restitucionem dampnorum . . . necnon ad emendas pro delacione armorum nobis debitas'). For his inability to do anything to Mirepoix, and his attempts to persuade the seneschal of Carcassonne to handle the matter, see ibid., no. 906. A similar case involved the bishop of Rodez: 'De la partie l'esvesque de Rodais n'est mie feste l'enqueste, quar l'en ne puet contreindre ses homes, qu'il ne sont pas de la jurisdicion mon segneur' (*Enquêtes administratives*, ed. Fournier and Guébin, no. 35, art. 3). For the royal domain, see *HL*, VIII: 1455–63.

[122] '[De] preconizatione quorumdam malefactorum clericorum et captione eorumdem et de delatione armorum . . . constiterit senescallo quod episcopus processit contra dictos malefactors quantum licet, si postmodum per suas patentes litteras requisierit senescallum, senescallus . . . quantum ad jurisdictionem domini comitis pertinet, faciet quod debebit; et inhibebitur senescallo ne se opponat nec impediat quin dictus episcopus in correctione et captione clericorum suorum jure suo et jurisdictione possit uti' (*Enquêtes administratives*, ed. Fournier and Guébin, no. 128, art. 479).

[123] There is a reference in 1265 to a 'statutum [regis] de armis non ferendis', but the statute appears non-extant (*Olim*, I: 626; see also n. 119, above; Jordan, *Louis IX*, 204). See also Perrot, *Les cas royaux*, 150–3; M. Toulet, 'L'incrimination de port d'armes au bas moyen-âge', *Mémoires de la Société pour l'histoire du droit et des institutions des anciens pays bourguignons, comtois et romands* 45 (1988): 435–48.

[124] See a 1320 *ordonnance* issued by the seneschal of Beaucaire (*HL*, X: 610–11) and one clause of a 1371 royal *ordonnance* for the bailliage of the Touraine (*Ord.*, V: 428–30).

broader range of violence than warfare.[125] The assimilation of war to this jumble of violence obscures the political and organizational aspects of war, as well as the difference in scale, that makes such wars – as opposed to violence in general – problematic for the growth of centralized, hegemonic authority. It also testifies to the continuing lack of a firm distinction between war and other forms of violence.[126] In this regard, it is particularly interesting that the charge of infractions of the peace, a more precisely defined crime that explicitly excluded minor types of violence, was used much less frequently than *portatio armorum* in judicial reactions to seigneurial warfare.[127]

There were also practical considerations that limited the implications of *portatio armorum*. Exceptions to the prohibition could be granted, and at least on one occasion lords attempted to use such exemptions in order to attack one another.[128] A related difficulty arose from the problem of fragmented jurisdiction. As long as justice over *portatio armorum* remained the purview of lords like Alphonse de Poitiers, then these lords had to have sufficient authority to carry weapons themselves and to use these weapons in order to stop wars and to enforce judicial decisions. Alphonse's example shows that such enforcement activity might very well involve waging a war of one's own against the recalcitrant seigneurs. In the early 1260s, for example, Alphonse had the seneschal of Toulouse enter the county of Armagnac with an army (*exercitus*) on account of the count of Armagnac's 'guilt, rebellion, and contumacy' in his war with Comminges (an expensive expedition for which Armagnac later repaid the seneschal), and there were other instances as well.[129] The imperative for lords to enforce justice coercively in their own domain effectively obviated any possibility of excluding seigneurs from engaging in violence legitimately.[130]

---

[125] Toulet, 'L'incrimination'.

[126] F. H. Russell, *The Just War in the Middle Ages* (Cambridge, 1975).

[127] The exclusionary clause in Gui Foucois's definition is 'Quod si private persone in civitatibus vel municipiis sese agresse fuerint, aut eciam pastores in pascuis multi, ut sepe contingit, occcasione eorumdem rixati, hec ad pacis non pertinent fractionem' (*HL*, x: 131–2).

[128] In 1270, the count revoked a licence to bear arms granted to a lord in Quercy because his opponent asked for a similar licence (*Enquêtes administratives*, ed. Fournier and Guébin, no. 128, art. 403). For the original licence, which was strictly given to deal with incursions from English Gascony and the bishop of Cahors, see ibid., no. 128, art. 206: 'proviso tamen ne in portatione armorum non excedat in aliis casibus non permissis'.

[129] Ibid., no. 56 and see no. 35, art. 14, n. 1. Other such military responses to war include the same seneschal's defence against Béarn (*Correspondance administrative*, ed. Molinier, nos. 1984–5) and his seizure of one of Isle-Jourdain's castles (*HL*, VIII: 1647); for involvement in the case of Anglise de Marestang/Ros, see *Enquêtes administratives*, ed. Fournier and Guébin, no. 128, art. 414.

[130] See O. Brunner, *Land and Lordship: Structures of Governance in Medieval Austria*, trans. H. Kaminsky and J. Van Horn Melton (Philadelphia, 1992), esp. 210; J. Firnhaber-Baker, 'Seigneurial War and Royal Power in Later Medieval Southern France', *Past & Present* 208 (2010): 62–6.

An apparent attempt by Louis to stop Alphonse from waging a judicial war against Foix in 1270 perhaps suggests some awareness on the crown's part that even such judicially authorized wars created a problem,[131] but there is no indication that this measure had broad implications for jurisdiction over violence.

In addition to these problems of law and jurisdiction, there were also administrative difficulties that would have impeded even the most enthusiastic effort to restrain seigneurial warfare in the South. The crown's hold on Languedoc, as everywhere in France, was relatively weak because there were very few Capetian agents in the South in proportion to the region's size. Even in the next century, when the crown had considerably greater authority in the South than it had under Louis, the administrators of the seneschalsy of Toulouse included the seneschal himself, his lieutenant, a *viguier*, a *sous-viguier*, a lieutenant to the *sous-viguier*, and bailiffs in three towns, as well as at least forty-two castellans holding down royal fortresses.[132] To this sum of about fifty officers, we must add their staffs and whatever garrisons were attached to the castellanies.[133] One could also include *paciarius* or *paciarii* in this accounting, but there is no evidence for the exercise of the office, and it is not clear that the position was under royal or comital supervision. All told, one can imagine that this came to a significant number of men, but it must be remembered that they were not all in one place at one time, that their mobility and communications were restricted, and that they had other responsibilities aside from dealing with seigneurial violence. In any case, whatever their numbers may have been in the fourteenth century, they were certainly fewer under Alphonse. Any efforts by him or by Louis to prevent or to punish seigneurial warfare would have been greatly circumscribed by this lack of manpower.

Even when men were available, it was not certain that they would do their job. As is well known, Louis's officers did not always conduct the king's business with efficiency and rectitude. Alphonse's representatives

---

[131] In 1270, Alphonse ordered the seneschal of Toulouse to be prepared to raise an *exercitus* to take back the castle of Montaut from the count of Foix if he did not return it peacefully (*Correspondance administrative*, ed. Molinier, no. 1394), but only ten days later he attenuated the order, telling him that on account of Louis IX's orders (*durante ordinancione . . . Regis*) he should not wage a war (*guerra*) against the count of Foix until he received further instructions (ibid., no. 1403).

[132] This estimate is based on the offices and castellanies whose existence is attested at least once between 1300 and 1400 in the *Gallia regia*. There were also about a dozen royal judges and several fiscal officers, but these men would not have been involved in employing force against warmakers or in the coercive execution of judgments. See also the map of royal administrative areas at the end of the fifteenth century in G. Dupont-Ferrier, *Les officiers royaux des bailliages et sénéchaussées et les institutions monarchiques locales en France à la fin du moyen âge* (Paris, 1902).

[133] An inventory of the armaments and supplies in the castle of 'Sumidrius' in the seneschalsy of Beaucaire in 1260 suggests a modest garrison and one probably not always in residence (*LTC*, III: no. 4626).

also seem to have been frequently delinquent. We know about the two wars in the Auvergne in the early 1250s because Alphonse's lieutenant, the constable of Auvergne, reportedly refused to intervene in them (*noluit se intromittere*).[134] On at least one occasion, this constable is said to have taken money in exchange for his aid, but then to have done nothing further.[135] The officers in the western districts of Alphonse's lands were not always as responsive as some might have wished either; in July 1269, Alphonse ordered the seneschal of Toulouse to handle the violence done to members of the abbey of Lézat, but he had to reiterate this instruction in October with evident irritation.[136] Such managerial difficulties acquired additional complexity when wars crossed jurisdictional boundaries, requiring the brothers and their officers to cooperate. While the seneschals of Toulouse and Carcassonne – the one working for Alphonse and the other for Louis – seem to have functioned in a complementary manner regarding the two wars of Albi in the 1250s,[137] other cases were less easily handled. Alphonse seems to have had no success at all in his efforts to persuade the seneschal of Carcassonne to force the marshal of Mirepoix to pay damages to Gaja-la-Selve and other villages for the violence he inflicted on them.[138]

These administrative shortcomings helped to ensure that 'self-help' without reference to royal or comital authority was a regular aspect of seigneurial disputes, in terms of both the actual violence and its aftermath. One may speculate that the seneschal of Carcassonne's foot-dragging may have been a factor in Gaja-la-Selve and its allies' attack on Mirepoix, during which they effectively took for themselves the reparations that Mirepoix owed.[139] Certainly, there were cases in which exasperation was evident. As Chatard de Saint-Germain explained in 1252, because the

---

[134] The quote is from *Enquêtes administratives*, ed. Fournier and Guébin, no. 4, art. 109 and regards the war between Guillaume de Vendat and Chatard de Saint-Germain. For the constable's reported obstinacy in the probable war between Uldin Cholet and Chatard, lord of Thiers, on account of which Chatard claimed to have 'amisit jus suum', see ibid., no. 3, arts. 2–6, and no. 4, arts. 53–8.

[135] '[I]dem dominus dedit dicto conestabulo 60 l., de quo dedit sibi litteras suas pattentes ut juvaret ipsum contra malefactores suos, qui terram suam comburunt: et nullum dedit sibi juvamen' (ibid., no. 3, art. 2).

[136] '[Si] nondum processum est, procedatis, ita quod propter deffectum juris vel vestrum ipsos ad nos non oporteat propter hoc ulterius laborare' (*Correspondance administrative*, ed. Molinier, no. 1350; original mandate at no. 1255).

[137] See also the seneschal of Toulouse's seizure of a castle belonging to Foix for the benefit of the king at ibid., no. 1394.

[138] Ibid., nos. 906, 1272.

[139] The communities' attack on Mirepoix, recounted in ibid., no. 1336, which dates from September 1269, came after efforts by Alphonse in November 1268 and July 1269 (ibid., nos. 906, 1272). Gaja-la-Selve and Plaigne were still seeking the count's assistance in procuring amends from Mirepoix in the late spring of 1270 (*Enquêtes administratives*, ed. Fournier and Guébin, no. 128, art. 412).

constable of the Auvergne refused to intervene in Guillaume de Vendat's war against him, he and his brother 'were forced to settle with Guillaume as best they could' (*choacti fuerunt componere prout potuerunt cum dicto W.*).[140] Such incidents recall an earlier period of history, when no princely power restrained noble disputes, and people were left to fight their own battles and settle their own disputes. While it has sometimes been assumed that such processes were replaced with institutional justice upon the arrival of Capetian authority in the South, this clearly was not the case.

It is true that neither Alphonse nor Louis endorsed these self-authorized violent initiatives; Gaja-la-Selve was fined for *portatio armorum* and the constable of the Auvergne was presumably punished for his dereliction of duty. But Louis and Alphonse's resistance to becoming involved in wars that bordered their southern domains suggests a certain reticence about overextending their authority in this region. At least partly because Louis prohibited his officers from interfering when the viscount of Béarn made war against the count of Bigorre, the latter was forced to give his county (*damus totum comitatum*) to Simon de Montfort in order that it be protected from these incursions.[141] When the two sides settled their dispute, they did so through the arbitration of the count of Foix, without any reference to Louis.[142] A similar dynamic seems to have been at work in the war between Montpellier and Marseilles, settled by Louis's brother Charles d'Anjou, without any apparent involvement by Louis or his officers.[143] With the exception of Montpellier, whose status was in dispute, none of these parties were royal vassals, and so the lack of royal involvement is in one way not surprising. But an accord made in 1258 between the viscounts of Lautrec and the count of Castres, all of whom did hold their lands from the king, was also made without evident royal participation.[144] Given Louis's well-known penchant for settling the disputes of others, his disinterest here seems to indicate that his ambitions in the South were limited and that he was not interested in using these incidents as an

---

[140] *Enquêtes administratives*, ed. Fournier and Guébin, no. 4, art. 109.

[141] '[Q]uod dominus Gasto Bearnensis devastavit nobis totam terram et nos non possumus defendere. Quare vobis et ordinio vestro damus totum comitatum Bigorre' (*LTC*, III: no. 4279). For Louis's prohibition (*nullum sucursum eidem Eschivato faciatis*), see *HL*, VIII: 1365. This donation caused a number of later problems in both England and France: J. R. Maddicott, *Simon de Montfort* (Cambridge, 1994), 134–5, 173, 183–4, 199–200; I. J. Sanders, 'The Texts of the Peace of Paris, 1259', *EHR* 66 (1951): 88–9, n. 4.

[142] *LTC*, III: nos. 4284, 4286–9.   [143] AD Hérault A 231, piece 3, fols. 21–3.

[144] *HL*, VIII: 1434–5. One of the arbiters, Pierre de Voisins, served as seneschal in both Louis's and Alphonse's domains, but he was not in office in the seneschalsies of Toulouse or Carcassonne in 1258 (*Enquêtes administratives*, ed. Fournier and Guébin, lxxvii–lxxix). The other two, Pierre de Graves and Bozo de Monestiès, were both titled *miles* and at least the former was a local landholder of some importance. For Graves: ibid., no. 128, art. 116; *HF*, XXIV: 651, 655, 679–81.

opportunity to increase royal influence. As for Alphonse, there is no indication that he was involved in the disputes of his neighbours, and his almost total absence from his southern lands during the more than twenty years of his reign as count suggests that his non-intervention came from the same conservative policy.

If the Capetians' impact on violence and justice in the South was limited, though, that does not mean that there was no impact at all. Some war-makers did pay fines, and Alphonse's officers' military intervention in the wars that took place in his domain demonstrates the count's ability to assert his authority coercively. Perhaps more importantly, some of their vassals had developed an expectation that officers could and even should interfere in these disputes, as complaints about their failure to do so make clear.[145] Although the officers' role was neither consistent nor based on consistent ideas about the relationship between greater authority and seigneurial warfare, some claims had been staked with implications for the restraint of violence and its submission to justice. There was certainly no coherent policy against seigneurial warfare in mid-thirteenth-century Languedoc, so judging its success or failure would be a futile exercise. Still, a number of developments had taken place that opened the door to increased oversight of seigneurial violence, particularly once Alphonse's appanages reverted to the crown after his death. There was some aware-ness that a war could harm higher authority even when that authority was not physically damaged by the violence, and a network of officers had been put in place. If a later administration were inclined to increase royal oversight of seigneurial violence, these were tools that it could use to do so.

As it happened, Louis's grandson Philip the Fair did have leanings in that direction. Philip would use these elements of his ancestors' legacy to revolutionize the crown's approach to seigneurial warfare, and he would cloak these efforts in Louis's saintly prestige. Before turning to Philip, though, it is important to emphasize that his initiatives were not Louis's, and that neither Louis nor Alphonse seems to have formulated a long-term policy. Under Gui Foucois's tutelage, Louis's measures against seigneurial warfare and violence developed in innovative ways, repurposing ideas from the Peace and Truce of God to bolster the crown's claims to oversight of violence and replacing the diocesan peace-forces with Capetian

---

[145] In addition to the incidents cited above, for Alphonse's administration in Rouergue see the complaint addressed to him by the lord of Sévérac against the bishop of Rodez (*LTC,* III: no. 4663).

officers. Yet, even though Languedoc seems to have been the main object of these measures, their practical effect is undetectable. There is no evidence that they dissuaded lords from warfare, the prevention of which was probably not an achievable goal given logistical realities. They also do not seem to have influenced the way in which Louis's and Alphonse's administrations handled these disturbances after they had erupted. One does not observe much effort to put the ideas elaborated in the normative documents into practice, but rather ad hoc reactions with no *modus operandi* or consistent justification for actions. Perhaps the most important constraint on Louis's and Alphonse's administrations, though, was the continued armed resistance to Capetian rule. By the mid-point of Philip IV's reign, southern lords would no longer wage war against the crown. In the post-Albigensian decades, though, the necessity of dealing with violent seigneurial opposition meant that politics remained a more important consideration than policy.

Chapter 2

PHILIP THE FAIR'S MISSION FROM GOD,
1270–1314

In 1270, Louis IX died while on crusade, and his brother Alphonse perished a year later. The kingdom, its domain lands now including Alphonse's appanages, was inherited by Philip III. Philip had good administrators, but his reign was brief by Capetian standards.[1] In 1285, he was succeeded by his son, Philip the Fair, whose twenty-nine-year reign is generally regarded as a watershed in French kingship and administration. Continually asserting the power and the dignity of his office, Philip IV literally and figuratively gave battle to challengers ranging from the Flemish towns to the king of England to the pope himself. Known as a cold and calculating man, he surrounded himself with lawyers who fostered and furthered his ambitions. Pierre Flote, Guillaume de Nogaret, Enguerran de Marigny, and other such capable and ambitious men helped Philip to transform the somewhat makeshift administrative structures that he had inherited into bureaucratic, professionally run institutions that increased the king's power over his lands and subjects.[2] Taxation was the primary way that they did this (and the primary reason that they were forced to do it), but the administration of justice, necessarily entailing restrictions on violence, also played an important role in the growth of royal dominion.

By the end of Philip's life, profound changes had taken place regarding seigneurial war. His reign saw a flowering of ideas about violence, justice, and royal authority, as well as major changes in the nature and treatment of actual seigneurial violence. In Languedoc, lords continued to wage war against one another, but by 1300 they had stopped doing so

---

[1] G. Sivéry, *Philippe III le Hardi* (Paris, 2003); C.-V. Langlois, *Le règne de Philippe III le Hardi* (Paris, 1887).

[2] The considerable bibliography on Philip the Fair and his reign includes J. Favier, *Philippe le Bel* (Paris, 1978); J. R. Strayer, *The Reign of Philip the Fair* (Princeton, 1980); and numerous essays by E. A. R. Brown, some of which are collected in *The Monarchy of Capetian France and Royal Ceremonial* (Aldershot, 1991) and *Politics and Institutions in Capetian France* (Aldershot, 1991). Most recently see her 'Moral Imperatives and Conundrums of Conscience: Reflections on Philip the Fair of France', *Speculum* 87 (2012): 1–36.

against the crown. In the context of this increased security, a network of royal courts and administrators developed to adjudicate disputes of all kinds and, at least in theory, to carry out the resulting decisions. The frenzy of legal and administrative activity that ensued meant that seigneurial wars fought in this period were often better documented than those that preceded them. Some of this success would be illusory, swept away by the Leagues of 1314–16, whose brief triumph will be discussed in the next chapter. But even under Philip's firm hand, royal development comprised not only centralized power encroaching on provincial society, but also an equally important, acephalous infiltration and co-optation of local power relations. Royal representatives continued to approach seigneurial warfare obliquely, working around the problems of power, violence, and justice in ways that expanded the crown's influence in a piecemeal but effective fashion, laying the foundation of a royal presence in local society which could endure even under the less favourable conditions that followed.

A MISSION FROM GOD: IDEOLOGICAL AND NORMATIVE DEVELOPMENTS

Ideologically, Philip the Fair's reign was a period of both continuity and growth. Philip and his councillors incorporated and expanded upon the ideas about royal power and the peace of the realm that had developed under Louis IX and Gui Foucois, justifying some of their new measures against seigneurial warfare by invoking Louis, whose authority Philip increased when he had him canonized. But Philip also exploited far more fully the opportunity to develop royal ideology through the proscription of warfare. Under Philip IV, the crown issued at least six *ordonnances* related to the limitation or prohibition of local warfare between 1296/7 and the king's death in 1314.[3] These measures are at once more pragmatically motivated and more elaborately theoretical than those of Louis. Confronted with wars that consumed unprecedented amounts of men and money, Philip tried to reserve the realm's military and economic resources for his own campaigns. He also used prohibitions against seigneurial warfare to articulate a theory of royal rule as the terrestrial execution of divine will whose implications for royal supremacy were no less great than military success in Gascony and Flanders. Losing some of the sacred associations it had in the mid-thirteenth century, peace

---

[3] *Olim*, II: 405 (1296/7); *Ord.*, I: 344–5 (1302), 390 (1304), 435–41 (1306), 492–3, XI: 426–7 (1311), I: 538–9 (1314).

under Philip IV became more fully connected with the king's justice and God's peace became sublimated to that of the king.[4]

In certain ways, this development of ideas meant that Philip's legislation broke with the inheritance from the Peace and Truce of God traditions so apparent in his grandfather's reign. Unlike peace legislation or Louis IX's regulations, Philip explicitly limited seigneurial wars for the benefit of the crown's diplomatic and military interests. By March 1297, Philip had prohibited wars when the king himself was at war, specifying that 'all other wars should cease until the king's war is finished', and furthermore forbidding recourse to judicial duel, the seizure of arms and horses for debts, as well as jousts and tournaments.[5] The interdictions against *guerra* and judicial battle would be reiterated in August 1314.[6] These statutes were promulgated in response to the wars in which Philip was engaged for most of his reign, wars that could not be effectively prosecuted if the energies of the fighting class and the fruits of the productive class were exhausted in petty internal conflicts.[7] Philip marshalled large armies for these conflicts, perhaps numbering between 17,000 and 26,000 men at one point.[8] Maintaining such a force was not only expensive but also logistically difficult. France would not have anything approaching a standing army until the reign of Charles V, and men were accustomed to serve only for the limited terms required by feudal dues.[9] Philip's edicts against seigneurial wars during royal wars were meant to ameliorate this situation by removing an impediment to recruitment. Moreover, decreasing the incidence of such warfare had economic benefits because it lessened the damage inflicted upon productive resources by the burning, pillaging, and murdering of peasants that seigneurial conflicts entailed.[10]

Philip's prohibitions against other wars during royal wars mark an innovation in royal normative thought, adding practical implications to

---

[4] J. Krynen, *L'empire du roi: Idées et croyances politiques en France, XIIIe–XVe siècle* (Paris, 1993), esp. 40, dates this transformation much earlier, but as argued in the previous chapter, even under Louis IX much peace-keeping remained an ecclesiastical concern, both practically and ideologically.

[5] 'Dominus Rex ... statuit quod durante guerra sua, nulla alia guerra fiat in regno ... aliae guerrae cessent, donec guerra Regis fuerit finita' (*Olim*, II: 405). The earlier prohibition is undated in the manuscript, though it is associated with business undertaken at the Parlement session that opened on All Saints' Day 1296. A *terminus ante quem* is provided by a *vidimus* of a letter of the lieutenant of Languedoc issued on 15 March 1297 regarding this prohibition (AD Tarn-et-Garonne A 297, fol. 931).

[6] *Ord.*, I: 538–9.

[7] Strayer, *Philip the Fair*, 314–46; Favier, *Philippe le Bel*, chs. 7–8; F. Funck-Brentano, *Les origines de la Guerre de Cent Ans. Philippe le Bel en Flandre* (Paris, 1897).

[8] Strayer, *Philip the Fair*, 376–9.

[9] P. Contamine, *Guerre, état, et société à la fin du moyen âge: Études sur les armées des rois de France, 1337–1494* (Paris, 1972), esp. 48–9, 151–70.

[10] G. Algazi, 'The Social Use of Private War: Some Late Medieval Views Reviewed', *Tel Aviver Jahrbuch für deutsche Geschichte* 22 (1993): 256.

what had been presented as simply a moral imperative. But Philip and his councillors were also aware of the sacral aspects of royal peace-keeping, and keen to extend their implications. In two *ordonnances* prohibiting warfare altogether, Philip elaborated and transformed the spiritual and moral underpinnings of Louis IX's regulations into a theory of king as divine judge. This made the suppression of warfare not just a moral duty related to the protection of peasants, but also a demonstration of the power with which the king was divinely invested. This conceptual evolution of the king's rights and duty with regard to his subjects' violence is most thoroughly explicit in a mandate of 18 January 1304 issued at Toulouse, which is worth quoting at some length:

> For the good of our realm, as befits the office of royal dignity, striving and desiring with all zeal and effort to counter the serious dangers to the people and things entrusted to us by God and the disturbances and various expenses which could arise from the criminal events of wars and battles, and thus noting that laws are ordained as a mediator (*in medio*) for this purpose, and the kings and princes of the earth [are] divinely deputized (*divinitus deputati*) for their defence and the execution of justice so that no one dare to make his own law (*sibi jus dicere*) or take up vengeance for himself, but that the force of justice (which we govern) might satisfy everyone, during our reign we want a solution to be supplied for everyone. Following the example of Saint Louis, the distinguished late Confessor-King of the French, and having made fuller deliberation with a number of our prelates and barons, by this general statute we expressly forbid and most strictly prohibit wars, battles, homicides, the burning of towns or houses, assaults of attacks on peasants or those who plough, or doing anything similar to our vassals and subjects, regardless of status or condition, in any place, or in any part of the realm; more expressly, we also prohibit challenges to judicial duel to be received or granted, or these duels to take place during our wars . . . Indeed we declare that for the purpose of the foresaid wars, the rash transgressors of these statutes and inhibitions ought to be punished as disturbers of the peace (*turbatores pacis*), regardless of contrary custom, or rather corruption, allegedly followed in any part of the said realm. . .[11]

This measure, whose provisions and language were recalled in a similar prohibition issued seven years later,[12] was clearly composed with Philip's military concerns in mind. This is to be expected as Philip was then preparing a very large expedition to Flanders for the summer of 1304

---

[11] *Ord.*, I: 390, here incorporating the corrections found in *Inventaire des archives communales antérieures à 1790: Ville de Toulouse*, ed. E. Roschach, 2 vols. (Toulouse, 1891), I: 61 and by consultation of AM Toulouse AA 4, no. 37, fol. 46. I have not been able to consult BN nouv. acq. fran. 7365, fol. 602v, notification of this *ordonnance* to the seneschal of Toulouse (cited in *Itinéraire de Philippe IV le Bel (1285–1314)*, ed. E. Lalou, 2 vols. (Paris, 2007), II: 234).

[12] *Ord.*, I: 492–3.

and was in Toulouse as part of a tour of the South to drum up support for the war.[13]

Despite this short-term objective, the prohibition evinces concerns inherited from the earlier ideas that imbued the regulations associated with Saint Louis. It specifically institutes the protection of peasants (*agricolae vel aratores*), and though this detail may strike a modern reader as ancillary, Philip's contemporaries apparently considered it a central feature since, in the register containing a copy of this letter, a fourteenth-century hand entitled (and interpreted) the entry *littere salvagardium agricolarum francorum*, or 'letters of safeguard for French peasants'.[14] The *ordonnance* also speaks of punishing transgressors as disturbers of the peace (*turbatores pacis*). This might just be a turn of phrase, but in 1302 Philip had sent a mandate to the southern seneschals in which he repeated almost verbatim Philip III's reference to the counsel given by Gui Foucois on violators of the peace.[15] Philip IV added that attacks on 'private people' (*private persone*, i.e. those not serving in an official capacity) and the violence of shepherds against one another did not pertain to infractions of the peace, but that anyone attacking someone on the roads should be considered a peace-breaker, even if acting alone.[16] As this suggests, peace-breaking was still a crime under Philip IV, as it had been under Louis IX and Philip III.

Yet, the crown's concept of the sacred aspects of kingship had consequences for the limitation of violence that went far beyond those implicit in Ludovician regulations. According to the reasoning of the 1304 *ordonnance*, Philip forbade wars and other destructive acts closely associated with warfare as a consequence of the king's role as God's minister of justice on earth. Self-help (*sibi jus dicere aut vindictam assumere*) could not be tolerated because it violated royal jurisdiction, not just because it caused destruction. The seeds of this conceptualization of royal power were clearly present in Louis's reign: Louis had a sense of himself as a divinely ordained judge and had prohibited warfare. But under Louis, the crown never made as explicit the connections between royal ideology and these provisions as this *ordonnance* of Philip's did. For

---

[13] *Itinéraire de Philippe*, ed. Lalou, II: 233–9; E. A. R. Brown, 'Royal Commissioners and Grants of Privilege in Philip the Fair's France: Pierre de Latilli, Raoul de Breuilli, and the Ordonnance for the Seneschalsy of Toulouse and Albi of 1299', *Francia* 13 (1985/6): 183–4.

[14] AM Toulouse AA 4, no. 37, fol. 46. There is also a marginal note: *non de guerris et duellis*.

[15] *Ord.*, I: 344–5 (Philip IV's mandate). For Philip III's mandate, see *HL*, X: 131–2, BN Latin 9988, fol. 117v; BN Latin 9989, p. 239, discussed on p. 28, above.

[16] For the importance of public roads, see *HL*, VIII: 1705–6; M. Toulet, 'L'incrimination de port d'armes au bas moyen-âge', *Mémoires de la Société pour l'histoire du droit et des institutions des anciens pays bourguignons, comtois, et romands* 45 (1988): 435–48.

Philip, the significance of his divinely authorized legal competency extended even beyond simply judging, to the annulling of customs contrary to God's will. Philip had inherited the claim to abolish custom from his father, and the 1304 *ordonnance* borrows the elder Philip's language wholesale, describing these customs as 'corruptions' (*consuetudines . . . seu pocius corruptelas*).[17] Philip IV would repeatedly push this claim about his precedence over custom in other promulgations, insisting upon the king's role as 'divinely appointed dispenser of justice, sovereign arbiter, and intermediary between God and his subjects'.[18]

There are some factors that suggest a more restricted interpretation of Philip's intentions for this measure: it survives only in a mandate to the seneschal of Toulouse and was issued at the same time as a number of privileges granted to the inhabitants of that city, who were at the time concerned about the war being waged between the counts of Foix and Armagnac.[19] But on closer inspection, these particular circumstances should not prevent a broad interpretation of this measure. Philip legislated on other generally applicable matters while in Toulouse,[20] and diplomatically, the prohibition bears a much closer resemblance to a general mandate for the upcoming war in Flanders issued at the same time than it does to the privileges for Toulouse.[21] It is true that Philip helped to negotiate a peace between the counts of Foix and Armagnac a few days after issuing the *ordonnance* against warfare and was in the South partly in order to settle their differences. When the crown referred to this incident several years later, though, it spoke of 'a *general* peace (*pax generalis*) pronounced there [in Toulouse] between all those of the lands of the seneschalsies of Toulouse, Carcassonne, Périgord, and Cahors and the

[17] *Olim*, II: 163–4 (1280 letter patent for Gascony, cited in P. Chaplais, 'La souveraineté du roi de France et le pouvoir législatif en Guyenne au début du XIVe siècle', *Le moyen âge*, 4th ser., 18 (1963), 463 and discussed by Langlois, *Le règne*, 291–2).

[18] E. A. R. Brown, 'Persona et Gesta: the Image and Deeds of the Thirteenth-Century Capetians, the Case of Philip the Fair', *Viator* 19 (1988): 230. See also E. A. R. Brown, 'The Prince is Father of the King: the Character and Childhood of Philip the Fair of France', *Mediaeval Studies* 49 (1987): 289; K. Wenk, *Philipp der Schöne von Frankreich, seine Persönlichkeit und das Urteil der Zeitgenossen* (Marburg, 1905), 50.

[19] R. Cazelles, 'La réglementation royale de la guerre privée de Saint Louis à Charles V et la précarité des ordonnances', *RHDFE*, 4th ser., 38 (1960): 539.

[20] T. N. Bisson, *Assemblies and Representation in Languedoc in the Thirteenth Century* (Princeton, 1964), 257.

[21] Privileges at *Ord.*, I: 392–3, 393–4, 394–7, II: 110–11. Mandate for the war in Flanders at *Ord.*, I: 391–2. Whereas all the privileges are written in the form of letters patent, the Flanders document and the war *ordonnance* were written as mandates. All the privileges state that they were sealed and are dated simply with the month and the year. The war *ordonnance* and the Flanders document do not bear sigillogic statements and are dated with a specific day. Both also specify that the king has consulted his prelates and barons in the matter, the advice of whom Philip does not mention in the privileges.

whole duchy of Aquitaine, which . . . we ordered to be observed between the two counts *and all others* . . .'[22] That the validity of this prohibition may have in fact extended beyond the South is further evidenced by a letter patent from 1306 modifying the 1304 ordinance's prohibition on judicial duel, in which the king observed, 'We have *generally* prohibited all manners of war and challenges to combat to *all* our subjects.'[23]

In December 1311, the king was once more moved to issue a prohibition on warfare. Addressed to 'all the justiciars of the realm' (*universis justiciariis regni nostri*), there can be no question of its general audience.[24] The 1311 ordinance was clearly intended to reiterate, not to replace, that of 1304, for reading between the lines one can observe the opposition that the 1304 ordinance had engendered. Like that of 1304, the measure of 1311 justified itself in terms of the common good, this time speaking of the harm that might befall the *res publica* if a remedy was not provided, and it attacked those who claim the right to engage in war because of local custom, which it twice likened to a corruption (*ex consuetudine . . . potius coruptela . . . consuetudine seu corruptela*). The custom/corruption language is significant. Although it was used in a measure of Philip III and ultimately derived from canon law, in my observation it was not regularly employed by the early fourteenth-century chancery.[25] Its appearance here suggests the 1304 *ordonnance*'s direct influence on composition, or at least a conscious effort to link this act with other measures claiming new royal power over local customs. The prohibition specified that its violators should be punished in body and goods, regardless of their status (*cujuscumque status aut conditionis*), and instructed the royal officers to publish it in their jurisdictions, making it known to all the barons, nobles, and other royal subjects so that they could not claim to be ignorant of it. It seems that there had

---

[22] '[D]e pace generali ibidem pronunciata inter omnes de illa patria senescalliarum Tholosane, Carcassonensis, Petragorircensis & Caturcensis ac tocius ducatus Aquitanie, quam pacem . . . servari inter dictos comites & omnes alios . . . statuimus' (*HL*, x: 490–7, also published in *Olim*, iii: 382–9).

[23] '[N]ous eussions deffendu generalement à tous nous subjets, toutes manieres de guerre & tous gaiges de bataille' (*Ord.*, 1: 435–41; *Textes relatifs à l'histoire du Parlement depuis les origines jusqu'en 1314*, ed. C.-V. Langlois (Paris, 1888), no. 122). Philip's evolving position on judicial duel is too complex to be dealt with here and will form the basis of a separate article, demonstrating that under Philip judicial duel became separated from the issue of public order and came to be seen mainly as an issue of procedural law rather than violence.

[24] *Ord.*, 1: 492–3. Another, almost identical version is to be found at *Ord.*, xi: 426–7, where it is addressed to the bailiffs of Vermandois, Amiens, and Senlis.

[25] An almost exactly similar phrase 'non consuetudo, sed corruptela potius sit censenda' appears in Book 1, Title 4, Chapter 5 of Gregory IX's *Liber extra* in reference to violations of interdict. It also appears in ibid., 1.4.11, where it is argued that custom ought to be in accordance with natural and divine law. The earliest example of the phrase of which I am aware is the first canon of the Council of Sardica (344 or 347), in which the wandering of bishops is characterized as 'Non minus mala consuetudo quam perniciosa corruptela' (Mansi, iii: 22), but other authors used the phrase or words like it repeatedly.

been objections to the 1304 measure both from those who claimed a regional dispensation and from those who claimed they had not heard about it. The new *ordonnance* was intended to obviate these excuses. But Philip's 1311 *ordonnance* also makes it clear that this was a work in progress, saying that the king planned to issue further instructions about the implementation of this measure (*quousque super hiis plenius fuerit ordinatum*), much as he had been forced to do in 1306 when tempering the 1304 ordinance's prohibition of judicial duel. Acting innovatively to privilege legal process over violent self-help, Philip also evinced awareness that the practical exigencies of government would require adjustment and perhaps attenuation.

Three years later, Philip issued a new act, again addressed to all the justiciars of the realm, in which he prohibited war and duels during his own projected war in Flanders.[26] This prohibition is difficult to understand in the context of the two previous *ordonnances*. It would seem as though the crown were relaxing the prohibition against warfare that it had made in very strong terms in 1304 and reiterated in 1311. The proscription of other wars during the king's war seems to suggest that when the king was not at war, then such wars were legal. This had been an explicit stipulation of the 1296/7 *ordonnance*, which was only a temporary measure, outlawing local war only until (*donec*) the royal war had ended.[27] But it is less clear that the 1314 ordinance should be read this way. It begins by referring to the prohibition of 1296/7, and then remarks that, these wars being over, 'many people presumed and presume (*presumpserint & presumant*) to make war among themselves'.[28] It does not say that their presumption was correct, and the choice of the verb *praesumere* seems almost pejorative. One might translate it as those who had gone to war had *dared* to do so. It is true that the measure specifies that wars are to cease during the king's war (*dicta guerra durante*), but the phrasing is much more ambiguous than the 1296/7 ordinance's provision (*donec guerra regis fuerit finita*). And the 1314 *ordonnance* also specifies that it should endure 'for as long as it should please the king' (*quandiu nobis placuerit*). The grammar is ambiguous here: this stipulation certainly was meant to apply to the prohibition on judicial duels, but it may also be construed to apply to the wars, as well.[29] Rather than relaxing the prohibition against all wars, then, the crown seems once more to have been reiterating it – like the

---

[26] *Ord.*, I: 538–9.   [27] Cazelles, 'La réglementation', 539.

[28] 'Cum nos olim tempore guerrarum nostrarum Vasconie, & Flandrie, omnia guerrarum genera . . . inhibuimus . . . post hujusmodi guerras nostras finitas, persone plures inter se guerras facere presumpserint & presumant . . .'

[29] '[O]mnes guerras in regno nostro, inter personas quascumque sub pena commissionis corporum & bonorum, guerra nostra durante inhibeamus fieri, & duellorum vadia quecumque quandiu nobis placuerit, precipiamus in suspenso teneri.'

1311 ordinance, that of 1314 placed special emphasis on the publication of the measure – and to have been conveying the particular importance of its observance during royal wars. Although we do not have evidence from Philip's reign that bears on the interpretation of the 1314 *ordonnance*, later judicial evidence supports the interpretation that making war during the king's war was an aggravating factor, but that war was not therefore licit during times of royal peace.[30]

In many ways, then, Philip's prohibitions developed the peace-keeping efforts of earlier Capetians in novel ways. While Philip's ordinances speak of peace, the same central concern of his father's and grandfather's measures, they seem to mean simply freedom from violence – in the sense of peace and quiet (*pax et quies*) – rather than peace in the older, more holistic, and sacred sense that seems to have been indicated in Louis's peace-keeping measures.[31] As the sacral connotations of *pax* disappeared from royal normative language, though, they were replaced by a new preoccupation with the common good and even the *res publica*, a term that might best be translated as 'state' or 'government' in this context.[32] The exposition of the 1304 *ordonnance* asserted that the prohibition was needed for the 'prosperous state of our realm' (*ad statum prosperum regni nostri*), and that of 1311 claimed that *guerrae* were 'a danger to the republic' (*in periculum Reipublice*), ideas also found in the *ordonnance* of 1296/7 (issued *pro communi utilitate & necessitate regni*) and in the interpretative mandate of 1306 (made *pour le commun prouffit de nostre Royaume*).

Here we may see an indication of the difference between Louis IX's councillors and those of Philip IV. While Louis's measures apparently derived from the ideas of Gui Foucois, whose career was divided between royal and ecclesiastical service, the ideas that resonate in Philip's prohibitions suggest input from his lawyers. In particular, we may discern the hand of Guillaume de Nogaret and/or of his protégé Guillaume de Plaisians. Trained at Montpellier and serving first as provincial judges and administrators in their native South, both men held expansive ideas about the reach of royal authority and law's role in the ordering of society.[33] Their understanding of Philip's power not only eschewed

---

[30] See Chapter 4, pp. 134–5.
[31] For 'pax et quies', see *Ord.*, I: 492–93. Cf. the same phrase in Louis's 1254 reform measure (*Ord.*, I: 65–75).
[32] See further discussion of the *res publica* at pp. 103, 119, 177, below.
[33] F. J. Pegues, *The Lawyers of the Last Capetians* (Princeton, 1962), 98–103; H. Wieruszowski, *Vom Imperium zum Nationalem Königtum. Vergleichende Studien über die publizistischen Kämpfe Kaiser Friedrichs II. und König Philipps des Schönen mit der Kurie* (Munich and Berlin, 1933), 157–64; C.-V. Langlois, 'Les papiers de Guillaume de Nogaret et de Guillaume de Plaisians au Trésor des Chartes', *Notices et extraits des manuscrits de la Bibliothèque nationale et autres bibliothèques* 39, pt. 1 (1909): 211–54; Brown, 'Moral Imperatives', 17–26.

subservience to the Church but also positively asserted the king's dominance over it within the confines of his kingdom.[34] Their hostility to ecclesiastical jurisdiction, particularly after the culmination of the Boniface controversy, may well account for the more secular tone of the crown's normative approach towards peace-keeping under Philip IV and the completion of its transformation from God's peace into that of the realm. It is likely that Guillaume de Plaisians accompanied Philip on his trip to the South in 1304,[35] which would have placed him at the scene for the promulgation of Philip's most expansive statement against seigneurial war.

Yet these apparently more worldly concerns of Philip IV and his councillors belie a strong, enduring sense that royal peace-keeping responsibilities had a divine origin. In Philip IV's measures his obligations are presented as delegated to him by God: the 1304 ordinance says that kings and princes were 'divinely deputized' (*divinitus deputati*) and that people and things had been 'entrusted to us by God' (*commissarum a Deo nobis*). But under Philip, the divine nature of the task was transformed into a justification for royal opposition to seigneurial war in a way that affirmed the superior rights and powers of kings, particularly relative to justice and violence. The 1304 *ordonnance* asserts these connections most strongly, explaining that prohibiting warfare and judicial duels 'befits the office of royal dignity' (*Regiae dignitatis decet officium*) and that it is intended to dissuade people from avenging themselves, when they ought to defer to kings and princes. Under Philip IV, the crown employed the Capetian inheritance from earlier peace legislation to support its ideological effort to extend royal power with explicitly governmental intentions. The execution of these aims was, as we shall see, problematic and its legacy insecure, but it is important to recognize the extent of the conceptual advance made. Philip and his councillors claimed control over justice and violence in the name of the public good not just because peace was a Christian ideal, but also because as a Christian king Philip had a duty and a right to do so.

A MORE LOCALIZED PHENOMENON: SEIGNEURIAL WAR UNDER PHILIP THE FAIR

At the same time that Philip's administration was developing this more ideologically sophisticated framework, the character of seigneurial war in

---

[34] See *Documents historiques sur le Gévaudan. Mémoire relatif au paréage de 1307 conclu entre l'évêque Guillaume Durand II et le roi Philippe le bel*, ed. A. Maisonobe (Mende, 1896).

[35] A. Henry, 'Guillaume de Plaisians, ministre de Philippe le Bel', *Le moyen âge* 5 (1892): 35–6; F. Maillard, 'À propos d'un ouvrage récent. Notes sur quelques officiers royaux du Languedoc vers 1280–1335', in *France du Nord et France du Midi: Contacts et influences réciproques*, vol. 1 of *Actes du 96e Congrès national des sociétés savantes (Toulouse, 1971)* (Paris, 1978), 325–58.

the South underwent some changes in character. Southern seigneurial war in the immediate post-Albigensian decades was mainly waged by great lords, sometimes waged against the Capetians, and sometimes spilled over the Rhône or the Pyrenees. During Philip the Fair's reign, all of these qualities largely disappeared. While the legacy of the Albigensian Crusade continued to cast a shadow, the real motor of dispute was the beginning of the 'little Hundred Years War' between the counts of Foix and Armagnac. The most significant change was that under Philip IV wars tended to be fought by smaller players over smaller stakes than they had been under Alphonse and Louis. Finally, as changes in royal thought and practice are reflected in the disposition of the sources, the wars of this period appear more sharply delineated, especially in the last years of Philip the Fair's reign.

For the reign of Philip III and the first half of his son's rule, however, the sources are few, and what we do hear about seigneurial war looks similar to events in the 1250s and 1260s. The scarcity of the records may be largely explained by the fact that Languedocian cases were heard in the short-lived provincial Parlement at Toulouse, the records of which have essentially disappeared.[36] The records we do have from the period 1270 to 1285 mainly pertain to wars fought by the semi-independent counts of Foix and Armagnac against the crown and against one another. The first of these occurred around 1272, when, as Guillaume de Nangis reported in his *gesta* of Philip III, Géraud de Casaubon, lord of the castle 'Sompuy', and the count of Armagnac were in conflict, 'daily challenging one another to battle'.[37] The conflict might have gone no further, but when Casaubon killed Armagnac's brother in an impromptu battle, things became serious. Fearful for his life and holdings, Casaubon placed himself under the king's protection, while Armagnac called upon his allies, particularly the count of Foix, Roger-Bernard III.[38] They besieged and burned Sompuy, killed the inhabitants, and laid waste to the surrounding area.[39] The crown's response was swift and mighty. A *guerra*

---

[36] The various copies of the 'Curie Francie domini regis de feudis et negociis senescalliarum Carcassone et Bellicardi et Tholosani et Caturcensis et Ruthenensis' (BN Latin 9988, 9989, 9990, etc.) are not related to the Parlement of Toulouse nor are they registers of the Parlement de Paris, as is sometimes mistakenly reported.

[37] '[S]e invicem ad bellum quotidie provocabant' ('Gesta Philippi regis Franciae, filii sanctae memoriae regis Ludovici', *HF*, xx: 490; Guillaume reported a less exciting account in his 'Chronicon', *HF*, xx: 564). The episode was also related in Guillaume de Puylauren's chronicle (*Chronique (1145–1275): Chronica magistri Guillelmi de Podio Laurentii*, ch. 50, ed. and trans. (into French) J. Duvernoy (Paris, 1976), 212–17). For the identification of Sompuy (probably Saint-Puy), see *The Chronicle of William of Puylaurens: the Albigensian Crusade and its Aftermath*, trans. and ed. W. A. Sibly and M. D. Sibly (Woodbridge, 2003), 123, n. 94.

[38] For this and what follows, see Langlois, *Le règne*, 59–63; *HL*, IX: 11–21, X: n. 2.

[39] '[O]bsidendo castra dicti Geraudi de Casali Bono ... eadem incendio concremando, depredando,

raged between Foix and the seneschal of Toulouse, while Philip III himself gathered an army and personally marched south.[40] Armagnac was immediately punished and Foix made to submit, but a final peace between Foix and the crown was only reached around 1277 when Foix did liege homage to Philip III, agreed to accompany him on crusade, and accepted a diplomatic role in Iberian affairs.[41] An inheritance dispute over Bigorre soon prevented any further violent collaboration between Foix and Armagnac, but far from quieting south-western Languedoc, it set off a war between the counties that would continue intermittently for most of the next century.[42] This war thus began a new chapter in the history of southern warfare, but the war over Sompuy had closed another. Except for the (rather different) case of collaboration during the Hundred Years War between the English and the counts of Foix, who remained essentially outside royal control for most of the fourteenth century, the war that began over Sompuy was the last war that southern lords fought against the crown, rather than just amongst themselves.

Aside from the wars of these great barons, there is little indication of seigneurial warfare from 1270 to 1300. In 1287, the viscount of Narbonne erected a gallows by 'armed power' (*armata potencia*) as part of his dispute with the city's cathedral chapter, a deed that may have been part of a larger conflict since he was suspected of peace-breaking and *portatio armorum*.[43] In 1294, the lord of la Voulte in the seneschalsy of Beaucaire was found guilty of destroying the bishop of Valence's castle during a truce in their *guerra*.[44] And in 1295 there were two possible wars: a dispute between the lords of Castelnau and Uzès over succession to the barony of Lunel was in danger of inciting the claimants to 'brawls and arms, unless quickly curbed by mediating justice' (*ad rixas veniat & arma, nisi mediante justicia celeriter refrenentur*),[45] and in English Gascony, the viscount of Béarn waged *cavalgade*, though the destruction may not have extended to French territories.[46] In the absence of the records from the

interficiendo homines et mulieres in castris existentes, extirpando vineas et ortos, et arbores fructiferas abscidendo' (*Olim*, I: 407–8, also published in 'Essai de restitution d'un volume des *Olim*', in *Actes du Parlement de Paris*, ed. E. Boutaric, 2 vols. (Paris, 1863–7), I: no. 121 with some omissions).

[40] *HL*, X: 88–93, and see 102–7; Guillaume de Nangis, 'Gesta Philippi regis Franciae, filii sanctae memoriae regis Ludovici', *HF*, XX: 490–5; Guillaume de Nangis, 'Chronicon', *HF*, XX: 564; 'Majus chronicon Lemovicense', *HF*, XXI: 778.

[41] *Olim*, I: 407–8; *HL*, X: 88–93, 138–40.

[42] No monograph exists on this long conflict. For some guide to it, see M. Vale, *The Angevin Legacy and the Hundred Years War, 1250–1340* (Oxford, 1990), 86, 88–90, 124–31; *HL*, IX: 146–8.

[43] *HL*, X: 211–12.

[44] L. Ménard, *Histoire civile, ecclésiastique, et littéraire de la ville de Nismes avec des notes et les preuves*, 7 vols. (Paris, 1750–8), I: no. 90 (based on BN Latin 11017, fols. 7v–8, 10v, 14r, 79v–80r); BN Latin 11017, fol. 66v.

[45] *HL*, X: 317; see also the account in *HL*, IX: 186–7.   [46] Vale, *Angevin Legacy*, 84.

Parlement of Toulouse, though, it is impossible to tell much about the actual incidence of seigneurial warfare.

At the turn of the fourteenth century, however, the sources become more consistent and more abundant. This may reflect institutional changes in the Parlement of Paris as it grew in importance for Languedoc owing to the closure of the Languedocian Parlement at Toulouse in 1291, and as the Parisian court gradually emerged as the supreme court of appeal and developed a section dedicated to criminal affairs by 1306.[47] Conflicts also become more clearly defined: five of the seven definite wars of Philip IV's reign, all termed *guerra*, occurred between 1310 and 1314, suggesting that there may have been a growing prosecutorial sensibility to large-scale, organized violence as different from a collection of murders and burnings. The resurgence in royal legislation on seigneurial war during the second half of the reign may also have played a role in bringing more conflicts to royal attention and more clearly describing them as wars, although, as discussed in the next section, there is little evidence for application of the *ordonnances*. The increase in visible warfare may also reflect an escalation in the amount of actual disorder in the South as inquisitorial excesses drove Languedoc almost to the point of rebellion,[48] and the Foix and Armagnac war tended to ignite other hostilities not directly related to the conflict.

During the first fifteen years of the fourteenth century, that is the latter half of Philip IV's reign, Parlement dealt with six definite wars and six other conflicts that may have been wars. Nearly all of the questionable conflicts are reported in the first ten years of the century. In 1302, Parlement confirmed the sentence pronounced by the seneschal of Carcassonne against certain communities in Foix and Andorra for excesses and bearing arms against the lord of Mirepoix, an indication that they had probably been at war.[49] Parlement did not convene in 1303 on account of the war in Flanders,[50] but in 1304, it was again ruling on significant seigneurial violence, ordering the viscount of Narbonne to return the castle of Leucate, which he had violently occupied *per vim et potenciam suam*, and the 'many excesses and injuries' that Jean de 'Chanlayo' committed against Guillaume Buisard, though this latter conflict may not have occurred in Languedoc.[51]

---

[47] On the appeal's development: L. de Carbonnières, *La procédure devant la chambre criminelle du Parlement au XIVe siècle* (Paris, 2004), 25–30; Strayer, *Philip the Fair*, 200. On the criminal/civil division: M. Langlois, 'Les archives criminelles du Parlement de Paris', in *La faute, la répression, et le pardon*, vol. 1 of *Actes du 107ème Congrès national des sociétés savantes (Brest, 1982)* (Paris, 1984), 7–8; A. Grün, 'Notice sur les archives du Parlement de Paris', *Actes*, ed. Boutaric, I: CCXXII.

[48] Strayer, *Philip the Fair*, 14, 260–7; W. C. Jordan, *Unceasing Strife, Unending Fear: Jacques de Thérines and the Freedom of the Church in the Age of the Last Capetians* (Princeton, 2005), 5–6.

[49] '[S]uper excessibus et armorum portacione illicita factis in terra domini Mirapicis' (*Olim*, III: 105–6).

[50] *Olim*, II: 467.

[51] For the viscount of Norbonne, *Olim*, III: 136–7. For Chanlayo and Buisard, *Olim*, III: 120.

Two years later, it dealt with Bernard de Roquefort's invasion of the priory of Moulin-Pessin in the Auvergne, convicting him of stealing animals, destroying property, and imprisoning the prior and his familiars.[52] In the seneschalsy of Toulouse before March 1309, Castelnaudry's army (*exercitus*) attacked Gaillac in arms and with raised banners after the latter complained that this army had stolen their livestock. Reportedly shouting, 'Peasant traitors ought to die!' (*moriantur rustici proditores*), they burned down seven houses, broke into other houses, robbed strong boxes of clothes, money, and charters, and attacked the church.[53] In the same seneschalsy that year, the *damoiseau* Eudes de Roquefort and his enemy, Guillaume Unaud, agreed to a peace agreement, which may indicate that a war had transpired.[54] In or before 1311, there may have been a war between Pierre d'Avène and Raymond de Sanséchelle because their peace treaty (*pacis federa*) is said to have been broken.[55]

The last four years of Philip's reign primarily saw conflicts that were definitely wars. In May 1312, the viscount of Polignac in the Auvergne came before Parlement for what seem to be two separate conflicts. The first took place with the church of Brioude over the possession of jurisdiction in the town of 'Alnerio', a dispute that incited the viscount to invade the town twice, once with three hundred and then with four hundred armed men, shouting that all should come to see the viscount's justice (*clamantes quod omnes venirent videre justiciam vicecomitis antedicti*).[56] The second was a war with the lord of Saint-Nectaire, in which the two allegedly 'tried to attack one another and to convoke crowds and to make raids' (*ipsi invicem nisi fuerunt se debellare et plures convocare et facere calvacatas*).[57] In 1312 as well, the bishop of Albi mustered the entire population of the town of Albi to attack Amblard de Pullan's bastide and castle, reprising this act the next year.[58] In 1313, Parlement took up the matter of Pierre de Maumont's misdeeds against several parties in the Auvergne, including two priories and the lord of Beaufort, against whom he was accused of mustering three hundred troops.[59] Finally, in the last year of Philip IV's reign, the Toulousain towns 'Helizona', Eauze, and Bretagne-d'Armagnac, on one hand, and Othon de Cazeneuve and the

---

[52] *Olim*, III: 182–3.   [53] *Olim*, III: 324–5.
[54] '[A]d tractandum de pace super quadam controversia mota inter eos reformanda' (*Olim*, III: 381–2).
[55] *Olim*, III: 626–7.   [56] *Olim*, III: 667–9.   [57] *Olim*, III: 672, and see also 787–8, 878–9.
[58] BN Doat 103, fols. 139–52; *HL*, IX: 347.
[59] '[I]dem miles, cum magna multitudine armatorum, feodalium suorum, ac aliorum plurium, tam peditum quam equitum, usque ad numerum trecentorum et amplius, cum armis prohibitis, in terra et juridicione domini de Bello-Forti plures excessus perpetravit' (*Olim*, III: 1270–1; see also *Olim*, III: 764; AN X2a 1, fol. 25; AN X2a 2, fol. 143r; *Actes*, ed. Boutaric, no. 6034).

town of Gondrin, on the other, made *guerra* against one another, raising their banners, cutting down trees, and burning houses.[60]

Overall, from 1271 to 1314, southern powers took part in at least eight and perhaps as many as seventeen seigneurial wars. As under Louis IX and Alphonse de Poitiers, wars took place with a greater incidence in the south-west than in the south-east. Of the eleven conflicts with known geographical information, seven took place in the seneschalsies of Toulouse and Carcassonne, while only two happened in the seneschalsy of Beaucaire and only three in the bailliage of Auvergne. But while the period from 1250 to 1270 is conspicuous for its wars' disregard for royal borders, seigneurial conflicts under Philip III and Philip IV largely lacked this element. The only exceptions are the Foix and Armagnac war of 1272, which seems to have involved King James of Aragon in some way, and the possible war against Mirepoix in 1302 which involved Andorrans (who were, according to Parlement, *de extra regnum*).[61] Both were relatively early and both involved Foix, the only southern power that would retain strong trans-Pyrenean ties throughout the fourteenth century.[62]

That lords increasingly seem to have looked inward and to have concentrated on local struggles is partly explained by changes in the identity of opponents. Fewer wars in this period involved very important lords or other kings and, except for Foix and Armagnac's war of 1272, none was waged against the French crown and its representatives. The rest of the wars during this period were small conflicts fought between fairly minor players. The increased incidence of this later type of war after the turn of the century may be more apparent than real owing to the uneven nature of the sources, and perhaps to patterns of prosecution and the growth of administrative networks that allowed better royal surveillance, as is discussed below. Richard Kaeuper thought that the preponderance of small lords in early fourteenth-century prosecutions simply indicated that the crown was less comfortable pursuing more important magnates.[63] Still, the absence of 'international' conflicts and of seigneurial wars against the crown after 1300 is striking and significant. There would still be uprisings and rebellions, some of them violent, but none of these was

---

[60] '[P]redicto defendentes, cum pluribus aliis malefactoribus aliunde venientibus … insultum faciendo et guerram, turba coadunata, vexillo ville de Helizona elevato … loca, domos, vineas et arbores fructiferas dicti militis et subjectorum suorum, per ignis immissionem, devastaverant, depopulaverant et pluries invaserant' (*Olim*, III: 887–9, additional accounts at 886–7, 903–5).

[61] *Olim*, III: 105–6. See also the works cited in note 62.

[62] C. Pailhès, *Le comté de Foix, un pays et des hommes: Regards sur un comté pyrénéen au moyen âge* (Cahors, 2006), 293–4; R. Viader, *L'Andorre du IXe au XIVe siècle: Montagne, féodalité, et communautés* (Toulouse, 2003), 132–5.

[63] *War, Justice, and Public Order: England and France in the Later Middle Ages* (Oxford, 1988), 237, n. 178.

primarily military in character. For the entire fourteenth century, the French crown was never again the object of its southern vassals' armed hostility in the way that it had been so often in the years following the Albigensian Crusade. Fifty years after the death of the last Raymondine count of Toulouse, the Capetians were finally secure in their Languedocian possessions.

POLICY, PROTECTION, AND PRIVILEGE: THE JUDICIAL PROSECUTION OF WARFARE

The development of royalist ideology in the *ordonnances* and the consolidation of the king's military and governmental position in the South reflect the growth of royal authority in both ideal and fact under Philip the Fair. Complementary changes were taking place in the judicial prosecution of warfare in the South, as the crown began treating warfare as more clearly a criminal than a political matter, and as it developed the kind of administrative network necessary to enforce its will. At the same time, there were also other developments that, while less coercive, royalist, or centralizing, none the less arose from and further enabled royal expansion in the South. Examining the reasons given for sanction against seigneurial war-makers reveals that while the *ordonnances'* assertion of a royal monopoly over justice and warfare was not central to officers' actions, a major innovation made in prosecuting warfare under Philip was to argue that it violated a special royal privilege of protection called the safeguard. The safeguard grew out of ideas that were somewhat at odds with those expressed in the *ordonnances* and demonstrates the variety of avenues through which the crown's role in local power struggles could grow, even in a period of relative royal strength.

A fundamental judicial change under Philip IV was to begin to treat seigneurial warfare not just as a social and political problem to be solved but also – or even exclusively – as a crime to be punished. In addition to civil penalties intended to restore the damage done to the opponent, eleven of the conflicts also resulted in fines paid to the king, and most of these were clearly criminal fines, not civil damages for harm done to the king's lands and justiciables, as had usually been the case under Louis and Alphonse. The fines were apparently linked to the financial status of the convicted. In 1312, Parlement refused to judge a case because the inquest did not contain such crucial information as whether the accused had sufficient resources to be fined.[64] But when there was money to be had,

---

[64] '[D]efectus sunt tales: Non apparet . . . si sunt divites vel non, ut competens emenda contra eos possit taxari' (*Olim*, III: 672).

the fines were large. As a sampling, the inhabitants of Foix and Andorra were fined more than 7,000 l.t.; Jean de Chanlayo was originally fined 4,000 l.t., though it was later reduced to 800 l.t.; Bertrand de Roquefort was sentenced to pay 1,000 l.t.; and while the town of Gondrin got off with a 1,000 l.t. fine, Helizona, Eauze and Bretagne-d'Armagnac were each slapped with a 10,000 small l.t. penalty.[65] A sentence pronounced against the viscount of Polignac condemning him to pay a year's income over two years suggests that the sums may have approximated annual revenues, certainly a heavy burden for anyone.[66] In addition to these steep financial penalties, Parlement also sometimes sentenced war-makers to royal seizure of their lands, or even the destruction or deprivation of castles, a penalty that struck at the heart of military lordship.[67] In the case of the Toulousain towns Helizona, Eauze, and Bretagne-d'Armagnac, they were deprived of their right to a consulate, effectively stripping them of their municipal identity and governmental authority.[68]

The shift from the political to the judicial partly reflected the increased security of Capetian rule in the South, and it probably also helped to make this security possible, because it grew out of the consolidation of a remarkably efficient network of royal courts and officers. Procedural indications in Parlement's records reveal a coherent hierarchy of courts where cases were heard and investigated in a systematic fashion. Most of the cases of seigneurial warfare in Parlement during this period were heard as an appeal to a sentence pronounced at a seneschalial court (the records of the latter rarely survive). Once at the great court, the parties made their case, and then the matter was investigated locally and the results (*inquesta*) were sent back to Parlement to be judged. Depending on what was proved (*probatum est*), the court issued its judgment, or, in the rare case that it did not have enough information, it ordered the inquest to be again conducted.[69] These inquests do not survive, but they must have been fairly detailed because Parlement often fined not just the principal parties to the dispute, but also numerous accomplices, many of whom seem to be of quite humble background.[70] The general impression is of a court that judged efficiently, based on a systematic investigative process, and whose

---

[65] *Olim*, III: 105–6, 120, 182–3, 887–9, 903–5.

[66] '[D]ictus vicecomes condempnatus fuit . . . ad solvendum nobis, pro emenda, valorem fructuum et reddituum terre ipsius vicecomitis de uno anno, solvendum ad duos annos' (*Olim*, III: 667–9).

[67] *Olim*, III: 182–3, 381–2, 626–7. For a contemporaneous case from the seneschalsy of Périgord, see *Olim*, III: 373–4.

[68] '[P]er suam sentenciam, omni consulatu, ita quod ipsi amodo non habeant consulatum, nec possint consules eligere vel creare in locis predictis aut alioquo eorumdem in futurum, privavit' (*Olim*, III: 887–9).

[69] Reinvestigations ordered at *Olim*, III: 672, 764, see nn. 57 and 59, above.

[70] E.g. *Olim*, III: 46–7, 667–9, 903–5, and see 1448–54, from the reign of Philip V.

constituents respected its authority. Unlike in later periods, defendants were almost never contumacious, and decisions were arrived at quickly, with a minimum of procedural wrangling.[71]

This court system was buttressed by the work of provincial officers. Under Philip IV, the old office (or offices) of *paciarius* was replaced by the king's own men, a change indicated by the substitution *nostre gentes* for *paciarius* in Philip's 1302 reissuance of his father's mandate on peace-breaking.[72] How often these royal officers were able to execute the judgments communicated to them is difficult to gauge given the surviving evidence, but they were clearly expected to do so.[73] A mandate from 1284 prohibits judges from daring to change or obviate *ordonnances* and *arrêts*, threatening that if they continued to do so the king would inflict such punishment as to put fear in their hearts.[74] At least in the case of Bertrand de Roquefort, we know that his sentence was carried out because a later remission relates that royal officers had executed the sentence to destroy his castles (*factaque per gentes nostras fuerit execucio dirucionis predicte*) and grants permission for their reconstruction.[75]

Officers also attempted to limit violence in their districts. The *viguier* of Toulouse was certainly punishing *portatio armorum* in the late 1270s, because the consuls and inhabitants of Toulouse complained that he was fining people much more for simply unsheathing a sword than the customary fine for actually wounding someone.[76] There are at least two instances in which royal officers reportedly physically arrested noblemen and their retinues when they suspected them of intending to do violence.[77] And there is evidence that it was incumbent upon officers to mediate disputes before they turned violent, as in 1295 when Philip IV ordered the seneschal of Beaucaire to seize a disputed barony and adjudicate the matter, lest the

---

[71] The only instance of contumacy in a case of southern seignuerial warfare in this period is that of Bernard de Saint-Nectaire (*Olim*, III: 878–9).

[72] Philip IV's mandate orders that peace-breakers be handed over 'sive ad manum gentium nostrarum sive ordinariorum' (*Ord.*, I: 344–5). Philip III's order was that they go 'sive ad manus paciarii sive ad sui ordinarii manus' (*HL*, x: 131–2). See also Bisson, *Assemblies and Representation*, 233.

[73] Records of the collection of fines, which would have been received by the Chambre de comptes, were probably destroyed with the vast majority of the institution's records in the fire of 1737 (M. Nortier, 'Le sort des archives dispersées de la Chambre des comptes de Paris', *BEC* 123 (1965): 460–537).

[74] '[J]udices nostre ordinationes curie & arresta . . . nullatenus observantes, ea retractare, immutare & eis obviare presumunt . . . transgressores . . . taliter puniemus, quod unius inmensitas pene terrorem inferat merito cordibus aliorum' (*HL*, x: 186–7).

[75] *HL*, x: 511–12.

[76] '[Q]uando aliquis vulnerat aliquem . . . tenetur domino Regi in sexaginta solidis Tholosanis. Nunc vicarius de novo, si aliquis extraerit gladium . . . & neminem vulneraverit . . . punit tales & dicit debere puniri in decem vel XX libris' (*HL*, x: 159–65).

[77] *Olim*, III: 281–2 (from the seneschalsy of Périgord), 667–9.

claimants take up arms.[78] Royal provincial administrators encountered the occasional bump – such as the poor lieutenant seneschal of Toulouse, caught between conflicting orders from his superiors in 1295[79] – but in general the system (and it was a system) seems to have functioned surprisingly smoothly.

The contrast between the response of Philip IV's administrators and the ad hoc, mainly political treatment of seigneurial conflicts under Louis IX and Alphonse de Poitiers is striking, but there were also other, less coercively 'royalist' developments afoot. First of all, an important exception to the move from the political to the judicial can be seen in the treatment of the great lordship of Foix, and to a lesser extent, that of Armagnac. In 1272 when these counts attacked Géraud de Causabon and the seneschal of Toulouse, Philip moved against them with overwhelming force, summoning an army drawn from all over France.[80] He ultimately imprisoned both counts, fining Armagnac 15,000 l.t. and reportedly leading Foix away in chains.[81] This was primarily a military operation, though, and there are few legal concerns evident in this display of royal power. Armagnac's fine can be viewed as a penalty for damage done to the king's lands, and as Guillaume de Nangis put it, Philip was moved to act 'mostly because it happened in the beginning of his reign' (*maxime quod in primordio regiminis sui*),[82] when his hold on the realm was not yet fully established, especially in Languedoc where royal rights to the county of Toulouse following Alphonse's death could potentially have been disputed. Moreover, Foix's disobedience was especially dangerous; he was probably a Cathar sympathizer, and his ties to Aragon were at least as strong as his links to France.[83]

The lesson that the crown wished Foix and Armagnac to learn seems to have been simply not to attack the crown and its representatives. When they began to fight one another, as they did throughout the later thirteenth and the fourteenth century, royal agents did not generally interfere in a judicial way and usually intervened only to try to orchestrate truces. Although Philip had explicitly told the count of Foix not to attack Armagnac in 1303 and to allow him to settle the problem, the arbitration of 1304 was only a civil settlement, carrying no penalties for his disobedience.[84] Indeed, unlike the smaller lords who found themselves called

---

[78] *HL*, X: 317.   [79] *HL*, X: 288–92.

[80] 'Majus chronicon Lemovicense', 778; Langlois, *Le règne*, 60.

[81] Armagnac: *Olim*, I: 407–8. Foix: Guillaume de Nangis, 'Gesta Philippi', 492.

[82] Guillaume de Nangis, 'Gesta Philippi', 492.

[83] Pailhès, *Le comté de Foix*, 293–4; Langlois, *Le règne*, 62; Jean Duvernoy's remarks to Guillaume de Puylaurens, *Chronique*, ch. 50, ed. Duvernoy, 212–17; *HL*, VIII: 215, IX: 14, n. 1, X: 138–40; cf. Vale, *Angevin Legacy*, 92–3.

[84] Pierre de Marca, *Histoire de Béarn*, 2 vols. (Paris, 1640), bk 8, ch. 29, II: 610–12.

before Parlement and fined for their war-making, the great counts of Foix and Armagnac never seem to have been criminally prosecuted for their activities in the fourteenth century, even though their war was definitely implicated in the prohibition of January 1304.[85] For Foix, at least, his apparent immunity may be explained by his very active and able lawyers, whose frequent jousting with royal proctors over comital prerogatives is discussed below, but it certainly also reflects the special relationships that the crown needed to maintain with these great lords on the borders of its kingdom and the fact that it was very difficult to police such important men.

Lesser lords could obviously be subjected to greater pressures, especially given the growth of Philip's judicial and administrative network. Still, his courts and officers do not seem to have understood their work as a defence of the idea of hegemonic royal justice articulated in the *ordonnances*. There is a near total lack of definite references to Philip's legislation in royal judicial records. The only possible explicit reference is a prohibition reportedly made in 1298 by the seneschal of Toulouse forbidding the count of Foix from making war on Armagnac because of the 1296/7 *ordonnance* against seigneurial war during the king's wars, but the reference is doubtful and does not jibe with the surviving evidence.[86] From the early fourteenth century, particularly in Périgord, there are regular citations of the 'statutes of the peace', and these may refer to Philip IV's *ordonnances*,[87] but as is the case for similar references under Louis IX, it is equally possible that these *statuta pacis* refer to Church canons, not royal legislation. For the seneschalsies and bailliages of Languedoc, Parlement's records on warfare make only two ambivalent references to laws emanating from the king: in 1312, the viscount of Polignac was accused of 'rashly contravening our prohibitions' (*contra nostras prohibiciones temere venientes*), and in 1314, Helizona's and Eauze's actions were described as 'rashly contravening the good of peace and the state of the county, and our statutes' (*contra bonum pacis et statum terre, ac nostra statuta, temere venientes*).[88] The similarity of the phrasing perhaps suggests an embryonic effort to standardize legal treatment of seigneurial warfare (at least from a prosecutorial point of view), and the appearance in Philip IV's waning years – at the same moment that

---

[85] See above, pp. 62–3.

[86] The only evidence for it is a remark made in the eighteenth century by the Languedocian historians Claude Devic and Joseph Vaissete (*HL*, IX: 205), which cited a text from Château de Foix, caisse 36 that was destroyed along with the rest of the comital archives in a fire in 1803. (My thanks to the staff of the AD de l'Ariège for information on the archives.) Devic and Vaissete's remark does not fit in with the rest of the evidence for citation of *ordonnances* under Philip, and the frequency of Auguste Molinier's corrections to their text makes me unwilling to take them at their word.

[87] E.g. 1301: 'contra pacis statuta' (*Olim*, III: 46–7); 1308: 'contra statuta pacis' (*Olim*, III: 245–7, 247–8); 1313: 'contra nostra pacis statuta' (*Olim*, III: 789–90).

[88] *Olim*, III: 672, 886–7.

conflicts were more consistently described as wars – may indicate a growing interest in war per se. Even these references are imprecise, though, and, particularly in the case of Polignac, should probably be understood to refer to specific warnings from a royal officer rather than general legislation.

There is more evidence that the prohibition of *portatio armorum* was being used as a tool against seigneurial warfare and that, unlike under Louis IX, royal courts and officers were able to judge the crime even when it did not take place in the royal domain.[89] Most of the war-makers who came before Parlement were accused of carrying arms, and in four cases – namely those of the viscount and the cathedral chapter of Narbonne; the inhabitants of Foix and Andorra against Mirepoix; the viscount of Polignac against Brioude; and Pierre de Maumont's various conflicts – legal prosecution seem to have been primarily justified by the prohibition against carriage of arms.[90] The crime of *portatio armorum* had significant implications for royal peace-keeping. Ernest Perrot believed it became *le cas royal type* – that is, the classic example of a case justiciable solely by the crown – and Richard Kaeuper hypothesized that the prohibition against carrying arms gave the crown 'significant jurisdiction' over seigneurial warfare.[91] There is evidence that the later years of Philip IV saw a concerted effort to monopolize jurisdiction over *portatio armorum* regardless of where or against whom the armed violence took place. As the lieutenant of the *juge-mage* of Carcassonne argued in 1306:

> jurisdiction and punishment of *portatio armorum* belongs to the lord king and his court throughout the whole realm and especially in the seneschalsy of Carcassonne and in the land of whatever baron ... wherever the said *portatio armorum* was made and by whatever persons, and it has been this way for such a long time that no one remembers a situation to the contrary.[92]

This effort to claim control over seignuerial violence, however, had only limited application. As is evident from the fairly low number of cases, royal officials did not often cite *portatio armorum* as a reason for judicial pursuit.

---

[89] The exposition of Philip IV's reissuance of Gui Foucois's guidance on peace-breaking suggests something similar for this category of crime (*Ord.*, 1: 344–5).

[90] This took place in other parts of the realm, as well, e.g. 'pour le port d'armes qu'il ont fait en Vermendois sus les deffenses le Roy noseigneur ... Et ont chevauchié parmi la baillie de Vermendois à trompes et à armes découvertes en foisant guerre ouverte' (edited in *Actes*, ed. Boutaric, no. 4183) and see Kaeuper, *War, Justice*, 243–4.

[91] E. Perrot, *Les cas royaux: Origine et développement de la théorie aux XIIIe et XIVe siècles* (Paris, 1910), 149–70, quote at 158; Kaeuper, *War, Justice*, 243–6, quote at 246. See also Toulet, 'L'incrimination', 435–6.

[92] '[C]ognitio & punitio portationis armorum spectat in toto regno & specialiter in tota senescallia Carcassone & in terra cujuscumque baronis ... ad ipsum dominum Regem & ejus curiam ... ubicumque dicta fiat armorum portatio & per quascumque personas, & fuit tanto tempore quod in contrarium memoria non existit' (*HL*, x: 453–7).

This may have been due to the problem of defining the crime, which had also been an impediment under Louis IX.[93] Officers may also have been loath to cite *portatio armorum* because the measure was evidently unpopular. One knight actually attacked the royal official publicizing a ban on arms.[94] But compunction probably also stemmed from the fundamental problem that seigneur-justiciars could not be forbidden from enforcing their own authority through violence. The lords themselves recognized this. A number of great southern lords, including the duke of Aquitaine, the marshal of Mirepoix, the count of Comminges, and *quidam alii* banded together to contest the prohibition of arms as a usurpation of their lordships.[95] As the count of Foix's proctor argued, the count had jurisdiction over *portatio armorum* and peace-breaking because 'all justice of a sovereign (*superioritatis*) belongs to the lord count just as to a prince of his land' (*velut ad principem terre sue*).[96] Such efforts were not always successful, but the crown's own position was not without exceptions. There is ample evidence that lords could still procure royal licences for arms in recognition of their need to exercise violence in the pursuit of justice.[97] Indeed, the final instructions of Philip's 1304 *ordonnance* against warfare clarify that those bearing arms 'for the execution of justice or licit defence . . . in places and cases belonging to them' were not to be considered culpable of bearing illicit arms.[98]

Through such actions, the crown showed itself flexible and able to respond to local conditions in a way that contrasts sharply with the hegemonic claims to universal jurisdiction asserted by the *ordonnances*. This flexible particularity was also a central principle in the development of a royal grant called the safeguard, which would become the most important tool in royal peace-keeping during the fourteenth century.

---

[93] In most cases from 1270 to 1314 the reference to arms is limited to a description (*cum armis*), and arms are often treated as an aggravating factor rather than the constituent element of the crime (e.g. *Olim*, III: 672).

[94] *Olim*, III: 507, cited in Kaeuper, *War, Justice*, 239–40.

[95] Chaplais, 'La souveraineté', 461; *Olim*, II: 514, III: 301–2. See Strayer, *Philip the Fair*, 194–5, Perrot, *Les cas royaux*, 162–70.

[96] *HL*, X: 453–7, and see 287–92.

[97] J. Firnhaber–Baker, 'Seigneurial War and Royal Power in later medieval Southern France', *Past & Present* 208 (2010), 62–3. In addition to examples cited there, see *Lettres de Philippe le Bel relatives au pays de Gévaudan*, ed. J. Roucaute and M. Saché (Mende, 1896), nos. 13, 15 (cited in E. A. R. Brown, 'Charters and Leagues in Early Fourteenth-Century France: the Movement of 1314 and 1315', Ph.D. dissertation, Harvard University and Radcliffe College (1961), 47); *Lettres inédites de Philippe le Bel*, ed. A. Baudouin (Paris, 1887), no. 98; BN Latin 11017, fols. 13r and 79r; Kaeuper, *War, Justice*, 240.

[98] 'Illicitamque, vel prohibitam dilationem armorum, non intelligentes in hoc casu, si qui pro exsecutione justiciae, vel defensione licita, cum moderamine debito in locis & casibus ad eos spectantibus arma portent' (*Ord.*, I: 390).

A safeguard entailed the assumption of a person and his or her goods, domicile, and *familia* into royal protection, meaning that any violence done to them was an offence against the king and fell under his jurisdiction.[99] In effect, safeguards were the opposite of the *ordonnances'* assertion of ubiquitous jurisdiction over the whole realm: while certain populations such as widows and orphans and anyone involved in a royal court case enjoyed the safeguard automatically, most safeguards were issued to individuals upon request and were restricted to protecting them for the grant's duration. Such limitations made the safeguard considerably easier to swallow than the unpopular prohibition on *portatio armorum* or the *ordonnances*, which as discussed in the next chapter, ran into serious opposition after Philip's death. Unlike the *ordonnances* or even royal claims to exclusive jurisdiction over certain crimes, safeguards did not impinge upon whole swaths of seigneurial jurisdiction. They were essentially privileges that grew out of a legal and political culture in which privilege was the main avenue for securing one's rights.[100]

Lords sometimes raised objections to safeguards granted to their justiciables.[101] In 1292 the count of Foix complained that the seneschal of Carcassonne had prejudiced his rights by protecting (*gardiare intenditis*) two *damoiseaux* under Foix's jurisdiction since it was up to Foix to defend and provide reasonable protection (*rationabiliter manutenere*) to these men.[102] But, particularly for lesser lords, safeguards offered obvious benefits in that one could request one against bullying overlords or irritating neighbours. The safeguard was advertised both through the grant's publication and by the affixing of pennants (usually called *penuncelli*) painted with the fleur-de-lis on the grantee's residence, which meant that the king's interest in the matter was immediately visible. Sometimes the grantee's enemy was even specially notified. These advantages, particularly in conflicts between asymmetrical enemies, are already clear in the Sompuy war. In 1272, when Casaubon killed Armagnac's brother and knew he could expect swift

---

[99] For the safeguard, see F. L. Cheyette, 'The Royal Safeguard in Medieval France', in *Post Scripta: Essays on Medieval Law and the Emergence of the European State in Honor of Gaines Post*, ed. J. R. Strayer and D. E. Queller (Rome, 1972), 631–52; Perrot, *Les cas royaux*, 98–148; Firnhaber-Baker, 'Seigneurial War', 70–2.

[100] This argument and what follows are discussed at greater length in Firnhaber-Baker, 'Seigneurial War', esp. 67–75.

[101] Perrot, *Les cas royaux*, 129–31; Cheyette, 'Royal Safeguard', 651; Kaeuper, *War, Justice*, 249.

[102] '[D]omicellos, & eorum parcionarios, qui sua foeda & hereditates infra limites terre & baronie dicti comitis habere dicuntur & in sua juridictione morari, ne eisdem domicellis per homines Appamiarum injurie vel molestie indebite inferantur, gardiare intenditis, licet dictus comes paratus sit & ad eum pertineat dictos domicellos & eorum parcionarios ab injuriis & violentiis hujusmodi deffendere & rationabiliter manutenere' (*HL*, x: 287–8; see 288–92, 453–7 for the development of the case).

retribution, he put himself under royal protection and had the king's banner (*vexillum*) affixed to his castle, believing (as Guillaume de Nangis tells it) that no one would dare attack him for fear of the king (*propter Regem*).[103]

The safeguard first appeared in the reign of Philip III, and from the beginning it was intended as a means to expand royal authority in a number of spheres, though it took a few decades for its full implication for royal oversight of warfare to be realized in practice. Aside from the Casaubon case, there are only two instances of the safeguard (or equivalent custodial action) being used to intervene in seigneurial violence in the South before the last years of Philip IV's reign. In 1295, Philip ordered the seneschal of Beaucaire to take a castle into royal custody (*ad manum nostram capiatis & teneatis*) in order to prevent violent conflict over its possession.[104] In 1306 the prior of 'Moulin-Pessin' successfully showed that Bertrand de Roquefort attacked him 'although he, his priory, and his goods were in the king's special guard, and the priory was marked (as safeguarded) by pennants and staves' (*licet dicuts prior, ejus prioratus et bona sint in nostra gardia speciali, et dictus prioratus esset palhonatus et brandonatus*).[105] The charge became much more common in the last years of Philip IV's reign, being cited in four of the six cases of southern warfare between 1311 and 1314,[106] and it would prove a durable tool. Safeguards were granted throughout the fourteenth and fifteenth centuries, with violation of the guard providing royal officials with grounds to intervene in about two-thirds of seigneurial wars in fourteenth-century Languedoc.

Less intrusive, more popular, and possibly more effective, the safeguard projected royal power in a different way than did the *ordonnances*, allowing the piecemeal judicial colonization of people and places normally outside direct royal supervision. Yet it is important to recognize that the safeguard was not second best to the *ordonnances*; it was not just what the king did because he could not enforce legislation. The safeguard is also indicative of an understanding of kingship that stressed the majesty of royal office. In granting safeguards exempting their holder from the violence, including the violence of their lord-justiciar, the crown temporarily suspended the normal workings of justice through an act of royal grace. It is no accident

---

[103] '[A]d alas protectionis regis Franciae se transtulit . . . putans quod hostes sui castrum illud invadere propter regem Franciae non auderent' ('Gesta Philippi', 490). It may be that Guillaume de Nangis overstates Casaubon's volition; Parlement's judgment against Armagnac indicates that Casaubon was in fact in prison awaiting justice for killing Armagnac's brother, and so royal tuition may simply have resulted automatically from his legal situation (*Olim*, I: 407–8; see also Guillaume de Puylaurens, *Chroniques*, ch. 50, ed. Duvernoy, 212).

[104] *HL*, X: 317.   [105] *Olim*, III: 182–3.

[106] The two exceptions are Pierre d'Avène vs. Raimond de Sanséchelle (1311), for which no prosecutorial rationale was stated, and the viscount of Polignac vs. Bertrand de Saint-Nectaire (1312).

that this happened at the same moment that the crown began issuing *lettres de rémission*, another gracious and very popular grant through which the normal progression of justice was halted by royal fiat. This, too, was an act of majesty that – far from exposing royal weakness – expressed the king's power to pardon, as well as to condemn.[107] The language and diplomatic attributes of safeguards and remissions have little in common, but their core assumptions about the king's ability to thrust aside the law have more than a passing similarity.

Almost paradoxically, this aspect of the safeguard connects it to the ideological positions that inform the *ordonnances*. Although safeguards (and remissions) are in a sense derogations of the law or at least of the legal order, the promulgation of positive law asserts the same fundamental claim to absolute authority over the legal universe. The king's legislative power is that which allows him to dispense with customs contrary to royal prohibitions (which 'should rather be called corruptions', as we have seen). Indeed the resemblance of safeguards to legislation is suggested by the rubric for the manuscript copy of Philip IV's 1304 prohibition: *littere salvagardium*.[108] Privileges sometimes buffered a beneficiary from the immediate effects of royal authority, but granting them was a signal demonstration of the king's power and an inventive way of insinuating it into the lives of his subjects and vassals. The flexibility and popularity of the safeguard meant that its availability as a tool of royal expansion was not limited to the period in which the crown's coercive power was at its height. When, in later decades, royal ability to force compliance became significantly weaker, safeguards remained a key method through which royal agents engaged with seigneurial violence.

CONCLUSION

Louis IX's son and grandson carried on and extended the peace-keeping work that the Capetians had begun in the South following the Albigensian Crusade. It is clear that some of their efforts were made in conscious imitation of their progenitor and with the intent of increasing royal oversight of violence. Like Louis and Alphonse de Poitiers, Philip III and Philip IV stressed the importance of peace and protection in their legislation, but their administrations also made substantial innovations to this inheritance, particularly in the latter half of Philip IV's reign. Philip the Fair's *ordonnances* introduced new elements about the relationship of

---

[107] C. Gauvard, 'Grâce et exécution capitale: les deux visages de la justice royale française à la fin du moyen âge', *BEC* 153 (1995): 275–90; see also Chapter 3, pp. 107–8.

[108] AM Toulouse AA 4, no. 37, fol. 46.

royal prerogatives and obligations to the maintenance of peace and the administration of justice, harnessing the duty of peace-keeping to the task of governance. These ideological and normative developments had parallels in the judicial and administrative work that was carried out both in Paris and by provincial judges and officers. It was also related to the development of the idea of crime, as the crown increasingly began to consider seigneurial warfare an offence against itself even when royal lands and subjects did not suffer actual harm. These developments had concrete effects: lords ceased to war against the crown in Languedoc, and royal engagement with wars waged between local lords increased considerably. There were impediments to this development, not least of them the need for seigneur-justiciars to execute justice coercively, but safeguards, an ingenious approach to the extension of royal power, could circumvent this. While safeguards may not have been invented to give the crown greater authority to intervene in seigneurial conflicts outside the royal domain, they certainly functioned this way in practice and were perhaps the most obvious example of the crown's opportunistic infiltration of seigneurial power relations.

At the end of Philip IV's reign, royal oversight of seigneurial warfare was at its apex, but this success came at a cost. It is under Philip the Fair that the relationship between crown and nobility can best be characterized as a struggle. This was, of course, especially true when it came to taxation, but Philippian claims about the king's right to arbitrate conflicts and suppress violence also chafed. Up until the autumn of 1314, it probably looked like the crown would ultimately prevail. As Philip breathed his last in Paris that November, however, sustained and organized opposition was already coalescing. This movement, followed by the vicissitudes of the 1320s and 1330s, interrupted the established trajectory and forced a renegotiation of royal/seigneurial relationships, particularly regarding violence and the law. Like Philip III and Philip IV, their successors would represent their peace-keeping as a continuation of Saint Louis's good works, but in the context of resurgent seigneurial power and deepening hostilities with England, a new, less royally directed period was about to begin. While the crown would never abandon the prerogatives expressed in Philip's *ordonnances*, in the decades to come a role for royal authority in seigneurial disputes would be assured as much by the flexibility and usefulness of the institutions and administrative network that had solidified under Philip as by the autocratic assertion of royal rights.

Chapter 3

THE LAST CAPETIANS AND THE HUNDRED YEARS WAR, 1315–1350

As Philip the Fair lay dying in November 1314, nobles and others were forming associations and alliances to protest against his high-handed ways. Initially motivated by taxation practices, their complaints also encompassed 'many other things ... by which the nobles and commons have been much damaged'.[1] When Louis X succeeded his father, he was soon forced to capitulate to these demands, issuing charter after charter that promised that the crown would not interfere in local rights, usually including the right to wage war. But the blow was hardly mortal. Louis was soon succeeded by his brother, Philip V. Relentless and shrewd, Philip succeeded in restoring many of the rights lost to the Leagues of 1314–16. But Philip's succession was problematic: lateral and resulting from the (possibly suspicious) death of his infant nephew, it gave rise to questions about the legitimacy of his kingship that the Capetians had not had to answer for centuries.[2] When first Philip V and then his brother Charles IV died in quick order and without male heirs, that long, lucky line came to an end. The problems of legitimacy created by the Valois succession in 1328 were exacerbated by Philip VI's personality and fortunes, and his accession also offered an excuse for a deadly escalation of the ancient rivalry between the English and French kings.

---

[1] Quote from the November 1314 charter of alliance between the league of Champagne and that of Burgundy edited in E. A. R. Brown, 'Reform and Resistance to Royal Authority in Fourteenth-Century France: the Leagues of 1314–1315', *Parliaments, Estates, and Representation* 1 (1981): 130, appendix 2. The definitive work on this movement is still Brown's doctoral dissertation ('Charters and Leagues in Early Fourteenth-Century France: the Movement of 1314 and 1315', Ph.D. dissertation, Harvard University and Radcliffe College, 1961), which replaces A. Artonne, *Le mouvement de 1314 et les chartes provinciales de 1315* (Paris, 1912). Brown published a summary of many of her conclusions in 'Reform and Resistance'.

[2] P. Lehugeur, *Histoire de Philippe le Long, roi de France (1316–1322)*, 2 vols. (Paris, 1897–1931), I: 73–105; C. Taylor, 'The Salic Law and the Valois Succession to the French Crown', *French History* 15 (2001): 358–77.

The war that started in 1337 loosed decades of violence upon a country that was already weakening demographically and economically, trends that escalated exponentially with the first outbreak of the plague in 1348.[3] In combination with military and diplomatic events, this economic crisis unleashed a flood of violence in the latter half of the fourteenth century. The reign of John II (1350–64) would see the worst of these troubles, but even before 1345, there were already worrying reports of brigandage around Toulouse, Agen, and Beaucaire, an ominous sign of the times to come.[4]

Yet if this period can be viewed as one of deepening difficulty for France and its kings, it was also one of bureaucratic efflorescence, as the professional corps that had coalesced under Philip IV matured. The Parlement of Paris, the Chambre des comptes, and the Trésor des chartes began to function independently of the king and sometimes in opposition to him.[5] As a result, new poles of power developed and new sources of authority could be called upon. Despite the deaths of kings, the change of dynasty, and the encroachments of war and disease, the personnel who staffed royal institutions experienced a remarkable continuity. Those serving as the king's ministers in 1340 were often the sons and grandsons of those who served Philip the Fair.[6] Despite the atmosphere of decline surrounding them, this bureaucratic class was on the ascent. Throughout the disappointments of the period and the disasters to come, these men, their families, and their descendants would be the bulwark that ensured the crown's institutional survival.

The decades between 1315 and 1350 were thus far more challenging than those experienced by Philip the Fair or his recent predecessors. Inevitably, this affected how the crown's various officers and institutions approached the problem of seigneurial violence. A wholesale retreat from the principles that emerged in the later thirteenth and early fourteenth century might be expected, as the crown's acknowledged duty to protect the weak and its ambitions to substitute royally controlled justice for seigneurial self-help gave way before the Leagues' opposition and later to the pressing need to ensure lords' military support for the war with England. In terms of royal ideology, this did not happen, and in fact some new ground was broken. Still, the increase in violence of all kinds and the logistical problems that the

---

[3] B. Campbell, 'The Agrarian Problem in the Early Fourteenth Century', *Past & Present* 188 (2005): 3–8; W. C. Jordan, *The Great Famine: Northern Europe in the Early Fourteenth Century* (Princeton, 1996); G. Bois, *The Crisis of Feudalism: Economy and Society in Eastern Normandy, c. 1300–1550* (Paris, 1984).

[4] *HL*, IX: 545–6, n. 3.

[5] R. Cazelles, *La société politique et la crise de la royauté sous Philippe de Valois* (Paris, 1958).

[6] F. J. Pegues, *The Lawyers of the Last Capetians* (Princeton, 1962), ch. 9. For the relative stability of Valois political society, see Cazelles, *La société politique ... sous Philippe*, 66–71, 231–4.

war with England and other disasters created for the judicial and administrative corps meant that a change in tactics was inevitable.

As the troubles mounted in the later 1340s, judicial and/or penal resolutions became less frequent, while extrajudicial settlements and pardons proliferated. These practices of negotiation and clemency were forced on the crown by circumstance, but they also allowed provincial officers to insert themselves into seigneurial conflicts in new ways, albeit less coercively than did their predecessors. Like the crown's central administrative organs, the provincial administrative system proved durable. Having embedded itself in local life over the previous century, it continued to assert a role for royal authority against the violent proclivities of local powers. At the same time, local powers adopted and adapted provincial administration to their own ends, using official avenues as another method of negotiating – or sometimes pursuing – their conflicts with one another.

LEGISLATION: SEIGNEURIAL REACTION AND ROYAL RETRENCHMENT

Although Philip IV's ideological legacy would ultimately endure, the years immediately following his death saw strong seigneurial reaction against royalist ambitions. The Leagues that were formed in the final months of Philip IV's life had largely been galvanized by opposition to taxation, but connected with and underlying this complaint was a profound opposition to Philip's penchant for annulling customary rights and practices. In the spring of 1315, when the Leagues forced Louis X to admit defeat, the agreement reached between them spoke of 'their ancient and good customs, privileges, liberties, franchises, and usages that had been infringed' and that were now to be set right.[7] In charter after charter issued to almost every part of the realm, Louis X had to disavow these excesses and to uphold the authority of customary rights. As he promised the inhabitants of the seneschalsy of Toulouse in May 1315,

Desirous of affirming the estate and customs of our counts, barons and other nobles and their men and subjects of the seneschalsy of Toulouse, we wish to maintain and to have our men firmly observe the laws, uses, customs, franchises, immunities, liberties, and privileges . . . just as they were in force beginning a long time ago. . .[8]

---

[7] Edited in Brown, 'Reform and Resistance', 136, appendix 8.

[8] Brown, 'Reform and Resistance', 135, appendix 7, and see 134–5, appendix 6 for Champagne, Auxerre, and Tonnerre, and 136–7, appendix 9 for Vermandois, Amiens, and Senlis, as well as *Ord.*, I: 557–60, 567–73, XI: 441–4.

The principle, trumpeted under Philip the Fair, that the king could make a universal stipulation irrespective of regional variation was thus discredited.

The collapse of this principle undermined the foundation upon which Philip's edicts against warfare were built, and as a direct consequence, his prohibition of warfare 'to all subjects in whatever part of the realm', was fully reversed in many parts of France and substantially gutted in others. Almost every charter of concession granted by Louis X in 1316 included a passage endorsing the nobility's customary right to wage war against one another.[9] The language of the charter granted to the nobles of Burgundy, Forez, Langres, Autun, and Chalons is typical:

First, about that which they assert, that they and their predecessors were accustomed to make war against one another, and to bear arms, for the conservation of their status, lands, and goods (*consuevisse guerras inter se ad invicem facere, & arma portare, ad conservationem status, terrarum, ac bonorum suorum*), and that they have been impeded in this against their customs (*consuetudines*) and have had fines levied against them on account of it, we will have what they were accustomed to do in previous times investigated, and according to the findings, we will make sure it is firmly observed, and we will have any novelty made during the time of our lord father [Philip IV] restored to its original state.[10]

Even in places where the nobles did not find it possible to argue that custom legitimized their wars, the right to wage war was extended as a consequence of the leverage the regional nobility had gained over royal authority. The nobles of the southern seneschalsies, whose laws were based on Roman law (the *lex scripta*) rather than customary law and who therefore had less leeway to claim the right to war by custom, received permission to make war against one another in January 1316. Unlike the recognitions of privilege given to the more northerly regions quoted above, the right was not granted because the nobles had it by custom. Rather, Louis X permitted the nobles to wage war 'by special grace' (*de speciali gratia*), a formula that the crown used in situations, such as the granting of remissions, where its actions had no authoritative basis other than royal will.[11] Ironically, the revolt against royal arbitrary power in this case required its exercise in order to confirm seigneurial privilege.

The Leagues' victory thus interrupted an ideological arc that can be traced from the reign of Louis IX (or even earlier), but the collapse was

---

[9] The exceptions are Champagne and Languedoc (Louis X's concessions to them at *Ord.*, I: 576–80, 644–5). However, Languedoc's nobles were granted the right to wage war against one another by the king's grace in 1316, as outlined below.

[10] *Ord.*, I: 569.

[11] 'Concedimus eisdem insuper de speciali gratia, quod nobiles & barones senescalliarum ipsarum guerram inter se possint facere' (*Ord.*, XII: 411–15, art. 22; also at *HL*, X: 547–55).

neither total nor even of long duration. Even at the nadir of royal fortunes, most of the practical limitations on violence were retained, either in the concessions themselves, or by *ordonnances* issued shortly thereafter. The grace issued to the nobles of Languedoc, for example, hedged the permission granted to wage war with provisions that protected non-combatants, encouraged settlement by law, and prioritized royal wars over local ones, while the confirmation of privileges given to Amiens and Vermandois – areas where the appeal to customary rights to warfare was insistent – required continued observance of the *quarantaine* (or forty-day delay before the onset of war). Although the Leagues fatally weakened Louis's rule, his premature death in 1316 enabled the crown to retrench its opposition to local war more fully under Philip V.

By the spring of 1318 – with his rule firmly established to the exclusion of Louis's female heir – Philip had reinstated his father's ban against local war during royal war.[12] And if those in the bailliage of Vermandois believed that custom still gave their wars priority over those of the king despite this ban, Philip soon dispelled the illusion. Stating in a mandate to the bailiff that he 'understood that a number of our subjects in your bailliage have had many wars ... even during our own',[13] Philip disavowed any grants made earlier. In language reminiscent of his father, he renewed the claim to disregard custom at will:

We who desire to provide for the good estate of our realm ... make an end to all manner of wars ... regardless of use, regional custom, graces or privileges granted or made to the contrary (*non contrestant Us, coustumes de pays, graces ou privileges octroiées, ou faisans au contraire*), which we suspend until such time as it pleases us.

While this mandate survives only in the copy sent to Vermandois, it or one similar to it was also published around this time in the seneschalsy of Carcassonne: a prosecution in 1321 in Parlement noted that a prohibition of warfare had been repeatedly published 'particularly beginning a year before the accusation in the seneschalsy of Carcassonne'.[14] With such

---

[12] The edict itself is no longer extant (or at least not currently locatable), but its former existence is attested by Philip's reissue of his father's 1306 measure to deal with problems this prohibition created (AN x2a 2, fol. 7r). This measure uses the text of Philip IV's instructions (at *Ord*, I: 435–41), which Philip V states that he had extracted from the criminal registers of the Parlement: 'a registris causarum criminalium curie nostre Parisis extrahi fecimus'.

[13] *Ord.,* I: 655–6.

[14] '[P]er nos pro bono pacis ac transquillitate Regni nostri fuisset ordinatum et statutum quod nullus cuiuscumque conditionis et status existeret armatorum congregationem facere auderet, nec arma portare seu Guerram facere in aliqua parte dicti Regni Quamvis etiam dictum statutum diu est & plures et specialiter ab anno citra ante tempus dicte perventionis publicatum in Senescallia Carcassone tam in civitatibus Carcassone & Bitterensis quam in locis insignibus Senescalle supradicte' (AN x1a 5, fols. 97v–98r).

notifications sent to locales as diverse as Vermandois and Carcassonne, the prohibition was probably generally applicable.

Philip's reign did see some setbacks. In the summer of 1319, the need for money forced him to confirm the privileges for the Auvergne and the Mountains of the Auvergne that restricted the extension of royal safeguards and granted greater scope to carry arms legally.[15] But later that year, Philip and his wife Jeanne issued a joint *ordonnance* against the violence associated with war in Franche-Comté, a territory that Jeanne had brought to the crown as dowry.[16] Although this promulgation does not prohibit war per se, it otherwise evinces a rebirth and even an expansion of the ideas expounded under Philip the Fair. Like Philip IV's measure of 1304, it was composed by a skilful rhetorician, who was familiar with the conceptual basis of Philip the Fair's *ordonnances*:

> Since in our county of Burgundy, on account of the damages resulting from frequent wars, above all fires, devastation of fields, vines, and trees, seizures of farmers (*agricolae*), the poor (*pauperes*), and their animals, and [since] all power was bestowed by God for the ruling of subjects, for the doing of justice, so that human recklessness might be corrected through his office (*ministerio*), so that the innocent should be protected, and so that the power of the guilty to do harm should be restrained ... by the right, power, and superiority that belongs to us (or which ought to belong to us), we have ... prohibited altogether and henceforth that no one of whatever status, importance, or condition, on account of hatred, malevolence, enmity, vengeance, or war (*guerra*), should dare or attempt to set fire in the county ... to cut, destroy or uproot vines, arbours, or orchards, or to capture for any reason whatsoever any beasts of burden, or men and things involved with ploughing, or anything belonging to ploughs or agriculture ... If someone does the above, or any part of it, or orders it to be done, or consents to it, he is to be considered a violator of the peace (*violator pacis*), an adversary, and a public enemy (*hostis publicus*) by everyone, and he and his accomplices and their goods are to be treated thusly until he makes appropriate restitution, regardless of any custom – which we consider an abuse – hitherto observed in the county, the which custom we wish and order to cease henceforth.[17]

This measure is a prohibition of the violence associated with war and vengeance, rather than an explicit prohibition of war, but it otherwise features every aspect of royal policy against local war as it had developed until Philip IV's death and the revolt of the Leagues in 1314. The concern for peasants and their animals and instruments and the instruction to treat

---

[15] *Ord.*, I: 688–91; AN JJ 59, no. 113, fol. 48. Immediately following these grants, the regions approved aids for war in Flanders (*Ord.*, I: 691–3; AN JJ 59, no. 114, fols. 48v–49r; AN JJ 59, no. 116, fols. 49v–50r). See also a similar grant to Périgord and Quercy in July 1319 (*Ord.*, I: 694–700).

[16] Lehugeur, *Histoire de Philippe le Long*, I: 220–2.   [17] *Ord.*, I: 701–2.

war-makers as violators of the peace echo the efforts of Philip IV and his predecessors.[18] This prohibition also shows an awareness of Philip the Fair's innovations. Like his father, Philip V justified his prohibitions on the basis that his rule was entrusted to him by God, from whom he evocatively claimed to hold a *ministerium*. Philip V also spurned the region's customary rights in this *ordonnance*, an innovative expansion of royal power that originated in his grandfather's reign and can be seen in his father's ordinance of 1304. In fact, whoever composed this *ordonnance* may have been familiar with the measures of 1304 and 1311, for he refers to contrary custom as 'use, or rather abuse' (*usum, abusum verius*) in a manner reminiscent of the 'custom, or rather corruption' (*consuetudo quin potius corruptela*) formulation found in Philip the Fair's *ordonnances*.

Philip V's reign has been characterized as 'a peak in the public order efforts of the monarchy',[19] and his normative efforts are certainly striking in their ideological development, particularly in light of the crown's recent troubles. But the moment was short-lived. Philip died in January 1322 without legitimate male issue, and his brother Charles IV succeeded him. Charles reigned only six years, dying like his brothers without an heir, and the crown passed to the Valois line. There are no surviving prohibitions from Charles IV, or from Philip VI (r. 1328–50), but the latter, at least, did issue such statutes. By April 1335, he had apparently prohibited all local wars because four mandates and a judgment from Parlement mention a measure that had been 'published throughout the realm of France' (*publice per totam regnum francie . . . proclamatum fuit*).[20] With the outbreak of hostilities with England, he then apparently issued another decree, first attested in April 1343, prohibiting war during the king's wars.[21]

How much these promulgations had in common with those of his Capetian predecessors is obviously impossible to say in the absence of the texts themselves. Philip's questionable right to accede to the throne weakened his rule, and his position was made more precarious by the onset of the Hundred Years War, which forced him to rely on the nobility for military aid. As Raymond Cazelles has shown, in one instance the war with England drove Philip to concede the right of provincial nobles to go

---

[18] It may also reflect imperial influence. In 1315, Louis X had re-promulgated an edict of Frederick III that, while mostly dealing with heresy, included a clause forbidding attacks on *agricultores, & circa rem rusticam* (*Ord.*, 1: 610–13).

[19] R. W. Kaeuper, *War, Justice, and Public Order: England and France in the Later Middle Ages* (Oxford, 1988), 249.

[20] Quote from AN x2a 3, fol. 71; other witnesses to the *ordonnance* at AN x2a 3, fols. 9, 79v–80r; AN x2a 2bis, fol. 2; AN x1a 8, fol. 143.

[21] '[A]licui non licet guerram facere in regno nostro guerris nostris durantibus' (AN x2a 5, fol. 186). See also AN x1a 9, fols. 492v–494r; *Ord.*, II: 511–12.

to war against one another in order to shore up military support on the frontier.[22] But the importance of this exceptional concession should not be overstated. It was made to the nobles of Gascony in 1339 in a moment of crisis, and even under such dire circumstances, the king retained the prohibition of seigneurial wars during royal ones.[23] In any case, as is discussed in Chapter 4, when Philip VI's son John issued his own general prohibition of warfare during royal war in 1352, he claimed to be simply reiterating the (now lost) prohibition of his father.[24] The presence in John's measure of certain elements common to earlier Capetian precedent suggests that Philip's lost *ordonnances* probably continued to assert the crown's central claims about royal authority and violence.

In so far as the material available allows judgment, it thus appears that Philip VI maintained the ideological and normative stance of his Capetian predecessors, despite his considerably weaker position. How much this had to do with the king himself is unknowable, but his military and financial disasters led the royal technocrats to take the governance of the kingdom into their own hands, at one point imprisoning Philip's familiars and threatening to exclude his son (the future John II) from inheriting.[25] This crisis was caused by the military loss at Crécy in 1346, but even in the early years of his reign, Philip, who succeeded his cousin Charles IV through consensus and political expediency rather than an unquestionable blood right, was forced to rule with considerable input from the professional cadres, particularly those from Parlement and the Chambre des comptes.[26] Given the perceptible role of royal councillors like Gui Foucois and Guillaume de Plaisians in the peace measures of Louis IX and Philip IV, the continuity with Capetian precedent apparent in Philip VI's normative efforts may reflect the stability of the royal professional class. As prosoprographical studies have shown, the staff of royal institutions in Paris was increasingly a closed group drawn from the same families whose children intermarried.[27] Peace-keeping ideas may thus have continued to pass from father to son among these bureaucratic

---

[22] R. Cazelles, 'La réglementation royale de la guerre privée de Saint Louis à Charles V et la précarité des ordonnances', *RHDFE*, 4th ser., 38 (1960): 530–8, which corrects the dating of this measure, erroneous in the edition.

[23] '[S]alvo tamen & retento Nobis & successoribus, quod dicti Barones & Nobiles, & eorum successors a guerris suis, pro facto guerrarum nostrarum & successorum nostrorum . . . cessarent seu qui cessare tenebantur' (*Ord.*, II: 61–3).

[24] *Ord.*, II: 511–12.   [25] Cazelles, *La société politique . . . sous Philippe*, 208–29, 427.

[26] Ibid., esp. 71–2.

[27] F. Autrand, *Naissance d'un grand corps de l'état: les gens du Parlement de Paris, 1345–1454* (Paris, 1981), 56–9, and above, n. 6.

families.[28] In this domain, as in many others, the corporate genius of the administration had begun to overshadow the personal rule of the king.

From the advent of Philip V's reign through to the death of Philip VI, the trend is thus one of continuity and even of growth. It is true that the objections of the Leagues forced a volte-face, particularly on the question of annulling custom, but this was only temporary. And while throughout this period a seigneurial right to go to war was habitually asserted either by claiming custom or by securing royal privileges extorted for military or financial aid, the core claims of Louis IX's and Philip IV's legislation remained: non-combatants, particularly agriculturalists, were protected; seigneurial wars had to cease when royal wars began; and (at least in Flanders, Picardy, and the Île-de-France) a significant delay was to be observed between the declaration of hostilities and the onset of violence. Just as importantly, we can observe a continuous tradition linking internal security to the responsibility of the king to ensure the public good. This tradition would not survive the upheavals of the next fifty years, but for nearly a century the French crown had repeatedly insisted upon the superiority of royal, institutional justice over violent self-help. This would remain the bedrock position of judicial and administrative engagement with seigneurial war-makers during even the most trying moments of the decades ahead.

THE FALL AND RISE OF SEIGNEURIAL WARFARE IN THE SOUTH

The trials of the early to mid-fourteenth century affected patterns of seigneurial warfare in the South in various ways. As one would expect, more violence is recorded towards the end of this period than at the beginning. Overall, the picture is one of stable or declining violence from the end of Philip IV's reign until the second half of Philip VI's, when the incidence of warfare picked up significantly. (See Figure 2.) The linkages between seigneurial war and the macro-historical trends of the period are not very clear, however. No seigneurial war seems to have been directly related to the Anglo-French conflict. Continuing the pattern established early in Philip IV's reign, the causes of seigneurial wars remained matters of limited geographic and political importance stemming from local lordship: who held that castle; who collected those taxes; who could try those men. It

---

[28] On ideological traditions among bureaucrats as a socially cohesive group, see J. Dumolyn, 'Nobles, Patricians, and Officers: the Making of a Regional Political Elite in Late Medieval Flanders', *Journal of Social History* 40 (2006): 431–52, and 'Justice, Equity and the Common Good: the State Ideology of the Councilors of the Burgundian Dukes', in *The Ideology of Burgundy: the Promotion of National Consciousness, 1365–1565*, ed. D. J. D. Boulton and J. R. Veenstra (Leiden, 2006), 1–20.

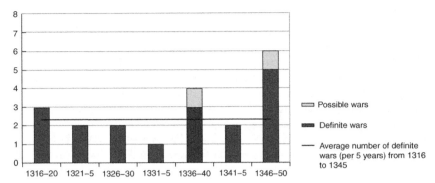

Figure 2   Seigneurial wars, 1316–50

seems possible that the reduced royal ability to enforce justice coercively after Crécy encouraged more lords to go to war, though there are no explicit indications in the sources themselves that this was so, at least initially.[29] The most that can be claimed is that the large-scale historical developments of this period created conditions favourable to the pursuit of conflict through violence; they did not themselves cause wars to break out.

There appears to have been no seigneurial war fought in the reign of Louis X. This is probably because his experience with the Leagues dissuaded his courts and officers from prosecuting seigneurial war.[30] Once Philip V succeeded Louis and a semblance of normality returned to royal affairs, Parlement began to prosecute warfare again. The first case that came before the court dated from 1316. That year, war broke out between Eleanor de Montfort, countess of Vendôme, and her nephew, Gui de Comminges, over lands in the Albigeois and Narbonnais that both claimed as heirs to Simon de Montfort's conquests during the Albigensian Crusade.[31] This war, lent impetus by Eleanor and Gui's additional contesting claims to the barony of Lombers, had been in the

---

[29] Patterns of enforcement are discussed in the next two sections.

[30] The one possible exception is a judgment rendered in 1315 against Pierre de Maumont for what may have been a new war with one of his vassals, though the violence 'cum armis & magna comitiva' may have been part of Pierre's earlier war with the lord of Beaufort (AN X2a 1, fol. 25). For the previous war, see above, p. 70.

[31] C. Higounet, *Le comté de Comminges de ses origines à son annexion à la couronne*, 2 vols. (Toulouse and Paris, 1949), I: 137–8, 151–6; *HL*, IX: 344–6, 407–9. See *HL*, X: 252–4 (11 May 1290) for the disposition of the Montfort lands after Jean de Montfort's death. On 24 January 1302, Parlement agreed to receive homage from Eleanor for the lands in question rather than the Comminges because the custom of Paris rather than written law governed succession to the lands since they 'erant de conquestis factis per quondam comitem, Symonem de Monte-Forti' (*Olim*, II: 453–5).

making for more than a decade and ignited when Eleanor orchestrated a revolt in Castres against Gui's authority.[32] Gui, along with his brother, the count of Comminges, and their allies, the viscounts of Lautrec, took quick revenge by attacking the community of Assac in early 1317.[33] In 1318, Parlement ordered the seneschal of Carcassonne to investigate the charges made by Eleanor against Gui and his accomplices, which included violence, rapine, rape, bearing arms, disobedience, and verbal attacks on the royal majesty (*verbis enormibus . . . contra nos et nostram magiestatam regiam*).[34] By 1320, Eleanor's officers in the castle of 'Amiaco' had apparently incited the castle's inhabitants to besiege a castle called Tourette in the manner of an army (*ad modum exercitus*), an operation that involved the use of a ballista and wounded many of Tourette's inhabitants.[35] In May 1321, Eleanor and Gui were still said to be raising troops 'in the manner of open war' (*amodum guerre apperte*).[36] In 1323, following a judgment from Parlement, the two sides agreed to an accord, but the truce soon failed, and pontifical correspondence indicates that the war continued throughout the 1320s.[37] It was only in 1332 that the parties agreed to an apparently final accord and the Comminges party obtained remission for the crimes that they had committed over the years.[38]

Contemporaneous with the Comminges/Vendôme war, in 1317, Parlement heard the case of the *guerra* between Othon de 'Temda' and the abbey of Belleperche.[39] The next year, it confirmed the seneschal of Carcassonne's sentence against 171 inhabitants of Bordes-sur-Arize for a series of attacks on the men and monks of Mas-d'Azil and of Severac, which involved armed attacks behind a raised banner (*vexillo explicato*) in violation of peace.[40] In 1321, the court heard accusations against the lord

---

[32] For Lombers, see *HL*, IX: 344–6; *Olim*, III: 894–9. For the revolt at Castres, see AN x2a 1, fol. 134r; *HL*, IX: 409, n. 1.

[33] AN x2a 1, fols. 55r, 136v; AN x2a 2, fol. 40r. It is possible that the attack on Assac preceded the Castres revolt. The first mention of violence at Assac, AN x2a 1, fol. 136v, is dated 21 April 1317 and says that the inquest 'diu est fuisse factam'.

[34] AN x2a 2, fols. 41v–42r; cf. *Olim*, III: 1293–6. In December 1318, the seneschal of Carcassonne was also ordered to continue the inquest into the murders of Eleanor de Montfort's men, killed by Gui's associates: AN x2a 2, fol. 42.

[35] AN x1a 5, fol. 14, partially edited in *Actes du Parlement de Paris*, ed. E. Boutaric, 2 vols. (Paris, 1863–7), no. 6017.

[36] AN x2a 2, fol. 44r.

[37] Higounet, *Le comté de Comminges*, I: 153–4; note on Gui de Comminges at *HL*, IX: 568–70; failure of the accord at AN x1c 1 (9 April 1325). A new accord was reached in 1326, but also soon failed (*HL*, IX: 407–9). I cannot verify Vaissete's assertion that Parlement confirmed this accord.

[38] The king confirmed this accord in October 1333 (AN JJ 66, no. 1207, fols. 514v–516v). For the remission, see *HL*, X: 736–40 (November 1333).

[39] AN x2a 1, fol. 70v.

[40] Bordes-sur-Arize's representatives claimed that the monks had begun the conflict and that they had only acted in defence of their own lords (*Olim*, III: 1448–54).

and community of Florensac for acting in a hostile manner and making *guerra* against a settlement called Méjan.[41] The next year, it confirmed the bailiff of the Mountains of the Auvergne's sentence against the lord of Pierrefort for attacking the lord of 'Bresons' over the erection of a gallows.[42] In 1326, Arnaud-Guillaume de Monlezun, count of Pardiac, and other noblemen from the county of Armagnac received pardon for the *guerra illicita* that they had waged with the *damoiseau* Genses de Montesquiou, this dispute having existed 'for a long time'.[43] At the same time and with exactly the same language, Loup de Foix, lord of Crampagna, and Fortanier de Durban were pardoned for undertaking their own 'illicit war' during a dispute over a castle.[44]

The Parlement records for the last years of King Charles IV's reign, winter 1327 to summer 1328, have largely been lost,[45] and there is little mention of wars in the South between his death and the outbreak of the Hundred Years War in 1338. Beside the Comminges/Vendôme war, there are records only for a conflict fought by Aymar, lord of Roussillon in the Dauphiné, who crossed the Rhône to attack a castle and came before Parlement in 1332, and a jurisdictional dispute in the Auvergne between Pierre de Maumont and the prior of Saint-Hilaire-la-Croix in the later 1330s that entailed some violence, though possibly not actual warfare.[46] This lull does not reflect a new reluctance to prosecute; legal action continued in the Comminges/Vendôme case, and north of the Loire, prosecution may actually have picked up.[47] The pause may instead indicate an actual decrease in the incidence of warfare in the South, possibly related to the settlement of the Comminges/Vendôme conflict. This was the last war to arise from the Albigensian Crusade's reapportionment of lands and realignment of the southern nobility, and it may be that the gradual elimination of this conflict helped to quiet the South.

---

[41] AN x1a 5, fols. 97v–98r.   [42] AN x1a 5, fol. 239.

[43] The king confirmed this remission in 1329. It is published in *Sceaux gascons du moyen âge (gravures et notices)*, ed. P. Laplagne-Barris, 3 vols. (Paris and Auch, 1888–92), II: 389–90.

[44] The pardon was confirmed in 1328 (*HL*, x: 662–4). Loup's mother, Esclarmonde de Foix, and brother, the abbot of Lézat, also received a related pardon (AN JJ 65A, no. 269, fol. 185).

[45] *Actes*, ed. Boutaric, II: 637, n. 1.

[46] Lord of Roussillon: AN x1a 6, fols. 269v–270r; Pierre de Maumont: AN x1a 8, fols. 30v–32r; P. Charbonnier, *Une autre France: la seigneurie rurale en Basse Auvergne du XIVe au XVIe siècle*, 2 vols. (Clermont-Ferrand, 1980), I: 422. It may very well be that these incidents actually pertained to Pierre's earlier, on-going hostilities with his various neighbours (see Chapter 2, p. 70, above). Pierre also invaded the *maison forte* of a certain Guillaume de Gimel around this time (AN x1a 9, fol. 315v).

[47] Mandates and judgments in cases of seigneurial wars in France outside Languedoc can be found at AN x2a 3, fols. 9 (9 April 1335), 71 (29 April 1336), 79v–80r (4 July 1336); AN x2a 2bis, fol. 2 (5 December 1338); and AN x1a 8, fol. 143 (12 January 1341). Each relates to a separate war.

The fall and rise of seigneurial warfare

The last decade of Philip VI's reign, however, saw a considerable increase in the number of conflicts. On 16 January 1339, Parlement fined Othon de Pardeillan, the lord of Lavardac, and his accomplices for 'making prohibited wars' (*guerras prohibitas faciendo*) against Avisantius de Caumont and the communities of 'Helizona' in the seneschalsy of Toulouse.[48] The same day that it dealt with Othon and company, Parlement fined the lord of Bazillac in Bigorre for numerous offences against the crown, including marshalling four hundred men to take Montastruc 'with trumpets and like an army' (*cum tubis et per modum exercitus*) and setting up a gallows, though he claimed total innocence.[49] The same year, the houses of Comminges and Isle-Jourdain waged open war against one another (*guerres publiques*) as a result of a succession dispute over the county of Comminges, whose dowager-countess's claim was supported by her Isle-Jourdain relatives.[50] In 1342 Loup de Foix (who had previously fought with Fortanier de Durban) had a *guerra* with Guillaume-Bernard d'Asnave.[51] Early the next year, Aicard de Miremont waged a *guerra* on behalf of his mother against her vassal Sicard de Paulin, who had refused to submit to her justice and whose rebellion may have extended to committing war-like activities against her.[52] In 1346, Pierre de Turlande, a knight from the Mountains of the Auvergne, complained to the king about the attacks *cum armis prohibitis, equester & pedester* made against his lands and familiars by Gibert, lord of Pierrefort, during a legal suit, and Gibert apparently had similar grievances against him.[53] In 1347, the lords of Crussol, Belcastel, and Solignac in the Auvergne challenged Jauserans, lord of Saint-Didier, 'publicly making war against him', which incited Jauserans to counter-attack in defence and retribution (*ad defensionem . . . & vindictam*).[54] Also

---

[48] AN x1a 8, fols. 19v–21r. It is not clear how or whether this war related to the one fought twenty-five years prior between 'Helizona', Eauze, and Bretagne-d'Armagnac and Othon de Cazeneuve and the consuls of Gondrin.

[49] AN x1a 8, fols. 17–18r.

[50] Higounet, *Le comté de Comminges*, II: 515–23. See AN JJ 73, no. 323, fols. 250v–251r; *HL*, x: 909–10; AN JJ 75, no. 312, fols. 183v–184; AN x1a 9, fol. 454v. For the complaints of Saint-Sulpice, the monks of Candeil, and other communities about the Comminges' behaviour in this war, see AN x2a 4, fols. 125r, 129r. There had been earlier disputes: the two houses had been reconciled by marriage in 1314 in order to prevent 'inimicias, discordias, guerras' (AN JJ 49, no. 233, fol. 103r), and the inheritance of a castle in 1322 had been cause for further dispute (AN x1a 8844, fol. 129r).

[51] *HL*, x: 944–6, 1000–1, 1077–9; AN JJ 81, no. 880, fol. 463r; AN x2a 4, fol. 126r; AN x1a 12, fol. 115r.

[52] AN x2a 4, fols. 112v, 125v–126r, 129v; x2a 5, fols. 14r, 66v; AN JJ 78, no. 45, fols. 23–6; AN JJ 68, no. 196, fols. 106v–107r; *HL*, x: 956–8. For more on this war, see J. Firnhaber–Baker, 'Seigneurial War and Royal Power in Later Medieval Southern France', *Past & Present* 208 (2010): 43–4, 56–7, 65, 74–5.

[53] AN x2a 5, fols. 65r, 190r.   [54] '(E)idem guerram publice faciendo' (*HL*, x: 1054–6).

in 1347, the viscount of Carlat and his officers waged a *guerra* against the priory of Saint-Michel-de-Laussac and numerous nobles of the Rouergue and the Auvergne, a conflict that arose over disputed rights of justice and taxation.[55] The pace picked up further from 1348. It was in the first half of that year that Géraud de la Barthe went to war (*guerra*) against Hugues and Jean d'Arpajon over the right to marry Hélène, the young heiress of Castelnau-Montratier, and took the barony by force.[56] The same year Parlement confirmed the remission that had been granted to Jean II de Lévis, lord and marshal of Mirepoix, for the violence done to François de Lévis, including the siege (*obsidio*) of his town, la Garde,[57] a conflict probably related to the dispute that Roger-Bernard de Lévis, who was Jean's son and François's son-in-law, had with Jean over his future inheritance, which he wished to preserve from his half-siblings. That conflict went on for a decade with the (ostensibly) final accord being reached only in 1362.[58] Finally, in 1350, the lord of Mirambel's refusal to pay homage to the lord of Herment in the Auvergne occasioned a war (*guerra*).[59]

Over the three and a half decades following Philip IV's death, the picture is one of stable or even declining warfare until the late 1340s, at which point the number of wars increases sharply. Surprisingly, this increase was not directly linked to the military or political events of the Hundred Years War. The war did engender some opportunistic behaviour: 'undue seizures' made by the viscount of Carlat in the later 1340s were said to have been made 'under cover of the royal wars' (*sub velamine guerrarum nostrarum*), and his quarrel with the region's nobles had much to do with his attempted muster of them, despite conflicting royal orders to go to Gascony.[60] But there are no cases in which events, alliances, or effects stemming from the Franco-English conflict are attributed as causing war in the South or, indeed, of preventing it.

---

[55] The main court records for this case are AN x2a 5, fols. 120, 192, 195v, 204v–207r, 207–8.

[56] AN x2a 5, fols. 109v, 118r, 119r, 177v–178r; AN JJ 77, no. 402, fol. 247; AN JJ 78, no. 250, fol. 139; AN JJ 80, no. 60, fols. 33v–34r. See the Introduction, above.

[57] AN x1a 12, fol. 252r.

[58] The king confirmed the accord in 1362 (AN JJ 91, no. 318, fols. 163v–165, partially published in *HL*, x: 1180–2). Earlier sources for this case include remissions granted to Roger-Bernard (*HL*, x: 1083–4) and to Jean (AN JJ 81, no. 768, fol. 414), and an abortive accord (*HL*, x: 1096–9). The quarrel between Roger-Bernard and his half-brother Thibaut continued after Jean's death. See P.-C. Timbal, *Un conflit d'annexion au moyen âge: l'application de la coutume de Paris au pays d'Albigeois* (Toulouse and Paris, 1949), 154–9; *Cartulaire de Mirepoix*, ed. F. Pasquier, 2 vols. (Toulouse, 1921), II: no. 34; and *HL*, x: 1769–70.

[59] Charbonnier, *Une autre France*, I: 410, 422; AN JJ 80, no. 606, fols. 384v–385r; AN JJ 81, no. 156, fols. 88v–89v.

[60] AN x2a 5, fols. 120, 192, 207r–208v.

Similarly, the first wave of plague in 1348 correlates with a further increase in warfare, but this may be coincidental, not causal. The disease may have halved the population of the South, particularly in the urban centres,[61] and such high mortality may have created an increase in the numbers of problematic inheritances, which were a prime cause of seigneurial war. But there are no explicit textual indications that this actually happened, and only one war fought between 1348 and the early years of John II's reign seems likely to have been caused by vacancy due to plague.[62] One can well imagine that the epidemic might actually have had a dampening effect on warfare, as people took flight and troops perished.

This insularity of seigneurial warfare from the period's macro-historical developments is striking and unexpected. One might easily have imagined that the Hundred Years War would have subsumed seigneurial war, or even that what we think of as the Hundred Years War might upon closer inspection be revealed as a collection of fragmentary seigneurial conflicts mostly unrelated to the dispute between the English and French kings.[63] This was not the case. There were certainly wars among the greatest lords – the near petty princes of France – that spilled over from or interwove themselves with the Hundred Years War: the Armagnac/Foix war and the war of Breton succession spring immediately to mind. The wars fought by local seigneurs and even those of viscomital status, however, remained essentially local affairs, incited by the same problems of cheek-by-jowl lordships and murky successions encountered in previous decades. It is possible that the weakness of royal government resulting from military defeats in Philip VI's later years was responsible for some of the increase in seigneurial war after 1346. As discussed below, patterns of prosecution and the growing prevalence of contumacy suggest that the crown was less able to enforce its will coercively in the later 1340s than it had been in earlier decades. The Black Death may also have played a role here, too, of course.[64] But there are no references in the sources to royal weakness encouraging seigneurial war in this period (as there were in later

---

[61] J.-N. Biraben, *Les hommes et la peste en France et dans les pays européens et méditerranéens*, 2 vols. (Paris, 1975–6), 1: 156–84. In Albi about half the population disappeared between 1343 and 1357 (G. Prat, 'Albi et la peste noire', *Annales du Midi* 64 (1952): 17–18). See also R. W. Emery, 'The Black Death of 1348 in Perpignan', *Speculum* 42 (1967): 614–16, whose estimate of mortality for Perpignan is more than 60 percent.

[62] The war *guerra* fought in 1352 between the lord of Puichéric and Pierre and Guillaume de Voisines happened because a castle's holder had died intestate and therefore possibly of plague sometime in the year just prior to 1351 (*HL*, x: 1073–4).

[63] H. Kaminsky, 'The Noble Feud in the Later Middle Ages', *Past & Present* 177 (2002): 72.

[64] For the effect of the plague on royal business, see below, pp. 106–7.

decades).[65] Indeed, since there is little or no evidence that prohibition and prosecution dissuaded lords from warfare even in periods of royal strength, there is little reason to assume prima facie that the absence of sanction would have encouraged them. Seigneurial warfare was not wholly isolated from the period's large-scale developments, but it appears substantially less affected by them than one might expect.

The localism of seigneurial war at mid-century may be at least partly explained by the geographical and political restriction of seigneurial war that was the fruit of the Capetian takeover of the South. As discussed in Chapter 2, after about 1300, seigneurial wars were no longer directed against royal authority. During Philip IV's reign such wars became conflicts that were fought only between local players and for reasons of local politics. Ironically, Capetian success may have meant not only that seigneurial wars were not directed against the crown, but also that royal fortunes had limited effect on local power struggles. The importance of this shift can be appreciated if one imagines the disintegrative effect that a defeat like Crécy might have had on the royal position in Languedoc in 1250 or even 1270. Over the next fifty years, the military vagaries of French fortunes would affect the waging of seigneurial war, but primarily by providing more or fewer available soldiers, not by creating new *casus belli*. Given the scope of the challenges, this was a remarkable achievement.

JUSTICE: A NEW ROLE FOR LEGISLATION

The geographically and politically restricted nature of seigneurial wars may have allowed the crown to break new ground in the legal pursuit of war-makers, for, despite many difficulties, royal lawyers and judges sharpened their arguments considerably during these decades. Although the Leagues' triumph seems to have stopped prosecutions in Parlement for seigneurial war under Louis X, prosecution not only resumed under Philip V but was also undertaken for the first time explicitly because the war in question had violated the *ordonnances* against warfare. This reasoning became regularly utilized under Philip VI, to the point that the redactors of Parlement's *arrêts* began using a formula to describe wars as violating *ordonnances*. It was also during this period that the first cases of seigneurial war were treated as offences against the crown in language that resembles that of treason or of

---

[65] There is no mid-century parallel, for example, to the remark made in 1395 by the count of Pardiac that even if war was illegal *toutesfois on en a ainsi usé au pais sans en estre reprins* (*Documents relatifs à la chute de la maison d'Armagnac-Fézensaguet et à la mort du comte de Pardiac*, ed. P. Durrieu (Paris, 1883), no. 3, discussed in Chapter 5, below).

lèse-majesté. Still, only a minority of cases of *guerrae* were brought up on the basis of *ordonnance* violation, and even fewer on the basis of royal injury. The complaint of safeguard violation, on the other hand, was almost universal, suggesting how useful this limited and flexible institution remained, perhaps especially because of the deteriorating political and military situation, as well as attendant administrative changes discussed in the next section.

The 1310s and 1320s saw fitful developments. In the last years of Philip IV's reign there had been at least two prosecutions of warfare in Parlement that had cited Philip's 'prohibitions' or 'statutes' (*nostras prohibitiones/statuta*), though the references are problematic.[66] The Leagues may have interrupted this nascent development, but in May 1317, with Philip V on the throne, a Parlementary mandate for an inquest into a conflict mentions *ordinati[one]s et statuta*.[67] One cannot claim very much for this statement: the passage may contain a clerical error, and the illicit associations and plans of which the men were accused do not seem to have included war. It also is possible that these 'ordonnances and statutes' may have been not general prohibitions, but rather specific admonitions to individuals, such as were mentioned earlier that year in relation to the *guerras orribiles* raging in the Périgord between Alexander de Caumont and Jourdain de l'Isle, said to be against certain 'statutes of our father made to them' (*sibi facta*).[68] In 1321, though, a clear citation of the *ordonnance* as grounds for judicial prosecution appears in a judgment about the war between Florensac and Méjan. The crown's proctor argued that the lord and inhabitants of Florensac had attacked Méjan 'although ... it had been decreed and established (*fuisset ordinatum et statutum*) ... that no one, regardless of their condition or status, should dare to muster armed groups, or bear arms, or make war in any part of the realm whatsoever (*in aliqua parte dicti regni quamvis*)'. He further observed that the statute had been published long ago and reiterated repeatedly (*diu est & plures ... publicatum*), that the defendants' actions had violated the *ordonnance*, and that they ought to be punished as the prohibition prescribed (*iuxta ... ordinationem*).[69]

The proctor's argument in this case suggests that by the last year of Philip V's reign the royal *ordonnances* against warfare were perceived (at least by some) as prescriptive law that ought to influence behaviour and to entail punishment for violators. Again, one's interpretation

---

[66] *Olim*, III: 672, 886–7; above, pp. 76–7.

[67] '[Nonobstantes?] ordinati[one]s & statuta cum matura deliberatione consilii edita & contra bonum statum patrie & regni nostri ... congregationes, colligationes, conspirationes illicitis, secreta consilia, conventicula & monopolia inter se ad invicem fecerunt' (AN x2a 1, fol. 137r).

[68] AN x2a 1, fol. 58v.   [69] AN x1a 5, fols. 97v–98r.

should be circumspect: the defendants in the case were totally absolved of punishment since the lord of Florensac proved that he had jurisdiction over Méjan and therefore the right to engage in violence against it and its people, regardless of royal prohibitions, thus reaffirming seigneur-justiciars' immunity from royal legislation in their own domains.[70] And there was no other effort in the 1320s to prosecute warfare on the basis of royal law, except for the rather ambivalent case of the lord of Pierrefort in 1322, whose carriage of illegal arms during his war against the lord of Bressons was said to have been 'against our constitutions' (*contra constitutiones nostras*). Much as Florensac had argued in 1321 that his jurisdiction legalized his violence against Méjan, Pierrefort claimed that the right to carry arms in his own jurisdiction had justified his actions.[71] Unlike Florensac, Pierrefort only saw a reduction in his fine, rather than its suppression, but seigneurial jurisdiction evidently remained a stumbling block to ubiquitous enforcement of royal promulgations.[72] North of the River Loire, other traditional objections remained, as well. In several cases from the 1320s, Parlement or the chancery accepted war as a licit pretext for violence, and defendants continued to appeal to customary practice as legalizing their wars, though the claim of custom was never accepted by Parlement for any region.[73]

A judicial watershed was reached in the reign of Philip VI when the illegality of seigneurial war seems to have become a judicial principle, though not one universally applied. In November 1330, the royal proctor charged that certain men had made armed assemblies, 'rashly contravening royal *ordonnances*' (*contra ordinationes regias temere veniendo*),[74] and from 1335, the explicit and extensive justification of prosecution for transgression of

---

[70] Firnhaber-Baker, 'Seigneurial War', 64–5 and pp. 51–2, 78–9, above.

[71] '[C]oncessimus Alvernigenisorum (?) quilibet possit portare arma in justicia seu iurisdictione sua ad justificandum et utendum ius suum et ipse ut dicebat coadunaverat predictos armatos ut ipse tueretur ius suum ... cum etiam istud sibi liceret de iure scripto ad regendam terram suam malis hominibus pro quod ipse et predecessores sui ut ipse dicebat ipsam terram ab antiquo rexerunt' (AN x1a 5, fol. 239). Pierrefort probably meant the grant to Auvergne made in 1319 (*Ord.*, 1: 688–91 and see above p. 88).

[72] Kaeuper, *War, Justice*, 260, n. 276 discusses another case from 1323. The immunity of seigneurial jurisdiction to royal interference had been among the concessions made by Louis X to the Leagues in some cases (e.g. *Ord.*, 1: 567–73, art. 12 and AN JJ 56, no. 127, fols. 49v–50r). Cf. Lehugeur, *Histoire de Philippe le Long*, 1: 317–23.

[73] War as an allegedly legitimate pretext for violence: AN x2a 2, fol. 91v; *HL*, x: 944–6; Cazelles, 'Réglementation', 542, citing AN JJ 61, no. 118, fols. 47v–48r. Invocation of custom: AN x2a 1, fol. 180v; AN x2a 2, fol. 132; AN x1a 8, fols. 19v–21r. For the rejection of customary right, see L. de Carbonnières, 'Le pouvoir royal face aux mécanismes de la guerre privée à la fin du moyen âge. L'exemple du Parlement de Paris', *Droits. Revue française de théorie, de philosophie et de culture juridiques* 46 (2007): 3–17, and see AN x1a 12, fols. 430v–431 for the argument that royal *ordonnances* overruled customary right.

[74] AN x1a 6, fol. 134.

ordonnances became a relatively frequent prosecutorial strategy. Lengthy statements about the law and the defendants' violation of it appear in Parlement's registers. In 1335, there are two such prosecutorial statements, one of which is this accusation against the lords of Sancerre and Sully:

> although after the deliberation of our council it was decreed by us and published and publicly prohibited throughout our kingdom of France that no one should presume to bear arms, to make wars in our kingdom or to take up arms under penalty of body and goods, nonetheless our beloved and faithful count of Sancerre and his people and accomplices on one hand and the lord of Sully and his people and accomplices on the other are preparing to make wars and to take up arms against one another, rashly contravening our *ordonnances*, proclamations, and prohibitions . . .[75]

In the year that followed, three more such accusations are recorded, followed by one in both 1337 and 1338.[76] In most of these cases, the language employed is nearly exactly the same as that used for Sancerre and Sully, indicating that the redactors drew upon language ready made for the circumstances and were probably using a formulary.[77] This suggests that Parlementary personnel considered the basis for these prosecutions to have been the same and that from the second quarter of Philip VI's reign the court had begun to react to seigneurial wars on a programmatic basis. That all of these texts are mandates directed to bailiffs indicates that Parlement also sought to transmit this understanding to the crown's provincial administrators.

The justification of prosecution on grounds of violating *ordonnances* remained frequent in the 1340s, though the formulaic language disappears. This probably reflects a change in the disposition of the sources rather than in policy. Whereas for the period from 1325 to 1340, only the mandates from Parlement's criminal section survive, the extant registers for 1340–5 contain only the court's judgments.[78] The lost mandates may well have employed the formula used in the 1330s. In any case, the language of the surviving documents does indicate continued efforts to enforce the prohibition on warfare. In 1341, there is a statement that a nobleman in Amiens contravened the *quarantaine* that had been instituted

---

[75] AN x2a 3, fol. 9. The other at AN x2a 3, fol. 20v (mandate regarding the Chartrain).

[76] 1336: AN x2a 3, fol. 71 (mandate to the bailiff of Bourges and prévôt of Paris); AN x2a 3, fols. 79v–80r (mandate to the bailiff of Anjou and Maine); AN x2a 3, fol. 80r (mandate to the bailiff of Orléans). 1337: AN x1a 7, fol. 217r (mandate, possibly to the bailiff of Bourges). 1338: AN x2a 2bis, fol. 2 (mandate to the bailiff of Senlis).

[77] J. Firnhaber-Baker, 'Formulating Opposition to Seigneurial War in the Parlement de Paris', in *La formule au moyen âge*, ed. E. Louviot (Turnhout, 2013), 209–18.

[78] *Actes du Parlement de Paris: Parlement criminel: Règne de Philippe VI de Valois: Inventaire analytique des registres x2a 2 à 5*, ed. B. Labat-Poussin, M. Langlois, and Y. Lanhers (Paris, 1987), 14.

by Saint Louis and other royal predecessors, and that he was thus to be punished as 'a traitor (*proditor*) and breaker of the truce and royal ordinances', having violated 'our public proclamations and prohibitions that no one should dare to bear arms or make war in our whole realm'.[79] In 1343 the accusatory portion of a Parlement *arrêt* for an inhabitant of the Vermandois asserted that 'during our wars it is not allowed to any of our subjects whatsoever in our realm to make war against anyone else'.[80] The same year, Parlement registered a remission for an inhabitant of Paris who assembled armed troops in order to attack someone 'against our prohibitions and the common good (*bien commun*) . . . in contempt of us and against our royal *ordonnances*'.[81] In 1346, a war in Senlis prompted the king's proctor to argue that 'by our *ordonnances* published through our entire realm all wars and vengeances were and had been prohibited and that [the defendant] made war against our previously mentioned *ordonnances*'.[82] Two remissions from 1349 for southerners mention wars in contravention of *ordonationes* among the recipients' crimes, and there are two further invocations of royal prohibitions in Parlementary prosecutions from the early months of 1350.[83]

The reign of Philip VI thus coincided with a significant change in how some royal representatives imagined the relationship between royal legal authority and seigneurial violence. Although the violation of royal legislation had appeared in local war cases before, most strikingly in 1321, under Philip VI this justification was invoked repeatedly and programmatically. Prosecution of these wars was justified on the basis that the king had prohibited it and because the decrees were well known throughout the kingdom. This demonstrates a new sense in Philip's reign that royal decrees about warfare should function as legislation subject to penal sanction, much as law is understood to work in modern states. There are also other indications of a nascent legal-judicial order resembling that of later polities in a renewed emphasis on the

---

[79] '[C]ontra ordinationes inclite recordationis beati Ludovici proavi nostri per nos & predecessores nostros . . . puniri debet tanquam proditor & fractor treuge & ordinacionum Regalium veniendo etiam contra proclamationes & prohibitiones nostras pub[l]ice factas quod nullus esset ausus portare arma nec guerram facere in toto regno nostro' (AN x1a 8, fol. 143).

[80] '[D]urantibus guerris nostris non liceat cuicumque subditorum nostrorum in Regno nostro contra aliquem guerram facere' (AN x1a 9, fols. 492v–494r). The *quarantaine* also came up in an *arrêt* from 1346 (AN x2a 5, fols. 75v–76r) and in another from 1346 for a war near Lille (AN x1a 10, fol. 418).

[81] '[C]ontre nos deffenses & le bien commun et de pais . . . laquelle chose estoit en contempt de nous et contre noz ordenances royaus' (AN x1a 10, fol. 35).

[82] '[D]ictus procurator noster inter cetera dicebat quod per ordinaciones nostras per totum regnum nostrum publicatas omnes guerre et vindicte erant et fuerant prohibite quodque contra dictas ordinationes nostris predictus Aubertus guerram fecerat' (AN x1a 11, fols. 111v–112r).

[83] Remissions at AN JJ 77, no. 402, fol. 247 (for Géraud de la Barthe); AN JJ 78, no. 45, fols. 23–6 (for Aicard de Miremont); 1350 prosecutions at AN x1a 12, fols. 430v–431; AN x2a 5, fol. 186.

damage that seigneurial war did to crown and commonwealth. Making war against the crown had been considered treasonable from late in Philip IV's reign,[84] but although wars between royal subjects were not explicitly prosecuted as a crime of *lèse-majesté* (*crimen leze majestatis* or *crimen legis Julie magistatis*) until the 1360s, in Philip VI's reign there were numerous charges that wars or related violence were *en contempt de nous, in offensam majestatis nostre, in nostrum nostreque majestatis regis prejudicium,* or similar.[85] From the 1340s, damage done to the *res publica* or to the *commune* was also invoked, and frequently such an accusation was made in connection with the claim that war harmed the royal majesty.[86] There were forerunners to this in isolated prosecutions from the reigns of Philip IV and Philip V.[87] But it was first under Philip VI that seigneurial war seems to have been regularly understood as harmful to the crown or community as an abstract entity.

The growing importance of the law and the state did not spell an end to prosecutions for other crimes of war, such as violation of safeguard or carriage of arms, which had different implications for royal authority over violence. Both *fractio salve gardie* and *portatio armorum* continued to predominate as prosecutorial justifications. In the South, nine of the twelve conflicts waged under Philip VI involved at least one allegation of safeguard violation, and eight included a claim of carrying illicit arms.[88] Comparatively, injury to the royal majesty/commonwealth appears in relation to only four cases, and the *ordonnances* were only invoked for two southern wars, that of Aicard de Miremont against Sicard de Paulin and that of Géraud de la Barthe against the Arpajons. Since those cases that

---

[84] S. H. Cuttler, *The Law of Treason and Treason Trials in Later Medieval France* (Cambridge, 1981), 31.

[85] Quotes from AN x1a 10, fol. 35 (1343); AN x2a 5, fols. 204v–207r (1350); AN x2a 3, fols. 196v–197r (1333).

[86] *Res publica*: AN x2a 5, fol. 65r (1346); AN JJ 78, no. 45, fols. 23–6 (1349), among others; paired with royal majesty at AN x2a 5, fols. 204v–207r (1350); paired with *patria* at AN x2a 5, fol. 120 (1346). *Commune*: AN x1a 10, fol. 35 (1343); AN JJ 75, no. 312, fols. 183v–184 (1344), both paired with royal majesty.

[87] See *Olim*, III: 247–8 (1308); AN JJ 46, no. 3, fols. 24–23v (1311); AN x2a 2, fols. 41v–42r (1318).

[88] Safeguard violation: Aymar of Roussillon vs. Briend de Lagnieu; Loup de Foix *et al.* vs. Guillaume-Bernard d'Asnave; Othon de Pardeillan *et al.* vs. 'Avisantius' de Caumont and Helizona; Bertrand Jourdain de l'Isle vs. Pierre-Raymond and Gui de Comminges; Aicard de Miremont *et al.* vs. Sicard de Paulin; lord of Pierrefort vs. Pierre de Turlande; lords of Crussol, Belcastel, and Solignac vs. Jauserans, lord of Saint-Didier; viscount of Carlat vs. prior of Saint-Michel de Laussac; Géraud de la Barthe vs. Hugues of Arpajon. Carriage of arms: Raymond Almeric, lord of Bazillac in Bigorre, vs. Bernard de Castelbajac; Othon de Pardeillan *et al.* vs. 'Avisantius' de Caumont and Helizona; Bertrand Jourdain de l'Isle vs. Pierre-Raymond and Gui de Comminges; Aicard de Miremont *et al.* vs. Sicard de Paulin; lord of Pierrefort vs. Pierre de Turlande; lords of Crussol, Belcastel, and Solignac vs. Jauserans, lord of Saint-Didier; and viscount of Carlat vs. prior of Saint-Michel de Laussac; Géraud de la Barthe vs. Hugues of Arpajon.

were pursued for reasons of legislation and/or injury to the polity always also included charges of safeguard violation or carriage of arms, royal representatives seem not to have considered these contradictory prosecutorial premises even though safeguards and the crime of *portatio armorum* in some ways came out of a more restricted view of royal power, as discussed more fully in Chapter 2.[89] Evidently, it was well understood that although safeguards entailed the admission of the restrictions on royal jurisdiction, the king's ability to issue them came from the same potentially absolute regalian authority as the king's legislative competence to issue (or to disregard) the law. In any case, the prevalence of the safeguard indicates that royal power continued to grow in this ostensibly limited, piecemeal fashion, even as a more universal vision of law and government came into focus.

ADMINISTRATION: THE EVOLUTION OF AUTHORITY IN DIFFICULTY

The dual expansion of royal authority through both direct and indirect means also took place in the administrative realm, with royal officers both coercing obedience and employing more cooperative methods of engagement. There is some evidence that the more expansive understanding of royal authority evident in judicial citation of the *ordonnances* also saw concrete application in the provincial administration of justice. Efforts to prevent wars or to restrain war-makers seem to have been routine. Among many examples, in the 1340s the judge of Rieux in the seneschalsy of Toulouse ordered the royal castellan of le Fousseret to prevent Guillaume-Bernard d'Asnave's son from attacking Loup de Foix, and the bailiff and judge of Vivarais and other royal officers prohibited the lord of Saint-Didier from attacking the lords of Belcastel and Solignac.[90] In early 1348, King Philip VI himself seems to have attempted – albeit unsuccessfully – to prevent the war that was in danger of breaking out between rival suitors to the young heiress Hélène de Castelnau, nominating special envoys and instructing them to take the girl somewhere where she might be suitably raised and to seize her holdings so that they might be properly governed until a solution could be worked out.[91] In the case of non-compliance with official decisions, there were

---

[89] For Philip V, see Lehugeur, *Histoire de Philippe le Long*, I: 316–17.

[90] Judge of Rieux at *HL*, x: 1077–9; officers of Vivarais at *HL*, x: 1054–6. Official preventive action was also presented as normal outside Languedoc and the Auvergne; see AN x1a 5, fol. 288; AN x1a 7, fol. 29r.

[91] AN x2a 5, fols. 109v, 118r.

often efforts made to enforce them coercively. Parlement ordered the seneschal of Toulouse to arrest Aicard de Miremont and his accomplices and to send them to await trial imprisoned in the Châtelet at Paris, and similar arrangements are reported for other cases.[92]

Such efforts were probably only exceptionally successful. The seneschals of Toulouse and Carcassonne, for example, were able to capture only a few of Aicard de Miremont's accomplices and were left to issue (probably toothless) proclamations of banishment against the rest. But the coordination of provincial administrative activity with orders from king and Parlement suggests the continuation of the hierarchical and systematic enforcement of justice seen under Philip the Fair. This was a framework that the lords themselves seem to have been willing to take advantage of for their own uses, frequently complaining (*conquerendo*) about their enemies' incursions. Investigations into Aicard de Miremont's war against Sicard de Paulin began at the behest of Sicard, who had requested a royal mandate to the seneschal for this purpose.[93] And Parlement ordered the bailiff of the Mountains of the Auvergne to investigate the war between Pierre de Turland and the lord of Pierrefort because of the former's complaints to the court (*ex gravi conquestione Petri de Turlanda*).[94] This bailiff was similarly notified about the viscount of Carlat's alleged misdeeds against many of the region's nobles.[95] The nearly universal allegations of safeguard violation also attest to the popularity of special royal protection even among lords otherwise opposed to the extension of royal jurisdiction beyond domain lands.[96]

Alongside the apparent continuity of the system that matured under Philip the Fair, however, the fourteenth century's challenges began to force changes in the functioning of royal judicial administration. Royal courts seem to have been less able to compel obedience beginning in the reign of Philip VI. For the first time, contumacy became a significant problem. In the first quarter of the century, individuals rarely failed to appear in court. In fact, contumacy was so unusual that when some defendants from the Périgord failed to come before the seneschal's court in 1313, they were initially sentenced to death.[97] By the 1340s, however,

---

[92] AN JJ 68, no. 196, fols. 106v–107r; AN x2a 5, fol. 66v. See also AN x2a 5, fols. 65r, 120, 190r.

[93] '[Q]uibusdam informationibus & processibus per senescallum Carcassone seu eius curiam vigore quarumdam litterarum a nobis per dictum Sycardum obtentarum' (AN JJ 68, no. 196, fols. 106v–107r).

[94] AN x2a 5, fol. 65r. [95] AN x2a 5, fol. 120. [96] See above, p. 103.

[97] AN x2a 1, fol. 15. These sentences were intended primarily to make a political point, however, and most were remitted a few months later: AN JJ 49, no. 83, fol. 40; AN JJ 49, no. 99, fols. 43v–44r; AN JJ 49, no. 108, fols. 46v–407r. See *Registres du trésor des chartes: Inventaire analytique établi par les*

contumacy had become a routine problem; during Philip VI's reign, five cases against war-makers in the South were complicated by a defendant's absence from court.[98] Although fines and other penalties continued to be levied against war-makers, the execution of sentences became less straightforward. Those sentenced *in absentia* were generally banished and their goods forfeited to the king's profit, but such a penalty was obviously difficult to carry out when one could not get hold of the person in the first place. A more or less lengthy delay in collection of fines may also have become more common, as there are cases in which heirs found themselves liable for their fathers' criminal fines.[99]

This new inefficiency was partly a logistical problem caused by the disordered state of a country at war, and it was exacerbated by the advent of plague at the end of Philip VI's reign. Although few of the crown's administrators died during the epidemic, the disease impeded royal business, interrupting the work of the king's council, which ceased to meet during the summer of 1349.[100] The disease further disrupted Parlement, already in a confused state because of the military reverses at Crécy and Calais. The epidemic meant that cases could not be heard, inquests made, or sentences carried out. The court observed in 1350, for example, that the investigation into the crimes committed by Pierre Turland in his war against Gibert de Pierrefort had not been completed 'on account of our wars and the disease that was in those parts'.[101] The same year, the court dealt with a case that was to have been heard in the previous year's session but had been postponed *occasione mortalitatis tunc vigentis*.[102] It is possible that plague hampered royal efforts to prevent the war between the Arpajons and Géraud de la Barthe over Hélène de Castelnau's marriage in 1348, though none

---

archivistes aux Archives nationales, ed. R. Fawtier *et al.*, 3 vols. in 6 (Paris, 1958–99), I: nos. 2003–9, 2011, 2015–20, 2026–32, 2036; J. Kicklighter, 'English Bordeaux in Conflict: the Execution of Pierre Vigier de la Rouselle and its Aftermath, 1312–24', *Journal of Medieval History* 9 (1983): 1–14.

[98] Othon de Pardeillan vs. Helizona (AN x1a 8, fols. 19v–21r); Aicard de Miremont vs. Sicard de Paulin (AN JJ 68, no. 196, fols. 106v–107r); Guillaume-Bernard d'Asnave vs. Loup de Foix (*HL*, x: 1077–9); viscount of Carlat vs. Laussac (AN x2a 5, fols. 207r–208v); and lords of Crussol, Belcastel, and Solignac vs. lord of Saint-Didier (*HL*, x: 1054–6).

[99] E.g. AN x1a 8, fols. 17–18r; AN JJ 81, no. 880, fol. 463r.

[100] R. Cazelles, *Société politique, noblesse et couronne sous Jean le Bon et Charles V* (Geneva, 1982), 125. For the much lower rates of mortality among royal officials as compared with the general population, see R. Cazelles, 'La peste de 1348–1349 en langue d'oïl: Épidémie prolétarienne et enfantine', in *Bulletin philologique et historique (jusqu'à 1610) du comité des travaux historiques et scientifiques, année 1962* (Paris, 1965), 293–305.

[101] '[M]andamentum ob guerras nostras & mortalitatem que fuit in illis partibus non fuerit ut dicitur executum' (AN x2a 5, fol. 190r).

[102] AN x2a 5, fols. 188r, 197v among other examples.

of the four commissioners sent to deal with it in the spring of 1348 died in the epidemic.[103]

The inability to pursue justice as effectively as before created or at least coincided with a change in the tenor of justice itself. The most striking sign of this change is the multiplication of letters of remission under Philip VI. The increase in pardons was a generalized phenomenon. While the chancery registers of the later Capetians include only around 70 of these letters, registers from Philip VI's reign contain about 450, almost two-thirds of which were issued during the 1340s.[104] In terms of seigneurial war, letters of remission were granted to participants in six of eight southern conflicts in the 1340s, as opposed to none of the conflicts under Philip IV and only two of those under his sons.[105] Many of these pardons were issued in light of the recipient's military service. That granted to Géraud de la Barthe in 1349 for his war with the Arpajons, for instance, was issued 'in consideration of the good and useful services that Géraud and those of his lineage have long supplied to us, both in our wars and elsewhere'.[106] This *quid pro quo* became almost standard under John II, even in the reign's less disastrous early period, and it would continue to figure as grounds for pardon for the rest of the century.[107] It is apparent that the war with England created favourable conditions for the pursuit of seigneurial privilege to the detriment of royal law and judicial prerogatives. Certainly, after Crécy, the pace of pardoning picked up considerably overall, and the war was also the context in which the nobility of Gascony won their concessions for waging war against one another.[108] But the granting of remission in exchange for military service is not a development that can be blamed solely on Philip VI's martial impotence; the first such pardons issued to war-makers in recompense for their military contributions were granted in 1326, following the War of

---

[103] All four were still alive and active in political society in the 1350s: Geoffrey de Charny famously died at the Battle of Poitiers (*Gallia regia*, no. 5871); his co-commissioner, Jean de St-Just was also still alive some years later, as were Ligier de Bardilly and Jean Hanière (Cazelles, *Société politique . . . sous Jean* (Geneva, 1982), 180, n. 26, pp. 256, 391).

[104] M. François, 'Note sur les lettres de rémission transcrites dans les registres du Trésor des chartes', *BEC* 103 (1942): 317–24.

[105] The exceptions under Philip VI were Pierrefort vs. Turlande and the viscount of Carlat's war.

[106] '[E]n consideracion aus bons & aggreables services que le dit Gerart & ceulz de son linage nous ont faiz longuement tant en noz guerres comme ailleurs' (AN JJ 77, no. 402, fol. 247). See also AN JJ 75, no. 312, fols. 183v–184 for Gui de Comminges in 1344; AN JJ 68, no. 196, fols. 106v–107r issued to Aicard de Miremont in 1347.

[107] E.g. *HL*, x: 1077–9 (1351), 1083–4 (1352), 1107–8 (1355); AN JJ 81, no. 880, fol. 463r (1353).

[108] P. Texier, 'La rémission au XIVème siècle: significations et fonctions', in *La faute, la répression et le pardon, vol. 1 of Actes du 107ème Congrès national des sociétés savantes (Brest, 1982)* (Paris, 1984), 200–2. For the Gascon privileges, see above, pp. 89–90.

Saint-Sardos in Aquitaine, and confirmed during one of Flanders' periodic rebellions in 1328–9.[109]

The war altered the legal pursuit of war-makers in other ways as well. From its debut, political and military considerations began to affect how and why royal officials became involved in seigneurial conflicts. Such factors are rarely explicitly mentioned, but often played an important role behind the scenes. The seneschal of Bigorre's prosecution of the lord of Bazillac in 1339 no doubt had as much to do with the latter's convocation of an assembly opposed to supplying money for the war in Flanders as it did with Bazillac's war against Bernard de Castelbajac.[110] The viscount of Carlat's contravention of royal orders for a military assembly probably similarly affected his treatment in his conflict with the regions' nobles, who were quick to point out his well-known English sympathies, and his request for a remission was refused.[111] Similarly, Roger-Bernard de Lévis's struggle to gain control over his father Jean II's barony was ultimately successful as a result of Jean's support for *inimici* and *rebelles* in the barony.[112] It is not necessarily true that justice was the victim of politics in these cases, but it does appear that military needs created an impetus to use judicial and administrative structures in novel ways.

This more flexible approach is also apparent in officials' involvement in arranging peace settlements between warring parties, a practice that developed significantly during this period. Subjects had long been accustomed to settle their conflicts between themselves, of course, and French kings had habitually arranged peace settlements between very powerful lordships, such as that made by Philip IV between Foix and Armagnac in January 1304.[113] But there was a noticeable increase in royal participation and interest in this sort of settlement under Philip IV's

---

[109] *HL*, x: 662–4 and AN JJ 65A, no. 81, fol. 66 (Loup de Foix and Fortanier de Durban); *Sceaux gascons*, ed. Laplagne-Barris, III: 389–90 (to Arnaud-Guillaume de Monlezun, his brothers and his son). For the War of Saint-Sardos, see J. Sumption, *The Hundred Years War*, 3 vols. to date (Philadelphia and London, 1990–2009), I: 91–9; P. Chaplais, *Introduction to The War of Saint-Sardos (1323–1325): Gascon Correspondence and Diplomatic Documents* (London, 1954).

[110] '[D]ictus Raymundus conspiracionem illicitam faciendo plures nobiles ... qui sic congregati per eum inducti concorditur statuerant quod suis subditis inhiberent ne Senescallio seu Thesaurario nostro Bigorre nomine nostro et pro nobis aliquid mutuarent, licet predicti senescallus & thesaurarius in promptu pecunniam non haberent de qua possent satisfacere hominibus dicte Senescallie destinatis et paratis de mandato nostro ad eundem in Flandriam' (AN x1a 8, fols. 17–18r).

[111] AN x2a 5, fols. 204v–207r.

[112] AN JJ 91, no. 318, fols. 163v–165 (partially published in *HL*, x: 1180–2) and *Cartulaire de Mirepoix*, ed. Pasquier, 71.

[113] References to accords between parties in various circumstances prior to 1314 include: *Olim*, II: 174, III: 121, 391, 504, 626–7, 629–30, 820; AN x2a 1, fol. 25; BN Latin 11017, fols. 7v–8. In addition to the Foix/Armagnac settlement negotiated by Philip IV (see Chapter 2, above), there is also the example from the later 1260s when 'peace was made' between the warring viscountess of Limoges and Bozon de Bourdeille 'by means of some of the members of the king's council'

sons. From the later 1310s, Parlement appears to have been keeping copies of accords, including those agreed without the help of a royal official, perhaps indicating an effort to exert greater royal authority over these agreements.[114] And with the intensification of hostilities with England and the overall weakening of coercive royal authority, administrative engagement in peace agreements gained greater scope. Although civil settlements made without any apparent royal involvement remained common throughout the whole fourteenth century, it was during the turbulent later 1320s – at the same time and reported in the same documents as the first remissions on the grounds of military service – that peace settlements appear that were made via a royal officer's assistance: *mediante senescallo ... pax amicabilis extitit*.[115]

Royal officials' involvement in *paces, concordiae*, and the like became increasingly prevalent in the later 1340s and beyond. In later decades, bailiffs and seneschals would do the bulk of such work, but initially special commissioners tended to represent royal authority in these agreements. Such commissioners, specially chosen by Prince John for this purpose, settled the accord for the war between Aicard de Miremont and Sicard de Paulin in the great hall of Toulouse in 1348.[116] The accord between Roger-Bernard and Jean II de Lévis in 1353 was made simply 'by the king at the relation of his council', without indication of who actually negotiated the settlement, but the final settlement of 1362 was made with the intervention of the Dauphin Charles's major domo, specially commissioned for this purpose.[117] Such special commissioners were also sent south to settle the conflict between Géraud de la Barthe and the Arpajons, and even when they failed, the parties eventually settled their conflict with the intervention of the king, whose 'full

---

('mediantibus aliquibus de consilio domini Regis, facta fuit pax inter partes' (*Olim*, I: 693–4)). See also J. Firnhaber-Baker, '*Jura in medio*: the Settlement of Seigneurial Disputes in Later Medieval Languedoc', *French History* 26 (2012): 441–59.

[114] AN X1c 1. The accords deposited with Parlement, of which there are thousands for the fourteenth century alone, are almost totally neglected. For their history, see M. Dillay, 'Instruments de recherche du fonds du Parlement de Paris, dressés au greffe de la juridiction', *Archives et bibliothèques* 3 (1937–8): 13–30, 82–92, 190–9; A. Grün, 'Notice sur les archives du Parlement de Paris', *Actes du Parlement de Paris*, ed. E. Boutaric, 2 vols. (Paris, 1863–7), I: ch. 7. There is no guide to the holdings except for a very incomplete *fichier* of names attempted in the nineteenth century (consultable at the *section ancienne* of the AN) and the lists of entries in the contemporary *registres de greffe* (AN X1a 8844–9). As far as I have been able to discover, the series does not contain all accords made between parties with cases in Parlement's criminal section because none of those made between warring parties which exist elsewhere (largely in local archives) is locatable in the X1c holdings.

[115] *HL*, X: 662–4; *Sceaux gascons*, ed. Laplagne-Barris, III: 389–90.

[116] '[C]onstitutus personaliter apud Tholosam in aula nova Regia Tholose dictus Aycardus de Miramonte ... coram ... commissaris in hac parte per illustrem principem dominum Johannem primogenitum & locum tenentum dicti domini nostri regis' (AN JJ 78, no. 45, fols. 23–6).

[117] *HL*, X: 1096–9, 1180–2.

power and royal authority' were needed to regularize their accord's problematic contents.[118]

As they became less able to enforce justice coercively, royal officials thus turned to more cooperative, flexible methods of engagement. Like the contemporaneous proliferation of remissions for warfare, the practice of ending conflicts through a negotiated agreement rather than through a formal judicial decision seems to indicate a weakening of royal authority. Indeed, the practices were connected; from the late 1340s the grant of remission was often linked to whether peace had been made between the parties.[119] By John II's reign there may even have been a sense that once peace had been made, further prosecution was superfluous; a remission from 1355, for example, complains that the seneschal of Beaucaire had continued his legal machinations, 'although peace had already been made on this matter between the bishop and the knight by the late Pope Clement [VI]'.[120] The dependence of remission on the reaching of a civil accord would become a prominent feature of royal procedure under John II and beyond, and the linkage does seem to have been an innovation of the second quarter of the fourteenth century.[121] Under Philip IV, for example, Parlement had flatly declared that regardless (*veruntamen*) of the civil agreement made by Agen in its dispute with the prior of Saint-Caprais, the community still owed the crown (*quantum ad nos*) the hefty sum of 10,000 l.t. for their violence and armed oppression of the priory.[122]

The shift in the crown's approach to seigneurial warfare seems to have been caused by military exigency, no doubt partly because there was greater need to shower favours upon one's vassals and subjects. Again, there were precursors in the remissions issued after the Saint-Sardos War, in which the peace made by the seneschal of Toulouse between the parties was cited as a reason for granting the remission.[123] But this attention to peace, negotiation, settlement, and mutual satisfaction also speaks to a growing preoccupation

---

[118] AN JJ 78, no. 250, fol. 139.

[119] E.g. remissions for Aimar de Roussillon made 'attento ... quod ... pax inter eos extitit reformata' (*HL*, x: 1107–8); the dual peace and remission for Aicard de Miremont (AN JJ 78, no. 45, fols. 23–6); the remission made to Jean II de Lévis, whose prosecution was resumed because 'consiliarius noster dictas partes ad concordiam ... minime reduxerat' (AN x2a 6, fol. 252). The linked language of abolition, remission, and peace in treaties during the Hundred Years War is suggestive: N. Offenstadt, *Faire la paix au moyen âge: Discours et gestes de paix pendant la Guerre de Cent Ans* (Paris, 2007), 50–5.

[120] '[S]enescallus noster Bellicadri, pro hujusmodi facto, lict de eodem pax inter ipsos episcopum & militem per bone memorie summum pontificem Clementem, ultimo deffunctum, refformata fuerit, prosequitur eundem militem & eorum eo posuit & traxit in causam' (*HL*, x: 1107–8). Earlier accords in cases with no criminal element had, of course, terminated the civil process.

[121] Cf. Texier, 'La rémission au XIVème siècle'.   [122] *Olim*, III: 121.

[123] AN JJ 65A, no. 269, fol. 185 in addition to those cited above at n. 115.

with order in a kingdom at war. From this point on, order became increasingly important as it became increasingly elusive, and the objective of royal efforts against seigneurial violence (and violence in general) shifted away from the assertion of royal prerogatives and towards the settlement of dispute.

Particularly given the apparent rise in seigneurial violence discussed above, this new emphasis on negotiated settlement suggests a move backward, towards the methods of self-help and informal dispute processing that the monarchical state's legal and administrative regime was supposed to have permanently replaced. According to John Baldwin, in the reign of Philip Augustus, 'the technique of allowing contending parties to arrive at their own decisions, then to be confirmed by royal authority, was the preferred method for resolving disputes in the royal courts'.[124] Indeed one of the hallmarks of the centuries that preceded Philip II's reign, during the long post-Carolingian period of weak central power, was the settlement of conflicts outside formal judicial systems and without reference to institutional authority.[125] As we have seen, the advent of Capetian rule in Languedoc did not obviate these practices, but there had been a moment during Philip IV's reign when court judgments, criminal prosecutions, and civil damages had begun to eclipse these cooperative arrangements. This trend had encountered serious checks after his death, however, and by the later 1340s – despite administrative precedent and a robust ideological tradition – officers simply could not compel obedience under the circumstances that confronted them.

It is important not to overstate the extent of the crown's retreat, even after Crécy. Parties did not settle their differences before royal representatives without some amount of pressure from those officials. Aicard de Miremont had been jailed in Toulouse for non-payment of a fine before agreeing to make his peace with Sicard, and the 1353 accord between Roger-Bernard and Jean II de Lévis was made with the parties 'submitting themselves by their good will entirely to [the king's] disposition', suggesting that the men were not free to disagree with the terms set. Certainly, the later accord that removed the barony from Jean II de Lévis's governance was made by royal fiat more than by cooperative negotiation. While many accords involved negotiation by non-royal parties – friends, overlords, ecclesiastical officials, and so on – from this period on even accords settled without royal involvement required royal permission and approbation if further pursuit in royal

---

[124] *The Government of Philip Augustus: Foundations of French Royal Power in the Middle Ages* (Berkeley, 1986), 37–44, quote at 43.

[125] See works cited in the Introduction, pp. 8–10, esp. n. 22.

courts was to be avoided.[126] Although remissions did have obvious negative implications for royal judicial power – the king's proctor observed in 1348 that a remission for Jean II de Lévis 'was evil and could be a bad example for the future' (*ipse erat inique et poterat esse res mali exempli in futurum*)[127] – in some ways their prevalence signals the criminal system's success because it indicates that royal courts and administrators could not be wholly ignored. Had it been otherwise, people would not have gone to the bother and expense of protecting themselves from prosecution.

Both accords and royal pardons can and should be understood *not just* as evidence for the deterioration of royal power, *but also* as alternative methods of asserting and participating in royal authority. In earlier periods, the only negotiators had been the parties' family, friends, and neighbouring monks, and the only condition of settlement was that both parties be satisfied.[128] Now, those brokering agreements frequently included the crown's representatives, meaning that royal administrators had inserted themselves into what had once been an essentially local affair. The development of criminal courts and a theory of crime meant that the king, too, had interests that must be addressed, even if only by requesting and paying for a remission.[129] Moreover, as Claude Gauvard has emphasized, the granting of remission was an act of obeisance by the

---

[126] E.g. AN JJ 66, no. 1207, fols. 514v–516. Parlement could annul accords, as it did in 1350: 'dicta accorda . . . anullavit & pronunciavit esse nulla' (AN x1a 12, fols. 430v–431). There is an early example of approbation from late in Philip IV's reign (AN JJ 49, no. 233, fol. 103r), but it does not appear that royal agreement was required in this case, only that it was sought.

[127] AN x1a 12, fol. 252r.

[128] For earlier negotiating parties, see G. Althoff, 'Vermittler' in *Lexicon des Mittelalters* (Munich, 1997); S. D. White, '"Pactum . . . Legem Vincit et Amor Judicium": the Settlement of Disputes by Compromise in Eleventh-Century Western France', *American Journal of Legal History* 22 (1978): 281–308; S. D. White, 'Feuding and Peace-Making in the Touraine around the Year 1100', *Traditio* 42 (1986): 252–7; F. Cheyette, 'Suum cuique tribuere', *French Historical Studies* 6 (1970): 291–3; P. J. Geary, 'Living with Conflicts in Stateless France: a Typology of Conflict Management Mechanisms, 1050–1200', in *Living with the Dead in the Middle Ages* (Ithaca, 1994 [1986]), 125–60. For the importance of satisfaction, see Cheyette, 'Suum cuique'; G. Althoff, 'Satisfaction: Peculiarities of the Amicable Settlement of Conflicts in the Middle Ages', in *Ordering Medieval Society: Perspectives on Intellectual and Practical Modes of Shaping Social Relations*, ed. B. Jussen, trans. P. Selwyn (Philadelphia, 2001), 270–84. See also *Le Conventum (vers 1030). Un précurseur aquitain des premières épopées*, ed. G. Beech, Y. Chauvin, and G. Pon (Geneva, 1995) for an eleventh-century dispute completely outside institutional judicial channels.

[129] For the development of the idea of crime, as distinct from civil tort, see Y. Bongert, 'Rétribution et réparation dans l'ancien droit français', *Mémoires de la Société pour l'histoire du droit et des institutions des anciens pays bourguignons, comtois et romands* 45 (1988), 59–107. Comparatively for England, P. R. Hyams, *Rancor and Reconciliation in Medieval England* (Ithaca, NY, 2003), ch. 7, esp. 220–4; P. R. Hyams, 'Does it Matter When the English Began to Distinguish between Crime and Tort?', in *Violence in Medieval Society*, ed. R. W. Kaeuper (Woodbridge, 2000), 107–28; P. R. Hyams, 'Nastiness and Wrong, Rancor and Reconciliation' and C. Donahue, 'The Emergence of Crime–Tort Distinction in England', both in *Conflict in Medieval Europe: Changing Perspectives on Society and Culture*, ed. W. C. Brown and P. Górecki (Aldershot, 2003), 195–218 and 219–28.

supplicant that created an opportunity for the crown to display the plenitude of royal power: the king's unique ability not just to condemn, but also to pardon.[130] Asserting royal authority through such displays of 'soft power' served to bind the crown more closely into local society. Certainly, these were practices adopted mainly by necessity not design, but they were still affirmations of royal authority, and in fact their usage signals a high level of support for royal administration from the governed. While the advent of coercively imposed, institutionalized justice and the rise of the French state are often considered inseparable phenomena,[131] the resolution of seigneurial conflicts through settlement indicates a growing role for royal authority despite the deterioration of judicial enforcement. Less forcefully than before but more insidiously, royal representatives and royal interests continued their penetration of the local struggles through which provincial power was arbitrated.

CONCLUSION

Over the decades that followed Philip IV's death, two patterns emerged. First was the gradual decrease in the incidence of seigneurial war (at least in Languedoc) through the 1330s, followed by a new upsurge coincidental with – though not directly caused by – the beginning of the Hundred Years War. The second pattern was a growing disconnection between what the king and his courts said about seigneurial war and what royal officers and administrators did about it. Despite the objections of the Leagues under Louis X and the troubles of his successors, the ideological basis for royal intolerance of seigneurial war changed little between Philip IV and the early years of John II. And in Parlement, the king's *ordonnances* at last began to be treated as a basis for judicial action, albeit relatively rarely and inconsistently. At the same time, the combination of logistical difficulties entailed by the war and later by plague and the loss of royal prestige suffered under Philip VI meant a waning of the crown's ability to enforce obedience. Consequently, royal representatives turned to other, less coercive means of engagement with war-makers, continuing to assert a role for royal authority but in a considerably less strident tone. These two patterns are obviously linked; the pressures that began to

---

[130] 'Grâce et exécution capitale: les deux visages de la justice royale française à la fin du moyen âge', *BEC* 153 (1995): 275–90; *'De grace especial:' Crime, état et société en France à la fin du moyen âge*, 2 vols. (Paris, 1991), II: 895–934; 'L'image du roi justicier en France à la fin du moyen âge, d'après les lettres de rémission', in *La faute, la répression, et le pardon, vol. 1 of Actes du 107ème Congrès national des sociétés savantes (Brest, 1982)* (Paris, 1984), 165–96.
[131] See the Introduction, esp. pp. 5–7.

mount in the later 1340s significantly altered the relationship between royal authority and seigneurial violence.

These developments bespeak considerable difficulties for the crown, but royal administrative resilience over these decades is striking. The elite professional administrators who counselled the king were no doubt primarily responsible for the recovery and maintenance of royal normative tradition as expressed in the *ordonnances*. And lesser such technocrats working in Parlement drew upon this tradition and related ideas in their prosecutions, articulating a direct relationship between justice and royal legislation for the first time. In a different – indeed nearly contradictory – way, those with provincial administrative responsibilities also asserted royal authority. The last group particularly was fighting a rearguard action in the face of mounting logistical and political difficulties. It is remarkable that they succeeded in preserving any role for the crown, let alone carving out new areas of activity more suitable to changed conditions. The decades ahead would prove much more difficult, though, as a great wave of violence washed over France, and John II's problems and follies dwarfed those of his father.

Chapter 4

THE CHANGING EXPERIENCE OF VIOLENCE,
1350–1364

France suffered a fundamental breakdown of public order under John II, whose reign intensified the governmental and administrative problems that had emerged after the military reversals of the later 1340s. In the abortive Treaty of Guines, drafted in 1354, France agreed to enormous territorial concessions to Edward III, and although the treaty was never ratified, John's prospects for holding the line against England were not good.[1] The crown's treasury was empty. Rebellion against taxation was rampant, and successive devaluation of the coinage was hardly a more popular expedient. Having inherited by primogeniture, John was not beholden to his supporters and his councillors the way his father had been, but there were other competitors for control over the kingdom. Impatient with royal fiscal and military incompetence, the Estates General (an assembly of burghers, nobles, and clerics) demanded a larger share in the government of the realm and the war in exchange for acquiescence to new subsidies. King Charles of Navarre, that wildcard of fourteenth-century politics, had many friends – and many soldiers – at his disposal. The time was ripe for a direct challenge to the king's rule.

John's capture at the Battle of Poitiers in 1356 obviated the otherwise very real possibility of a coup against him.[2] But it was disastrous for royal prestige, and the enormous ransom required for John's release created an unbearable tax burden for a population already in economic and demographic crisis. In Paris, the Estates met to approve an aid, and to demand oversight of the war and the government. As tensions mounted during the winter of 1357/8, Étienne Marcel, the chief of Paris's

---

[1] For the Treaty of Guines, see J. Sumption, *The Hundred Years War*, 3 vols. to date (Philadelphia, 1990–2009), II: 132–42; R. Cazelles, *Société politique, noblesse et couronne sous Jean le Bon et Charles V* (Geneva, 1982), 163–72. My thanks to Chris Given-Wilson for clarifying my understanding of this treaty.

[2] R. Delachenal, *Histoire de Charles V*, 5 vols. (Paris, 1909–31), I: 115–19; Sumption, *Hundred Years War*, II: 199–201.

merchants and a key figure at these assemblies, directed a revolt against the Dauphin with the cooperation of Charles of Navarre, an event that led to the encircling of Paris by military troops, and consequently the explosion of violence against these garrisons that became known as the Jacquerie.[3] Although the Dauphin regained control – and the Jacquerie was answered with a wave of bloody revenge by the nobility – the crown's political and financial situation remained dire. The unpopular Treaty of Brétigny, agreed in 1360, forced the cessation of much of the south-west to be held in full sovereignty by Edward III and set a ransom for John II's freedom that could no more be raised than the previous sum. After a brief visit to his realm to implement the treaty and to try to raise his ransom, John returned to England, dying in captivity in 1364.

Throughout these troubled years, the signature experience for many, perhaps even most, French men and women was violence. As the Hundred Years War became an inland affair no longer confined to naval skirmishes and battles in Flanders and Gascony, an increasing number of people came to have direct experience of warfare. What they experienced was searing. In the run up to Poitiers, England and France raised large armies, sometimes numbering in the tens of thousands,[4] and many men saw violent action while in military service. But most people experienced the war as its victims. In the decade and more that followed Poitiers, most of the Hundred Years War's violence was, like that of seigneurial warfare, concentrated not on battles but on raids (*chevauchées*) of unprotected settlements, in which troops captured livestock and booty, raped the women, and burned the houses.[5] In 1355, Edward, prince of Wales undertook a great *chevauchée* from the Gers to the Mediterranean, during

---

[3] The foundational work remains S. Luce, *Histoire de la Jacquerie d'âpres des document inédits*, new edn (Paris, 1895). See also D. Aiton, '"Shame on Him who Allows Them to Live": the Jacquerie of 1358', Ph.D. thesis, University of Glasgow, 2011; B. Bommersbach, 'Gewalt in der Jacquerie von 1358', in *Gewalt im politischen Raum. Fallanalysen vom Spätmittelalter bis ins 20. Jahrhundert*, ed. N. Bulst, I. Gilcher-Holtey, and H.-G. Haupt (Frankfurt, 2008), 46–81; Sumption, *Hundred Years War*, II: 327–36; D. M. Bessen, 'The Jacquerie: Class War or Co-opted Rebellion?', *Journal of Medieval History* 11 (1985): 43–59; M.-T. de Medeiros, *Jacques et chroniqueurs. Une étude comparée des récits contemporains relatant la Jacquerie de 1358* (Paris, 1979); R. Cazelles, 'La Jacquerie fut-elle un mouvement paysan?' *Académie des inscriptions et belles lettres. Comptes rendus* 122 (1978): 654–66; P. Durvin, 'Les origines de la Jacquerie à Saint-Leu-d'Esserent en 1358', in *Actes du 101e congrès national des sociétés savantes (Lille, 1976)* (Paris, 1978), 365–74; J. Flammermont, 'La Jacquerie en Beauvaisis', *RH* 9 (1879): 123–43.

[4] P. Contamine, *Guerre, état et société à la fin du moyen âge: Études sur les armées des rois de France, 1337–1494* (Paris, 1972), 65–74.

[5] J. Firnhaber-Baker, 'Techniques of Seigneurial War in the Fourteenth Century', *Journal of Medieval History* 36 (2010): 90–103; N. Wright, *Knights and Peasants: the Hundred Years War in the French Countryside* (Woodbridge, 1998); M. Bennett, 'The Development of Battle Tactics in the Hundred Years War', in *Arms, Armies, and Fortifications in the Hundred Years War*, ed. A. Curry and M. Hughes (Woodbridge, 1994), 1–20.

which he amassed a fortune in booty and spread terror among the inhabitants, a feat he repeated the next year on a northern route that culminated at Poitiers.[6] From the mid-1350s, violence that was not directly inflicted at English or French command also became a growing problem as mercenaries, left masterless during truces, formed companies and took up arms on their own behalf, raiding villages and holding towns to ransom for their own profit and destroying property at will. Their effect on individuals was especially acute as they frequently captured non-combatants, forcing them to ransom themselves (often under threat of torture) or to work for them essentially as slaves.[7] At the end of 1360, a huge gathering of these groups combined to form a 'Great Company', capturing the pope at Pont-Saint-Esprit outside Avignon and holding him for ransom. These mercenary groups, often called free companies for their characteristic absence of any higher command, would plague the countryside for the rest of the century and beyond, laying waste to all but the strongest and most determined regions. Finally, the Jacquerie of 1358 was only the most famous of the riots and uprisings that periodically erupted in every part of France as the difficulties that beset ordinary people – taxation, poor harvests, high prices, the effects of plague, and so on – combined with anger at authorities for not adequately addressing this violence to set off episodes of civil unrest.[8]

In this context of new types of violence and greater popular exposure to it, seigneurial war became only one aspect of large-scale public disorder, and not necessarily the most pressing one for the crown and its agents. Consequently, there was an amplification of the shift already visible in the later 1340s away from limiting violence in order to assert royal rights and towards the restoration of peace and quiet through whatever means available. Again, the ability of royal

---

[6] Sumption, *Hundred Years War*, II: 175–87; H. J. Hewitt, *The Black Prince's Expedition of 1355–1357* (Manchester, 1958). For the *chevauchée* as an effort to provoke battle, see C. J. Rogers, *War Cruel and Sharp: English Strategy under Edward III, 1327–1360* (Woodbridge, 2000), 7–8 and ch. 10.

[7] K. Fowler, *The Great Companies*, vol. 1 of *Medieval Mercenaries* (Oxford and Malden, MA, 2001); Sumption, *Hundred Years War*, II: ch. 8; H. Denifle, *La désolation des églises, monastères et hôpitaux en France pendant la Guerre de Cent Ans*, 2 vols. (Paris, 1897–9). The old nineteenth- and early twentieth-century antiquarian regional histories of the companies retain great value as they are mostly based on local documents: e.g. M. Chanson, *Les grandes compagnies en Auvergne au XIVe siècle: Seguin de Badefol à Brioude et à Lyon* (Brioude, 1887); G. Guigue, *Les tard-venus en Lyonnais, Forez et Beaujolais, 1356–1369* (Lyon, 1886); J. Monicat, *Les grandes compagnies en Velay, 1358–1392*, 2nd edn (Paris, 1928).

[8] S. K. Cohn, *Lust for Liberty: the Politics of Social Revolt in Medieval Europe, 1200–1425: Italy, France, and Flanders* (Cambridge, MA, 2006); J. Rogozinski, *Power, Caste, and Law: Social Conflict in Fourteenth-Century Montpellier* (Cambridge, MA, 1982). Cf. G. Fourquin, *The Anatomy of Popular Rebellion in the Middle Ages*, trans. A. Chesters (New York, 1978); M. Mollat and P. Wolff, *The Popular Revolutions of the Late Middle Ages*, trans. A. L. Lytton-Selis (London, 1973).

officers to maintain a role for the crown in local power disputes is striking. But it is clear that the crown lost control of events over the course of John II's reign, becoming even less able to compel obedience than in the 1330s and 1340s. Simultaneously, the role of judicial pursuit – including criminal processes – became increasingly open to political manipulation. None the less, there was no total breakdown of public order in this period, largely because institutions and associations at the local and regional level reasserted their role in peace-keeping activities, formulating ideas about government and security both to defend their own actions and to articulate their disappointment about royal inaction. The most important developments during this period thus came from outside royal official milieux, as ideas about legitimate authority for violence became more prominent in the face of the much broader social constituency responsible for the increase in large-scale violence experienced by ordinary people.

LEGISLATION: THE VALORIZATION OF ORDER

The growing urgency of the crown's need to quell violence is starkly evidenced in royal normative efforts to limit or prohibit non-royal warfare. For John's relatively short reign of thirteen and a half years – four and a half of which he spent as a captive in England – there are seven extant *ordonnances* against warfare. Most of these were narrow measures for certain, mostly northerly regions of the realm, where, as we have seen, a basic right to wage war may have been more established than in Languedoc. But two were general statutes applicable to the entire kingdom. The ideas about justice and protection inherited from John's predecessors are still apparent in many of these measures, but the text of a general *ordonnance* that John issued in 1361 suggests that the explosion of violence after Poitiers caused a break in this normative tradition, forcing the crown to focus more on the practical necessities of peace-keeping and less on its ideological imperatives and implications.

John's first regulatory statement on seigneurial violence, which is the provisions of a charter for the Vermandois issued following the grant of an aid in 1351, asserts royal claims to the limitation of warfare that recall those of his Capetian predecessors. Although the measure accepts the rights of the regions' nobles to make war with one another, it prohibits warring parties from damaging houses and agricultural structures and materials (*ne pourront abatre ... Maisons, ne Moulins, rompre ... Estangs, tuer Chevaux, ne Bestes, rompre Guerniers, Huches ... effondrer Vins*), forbids the involvement of non-nobles in warfare, and requires a modified observance of the *quarantaine* or forty-day delay before hostilities, despite custom to the contrary (*combien que les nobles . . . aient usé ou accoustumé*).[9] These regulations for Vermandois were followed by a measure for Normandy that included a provision that prohibited the wars that nobles fought against one another, instructing royal officers to imprison offenders in Rouen.[10]

In 1352, John issued an *ordonnance* mandating the reiteration of the general ban against local war during royal wars. The measure's exposition begins by explaining that

all wars among all of the subjects of the realm ought to cease entirely during royal wars, especially because our wars involve all inhabitants of the realm, and everyone should be concerned by them just as they are concerned with their own matters.[11]

John noted that his late father had publicly prohibited local war to 'all the inhabitants of the realm of whatever status or locale ... regardless of local privileges, customs, and uses, or observances' and had ordered this prohibition to be published in Parlement and throughout the kingdom. Nevertheless, many people were making war against one another 'under the pretence of local privileges . . . during our wars and those of our realm'. This, the measure observes, was 'the greatest prejudice, scandal, and danger to us, and the whole realm and to the commonwealth (*res publica*), and to all the subjects and inhabitants of our realm'. John therefore ordered his officers (this prohibition survives in copies addressed to the *prévôt* of Paris, the bailiff of Vermandois, and the seneschal of Carcassonne) to publish the prohibition again (*iterato*) and to see it enforced, regardless of any custom to the contrary.

This measure's insistent disregard of local customs recalls the royal prerogative claimed by Philip IV and Philip V. Like Philip the Fair's *ordonnance* of 1311, John's measure also refers to the *res publica*, a term that I have translated as commonwealth. In fact, the measure of 1352 extends the logic of royal power and the common good found in earlier

---

[9] *Ord.*, II: 391–6, arts. 15–17. Later that year, the crown agreed to reduce the delay for the principal parties to the war (*Ord.*, II: 447–8), though further measures in 1352, 1353, and 1354 reinstated the original delays (*Ord.*, II: 505–8, 529–32, 567–70, arts. 13–15 in all). Vermandois was also apparently included in the general *ordonnance* of 1352 prohibiting warfare during royal wars since a mandate was sent to the region's bailiff, as well as other royal officers (see n. 13, below).

[10] *Ord.*, II: 400–10, art. 27.

[11] '[M]axime cum dictae guerrae nostrae, omnies regnicolas, tam universaliter, quam particulariter, tangant & concernant, ut unusquique circa tamquam suas proprias debeat occupari' (*Ord.*, II: 511–12, based on AN Y 4, fols. 5–6r, to the *prévôt* of Paris. See also AN X2a 6, fols. 5v–6r for Vermandois and AM Narbonne FF 722, piece 2, the latter containing a little known copy addressed to the seneschal of Carcassonne).

prohibitions. It argues that non-royal wars ought to stop because the realm's inhabitants have a stake in royal warfare, which is referred to not just as 'royal wars' (*guerrae regiae*), but also as 'wars of the realm' (*guerrae regni*), and asserts that such wars concern all of the realm's inhabitants, just as their own affairs do. To be sure, regulations from Philip IV and Philip V had mentioned the 'common profit' to be had from the cessation of local wars during royal ones,[12] but this measure was the first to say in this context that the king's war was also that of his subjects.

Like Philip the Fair before him, John was anxious to connect his peace-keeping measures with those of his predecessors. The *ordonnance* of 1352 prominently mentions the (now lost) prohibition made by Philip VI and claims simply to be reissuing it. A year or two after this measure, the crown went further and attempted to cast John as the continuator of Louis IX's peace-work. In April 1353 or 1354, John promulgated an act billed as the reiteration of Saint Louis's *quarantaine*.[13] Issued to the *prévôt* of Paris, the bailiffs of Vermandois, Amiens, and Lille because the inhabitants of Amiens had not been observing the required delay, its import was probably limited to this particular slice of France. Although it is possible that, as happened for other statutes, this measure only survives in the copy intended for Amiens and neighbouring locales, there is no evidence that the *quarantaine* was ever enforced outside these areas. Despite its narrow audience, though, this decree was at pains to suggest that by enforcing the *quarantaine* John II was participating in a long-standing royal programme whose origins lay with his most illustrious predecessor, Saint Louis. The measure asserts that Louis first instituted the measure (*perfelicis recordationis Beati Ludovici praedecessoris nostris . . . ordinationes fecisset statutum*), and expresses the king's desire to follow in the footsteps of his praiseworthy predecessors (*vestigia Praedecessorum*).[14] The ordinance goes on to mention *beatus Ludovicus* twice more over the course of 750 words, spacing out the references for greatest rhetorical effect.

In the early years of John II's reign, royal promulgations about large-scale violence thus maintained the rhetorical and ideological tradition that stretched back at least to Philip IV. John's *ordonnances* justified prohibitions or limitations of warfare by invoking the responsibilities of the crown and

---

[12] '[P]ro communi utilitate' (*Ord.*, I: 328–9); 'pour le commun profit de nostre Royaume' (*Ord.*, I: 435–41). Philip V also spoke of the 'grans domages à nous, & à tout nostre Royaume' inflicted by local wars during royal wars (*Ord.*, I: 655–6).

[13] The act (published at *Ord.*, II: 552–3) is dated 9 April 1353. In 1353, Easter fell on 24 March, and in 1354, it came on 13 April, which means that the measure could have been promulgated in either 1353 or 1354.

[14] John and his councillors were (perhaps wilfully) mistaken about the origins of this restriction, which more probably dates to the reign of Philip II. See the discussion in Chapter 1, above.

the protection of the commonwealth, and even the recognition of the Vermandois nobility's right to wage war in 1351 had provided for the traditional protection of agricultural resources that John had inherited from his Capetian predecessors. But mid-way through John's reign the crown's normative approach to peace-keeping changed as the violence of the mid-1350s and 1360s drove a shift from the ideological to the practical. In 1361, John issued a new general *ordonnance* prohibiting warfare during times of both royal warfare and peace, which, although it shared many features with previous seigneurial war *ordonnances*, also broke with this heritage, emphasizing the maintenance of order over the assertion of royal prerogatives.[15]

On the surface, the 1361 promulgation was among the more ambitious such measures issued by French kings, as it was ostensibly intended to outlaw all non-royal wars indefinitely. It opened with the observation that the wars that 'some nobles and others' waged against each other by dint of custom had been repeatedly prohibited on account of the king's wars, and that under the pretext of the newly made peace, these people now wished to take up arms against one another again. Therefore, the king prohibited all such wars and self-help (*voies de fait*) until such times as should please him, 'despite the nobles' privileges or customs' (*nonobstant lesdiz Privileges ou usages des Nobles*). Royal officers were ordered to publish the prohibition and to seize and punish transgressors so as to serve as an example to others. If one concentrates on these aspects, it is possible to read the measure as a universal and absolute prohibition of seigneurial warfare, repudiating the nobility's violent prerogatives in favour of peace and royal justice much in the same manner as Philip IV's *ordonnance* of 1304.

But while the broad outlines of this edict would have been familiar to John's predecessors, the measure also reflects the military and diplomatic pressures weighing on crown and kingdom. Although it begins by addressing the usual 'nobles and others' with pretensions to privilege, it quickly moves on to other unspecified people (simply *plusieurs*) who, 'since our return from England', have been conducting evil musters, assemblies, and armed raids (*mauvaises convocations, assembléees & chevauchiées en armes*) without reference to formal justice (*sanz ... ensuyvre les voies de droit & de Justice*). Along with commanding the nobles' wars to cease, the measure orders an end to these

assemblies, musters, and raids of men-at-arms or archers – whether on foot or on horse – except by our permission (*congié*) or order or by that of our officers, and

[15] *Ord.*, III: 525–7. J. Firnhaber-Baker, 'From God's Peace to the King's Order: Late Medieval Limitations on Non-Royal Warfare', *Essays in Medieval Studies* 23 (2006): 23–6.

also all pillages, seizures of goods and persons without [resort to] justice, vengeances and counter-vengeances, robberies, and surprise attacks.[16]

This was not just a laundry-list of violent crimes; it was a pointed reference to the problems caused by the mercenary companies, as the allusion to John's return from England (*depuis nostre revenue d'Angleterre*) makes clear. Although mercenary activity had been a problem since the later 1340s, if not earlier, the situation had become terrifyingly acute following the Treaty of Brétigny in 1360 and the display of unstoppable strength manifested by the Great Company at Pont-Saint-Esprit. Moreover, the crown's inability to address this violence effectively had forced many individuals and communities to take defence into their own hands, which, while intended to restore order, also had the effect (at least from the crown's perspective) of contributing to disorder by privileging vigilantism (the *voie de fait*) over institutional justice (the *voies de droit & de Justice*).[17]

As the measure continues, it becomes clear that the control of these groups constituted its major objective. After prohibiting the violence associated with mercenaries, it went on to decree 'also that all people noble and non-noble, privileged and non-privileged who have travelled away from their homes in our realm should return to them within a month after these letters are published'.[18] Following the instructions to the king's officers to execute his orders against other aspects of war and private vengeance, the ordinance then turns back to the particular problem of dangerous vagabonds:

And if any people leave their homes or do not return to them, according to what we have ordained, seize all of their goods without *recreance* [the use of seized goods during judicial proceedings] . . . so that they come before you to receive law and judgment . . . and if they do not come, having been cited once [as opposed to the normal four times[19]], proceed to the banishment of their persons and the confiscation of their goods, and hold them and declare them disobedient and rebels against us and the crown . . . And if any of these malefactors and rebels are in fortresses or elsewhere in your jurisdiction, of which you cannot secure the obedience, on our authority order them and their supporters and accomplices to

---

[16] '[T]outes assamblés, convocations & chevauchiées de Gens d'armes ou Archiers soient de pié ou de cheval, se ce n'est par le congié ou ordennance de Nous ou de noz Officiers, & aussi tous pillages, Prinses de biens & de personnes sanz Justice, venjances & contrevenjances, desroberies & aguez'.

[17] See pp. 137–40, 142–8, below.

[18] 'Et oultre que toutes manieres de Gens . . . se sont absentez ou esloignez de leurs vrais domiciles . . . retournent & reviegnent en yceulz domiciles & habitacions, dedenz un mois après ce que ces presentes seront publiées'.

[19] For the defaults habitually allowed, see L. de Carbonnières, *La procédure devant la chamber criminelle du Parlement de Paris au xɪᴠe siècle* (Paris, 2004), 200–6.

render it without delay ... And if they do not wish to obey, do such things as are possible by men-at-arms and assemblies of nobles and others, such as laying siege to the place and other methods as you see fit ...

This measure suggests the extent to which the crown's most pressing order of business had become the maintenance of internal order, which had spun away from its control as its military and financial disasters mounted. The 1361 *ordonnance* is remarkable for the absence of ostentatious justifications of royal authority and its lack of rhetorical flourish. It does mention that John wished to maintain his realm and subjects in peace and to 'govern by good justice', and the king's *souverainneté* is mentioned, as is the *couronne*, both of which are presented as abstractions capable of injury by subjects' bellicose predilections. But whereas the later Capetian *ordonnances* feature elaborate expositions on the relationship between royal authority, justice, and subjects' wars, and even John's 1352 prohibition took care to explain why the king's wars ought to take precedence over those of his subjects, the 1361 prohibition does not explain why royal sovereignty was so vulnerable on this front, or why the crown should have the right to interfere in this violence.

The *ordonnance* also breaks with the past by ignoring the spiritual concerns that had been essential to the measures of John's forebears and which had made appearances in some of his own earlier measures. While one can easily imagine that *agricolae* (peasants) were at greater danger in 1361 than they had been at any time in the previous two centuries of French royal peace-keeping, the *ordonnance* does not even mention them or their instruments, let alone the king's God-given responsibility to protect them. It is apparent that after 1356, John and his councillors were not as interested in using such *ordonnances* as showcases for royal ideology as their predecessors had been. Indeed, the purpose of this measure may also differ in other ways from those of earlier kings because it may be best to read the 1361 measure not – or at least not solely – as a peace-keeping measure in the manner of earlier *ordonnances*, but also as a regulation for those fighting in the king's own war. Many if not most of the earlier royal *ordonnances* forbidding warfare had been similarly intended to ameliorate the king's military situation by reserving manpower and other resources for royal conflicts. But in the 1361 *ordonnance*, royal military concerns are more nakedly apparent and the social background of those concerned is broader than in earlier *ordonnances* aimed primarily at the nobility.

The measure, equally concerned with both nobles and non-nobles, orders those of both estates (*Gens Nobles & non Nobles*) who 'are absent from their homes' to return within a month, not specifically in order that they would cease creating violent disorder, but so that 'their state might be better known, and that they might be easier to assemble, if there is need' (*à ce que leur estat soit miex cogneu, & eulz soient plus aiables à convenir; s'il est mestier*). John and his councillors may also have been concerned to restore internal order as a way to ensure that the Peace of Brétigny would actually hold. The king and many of those within royal administration were desperate for peace by 1361 and had bitter experience of past peace agreements destroyed by the quasi-independent activities of captains attacking enemy positions in times of supposed truce.[20] This effort to empty the fortresses and clear the landscape of footloose fighters may have been intended to ensure that no accidental breaches of the peace took place. The effort clearly did not work – the difficulties of enforcing Brétigny are well known – but one should probably think of this *ordonnance* as a military regulation as well as a prohibition of seigneurial war.[21]

John's *ordonnance* is the last known surviving medieval French prohibition regarding seigneurial warfare. It is possible that Charles V and perhaps Charles VI may also have issued such measures since Parlement's *arrêts* from their reigns regularly mentioned *nostrae ordinationes* against seigneurial wars, though such references are ambivalent.[22] In any case, the lack of evidence is probably not a simple accident of survival. From Parlement's records and from other evidence, it is clear the royal *ordonnances* targeting seigneurial warfare had become generally known and more frequently employed in the latter decades of the fourteenth century, perhaps obviating the need for frequent reiteration. But perhaps more compelling, the conditions operating from mid-century onward were radically different than those that produced the prohibitions promulgated by John's predecessors, as his own last *ordonnance* shows. From mid-century, responsibility for large-scale violence no longer lay primarily with the nobility, and the purposes of that violence were no longer confined to the troublesome but quasi-judicial problems of lordship. It no longer made sense to promulgate elaborate statements about the relationship between violence, justice, and royal authority when so many of those creating public disorder had no regard for the latter two concepts. After mid-century, the crown was too busy with the practice of peace-keeping to attend to the theory.

---

[20] E.g. the difficulties of enforcing the Truce of Calais (1347): Sumption, *Hundred Years War*, II: 44–8.

[21] L. Cazaux, 'Réglementation militaire royale et usage de la force dans le royaume de France (XIVe–XVIe siècles)', *Inflexions. Civils et militaires: pouvoir dire* 13 (2010): 97. For the trouble enforcing Brétigny, see *La Guerre de Cent Ans vue à travers les registres du Parlement (1337–1369)*, ed. P.-C. Timbal (Paris, 1961), ch. 5 and 'Some Documents Regarding the Fulfillment and Interpretation of the Treaty of Brétigny (1361–1369)', ed. P. Chaplais, *Camden Miscellany* 19 (1952): 5–50.

[22] See Chapter 5, p. 153.

A RISING TIDE OF VIOLENCE: SEIGNEURIAL WAR BEFORE
AND AFTER POITIERS

These new realities are readily apparent in the seigneurial wars waged in Languedoc during John's reign. Already in the last years of Philip VI's reign the incidence of seigneurial war had increased sharply. This was not an isolated or accidental increase. Over the next decade and a half, the rate of seigneurial war would be more than double that experienced from the death of Philip IV to the last, violent years of John's predecessor. (See Figure 3.) As was the case in the previous decade, neither the war nor the plague can be considered responsible in itself for inciting this violence, but they had two identifiable knock-on effects. First, the further erosion of royal agents' ability to compel obedience, the evidence for which is discussed in the next section, contributed to the increase in violence, as lords themselves explicitly avowed. Second, the increase in the number of soldiers for hire after the decommissioning of royal armies post-Poitiers – a development which had socio-economic roots as well as military and political ones – enabled more lords to pursue their disputes through warfare.

In the first five years of the 1350s, the amount of violence was consistent with the higher levels seen at the end of the 1340s, with between three and five wars fought (as compared with five or six from 1345 to 1350). In 1351, the struggle between Jean II de Lévis and his son broke out into open hostilities, though this may have simply been a continuation of the conflict first apparent in Jean's attack on la Garde in 1348 and it is not clear that the

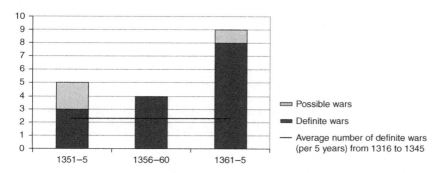

Figure 3   Seigneurial wars, 1351–65

violence reached the level of warfare.[23] In 1352, the lord of Puichéric in the seneschalsy of Carcassonne received remission for many instances of bearing arms against various castles and other locations which he claimed to have inherited from a relative, but which Pierre and Guillaume de Voisines had been occupying, though again the extent of actual violence is not clear from the surviving documents.[24] Prior to August 1352, Aimar de Roussillon, lord of Peyraud and several other castles in the seneschalsy of Beaucaire, engaged in warfare (*guerra*) against the citizens of Lyon, raiding near the city, transporting captured citizens from the realm to the Empire and torturing those imprisoned.[25] Also in 1352 or just prior to it, Hugues Adhémar, lord of Garde-Adhémar, waged a *guerra* against the bishop of Viviers, damaging his subjects and setting fire to their goods.[26] And sometime before April 1355 there was a new episode of war between Gui de Comminges and the Isle-Jourdain clan, which was settled through the mediation of local notables.[27]

The next five years may have seen some decrease in violence, though the lull probably simply reflects the disorder in Paris that followed Poitiers. The four wars for which we have evidence for this period all took place in the Auvergne in or around 1359. The first two appear to have been minor: Garin and Pierre de Pouzols were attacked by the family of a girl whom they had kidnapped and held in their castle,[28] and a remission notes that a war occurred around this time between a squire of the Velay, one Guillaume de Jagonas, and the lord of Faugerolles, whose castle was said to have been besieged.[29] But the third war was an extensive, violent, and long-running conflict between Armand, lord of la Roüe, and his nephew Robert Dauphin, lord of Saint-Ilpize, on one hand, and the viscount of Polignac, on the other, all of whom were great local powers with numerous castles under their obedience.[30] At issue was the barony of Solignac in the Velay. Armand believed that he had a better claim than the

[23] See Chapter 3, p. 96.   [24] *HL*, x: 1073–4.

[25] AN x2a 6, fols. 43v, 65r; AN JJ 93, no. 237, fols. 95v–96r (confirmation of a remission published in Guigue, *Les tard-venus*, no. 5); 'Compte en dialecte lyonnais du XIVe siècle', ed. E. Philipon, *Revue de philologie française et de littérature* 19 (1905): 249–59. See also the account in A. Mazon, *Essai historique sur le Vivarais pendant la Guerre de Cent Ans (1337–1453)* (Tournon, 1890), 14–18.

[26] *HL*, x: 1107–8. The remission relating the conflict was issued in 1355, but mentions that the parties had been reconciled by the late Pope Clement VI, who died in early December 1352.

[27] BN Doat 191, fol. 203r and see A. Molinier's note at *HL*, IX: 568–70.

[28] The conflict, which involved 'gentibus armorum & peditum' and efforts to destroy the castle's towers, is mentioned in a remission for a squire who participated in it 'ab anno citra' (AN JJ 90, no. 411, fols. 207v–208r).

[29] AN JJ 93, no. 212, fol. 85r; some discussion in Monicat, *Les grandes compagnies*, 154.

[30] An account of this war can be found in Monicat, *Les grandes compagnies*, 141–8. It seems mainly to be based on the account given by Vaissete and Molinier in *HL*, IX: 733–5 and on a 1372 confirmation of a 1361/2 remission issued for the viscount of Polignac (AN JJ 103, no. 83, fols. 51–52r; original

viscount's infant son, who had inherited it through his mother, the late baron of Solignac's daughter. This conflict grew to an unusual scale, involving at least ten castles and lasting well into the 1360s.

The dispute over Solignac drew in most of the neighbouring nobility.[31] It is not clear whether this conflict bore any relation to the two other Auvergnat wars fought around 1359, but this big war did have likely connections to at least two other conflicts fought in the Velay during the late 1350s and 1360s. One was fought by Arnaud d'Allègre against Guillaume de Chalençon, the two having allied with opposite sides in the Solignac dispute, though the remission for Guillaume does not mention this circumstance.[32] Stephen de Vissac, lord of a castle outside le Puy-en-Velay, fought the other. He directed his efforts mainly against the holder of a neighbouring castle, but Parlement also found him culpable of aggression against the castle of his brother Jean and that of an older relative, Louis de Vissac, as well as raping women and girls (*mulieres* and *juvencule*) and numerous other violent incidents against local people and merchants.[33] None of the sources for Stephen's various campaigns mentions the contemporaneous war over Solignac, but Robert Dauphin's party in the Solignac war is said to have conquered a castle called Saint-Romain around the same time that Stephen is said to have taken a castle by the same name.[34] A remission for the viscount of Polignac states that the viscount retook Saint-Romain from Armand and Robert's men, restoring it to the cardinal of Ostia and his nephew, and we know from another remission that this nephew was Bertrand Bertrand, Stephen

published in *Preuves de la maison de Polignac. Recueil de documents pour servir à l'histoire des anciennes provinces de Velay, Auvergne, Gévaudan, Vivarais, Forez, etc., (IXe–XVIIIe siècle)*, ed. A. Jacotin, 5 vols. (Paris, 1898–1906), II: no. 229). Other important sources for this war include a remission for Armand de la Roüe (*Preuves . . . Polignac*, ed. Jacotin, II: no. 240); remissions relating the actions of Robert Dauphin and his partisans (*HL*, X: 1291–3, 1300–1, 1475–6, 1641–2, 1698–9; AN JJ 93, no. 142, fol. 59r; AN JJ 117, no. 118, fol. 85v); and an *arrêt* of 1380 (published in Monicat, *Les grandes compagnies*, no. 16). The succession was apparently still an open question in 1414, when the bishop of le Puy presided over an accord between the viscount of Polignac and Armand de la Roüe's grandsons (*Preuves . . . Polignac*, ed. Jacotin, IV: no. 712 and discussion in Chapter 5, below).

[31] Monicat lists the lordships allied with Armand de la Roüe and Robert Dauphin (*Les grandes compagnies*, 142). Among those fighting in this war was the royal bastard Thomas de la Marche, for whom see M. Boudet, *Thomas de la Marche, bâtard de France et ses aventures (1318–1361)* (Riom, 1900), 189–94 and no. 47 (includes remission published at *HL*, X: 1291–3); P. Charbonnier, *Une autre France: la seigneurie rurale en Basse Auvergne du XIVe au XVIe siècle*, 2 vols. (Clermont-Ferrand, 1980), I: 446, n. 1; Sumption, *Hundred Years War*, II: 412–17, 463.

[32] *HL*, X: 1255–9. See also Monicat, *Les grandes compagnies*, 142, 147–8. Polignac and Chalençon's alliance is suggested by their association in a letter of grace published in *Étude sur la vie d'Arnoul d'Audrehem, maréchal de France, 1302–1370*, ed. E. Molinier (Paris, 1883), no. 32.

[33] Major Parlement documents are AN X2a 7, fols. 13–16r, 80–4, 192v–198; AN X1a 18, fol. 103r; AN X1a 25, fols. 13v–14. A remission from 1362 for one of Stephen's enemies is published in Monicat, *Les grandes compagnies*, no. 6.

[34] *HL*, X: 1300–1.

de Vissac's enemy and holder of the castle of Saint-Romain.[35] It seems evident that both the records for the Solignac war and those for Stephen de Vissac's conflicts refer to the same castle. But it is unclear whether the capture and recapture of this castle happened once but produced two different stories, the documents of which do not explicitly refer to one another, or whether the castle underwent two separate invasions and restorations in the course of two, fairly distinct wars.

The dispute over Solignac seems to have been mostly played out by the early 1360s, but elsewhere, we can observe an elevated number of wars. In November 1361, Aimar, lord of Roussillon and Annonay, took by force the castle of Colombiers which the cardinal of Ostia, Guillaume Bertrand, had willed to some Celestine monks.[36] Although he was forced to render it to them, he and his descendants would be a thorn in the monks' side for decades. Around the same time, a minor noblewoman named Mura Causit and her husband Guillaume forcibly occupied a castle near Béziers that she believed herself to have inherited, though it is not clear whether large-scale violence ensued.[37] In 1362, a conflict over the inheritance of the viscounty of Murat in the seneschalsy of Beaucaire and bailliage of the Velay moved from the courts to the battlefield, as Guillaume de Cardillac took up arms against Pierre and Reginald de Murat, a conflict which would produce episodic outbreaks of war for the next several decades.[38] This war also briefly drew in the bishop of

---

[35] 'Castrumque de Sancto Romano, de quo etiam dicti vicecomiti [Podompniaci] et suis dictus Robertus inferebat guerram, obsedit, insultavit et demum cepit, idem vicecomes [Podompniaci] armorum potencia et gentibus Reverendi in Christo patris Cardinalis Ostiensis et eius nepotis dominorum dicti loci restituit' (AN JJ 103, no. 83, fols. 51–52r). For the relationship between the cardinal of Ostia (Pierre Bertrand de Colombier, d. 1361) and Bertrand Bertrand, see the remission published in Monicat, *Les gandes compagnies*, no. 6.

[36] AN JJ 93, no. 183, fols. 74–75r, published from other copies in *Titres de la maison ducale de Bourbon*, ed. J.-L.-A. Huillard-Bréholles and L. de la Marche, 2 vols. (Paris, 1867–74), I: no. 2869, and see nos. 2835, 2849–51, 2871, 2874–5. Records of a criminal case in Parlement related to Aimar or Adhémar de Roussillon date from 1357 (AN x2a 6, fols. 318r, 318v–319r, 319, 349v–350). Albin Mazon demonstrated that this Aimar de Roussillon, lord of Roussillon and Annonay, was not the same as the Aimar de Roussillon, lord of Peyraud and Anjou, who attacked Lyon around 1352. The former Aimar is probably the same as the one who attacked the castle of Thorrenc around 1332, discussed in Chapter 3, above (Mazon, *Essai historique*, 14–15, 19–23, 108–23; Guigue, *Les tard-venus*, 7–10, 81–3).

[37] The first document from this war is a remission of June 1362, but it mentions that another remission had previously been issued (AN JJ 91, no. 317, fol. 163). Criminal and civil Parlement records for the conflict date from 1362 to 1365 (AN x2a 7, fols. 40, 92v; AN x1a 19, fol. 54). The greater part of the information about the case comes from AN JJ 98, no. 395, fols. 127–8, a remission of May 1365.

[38] For this war, see L. de Carbonnières, 'La vanité de dire le droit ou l'inexécution des arrêts: l'affaire de la succession à la vicomté de Murat (vers 1360–vers 1470)', in *Dire le droit: Normes, juges, jurisconsultes*, ed. B. Anagnostou-Canas (Paris, 2006), 191–22. Major documents include AN x2a 8, fols. 24v–29r; AN x2a 13, fols. 30–1, 284–91r; AN x2a 15, fols. 116v–118, 119–20.

Saint-Flour and the consuls of Murat, though their role seems to have been finished by the early 1360s.[39]

The Albigeois was the theatre for a number of wars during the early 1360s. In 1361, Gui de Lévis, one of the viscounts of Lautrec (the viscounty was customarily divided among several holders), and the bishop of Albi publicly and openly (*patenter et publice*) fought a *guerra* over territory in the Albigeois, 'inflicting all the damage upon one another that is customary in war' (*omnia dampna que per guerras assueta sunt fieri inferendo*).[40] That year or the next, another viscount of Lautrec and his allies fought an apparently separate war (*guerra*), against one Sicard Hébert, lord of Aigrefeuille, over jurisdictional disagreements.[41] In February 1363, the bishop of Albi again found himself at war (*guerra*), this time with the lord of Lescure, a conflict he pursued in tandem with the consuls and inhabitants of Albi.[42] In 1363 and 1364, the viscount of Montclar (-de-Quercy) attacked his neighbour Guillaume Agasse, the co-lord of Saint-Urcisse just west of Albi. Guillaume himself was not innocent of violence and admitted that he had made open war (*guerra publica*) against Montclar.[43] Finally, in 1364, around three hundred of the citizens of the *bourg* of Carcassonne made *guerra publica*, attacking first the neighbouring royal castle at Trèbes and then the walled *cité* of Carcassonne and claiming that those within the fortress were protecting mercenaries.[44]

The notable increase in the rate of seigneurial warfare from the late 1350s to the mid-1360s was fuelled primarily by the consequences of Poitiers. The temporary collapse and overall weakness of John's governmental administration after 1356 certainly contributed to the disorderly environment and may have encouraged the prolongation of some conflicts, as we will see. But the immediate cause of the increase in

[39] AN X2a 7, fol. 210v; *HL*, x: 1363–6.
[40] *Étude … Arnoul d'Audrehem*, ed. Molinier, no. 33, p. 101.
[41] AN X2a 7, fols. 239v–243, which notes that the war began 'anno domini Mo CCo LXI mense marcii', but because Easter fell on 28 March in 1361 and came in April in 1361, there is some scope for the war to have begun in 1361. Other related documents are AN X2a 7, fols. 157v–158r, 317v–318r; AN X2a 8, fols. 29v–30r.
[42] For this war, see J. Firnhaber-Baker, '*Jura in medio*: the Settlement of Seigneurial Disputes in Later Medieval Languedoc', *French History* 26 (2012): 441–59; Firnhaber-Baker, '*Guerram Palam et Publice Faciendo*: Local War and Royal Authority in Late Medieval Southern France', Ph.D. thesis, Harvard University, 2007, ch. 1. Documents include AD Tarn Edt 4 FF 41; BN Doat 110, fols. 164–98, 208–11r, 240–5r, 246–9, 277–81r; AN X2a 8, fols. 56v–58r; *HL*, x: 1332–5, 1424–5, 1433–4, 1435–40; *Étude … Arnoul d'Audrehem*, ed. Molinier, no. 63; Gregory XI, *Lettres secrètes et curiales du pape Grégoire XI (1370–1378) relatives à la France extraites des registres du Vatican*, ed. L. Mirot et al. 5 vols. (Paris, 1935–57), nos. 945–6.
[43] E.-A. Rossignol, *Monographies communales; ou, Étude statistique, historique et monumentale du département du Tarn*, 4 vols. (Toulouse, 1864–6), IV: nos. 2–3, quote at no. 3.
[44] *HL*, x: 1329–31.

seigneurial warfare was the battle's military consequences. The formation of the 'free companies' of unemployed mercenaries in the truce after Poitiers created a ready supply of soldiers, which gave small powers greater ability to fight than they had previously had available.[45] About half of the period's wars involved mercenary participation, and the geographic pattern of seigneurial war roughly mirrors the known movements of mercenary groups. The outbreak of numerous wars in the Velay at the end of the 1350s and in the early 1360s coincided with the free companies' virtual takeover of the Auvergne mountains, while mercenary penetration of the deeper South around Albi and Toulouse in the early 1360s corresponds to a constellation of wars in that area breaking out around the same time.[46] The great, on-going seigneurial war between Foix and Armagnac, which had broken out again in 1359, had absorbed some of these men, but the truce reached in 1363 left their troops free for other opportunities, particularly in the deep South.[47] Such men may have numbered among the 'captains and men of the great company of thieves and evildoers' (*capitaneis & gentibus latrunculorum & malefactorum magne societatis*) used in the war between Sicard de Lescure and Albi and among the *malefactores* associated with the viscount of Montclar's war against Saint-Urcisse.[48]

Allegations of employing mercenaries were no doubt as subject to exaggeration and mendacity as any of the other charges levied against war-makers, but the claim was a novel one in the later 1350s and 1360s and often alleged against both sides, suggesting that this was a new development in the waging of seigneurial war and not just a rhetorical trick. While such charges were often vague allegations of employing evildoers, thieves, pillagers, or murderers, in many cases, close links between specific mercenary bands and particular wars are alleged. The viscount of Montclar reportedly associated with the famous captains John Amory and Seguin de Badefol, the latter of whose troops were also allegedly employed by Guillaume de Cardaillac in the war over Murat.[49] Robert Dauphin's part in the war over Solignac was linked with the captain Walli de

---

[45] Firnhaber-Baker, 'Techniques', 98–102.

[46] Fowler, *Great Companies*, 3–4, 39, n. 53; Sumption, *Hundred Years War*, II: ch. 8.

[47] P. Tucoo-Chala, *Gaston Fébus et la vicomté de Béarn (1343–1391)* (Bordeaux, 1959), 81–92; Fowler, *Great Companies*, 61–71. In the first year of this conflict, Foix had declared war not only against Armagnac, but also against his father-in-law Prince Jean, count of Poitiers (eventually duke of Berry). As Jean was then serving as lieutenant of Languedoc, Foix took the fight to the communities of the three seneschalsies. See *HL*, IX: 709–11, X: 1183–97, 1197–8, and see below.

[48] Fowler, *Great Companies*, 70–2. Albi: quote from *HL*, X: 1332–5; see also *Étude . . . Arnoul d'Audrehem*, ed. Molinier, no. 63. Saint-Urcisse: Rossignol, *Monographies . . . Tarn*, IV: no. 2.

[49] Rossignol, *Monographies . . . Tarn*, IV: no. 2; *HL*, X: 1363–6

Boeuf and possibly Robert Knolles (*Robinus Canola* in the text).[50] The mercenary captains employed by Mura Causit in her attempt to claim her ancestral castles – *le Negre, le Bastard d'arse, Briconseil,* and *le Mervaz* – were perhaps less famous, in keeping with Mura's less exalted social (and probably financial) status as a castellan's daughter married to a burgher, but if their names are any indication, they were certainly men of the same ilk.[51]

The availability of mercenaries caused the increase in violence not just by providing more soldiers, but also by destabilizing local power relations. The threat that mercenary groups posed was considerable; basing themselves in networks of castles, they stripped the surrounding countryside bare through pillage and extortion. Defence against their incursions necessitated the military mobilization of local populations and the fortification and garrisoning of local strongholds, creating new loci of military strength, which could be perceived as threatening in their own right.[52] The war between Pierre, viscount of Lautrec, and his alleged vassal Sicard Hébert seems mostly to have been about asserting lordship – Lautrec's agents repeatedly erected a gibbet before Sicard's castle and destroyed Sicard's mills (gibbets and mills being markers of the judicial and fiscal powers of lordship) – but the flashpoint in the struggle between the men came when Pierre marched into mass one Sunday and announced that he would do all he could to harm anyone who garrisoned Sicard's castle, or indeed who took refuge in it.[53] As Sicard insisted, the castle may have been fortified according to the orders of the seneschal of Carcassonne, but for Pierre, this may have looked like an intolerable assertion of independence by an overbearing vassal.

In the case of the war between the bishop of Albi and Gui de Lévis, viscount of Lautrec, the mercenaries' presence was similarly decisive in turning a pre-existing quarrel violent. Gui's remission recounts that the parties' disagreement over a castle 'had been wrangled over for a long time before certain arbiters chosen by the parties and also in the royal court, until last year the companies of our lord king's and the realm's enemies, roaming the Albigeois, occupied Villeneuve d'Albi'.[54] In response to the bishop's association with these people, the viscount found it necessary to

---

[50] *HL*, x: 1291–3. [51] AN JJ 98, no. 395, fols. 127–8. [52] See pp. 145–8, below.

[53] '[C]oram populo ad audiendum missam quadam die dominica ibidem congregato publice proclamari & suis subditis sub omni eo quod erga ipsum forefacere possent inhiberi fecerat nequis ipsorum dictum fortalicium custodiret, defenderet, in eo vigilaret seu excubias faceret vel se aut bona sua ibidem retrahere seu refugium postulare presumeret' (AN x2a 7, fols. 239v–243).

[54] '[C]oram certis arbitris electis per ipsas partes et eciam in curia regia fuisset diucius altercatum, tandem dum anno preterito societates quorumdam inimicorum domini nostri regis et rei publice

pillage and rape in the bishop's lands, ostensibly as retribution for the episcopal support for the mercenaries. To what extent the bishop was using the mercenaries to pursue his enmity against the viscount – or to what extent the viscount's perception of the bishop's actions was opportunistically mistaken – is impossible to know, but in this instance and others like it, the presence of mercenaries clearly functioned as a destabilizing factor that encouraged recourse to violence.

The availability of mercenaries was connected to the social and economic difficulties of the mid-fourteenth century. It is difficult to trace the background, let alone the motivation, of those who made up the rank-and-file composition of freebooting bands.[55] But this was a period of severe economic contraction, exacerbated by a major outbreak of plague in 1361 and by the burden of royal taxation and monetary devaluation. Although many freebooters may have been *aliunde oriundi* (born elsewhere, i.e. foreigners), as was alleged of Sicard de Lescure's troops, economic pressure and demographic decline motivated some people to take up a life of military adventure and outright pillage.[56] Guillaume de Sauvent, originally of the Loire valley, was forced to join up with mercenaries, including Petit Meschin, in order to support himself, a credible claim also made by others drawn into such activities.[57] Such motivations were given added impetus by the militarization of local society caused by mercenary activity, which made soldiers from unlikely material. Most communities formed local defence forces, whose duties included counterattacks on mercenary groups, a development discussed further below. But this also meant that these men (and some women) engaged in the same sort of activities as those they were fighting against. Some of those thus militarized by circumstance could become candidates for a local lord's *comitiva*, the group of warrior-clients who made up the nucleus of seigneurial troops. Jacques Dupré, for example, was an eighteen-year-old cleric of le Puy-en-Velay, but made his reputation attacking the inhabitants of Sauxillanges and was subsequently approached to join a local nobleman's military retinue.[58] The category of those who would fight had greatly expanded, and the number of wars fought increased along with it.

---

patriam Albiensem discurrentium (sic), locum de Villanova Albiensi tirannice occupatum' (*Étude . . . Arnoul d'Audrehem*, ed. Molinier, no. 33). Villeneuve d'Albi does not currently exist; 'Villanova Albiensi' is probably either Villeneuve-sur-Vère or Villeneuve-sur-Tarn.

[55] Fowler, *Great Companies*, ch. 1 and appendix B.   [56] Quote from AN x2a 8, fols. 56v–58r.

[57] Firnhaber-Baker, 'Techniques', 101–2; see also Wright, *Knights and Peasants*, 89–91. For Guillaume, *HL*, x: 1339–40, also published in Guigue, *Tard-venus*, no. 33.

[58] AN JJ 93, no. 212, fol. 85r.

JUSTICE, CORRUPTION, AND SELF-HELP

Faced with a weak king and an increase in violence that included, but was not limited to, seigneurial war, royal agents extended the innovations that they had begun to make under Philip VI. Processes of reconciliation and clemency – the double action of accord and remission – became a standard, almost universal way of dealing with seigneurial conflicts. Beyond this, individual parties began to take a greater role in the resolution of their own conflicts, again marking a move away from the official arbitration of disputes by royal justice and towards their informal settlement by individuals. Of particular note is the evidence for the manipulation and perhaps even corruption of justice by those with connections to royal administration. These developments reflect the frailty and impotence of royal government under John. Again, however, the striking thing is not just that royal government became less coercive, but also that royal justice and royal agents remained an important part of the way that seigneurial disputes were processed and resolved.

This survival of royal authority even in a time of obvious governmental disarray had a great deal to do with the sophistication of royalist ideology, and in this area, Parlement held the line without apparent difficulty. As had been the case since early in the century, making war was dealt with as a crime, meaning an offence against the crown that was distinct from the civil injury done to other parties. Violation of special royal protection (the safeguard) remained a commonly cited rationale for prosecution, though perhaps somewhat less so than previously the case: under John, about two-thirds of southern wars were judicially prosecuted on account of the safeguard, while nearly 85 per cent of those under Philip VI had been said to involve it. Royal proctors and civil claimants also frequently invoked the carriage of illicit arms (*portatio armorum*) during the war as constituting a criminal offence.

The understanding of royal legislation (the *ordonnances*) as entailing criminal prosecution for violation – first observable in the 1320s and 1330s – also continued. In at least twelve instances under John, the crown and/or the civil plaintiffs invoked the defendant's violation of the royal *ordonnances* against warfare as a reason to find against him in Parlement,[59] often using

---

[59] AN x2a 6, fols. 23v (1353 for a war, possibly in Picardy), 62–65r (1353, Macon and Auvergne), 232–233r (1355, Laon), 244–246r (1355, Bourges), 273–4 (1356, Sens), 299v–304r (1356, Normandy), 353–354r (1357, Tournai), 363–365r (1357, Touraine), 449v–452 (1360, Maine); AN x2a 7, fols. 24 (1361, Nivernais), 34–35r (1361, Douai), 63v–66 (1362, Chartrain). AN x2a 6, fol. 59 (1353, Vermandois) probably also alludes to *ordonnances*, though its language is somewhat unclear.

formulaic language to express the crown's opposition to warfare.[60] The frequency with which legislation provided grounds for prosecution remained relatively rare, as it had in previous decades. Indeed, none of the Parlement cases of southern seigneurial war heard during John's reign were brought on account of transgression of the *ordonnances*, though violation of *ordonnances* is cited as an offence in two remissions.[61]

The one judicial innovation under John characteristically had to do with military matters: the court clarified in some cases that non-royal wars were illegal both during the king's wars and during times of truce. In 1355, an *arrêt* for a case of seigneurial warfare near Laon specified that war was prohibited '*especially* during our wars' (*guerram movere precipue nostris durantibus guerris*),[62] a clarification that became more important after Poitiers forced a cessation of hostilities. The first invocation of the *ordonnances* after Poitiers adds *sive treugis* (or truces) after the usual *durantibus nostris guerris* (during our wars), and the other citation from 1357 simply omits the phrase *durantibus nostris guerris*.[63] The next time the *ordonnances* appear in a prosecution, in 1360, the illegality of warfare during truces as well as wars is again asserted (*nostris guerris sive treugis durantibus*).[64] In 1362, the crown's proctor noted that a war had been waged despite the prohibition against all war (*omnes guerre*), and observed that at the time of the war 'peace had long been declared between us and our brother [the king of England]'.[65] A case from 1361 involved a war 'against the royal ordinances' (*contra ordinationes nostras Regias*) with no reference to the state of the king's war, and the remissions for southern wars in 1363 and 1364 that mention the *ordonnances* against warfare are similarly silent regarding the state of the king's war.[66] If one assumes that the *ordonnances* that prohibited seigneurial war during royal war tacitly allowed it during peacetime, it appears the

---

[60] The standard language, which runs along the lines of 'necnon inhibicionibus nostris ne quis cuiuscumque status aut conditionis existeret nostris durantibus guerris sub penis averi corperis & bonorum guerrarum movere seu facere quovismodo presumeret vel auderet et tam in nostris (sic) presentia quam undique per regnum nostrum solemniter publicatis', is used in AN x2a 6, fols. 62–65r, 232–233r, 244–246r, 299v–304r, 353–254r, 363–365r, 449v–452; AN x2a 7, fols. 34–35r. In 1365, it also appears in AN x2a 7, fols. 164v–167r, 178v–179. The grammatical oddity 'nostris presentia' is employed in several instances, suggesting unreflective copying: J. Firnhaber-Baker, 'Formulating Opposition to Seigneurial Warfare in the Parlement de Paris', in *La formule au moyen âge*, ed. E. Louviot (Turnhout, 2013), 216.

[61] AN JJ 93, no. 142, fol. 59r (remission for a participant in the Solignac war) and Rossignol, *Monographies...Tam*, IV: no. 2 (remission for Bertrand, viscount of Montclar, for his war against Guillaume Agasse, co-lord of Saint-Urcisse).

[62] AN x2a 6, fols. 232–233r.   [63] AN x2a 6, fols. 353–354r, 363–365r.

[64] AN x2a 6, fols. 449v–452.

[65] '[L]icet tunc & longo tempore antea pas inter nos & dictum fratrem nostrum facta fuisset & ubique proclamata ... ac etiam quod omnes guerre fuissent & essent atque sint omnibus subditis nostris & aliis in Regno nostro specialiter expresse & publice prohibite' (AN x2a 7, fols. 63v–66).

[66] AN x2a 7, fol. 24; AN JJ 93, no. 142, fol. 59r; Rossignol, *Monographies ... Tam*, IV: no. 2.

crown thus pulled a 'bait-and-switch' on its subjects.[67] But in light of the prosecutions in the mid-1350s – and particularly given the statement made in 1355 while the war with England was on-going – it may be that earlier statements that the war 'took place during the king's war' should be read as a circumstance that strengthened the prosecution's case: that is, an aggravating factor.[68]

The ideas about royal authority over violence apparent in some Parlement cases were one reason that the challenges of mid-century did not wholly obviate royal involvement in seigneurial conflicts, a point discussed further below, but there were significant changes in how people used and experienced royal justice in this period. The trend, first visible in the later 1340s, towards selective, opportunistic engagement with royal authority continued and increased. Contumacy, for example, which was first a significant problem under Philip VI, became a regular feature of cases under John II. Of the five cases for which there is evidence of a judgment and sentence (as opposed to the majority of cases in which only preparatory or interlocutory documents are locatable), in four of them the defendants were condemned for obdurate contumacy.[69] Logistical difficulties certainly caused some of the absenteeism. Stephen de Vissac, for example, found himself in violation of his parole and contumacious in March 1361 during the plague epidemic because he precipitously returned home from Paris, having been 'informed – as turned out to be true – that his wife and children were deathly ill' (*certioratus quod uxor sua & liberi laborant in extremis prout & verum fuit*).[70] The dangers of travelling when freebooters and bandits roamed the land were also an excuse, and perhaps a reasonable one, for failure to get oneself to Paris.[71]

---

[67] E.g. R. Cazelles, 'La réglementation royale de la guerre privée de Saint Louis à Charles V et la précarité des ordonnances', *RHDFE*, 4th ser., 38 (1960): 539. See discussion of Philip the Fair's *ordonnances* prohibiting war during royal wars above, Chapter 2, pp. 64–5.

[68] The problem of war during times of royal truce had come up once prior to Poitiers, in a case from Vermandois in 1343 where the plaintiff argued that subjects' wars were prohibited during times of royal war, and the defendant replied that 'tempore quo premissa facta & perpetrata fuisse dicebatur treuge prorogare erant & fuerant inter nos ac Regem Anglie' (AN x1a 9, fols. 492v–494r). However, while as usual the court did not comment on the defendant's argument, it did imprison and fine him. For the argument later in the century, see Chapter 5, below.

[69] Aimar de Roussillon (AN JJ 93, no. 237, fols. 95v–96r, absence from the court of the bailliage of Vivarais); Stephen de Vissac (AN x2a 7, fols. 11, 80–4, Parlement); Guillaume de Cardillac (AN x2a 8, fols. 24v–29r, Parlement); Sicard de Lescure and associates (AN x2a 8, fols. 56v–58r; *HL*, x: 1435–40, Parlement and the seneschalsy of Toulouse). Only the Causits, condemned by the rector of Montpellier and the viguier of Béziers, seem not to have been convicted in absentia (AN x1a 19, fol. 54r). Guillaume de Chalençon had also once failed to appear when cited before Parlement, but reached an accord with Arnaud d'Allègre before the matter developed further (*HL*, x: 1255–9).

[70] AN x2a 7, fols. 192v–198.

[71] E.g. AN x2a 7, fols. 190v–191r (argument made in a case from 1365 involving violence in the Auvergne).

Not only did people fail to show up for court, it also seems that fewer cases came to court in the first place. As mentioned previously, no cases of southern seigneurial war were heard in Parlement between 1356 and 1359, a lull that probably reflects the Estates General's removal of many members of the royal bureaucratic elite, including prominent *parlementaires*.[72] Failure to prosecute is also indicated by remissions issued not because the recipient had been convicted of a crime or was even under investigation, but because he wished to preclude future, hypothetical pursuit. Jacques Dupré, for example, requested remission in 1363 or 1364 simply because he 'feared the rigour of justice' (*formidans rigorem justicie*) for crimes he had committed several years before.[73] Such delays continued into the next decade; in 1372, Guillaume Chaberi, a participant in the Solignac war of the previous decade, asked for his pardon, 'although he has not been pursued about this, but none the less fears being prosecuted by royal officers in the future'.[74]

The weakness of royal administration under John and in the early reign of his son naturally meant the persistence and strengthening of the development from the late 1340s towards settlement of cases through an accord with the injured party and a remission from the king in place of civil and criminal conviction. Indeed the practice of addressing criminal offence through granting a remission of the crime and its punishment – that is, the gracious extension of royal amnesty – was generalized in the 1360s, with universally applicable remissions issued to anyone involved in the Jacquerie and counter-Jacquerie of 1358 and then in 1360 for 'the many and innumerable pillages, larcenies, robberies and other misdeeds' committed during the war with England.[75] As had been the case under Philip VI, royal military needs seem to have been a key impetus for the extension of amnesty. Following Poitiers, the ransoms and other inconveniences encountered in royal wars also became a bargaining chip. As a remission for Armand de la Roüe observed, he ought to be remitted since he 'loyally served our late father, the king (John II), and us (Charles V), in our wars, and was taken in the Battle of Poitiers and [that] of Brignais and held for very excessive ransoms' (*ait loyalement servi nostredite feu pere, mons. le Roy & nous ou fait des guerres & a este prins es bataille de Poitiers et de*

---

[72] Sumption, *Hundred Years War*, II: 278–81; Cazelles, *Société politique . . . sous Jean*, 258–9.
[73] AN JJ 93, no. 212, fol. 85r. See also *HL*, x: 1641–2; AN JJ 90, no. 411, fols. 207v–208r.
[74] '[L]icet de & super predictis exinde non fuerit impetitus, attamen dictus Guillemus formidat ne per aliquos justiciarios regni nostri super hoc futuris temporibus prosequatur' (*HL*, x: 1475–6).
[75] Luce, *La Jacquerie*, no. 23 (1358) and *Ord.*, III: 407–8 (1360). One of the partisans to the Solignac war argued that his remission should be granted on account of the general remission of 1360 (*HL*, x: 1300–1).

Brignays & mis a tres excessives rencons).[76] Mura and Guillaume Causit, who
were unlikely to have given any military service, none the less noted in
their supplication for remission that they had been much harmed by
the wars (*ont grandement este domages pour le fait de noz guerres*).[77] And the
bourg of Carcassonne was remitted its crimes against the crown in light of
the damages incurred when it was burned and destroyed by enemies
(*dampnificationibus ipsius burgi in concremacione & destruccione ipsius loci per
inimicos nostros factis*), a reference to the Black Prince's infamous treatment
of the town during the *chevauchée* of 1355.[78]

A negotiated settlement entailing a civil accord and remission of crimes
was the outcome for nearly all the wars that took place from 1350 to 1364,
and even when a case was decided in court the decision seems not to have
been final. Except for the Vissac/Bertrand case (for which other factors
discussed below seem to have precluded further negotiations), in each of
the five cases in which I have been able to locate a final judgment, the
decision was subject to further negotiation through remissions and/or civil
accords in the years and decades that followed. Such further wrangling
often also touched off further violence. The war over the viscounty of
Murat, for which judgment was rendered against Guillaume de Cardillac
in 1368, none the less went on throughout the 1370s and 1380s, the 1368
arrêt going unexecuted well into the fifteenth century.[79] Similarly Aimar
de Roussillon's violence against the Celestine monks of Colombiers
continued into the next generation and beyond, and in this conflict,
too, the arrangements for compensation that were made in a remission
of 1363 proved hard to carry out. The monks had the greatest difficulty in
collecting the damages awarded to them, and the crown simply never
received the 2,000 florins that Aimar had agreed to pay for his remission,
finally discharging the debt in 1411.[80]

Increasingly, responsibility for redress fell on private parties, with the
crown's officers and institutions involved mainly as facilitators or as points
of reference. During the 1350s and 1360s, parties in conflict frequently
worked both in conjunction with the crown and independently of it to
ensure their own interests. This interweaving of public authority with
private initiative could take many forms. For example, in the Solignac
war, after the seneschal of Beaucaire's lieutenant forcibly seized a castle

---

[76] *Preuves . . . Polignac*, ed. Jacotin, II: no. 240. See also AN JJ 90, no. 411, fols. 207v–208r; AN JJ 93, no. 183, fols. 74–75r; *HL*, x: 1107–8, 1255–9; *Étude . . . Arnoul d'Audrehem*, ed. Molinier, no. 33; Rossignol, *Monographies . . . Tarn*, IV: no. 2. Such arguments also began to be made in Parlement cases, e.g. AN X2a 7, fols. 192v–198; AN X2a 8, fols. 24v–29r. See also F. Bériac-Lainé and C. Given-Wilson, *Les prisonniers de la bataille de Poitiers* (Paris, 2002), 241–2.

[77] AN JJ 98, no. 395, fols. 127–8.   [78] *HL*, x: 1329–31.   [79] See n. 38, above.

[80] Mazon, *Essai historique*, 120–3.

from Armand de la Roüe when he refused to stop his war against the viscount of Polignac, Armand first pursued a legal solution, presenting himself before the king's lieutenant and requesting royal letters for the castle's restoration. But when he saw that this would not be sufficient, he associated himself with others who 'had a quarrel with the castle' and took it back *per force & a armes*. Despite this pursuit of the *voie de fait*, he then turned back again to royal authority, having a royal sergeant present the letters he had previously obtained in order to rid the castle of this third party and requesting a remission, which both protected him from criminal prosecution and reconfirmed once more his possession of the castle.[81] A similar dance of public and private, judicial and violent moves took place in the aftermath of the Albi/Lescure war.[82]

There is also significant evidence of aggrieved parties' participation in forcible – even military – actions undertaken under royal aegis for the punishment of offenders and/or the recuperation of seized property, and such partnerships could blur the line between 'private' violence and that which was state sponsored. The citizens of Lyon, for example, apparently not only paid for the judicially decreed destruction of the lord of Roussillon's castles, but also provided most of the labor themselves.[83] Jean de Colombiers and Sicard Hébert similarly joined their men and resources to royal officers' forcible efforts to repossess the castles taken from them by illegal seizure.[84] And the viscount of Polignac and his troops accompanied the seneschal of Beaucaire in military expeditions against Robert Dauphin in the Solignac war.[85] North of the Loire, such efforts were even legislatively endorsed by the Estates General of Languedoïl in 1357, whose promulgation orders royal officers to work with individuals (*les bonnes Gens du pays*) to force war-makers to come to terms.[86]

It was the crown's inability to enforce its will that necessitated the civil party's participation in the execution of justice and encouraged parties to act violently in their own interests. As the viscount of Polignac later claimed, his violence during the Solignac war was committed 'sometimes on his own account and sometimes at the behest of royal

---

[81] *Preuves. . .Polignac*, ed. Jacotin, II: no. 240.   [82] Firnhaber-Baker, '*Jura in medio*'.

[83] Mazon, *Éssai historique*, 14–18.

[84] AN JJ 91, no. 317, fol. 163 (Jean de Colombiers); AN x2a 7, fols. 239v–243 (Sicard Hébert).

[85] *Preuves. . .Polignac*, ed. Jacotin, II: no. 229.

[86] '[D]effendons . . . à tous Nobles et non-Nobles, que durant . . . ces presentes Guerres, aucuns d'eulz à l'autre ne meuve ou face Guerre . . . ordonnons se aucuns fait le contraire, la Justice du lieu, Seneschal, Bailiffs, Prevosts ou autres, appellés ad se, se mestier est, les bonnes Gens du pays, pregnant telz Guerriers, & les contraingnent senz delay . . . à faire paix & à cessier du tout de guerriers' (*Ord.*, III: 121–46, art. 34).

officers' (*quandoque per se quandoque ad requisitionem gentium regiarum*), who, he noted, needed his services because otherwise they could not execute their legal processes (*processus suos quos vi armata excequcioni, quia alias non poterant, demandarunt*).[87] The royal impotence that this comment reveals encouraged outright self-help as people were forced (or at least found it possible to argue that they were forced) to take their own defence into their own hands. Many of the supplications for remission for southern warfare in this period included the argument that the supplicant had had no other recourse to protect himself against his enemy's violence. The viscount of Polignac argued that his war was waged *pro defensione sua*, an assertion that the bishop of Saint-Flour made in somewhat different terms regarding his conflict with the viscount of Murat.[88] As the consuls of Albi argued, they attacked Sicard de Lescure because they

> could not easily resort to the king for a solution, and although the bishop [of Albi] and his subjects had asked royal officers [that the matter be handled] by formal judicial procedures (*per viam justicie*) or otherwise, they were busy with the difficult problems of defence, and because of the evil times and Sicard's power, they could not help.[89]

This renaissance of self-help seems also to have coincided with a re-valorization of the concept of vengeance. For the first time since the late thirteenth century there are claims that violence was necessary in order to exact vengeance or to conserve honour. The consuls and inhabitants of Albi argued that they had acted 'in the heat of anger and to have restitution and for vengeance' (*calore iratundie & restitutions habende & ex causa vindicte*), while the viscount of Polignac appealed to the need to conserve honour and exact vengeance (*statu et honore observandis seu alias causa vindicte*).[90] It is important to note, however, that the wars involving such claims were still being fought over the usual conflicts regarding land, castles, wealth, and power. The dispute between Albi and Lescure was related to the bishop of Albi's fortifications, while the viscount of Polignac was at war for the barony of Solignac. What changed was not the impetus for violence or the emotions incited by such conflicts, but the acceptability

---

[87] *Preuves...Polignac*, ed. Jacotin, II: no. 229.

[88] *Preuves...Polignac*, ed. Jacotin, II: no. 229. The bishop argued that he had to fortify his fortress 'ad dicti vicecomitis & suorum hujusmodi alligatorum perverse opinioni resistendum' (*HL*, X: 1363–6).

[89] '[A]d dictum dominum nostrum comode recurrere non poterant, pro salubri remedio adhibendo seu obtinendo, & quod gentes seu officiarii regiis dictarum Senescalliarum licet predictum episcopum, & subditos suos requisiti per viam justicie, vel aliter aliis arduis negociis deffencionem presente(?) tangentibus occupati, propter malicia tempus & pronominati Sicardi & suorum consortum potenciam non poterant remediare' (AD Tarn Edt 4 FF 41).

[90] AD Tarn Edt 4 FF 41 and *Preuves...Polignac*, ed. Jacotin, II: no. 229.

of vindictive language and emotion, a shift towards a more affective, narrative, and personal rhetoric that is found across *lettres de rémission* of the period for crimes of all sorts.

The emphasis on private concerns heralded by such language was a fundamental characteristic of the period. Even when parties used royal courts rather than (or in conjunction with) open war for the pursuit of their conflicts, there was greater scope to do so in a way that maximized self-interest. Beyond the preference shown to those loyal to the French crown in the war with England in the previous decades, the 1350s and 1360s saw the manipulation, perhaps even corruption, of royal administration and justice for private ends. Some of this was simply unsurprising pecuniary *quid pro quo*. The townspeople of Albi, for example, though already under investigation by the seneschal of Toulouse for their violence against Lescure, turned the tables by acquiring a mandate from King John that took the matter away from the seneschal and referred it to Parlement.[91] It cannot be proved that Albi received this mandate by offering the crown money, but the document was procured from John while he was at Villeneuve-lès-Avignon during the trip he took to Languedoc in 1362–3 in order to raise his ransom with the help of the southern towns.[92]

In other cases, one party's connections to power seem to have altered the balance. Sicard Hébert, for example, who was remarkably successful in his case against his overlord, the viscount of Lautrec, was the *prévôt* of a royal castle and is also described as a royal sergeant at arms (*serviens noster armorum*).[93] In the conflict over the viscounty of Murat, whose initial facts seem unfavourable to Reginald de Murat, Reginald may none the less have seized the advantage because he entered royal service.[94] Stephen de Vissac lost his case, was heavily punished, and never seems to have been remitted or to have regained anything that he lost,[95] a remarkably harsh outcome of unparalleled severity that came at the hands of the Bertrand clan, whose most prominent member, Pierre Bertrand, just happened to be the cardinal of Ostia, a royal diplomat, papal favourite, former *parlementaire*, and nephew of and successor to one of the century's

---

[91] Letter patent mentioned in the *arrêt* at AN x2a 8, fols. 56v–58r. I have not been able to locate the letter itself.

[92] See J. B. Henneman, *Royal Taxation in Fourteenth-Century France: the Captivity and Ransom of John II, 1356–1370* (Philadelphia, 1976), 180–4.

[93] AN x2a 7, fols. 239v–243.   [94] AN x2a 8, fols. 144v–145r.

[95] In the 1370s we find him arguing not that he should regain one of his castles (given to Bertrand Bertrand in lieu of an 8,000 l.t. fine) but simply that Bertrand ought not to have alienated it by selling it to the duke of Berry (AN x1a 25, fols. 13v–14r). The Vissacs did eventually pay Bertrand the money (BN Français 20692, p. 344).

most prominent royal lawyers.[96] This family's influence was probably also at work in the favourable outcome enjoyed by the Celestine monks of Colombiers, who were beneficiaries of the same well-connected cardinal, though their enemy, Aimar de Roussillon, had English and Navarrese sympathies that could not have helped his case.[97]

Just how easily insiders might have been able to game the judicial system or how much this had really changed from earlier periods should not be overstated. Part of the reason that those with connections had greater success was surely that they were or had access to better lawyers. One can hardly fault the court for finding against Stephen de Vissac, who, though faced with a family of fine legal minds, seems not even to have employed a proctor, his defence consisting solely of the argument that he was 'stupid and young and ignorant of the law' (*simplex & juvenis ac juris & justitie ignarus*).[98] Nor were political considerations all controlling. The viscount of Montclar managed to secure remission despite his alliance with a famed English mercenary and reports that his troops shouted 'Guienne, Guienne for Montclar' (*Guiana, Guiana per Monclar*) when invading his enemy's fortress.[99] Patronage and politics had probably always had some sway over justice in earlier decades; perhaps this sort of manipulation of justice and government was simply more apparent during these years than previously. But from the reign of Saint Louis, the 'public spirit' of service to the state as an abstract and disinterested entity – the sense that officials ought to serve the commonwealth's interests rather than their own – had been a central element of French royal government and a primary characteristic (at least ideally) of its bureaucratic staff.[100] That there seems to have been even a temporary loss of this professional detachment – or even just less caution in letting personal interest show through – suggests the profundity of the problems afflicting royal government at mid-century.

---

[96] Monicat, *Les grandes compagnies*, no. 6; *Preuves . . . Polignac*, ed. Jacotin, II: no. 229. For Pierre Bertrand, see Mazon, *Essai historique*, 58–86; R. Cazelles, *La société politique et la crise de la royauté sous Philippe de Valois* (Paris, 1958), 68, n. 2. I have not been able to read 'Discours généalogique de la noble maison de Bertrand et de leur alliance avec celle de Colombier', a manuscript history of this family.

[97] AN JJ 93, no. 183, fols. 74–75r. For Aimar's Anglo-Navarrese sympathies, see Mazon, *Essai historique*, 22 and Guigue, *Tard-venus*, 82.

[98] AN X2a 7, fols. 13–16r. Reginald de Murat and Sicard Hébert seem similarly to have had better counsel and to have presented better arguments.

[99] Rossignol, *Monographies . . . Tarn*, IV: no. 2.

[100] W. C. Jordan, 'Anti-corruption Campaigns in Thirteenth-Century Europe', *Journal of Medieval History* 35 (2009): 204–19; R. Cazelles, 'Une exigence de l'opinion depuis Saint Louis: la réformation du royaume', *Annuaire-bulletin de la Société de l'histoire de France* (1962–3): 91–9. For the *ésprit* of the *parlementaires* in particular, see F. Autrand, *Naissance d'un grand corps de l'état: les gens du Parlement de Paris, 1345–1454* (Paris, 1981), esp. 103–8, 264–5.

The extent of these problems is quite striking, but so is the fact that royal government and officials retained a significant role in the pursuit and resolution of conflicts. Royal crises may have forced further the evolution of royal officers' engagement with war-makers that began after Philip VI's military defeats, requiring them to negotiate and cooperate more than to command and compel, and it is undeniable that this development entailed a 'privatization' of some activities that in modern polities (or even perhaps under Philip the Fair) belong exclusively to the state. Yet, one must also note that even during these difficult years, the crown's judicial-administrative system not only survived but also remained engaged with and attractive to local elites. Just as in the 1340s, the negotiation of accords, the granting of remission, and the efforts – if only partially successful – to enforce judicial decisions all attest to the creativity and flexibility of the king's administrative network under difficult circumstances. The partnerships between royal officers and private parties demonstrate that the crown's resources were few, but they also show that royal representatives continued to play a role in local power struggles: the Albigensian townspeople, the viscount of Polignac, the citizens of Lyon, and others could not sit idly by, waiting for the state to guarantee their rights and redress their wrongs, but their initiatives were all made with reference to royal judgments or mandates which provided the legitimate legal backing for their undertakings. This was not conflict resolution in the absence of a state, but rather the strategic employment of governmental power by both officials and subjects in a way that recognized and therefore to some extent reinforced royal authority. In this way, the crown's role in local society could be maintained, perhaps could even grow in certain ways, even as its ability to compel obedience continued to wane.

LEGITIMATE VIOLENCE: THE REDEFINITION OF AUTHORITY

While the continued appeal to and use of the king's courts and officers attests to the survival of the ideal of royal government at a time when the reality had become dramatically less effective, a complementary development was taking place outside the royal/seigneurial relationship. Because the crown was unable (some thought unwilling) to protect people from the large-scale violence caused by mercenaries and others, local communities and regional associations began to take matters into their own hands, much as civil claimants in seigneurial wars were finding it necessary to do. Frequently it was more expeditious for local communities to cooperate with the men holding the country to ransom, paying them protection money and providing their victuals, their horses, and often their women. But there was also resistance on a wide scale.[101] Communal self-defence measures directed by municipal or regional associations, such as town militias and watch duties, became ubiquitous, and many individuals also found themselves engaged in spontaneous, ad hoc resistance under their own authority.[102] In parallel fashion to developments in seigneurial warfare, responses to the violence of mercenaries and other troops were thus frequently directed or sponsored by non-judicial and non-institutional entities, whose aim was simply the limitation of violence rather than any ideological imperative. Yet, as can be observed in the processes related to seigneurial warfare, these initiatives were often undertaken not in opposition to royal authority but in dialogue with it. The increased scale of violence and the more varied social background of those directing or defending against violence seem to have raised questions about legitimate authority for violence, suggesting to many that the right to control violence was a royal prerogative that could only be delegated to public representatives, not devolved to private individuals.

This interplay of ideas about violence, self-defence, and legitimate authority is observable in the important assemblies of the Estates General of Languedoïl held in 1355 and 1357, which responded to the increasing disorder around Paris by enshrining in law some measures of popular, autonomous self-defence.[103] The 1355 provisions of the Estates address the crisis of order occasioned by the crown's inability to control (because it could not pay) its troops by authorizing organized resistance to them. The measure speaks of the soldiers hired *pour fournir nostre Guerre* who 'sometimes pillage and rob the towns and churches and other subjects of our realm',[104] and stated that if such men seized anything, then everyone (*chascun*) should resist them by force (*par voie de fait*), assembling as seemed good to them to oppose the pillagers. In addition to ordering *les bonnes Gens du pays* to help end wars,[105] the provisions of

---

[101] Resistance and cooperation were not mutually exclusive strategies. For example, two remissions were issued in the same month to the communities of the seneschalsy of Beaucaire, one of which is for opposing the companies and the other for assisting them (*HL*, x: 1360–1).

[102] See Wright, *Knights and Peasants*, chs. 4–5; *La Guerre de Cent Ans*, ed. Timbal, 168–208; Sumption, *Hundred Years War*, II: 385–6, 395–400.

[103] J. Firnhaber-Baker, '*À son de cloche*: the Interpretation of Public Order and Legitimate Authority in Northern France, 1355–58', in *Espacio público, opinión y comunicación política a fines de la Edad Media*, ed. H. R. Oliva Herrer (Seville, forthcoming) and citations therein.

[104] '[P]our ce que pour fournir nostre Guerre, il Nous convient avoir des Soudoiers dehors nostre Royaume, tant de Genz de cheval comme de pié, lesquelz aucunes foiz pillent & robbent [derobent] sur les Villes & sur les Eglises, & autres subgiez de nostre Royaume' (*Ord.*, III: 19–37, art. 30). In the later 1350s the crown allowed royal troops to pillage in lieu of the wages that it could not afford to pay (Sumption, *Hundred Years War*, II: 305, 373).

[105] See above, n. 86.

the 1357 assembly repeated these instructions, mandating that if anyone from the realm or elsewhere took things or attacked anyone in the *bonnes villes*, they should be resisted by all the people (*par tout le peuple*), reiterating that *li peuples* should oppose them by force of arms and with all their power.[106] Both assemblies also authorized resistance *de fait* to royal officers who interfered in tax collection (to be carried out instead by the Estates' deputies) and to any royal seizures made by the king's people (identified as everyone from the queen down to masters of garrisons, castellans, captains, 'or other officers whatsoever').[107] Such prescriptions issued under royal authority – though not with voluntary royal assent in the case of 1357 – essentially authorized popular, autonomous self-help against the crown itself and signal another reversal of the long-term trend away from private remedy and towards public justice. Indeed, the provisions of 1355 regarding mercenaries explicitly privileged violent self-help over official judicial remedies. Only if the victims could not muster sufficient resistance (if they *ne sont assez forts*) was the problem to be taken to the nearest official (*la plus prochaine justice*).

The assemblies of 1355 and 1357 were anomalous, and the provisions of 1357 were soon repudiated.[108] Indeed, John II's *ordonnance* of 1361 forbidding armed violence *sanz Justice* may have been directed as much at those defending against the companies as against the mercenaries themselves; one could conceivably even read the measure as a pejorative reference to the Estates' provisions advocating self-help. But though ephemeral and contested, the assemblies' decrees accurately reflect the problems involved in restoring 'public order' when 'public authority' was in abeyance and when, indeed, many of the agents of disorder were effectively royal representatives. In the southern seneschalsies, the design of royal administration (entrusted to the lieutenant of Languedoc who had regalian powers and to seneschals with full military and judicial prerogatives) and the solidarity of the meridian towns meant that the increasing incidence of violence did not at first occasion the sort of breakdown of public order as occurred in the acephalous Île-de-France.[109] The

---

[106] *Ord.*, III: 121–46, art. 57.

[107] *Ord*, III: 19–37, art. 5, and 12–13. Similar statements in *Ord.*, III: 121–46, art. 2, and 16–17. The Languedocian assemblies of 1356 and 1358 similarly forbade royal interference in regional administration of tax collection and distribution, though in lieu of forcible resistance they threatened cessation of the aid (*Ord.*, III: 99–109, IV: 187–94).

[108] Sumption, *Hundred Years War*, II: 282.

[109] For the lieutenant of Languedoc, see P. Dognon, *Les institutions politiques et administratives du pays de Languedoc du XIIe siècle aux guerres de religion* (Toulouse, 1895), 345–63. The close relationship between the lieutenant and the communities is demonstrated by the count of Foix's attacks against the towns of the seneschalsies when the lieutenancy passed to Jean de Berry, linked by marriage to Foix's Armagnac foes (see above, n. 47). On the greater powers of southern seneschals, as opposed

Auvergne experienced more problems on this front, though it, too, could look to the lieutenant and depend upon vigorous communal alliances.[110] Nevertheless, as was the case north of the Loire, in the South, autonomous, ad hoc self-defence measures became common everywhere, creating problems of authority and legitimacy. At least eleven remissions were granted to individuals or communities between 1357 and 1364 for crimes committed in violently opposing these enemies (or people allegedly thought to be enemies), and this no doubt represents a vast underestimate of the real extent of opposition.[111]

As the evident need to obtain remission indicates, communities' and individuals' ostensibly laudable efforts to combat the companies and other enemies created legal and political ambiguities. It was easy for those engaged in resistance to slip into a life of brigandage, and in any case, their efforts could always be misconstrued.[112] As Nicholas Wright has stressed, the autonomous self-defence measures that became common from the 1350s onward were frequently perceived as challenging to traditional authority accustomed to monopolizing defence efforts.[113] Indeed, the most shocking challenge to established authority, the Jacquerie of 1358, was strongly motivated by the need to rid northern France of predatory troops and was understood by many of its participants as an effort to restore public order at a time when traditional authorities were either absent or actively abetting the violence.[114] As the control of violence thus became a responsibility that was shared by both crown and society (in fact if not in law), questions arose about who possessed authority to make decisions about violence and to carry those decisions out. Thus, while there was general agreement that violence ought to be restrained – by violent force if necessary – there was wide scope for disagreements about who could or should impose such limitations.

---

to northern *baillis*, see H. Takayama, 'The Local Administrative System of France under Philip IV (1285–1314) – Baillis and Seneschals', *Journal of Medieval History* 21 (1995): 167–93. While Philip VI's seneschals had mostly been lawyers, those of John II and Charles V were drawn primarily from military backgrounds (Sumption, *Hundred Years War*, II: 385). For regional solidarity, see Cazelles, *Société . . . sous Jean*, 352–3; Sumption, *Hundred Years War*, II: 352–5, 368, 411, etc.

[110] For the Estates of Auvergne, see Charbonnier, *Une autre France*, I: 451–2. Cf. Sumption, *Hundred Years War*, II: 354–5.

[111] *HL*, X: 1126–7, 1128–9, 1294–5, 1304–6, 1306–8, 1317–19, 1329–31, 1360–1; Guigue, *Les tard-venus*, no. 32; *Le Languedoc et le Rouergue dans le Trésor des Chartes*, ed. Y. Dossat, A.-M. LeMasson, and P. Wolff (Paris, 1983), nos. 1870, 1942 (no. 1870 recounts the same incident as *HL*, X: 1294–5 for a different beneficiary).

[112] E.g. Charbonnier, *Autre France*, I: 461, n. 3.

[113] *Knights and Peasants*, ch. 4, esp. pp. 91–3, 113. Cf. Charbonnier, *Une autre France*, I: 463.

[114] Sumption, *Hundred Years War*, II: 327–36; Wright, *Knights and Peasants*, 56, 84–7; Durvin, 'Les origines de la Jacquerie'; Luce, *La Jacquerie*, 50–4; Firnhaber-Baker, '*À son de cloche*'. See nn. 119–20, below.

In this context, a new emphasis on the concept of licence (*licentia*/*license* or *congé*) for violence can be discerned. Licence – the delegation of authority – was a key idea behind the regional assemblies that met so frequently during this period.[115] As discussed above, John II's *ordonnance* of 1361 against seigneurial war and other large-scale violent activities was preoccupied with the problem of such authority, complaining bitterly of the *plusieurs* who had made illicit assemblies and *chevauchées*, and forbidding such activities except by royal 'permission or order' (*congié ou ordennance*).[116] Those who undertook autonomous measures for self-defence seem to have been increasingly vulnerable to the accusation that they had acted without sufficient authority. The people of Béziers were accused of fortifying the town *absque licentia curialium* (without royal officer's permission), an offence for which they had to seek remission.[117] And the remission for the *bourg* of Carcassonne's attacks against fortresses thought to be harbouring mercenaries included both the complaint that the citizens had taken up arms 'without … asking or obtaining any licence (*licentia*) from the marshal (Arnoul d'Audenham) or the king's lieutenant (of Languedoc) … or from any other royal officer of Carcassonne', and their defence that, in fact, they had thought the men were heretics and were acting for Carcassonne's inquisitor.[118]

Even those whose actions might first appear inexcusable sought the cover of licence or delegated authority. At least two of the Jacques, whose rebellion, as noted above, could be construed as an effort at self-defence, did claim legal authority for their actions: Jean de Jaqueminart noted, 'it being common knowledge [that] … enemies of the realm meant to pillage and burn the region, it was decreed, by our [the Dauphin's] permission (*eust esté ordené, de nostre license*) … that the pillagers and enemies of the realm … could be pursued by the villagers'.[119] Indeed,

---

[115] The Estates of Languedoc declared in 1356 that they could congregate 'with impunity and without any new [grant of] licence' (*impune & absque nova licentia*), a right that they again granted themselves in 1358, albeit on more limited terms (*Ord.*, III: 99–109, IV: 187–94; see also Cazelles, *Société … sous Jean*, 235, 340). On a smaller scale, citizens of Montpellier had to obtain a royal grace for assembling and approving taxation *absque … nostrum obtinuissent assensum* (*HL*, X: 1293–4).

[116] *Ord.*, III: 525–7. See above, p. 122.   [117] *HL*, X: 1126–7.

[118] '[N]ulla … a dicto marescallo & locumtenente domini genitoris nostri … seu ab aliquo alio de curialibus nostris Carcassone licentia petita seu obtenta … predicta facta fuerint ad requisicionem seu mandatum inquisitoris heretice pravitatis in senescallia Carcassone residentis seu ejus locum tenentis, pretendentis dictos capitaneos hereticos esse' (*HL*, X: 1329–31). The accusation of heresy may stem from papal bulls excommunicating those in the mercenary companies. For the excommunication of mercenaries, see p. 160, n. 50, below.

[119] Luce, *La Jacquerie*, no. 33 and see no. 40 which also speaks of this 'ordenance'. Luce thought that the Jacques could have defended themselves by pointing to the provisions of the Estates General authorizing resistance by *voie de fait* (*La Jacquerie*, 160–4, followed by Durvin, 'Les origines de la Jacquerie', 368–70, 373).

the participation by the brother of a judge in Parlement and a number of royal functionaries suggests that the Jacquerie was probably understood by at least some of its participants not as an anti-social uprising, but as an effort to restore and maintain public order.[120] Although it was clear that the companies did not have sufficient authority to wage war on their own account, even they frequently tried to avoid punishment by arguing that they were actually fighting under the legitimate authority of the English, the Navarrese, or a lord.[121]

This stress on licence and delegated authority was prompted by the same sorts of logistical and political concerns that necessitated greater participation by 'private persons' in the execution of justice. Yet, while such considerations obviously had implications for seigneurial warfare, judicial interference in these more traditional conflicts seems not to have raised the issue in previous decades. This is surprising since in just war theory the idea of sufficient authority had an ancient pedigree[122] and because there is also some evidence that under Louis IX it had been possible to license warfare: a letter from Alphonse de Poitiers to the seneschal of Agen speaks of 'cavalcades or marches' made *sine nostra licencia speciali*, and Louis gave his subjects permission (*licentiam concedamus*) to participate in the war between Montpellier and James of Aragon.[123] But the concept then disappeared from the sources for nearly a century; during the first half of the fourteenth century, when problems of large-scale disorder were mainly associated with seigneurial warfare, the problem of licence is apparently completely absent from the discussion. No doubt this had to do both with the nobles' frequent (albeit frequently refuted) argument that customary law gave them the right to wage war, and with lord-justiciars' undoubted right to act violently in execution of their fiscal and judicial prerogatives.

It also stemmed from cultural and social considerations: only when the social constituency of those engaged in large-scale, organized violence broadened beyond lords and their followers to encompass the more varied types of people involved in the companies, on one hand, and the burghers and peasants defending against them, on the other, did the problem of authority for violence take on a new importance. Indeed, of the many

[120] Cazelles, 'La Jacquerie', 657; Cazelles, *Société politique . . . sous Jean*, 323. See also John Watts's discussion of the role of disappointed expectations about government in popular uprisings in *The Making of Politie: Europe, 1300–1500* (Cambridge, 2009), 271–4.

[121] P. Contamine, 'Les compagnies d'aventure en France pendant la Guerre de Cent Ans', *Mélanges de l'École française de Rome. Moyen-âge, temps modernes* 87 (1975): 371–4.

[122] F. H. Russell, *The Just War in the Middle Ages* (Cambridge, 1975), 45–8, 68–70, 100–5, etc.

[123] *Correspondance administrative d'Alfonse de Poitiers*, ed. A. Molinier, 2 vols. (Paris, 1894–1900), II: no. 1879; *HL*, VIII: 1394.

seigneurial wars waged in the 1350s and 1360s, it is notable that only the actions of Carcassonne – carried out by ordinary burghers rather than by noble lords – raised the question of licence. In future decades, the idea of royal licence for violence would spread to the more traditional conflicts of the seigneurs, becoming a consideration in the hereditary aristocracy's wars, strengthening the idea of royal authority, even as the crown's actual ability to enforce obedience weakened.

CONCLUSION

The middle decades of the fourteenth century saw serious dangers to the long-term health of crown and kingdom. Military victory, fiscal stability, and administrative reform were urgently needed, and the appearance of unabashed corruption in judicial and administrative circles where the *bien commun* had once been highly prized was an ominous sign. The key factors were the related problems of the mercenaries and the collapse of royal government after Poitiers. By acting on their own authority or by contributing troops to enable the pursuit of more traditional conflicts, the mercenaries were directly behind much of the increase of violence during these decades. Their availability further contributed to the disorder by upsetting local power relations.

Some of the blame for the scale of the problem can be laid at the crown's doorstep. In the power vacuum left by John's capture, there was no adequate leadership to address the kingdom's many ills, including that of the freebooters. The king having failed at Poitiers, his agents then failed to protect his subjects from the consequences. Neither the crown's military powers nor its institutional and administrative arms were up to the task of controlling violence and mitigating conflict in the decade after the French disaster. As a result, the de facto responsibility for the maintenance of order devolved away from the crown, back into the hands of individuals and communities. Communal efforts at self-defence became ubiquitous, and individuals took on an increased role in conflict resolution. As the king's justice became less coercive and less effective, the interested parties pursued the execution of judgment themselves, sometimes without the help of royal agents, and they frequently bypassed royal judgment altogether, pursuing agreements and settlements extra-institutionally.

Yet, while these developments signal a weakening of French royal power, the growth of self-help that began in this period did not entail the abandonment of the judicial-administrative system that had been put in place by the Capetians, let alone a return to the sort of unrestrained violence that many historians see taking place around the year 1000.[124] Individuals and associations were forced to take on a greater role in the limitation of violence and the protection of rights, but they tended to work as often in concert with royal officials and institutions as they did in disregard of them. Private parties undertaking their own efforts at redress for damages incurred in seigneurial wars sought legal backing from royal judgments and mandates, and the accords brokered by royal agents speak to the crown's continued role in the settlement of local disputes. Even the rise in remissions signals that the crown's subjects had to respect the king's authority, though they might not fear it much. Communities and individuals who took up arms against those whom they considered (or claimed to consider) public enemies also took cover behind the idea of royal authority, delegated to them by royal licence. Ironically, although the crown's ability to coerce and compel weakened significantly, its authority – the recognition of its *right* to coerce and compel – did not suffer the same fate and may even have become somewhat more robust, as the absence of effective government made desire for it all the more acute.

---

[124] See Wright, *Knights and Peasants*, 50, 60–1.

Chapter 5

VIOLENCE AND THE STATE, 1365–1400

By the time Charles V was anointed king in May 1364, the prospects for public order in France had begun to improve significantly. With the introduction of a *fouage* or hearthtax for Languedoïl in late 1363 royal finances had been placed on a firmer footing, and there would be no return under Charles to the monetary instability of his father's years.[1] The mercenaries were taken care of at least temporarily, having been sent off to greener pastures with the aid of Louis d'Anjou and the Constable Du Guesclin.[2] But Charles's primary task was no less than the restoration of the realm, so greatly diminished by the Treaty of Brétigny in 1360. In this he was aided by factors in England. By the later 1360s, Edward III was old, the prince of Wales sick, and the English crown in dire need of money. Taxation in Aquitaine was one possible source of revenue, and the inhabitants were squeezed hard.[3] With more than a little cunning, they appealed to Charles V, who summoned Prince Edward to appear before Parlement. The latter failed to show. Whether born of pride or bodily frailty, this was a mistake. His contumacy gave Charles the pretext under which to confiscate the duchy of Aquitaine and to reignite the temporarily dormant Anglo-French conflict. This time military events favoured the French. From 1369 to 1374, the French reconquered all the territory lost over the previous thirty years and pushed the English back nearly to the sea. When the Truce of Bruges was agreed in 1375, England's French

---

[1] J. Sumption, *The Hundred Years War*, 3 vols. to date (Philadelphia, 1990–2009), III: 54–60, 268; J. B. Henneman, *Royal Taxation in Fourteenth-Century France: the Captivity and Ransom of John II, 1356–1370* (Philadelphia, 1976), 226–9; R. Cazelles, *Société politique, noblesse et couronne sous Jean le Bon et Charles V* (Geneva, 1982), 558–60, 565–8. Languedoc had been contributing via *fouages* for decades: J. B. Henneman, *Royal Taxation in Fourteenth-Century France: the Development of War Financing, 1322–1356* (Princeton, 1971), 162–7.

[2] See below, pp. 159–60.

[3] For the Gascon taxes and their consequences, see Sumption, *Hundred Years War*, II: 574–80; Henneman, *Royal Taxation . . . the Captivity*, 247–55; R. Delachenal, *Histoire de Charles V*, 5 vols. (Paris, 1909–31), IV: chs. 3–5.

possessions had been reduced to Calais and the stretch of land between Bayonne and Bordeaux.[4]

These triumphs, of course, would all be extinguished under the rule of Charles V's young, foolish, and finally mad, successor, Charles VI. But even before the wise king's death in 1380, trouble was brewing. Socially and economically, the common people had been pushed past their limit once again. From the point of view of royal finances, the *fouage* was an innovative improvement that finally provided the crown with a sufficient and predictable income stream from which to fund administration, warfare, and luxurious pageantry. But from the point of view of the average town dweller, the *fouage* was simply suffocatingly expensive. And it was being collected against a backdrop of increasing misery. In 1374 and 1375, not only plague but also famine hit hard. In Toulouse, the memory of the latter was so searing that even thirty years later, people still spoke of the time of *magna caristia*.[5] Plague returned regularly, reducing the taxbase still further and increasing the fiscal burden on the survivors. In the last years of the 1370s, rebellions broke out from Languedoc to Flanders. Conscious of his subjects' objections, Charles V revoked the hearthtax on his deathbed, but revolts continued well into the 1380s – partly inflamed by the rumour that Charles had abolished *all* taxes – and had to be put down by the sort of military force that created not only fear but also permanent, simmering anger.[6]

When Charles VI acceded to the throne at the age of eleven in 1380, Louis d'Anjou and the dukes of Berry, Bourbon, and Burgundy undertook to govern in his stead during his minority. By the terms of his father's celebrated *ordonnance* of 1374, which outlined the rules of succession, Charles should have come of age in less than three years, but he was effectively kept in tutelage until 1388.[7] For a few brief years, Charles VI ruled in his own right and with the aid of a bureaucratic corps bent on efficiency and reform.[8] But in August 1392 he suffered a violent psychological breakdown, which left him in a state of mental incapacity that would recur at intervals for the rest of his long and wretched life. The royal uncles stepped back in to the vacuum that followed, joined now by the

---

[4] Sumption, *Hundred Years War*, III: ch. 6.

[5] P. Wolff, *Commerces et marchands de Toulouse (vers 1350–vers 1450)* (Paris, 1954), 183.

[6] Sumption, *Hundred Years War*, III: 400–5, 413–18, 443–53, 456–8, 479–92; H. A. Miskimin, 'The Last Act of Charles V: the Background of the Revolts of 1382', *Speculum* 38 (1963): 433–42; L. Mirot, *Les insurrections urbaines au début du règne de Charles VI (1380–1383), leurs causes, leurs conséquences* (Paris, 1905). And see below, pp. 163–4.

[7] *Ord.*, VI: 26–30.

[8] J. B. Henneman, *Olivier de Clisson and Political Society in France under Charles V and Charles VI* (Philadelphia, 1996), 131–61; J. B. Henneman, 'Who were the Marmousets?', *Medieval Prosopography* 5 (1984): 19–63; F. Autrand, *Charles VI: la folie du roi* (Paris, 1986), chs. 10–11.

king's younger brother, Louis d'Orléans, and the young queen, Isabelle of Bavaria. Suspicious, avaricious, and eager for advantage, they created factions that would tear the kingdom to pieces over the next several decades. But even in the relatively placid 1390s, they used their position to pursue their own interests, parcelling out the kingdom and its finances amongst themselves for private projects in Italy, Flanders, and Languedoc.

The kingdom's trajectory over the last two decades of the century was, however, not immediately catastrophic. It is true that the loss of the hearth-tax cut to the heart of the royal finances; Édouard Perroy famously claimed that, 'with a stroke of the pen [Charles V] deprived his successor of the means of governing'.[9] But the establishment of the *taille* in 1384 somewhat ameliorated the situation, and with England similarly preoccupied with a royal minor of irascible temperament dominated by fractious uncles, the war could stumble on without greatly endangering Charles V's reconquests.[10] While the duke of Burgundy was more interested in building up his quasi-principate than in the long-term health of his nephew's kingdom, his strategic interests in peace with England helped preserve the status quo.[11] The papal schism, which began in 1378, and the Turks' inexorable push westward lent a melancholy air to the time. But the story of the last twenty years of the fourteenth century is more one of disheartening drift than of disaster. Had Henry Bolingbroke not seized the English throne in 1399, Charles VI's *folie* might have left a less bitter legacy.

The effects of all this were that even during Charles V's reign, the emphasis was on war, diplomacy, and finance, rather than internal administration. Even before Charles VI's minority and later incapacity, responsibility for the governance of the provinces had become increasingly devolved to great nobles, like Berry and Burgundy, who served as lieutenants with near regalian powers.[12] The brief reign of the reformist royal councillors known as the *marmousets* in 1388 did not significantly change the crown's extramural orientation as they were primarily focused on peace with England, a solution to the papal schism, and quixotic dreams of a new crusade.[13] In fact, while the *marmousets* are credited with revolutionary advances in state-building, few or none of their initiatives seem to have concerned public peace.[14] Indeed, Charles V's

---

[9] *The Hundred Years War*, trans. W. B. Wells (London, 1951), 174.

[10] For the *taille*, see Sumption, *Hundred Years War*, III: 535–7.

[11] R. Vaughan, *Philip the Bold: the Formation of the Burgundian State*, new edn (Woodbridge, 2002), 47–51.

[12] See Cazelles, *Société politique . . . sous Jean*, 498–503.

[13] J. Magee, 'Crusading at the Court of Charles VI, 1388–1396', *French History* 12 (1998): 367–83; Autrand, *Charles VI*, 192–4.

[14] See below, pp. 154–5.

famous strategy of avoiding battle and letting the English exhaust themselves on the countryside was militarily effective, but it essentially meant
that the crown abandoned the cause of public safety, at least as far as the
common people were concerned.[15] As a result, there was little effort to
use royal administrative and judicial powers to enforce internal order
through the limitation of seigneurial violence. This, however, did not
mean that the issue was dead. Far from it. Rather, the problem of
seigneurial war became subsumed into a larger conversation about the
meaning of licit force and sufficient authority in military contexts. As the
nascent movement in this direction had done in the decade at mid-
century, this provided opportunities for local powers to use both the
ideas and the infrastructure of royal authority in order to buttress their
own claims and to resolve (or further) their own disputes.

THE 'LAWS OF WAR': SOCIAL AND IDEOLOGICAL DEVELOPMENTS

The crown's lack of interest in using public order to buttress its own
power is apparent from the dearth of normative material of royal provenance generated in the period. Although Charles du Cange's essay on
guerre privée – the first scholarly treatment of the subject – identified the
reign of Charles V as the culmination of the royal programme against
seigneurial warfare that had begun with Louis IX's promulgation of
1258,[16] in truth, under Charles V the crown essentially abandoned that
project. Royal proctors continued to cite violation of this legislation as
one basis for prosecution, and the phrasing sometimes makes it sound as
though these measures had been issued under the current king, speaking
of *ordonationes nostrae regiae* throughout the reigns of both Charles V and
Charles VI.[17] But the phrase *ordonationes regiae* without the possessive
adjective also occurs with some frequency in both reigns.[18] Such language
may thus simply reflect formulaic tradition or an assumption that all royal
promulgations in force belonged to the current king, regardless of their
original author. In any case, as discussed in Chapter 4, there are no

---

[15] John Henneman argued that this was a policy that originated with Olivier de Clisson and the
marmousets ('Who were the Marmousets?', 28).

[16] C. du Fresne du Cange, 'Des guerres privées, et du droit de guerre par coutume', in *Glossarium
mediae et infimae latinitatis*, new edn, 10 vols. in 5 (Niort, 1883–7), X: 100–8.

[17] E.g. AN x2a 7, fols. 178v–179, 239v–243, 332v–333, 351–353r; AN x2a 8, fols. 110–114r, 126–
130r, 163–165r; AN x2a 9, fols. 35, 138v–140, 179v–181, 216v–219r, 240–242r, 277–9; J. Monicat,
Les grandes compagnies en Velay, 1358–1392, 2nd edn (Paris, 1928), no. 16; AN x2a 13, fols. 19v–21r,
21–23r, 23v–24r, 80, 145–6, 171v–178r, and 292–7.

[18] E.g. AN x2a 7, fols. 164v–167r, 170–2; AN x2a 8, fols. 47v–52r, 155v–156r; AN x2a 9, fols. 238–
240r; AN x2a 10, fols. 246v–247; AN x2a 11, fols. 179v–183r.

surviving *ordonnances* from the reign of either Charles V or Charles VI, and it seems that the French crown never issued any further legislation on the matter during the Middle Ages. Although du Cange cited a promulgation of 17 September 1367, issued in mandate to the *prévôt* of Paris, which he said outlawed war despite custom to the contrary, he (uncharacteristically) did not provide a citation for the document, and I have not found any trace of it in either the surviving records of the Châtelet or those of Amiens, whose municipal holdings were du Cange's main source of information.[19] It is probably telling that when in the 1380s the townspeople of Narbonne wished to call attention to the traditional royal prohibition on warfare, they had nothing more recent to cite than John II's promulgation of 1352.[20]

It may be that the *ordonnances* against warfare had been published with sufficient repetition by the 1360s not to need reissuance. They were certainly referred to in Parlement, as the evidence cited above demonstrates, and there are also indications, discussed more fully below, that the king's subjects and vassals were more conscious than ever of the constraints and opportunities that these promulgations offered. But there was no detectable effort to develop ideas about royal authority, justice, and public order through normative pronouncements as there had been in previous reigns. Indeed, the extant evidence from the latter half of the fourteenth century suggests that the main thrust of royal prescription was to grant exceptions to the prohibition against warfare in a narrow, political, ad hoc way. The smattering of prescriptive texts of royal provenance from Charles V includes an article from *ordonnances* issued following an Estates General held at Sens in July 1367, which forbade nobles and others from making war unless by common consent of the principals (in which case they were simply forbidden from harming royal subjects), and a confirmation of privileges granted the same year for the Dauphiné, which specified that unless a special prohibition had been made, there would be no investigation or punishment of nobles who made war against one another.[21]

As for Charles VI, an agreement in 1383 with the bishop of Viviers confirmed his right to wage war outside the realm without impediment from royal officers, and in 1394, Charles confirmed privileges made in 1182 to the town of Beauvais, including the right to undertake *vindicta* against the goods and inhabitants of a fortress where a wrong-doer was

---

[19] 'Des guerres privées', 107. [20] AM Narbonne FF 722, piece 2; 1352 edict at *Ord.*, II: 511–12.
[21] Sens: *Ord.*, V: 19–22, art. 10; Dauphiné: 'non fiat inquisitio & punitio contra Nobiles inter se guerram facientes, , nisi esset facta specialis inhibitio' (*Ord.*, V: 34–56, art. 14).

sheltering.[22] As this meagre list suggests, there simply seems to have been little interest in promulgating new *ordonnances* in the last decades of the fourteenth century. One possibly dissuasive factor was the confirmations of local privileges in exchange for taxation that Charles granted soon after his accession.[23] In at least one case, some of these privileges were those issued on the demand of the Leagues of 1314–16.[24] None of the privileges granted directly references subjects' wars, vaguely referring instead to the upholding of local custom, but such custom, as we have seen, often endorsed warfare as licit.[25] Given the restive nature of the king's subjects in this period, it might have seemed prudent just to avoid the issue altogether.

As the legislative tradition against seigneurial war fell into abeyance, however, a new genre of royal military regulations was nascent. In 1374, Charles V issued a major organizational *ordonnance* for the army, solidifying a prescriptive practice that would endure through the sixteenth century.[26] As Loïc Cazaux observes, a central element of these acts was their effort to define the proper relationship between soldiers and non-combatants.[27] The act's exposition notes two major problems in the army's function: first, that captains often fail to distribute wages, and second, that many of the soldiers are of *petit estat* and poorly equipped, on account of which they have robbed and pillaged in both the towns and the countryside.[28] In order to alleviate the situation, the *ordonnance* mandates a hierarchy of command in which the onus for the recruitment of proper soldiers and payment of their wages rests on the individual captains. The captains are to forbid their troops from doing any damage to the people of the realm while in the king's service and from taking anything without paying for it.

---

[22] *Ord.*, VII: 7–14, art. 19 (Viviers) and 621–5 (Beauvais), both cited by J.-P. Juchs, 'Vengeance et guerre seigneuriale au XIVe siècle (royaume de France–principauté de Liège)', Ph.D. thesis, 2 vols., Université Paris 1 Panthéon–Sorbonne, 2012, II: 90. Juchs also interprets *Ord.*, VII: 424–38 (1391, privileges of Vienne) as a recognition of limited rights to what he refers to as 'faide', but I only find references to judicial duel in this document. For judicial duel, see p. 63, n. 23, above.

[23] *Ord.*, VI: 552–4, 564–6; Mirot, *Les insurrections*, 31–60.

[24] *Ord.*, VI: 549–52 (for Normandy), noted in A. Artonne, *Le mouvement de 1314 et les chartes provinciales de 1315* (Paris, 1912), 151; Sumption, *Hundred Years War*, III: 405. For the Leagues, see Chapter 3, above. My thanks to Elizabeth A. R. Brown for help here.

[25] E.g. *Archives administratives de la ville de Reims*, ed. P. Varin, 3 vols. in 5 (Paris, 1839–48), III: 512–16.

[26] L. Cazaux, 'Réglementation militaire royale et usage de la force dans le royaume de France (XIVe–XVIe siècles)', *Inflexions. Civils et militaires: pouvoir dire* 13 (2010): 93–104; Ordonnance of 1374 in *De la France des premiers Valois à la fin du règne de Françis Ier*, vol. 1 of *Construire l'armée française. Textes fondateurs des institutions militaires*, ed. V. Bessey, P. Bonin, and A. Crépin, 3 vols. (Turnhout, 2006), no. 6 (= *Ord.*, V: 657–61).

[27] 'Réglementation militaire', 93.

[28] '[G]rant nombre de gens de petit estat. . .armez & montez moin souffisans, ilz ont pillé & robbé, tant ès bonnes villes comme au plat pays'.

Marginal individuals (*qui ne soient . . . gens nécessaires pour servir l'ost*) are to be sent home.

This regulation and those that followed it in the early fifteenth century were much less ideologically charged than the edicts against seigneurial war had been.[29] But this promulgation did articulate and codify standards for the use of licit force and the delegation of sufficient authority relevant to violence generally. It is insistent that such authority could only come from the crown. 'From now on', Charles stipulated, 'no one will be a captain of soldiers without our letter and authority, or [that] of our lieutenants or *chefs de guerre*, or other princes and lords of our realm . . .'[30] And the soldiers were to be rigorously subject to the authority of their captains, who must give them permission (*congé*) to leave the host and who were to be responsible for any misdeeds committed by their men.[31]

These contentions about the transmission of authority were already visible in John II's edict of 1361, which forbade all assemblies of soldiers or archers 'except by our permission or order (*congié ou ordennance*) or that of our officers'.[32] John's assertion was made necessary by the unbridled disorder that followed Poitiers and may have been meant as a corrective to the claim made by the Estates General of 1355 and 1357 – a claim that perhaps lay behind some of the violence of the Jacquerie of 1358 – that communities and even individuals could carry out military defence on their own authority.[33] Indeed, the crown remained concerned to counter this claim. In 1388, a royal act observed that there was substantial disregard for the prohibition that captains, soldiers, and archers not seize anything without paying for it or assemble in companies, except by royal permission or command (*s'il n'ont adveu & retenué de Nous, de noz Oncles, ou d'autres Capitaines*), and it therefore commanded that such malefactors be forcibly resisted (*ordonnons que par voïe de fait [&] de force d'armes, l'en y résiste*).[34] But although this language sounds borrowed from the promulgations of the revolutionary assemblies of 1355 and 1357, the document stipulates that such resistance be carried out under the authority of royal

---

[29] For the fifteenth-century military regulations, see the Conclusion, p. 182, below.

[30] 'Doresenavant nul sera Capitaine de Gens d'armes sans nostre Lettre & auctorité, ou de noz Lieuxtenans ou Chefz de guerre, ou d'autres Princes & Seigneurs de nostre Royaume . . .'

[31] 'Se les gens d'armes . . . font aucune pillerie, roberie, ou aucun donmaige durant leurs services, les Capitaines les contraindront à dresser & repparer iceulx donmaiges, ou iceulx Capitaines les païeront de leur mesmes.'

[32] '[A]ssamblés, convocations & chevauchiées de Gens d'armes ou Archiers soient de pié ou de cheval, se ce n'est par le congié ou ordennance de Nous ou de noz Officiers' (*Ord.*, III: 525–7).

[33] See Chapter 4, above.

[34] *Ord.*, VII: 186–9. Similarly in 1375 the communities of Languedoc were given *licentia* to resist pillagers, but it was specified that they were to do this 'una cum ordinariis locorum sub cujus districtu tales malefactores venire contingeret' (*HL*, X: 1512–22).

officers specifically commissioned by royal letters: *pour ces choses mettre à execution, avons mandé & commis par noz autres Lettres à chascun Bailli de nostre Royaume, & à autres Commissaires que Nous y avons ordonnez avecques eulx, que ces choses acomplissent par force d'armes & autrement.* In other words, resistance was only to be made by royal representatives; no provision was made for violent action by the broader political community of *bonnes gens* acting for the manifest common good. This injunction was repeated in 1396, again with specification that royal officers were to carry it out.[35]

In actual practice, however, this was difficult to manage, and the crown sometimes permitted individuals to pursue redress through private initiative under grants of royal authority, as will be further discussed below. This was a move born of necessity, certainly, but the shift coincided with and may also have owed something to newly developed ideas about the 'laws of war'. For the most part, this *jus guerrae* was not a codified collection of rules, but rather a generally shared, mostly unwritten set of standards for conduct in military contexts, some of which could be categorized under that capacious label 'chivalry'.[36] From the mid-fourteenth century, however, a few lawyers began to produce treatises dealing with the laws of war. One significant feature of these works was their interest in a category of hostilities called 'reprisals' or 'letters of marque', that is, violence or even small wars undertaken by private individuals in order to carry out justice 'arising from the neglect of those who govern and rule people', in the words of the law professor Giovanni da Legnano.[37]

Up to this point, such actions had been treated in learned law as illegal usurpations of public justice, even though, particularly in the multinational port cities of the Mediterranean, they were frequently granted.[38] The new treatises turned this on its head. As Giovanni explained it, although reprisals were once unnecessary because 'all were in subjection both in law and in fact' to a superior ruler (here meaning the emperor and the pope), 'now there are some who in fact recognize no

---

[35] '[Q]u'il y soit resisté par voïe de fait . . . & mandons aux Seneschaulx & Baillis de nostre Royaume, à qui autresfoiz en avons envoïé noz Lettres, que icelles exécutent diligemment' (*Ord.*, VIII: 61–6, art. 9).

[36] M. H. Keen, *The Laws of War in the Later Middle Ages* (London, 1965).

[37] Giovanni da Legnano, *Tractatus de bello, de represaliis, et de duello*, ch. 123, ed. and trans. T. E. Holland (Oxford, 1917), 307–8. Giovanni drew much from Bartolus of Saxoferrato's *Tractatus de repraesaliis* of 1354 (printed in *Interpretum iuris civilis coryphaei, in Institutiones et Authenticas, commentaria. eiusdem tractatus XXXIX . . .* (Basel, 1562), 593–605). See also Alberico de Rosate's discussion (explicitly drawing upon Bartolus) in *Commentarium de Statutis, libri quator*, I, quaest. 53, printed in *Tractatus de statutis diversorum autorum et Jc. in Europa praestantissimorum . . .* (Frankfurt, 1606), 31–5.

[38] J. Grabher O'Brien, 'In Defense of the Mystical Body: Giovanni de Legnano's Theory of Reprisals', *Roman Legal Tradition* 1 (2002): 25–55; R. de Mas-Latrie, 'Du droit de marque ou droit de représailles au moyen âge', *BEC* 27 (1866): 529–77; 29 (1868): 294–317.

superior, and by them justice is neglected'.[39] He defended reprisals as a type of self-defence undertaken to protect the 'mystical body' (*corpus mysticum*) of the community.[40] Giovanni and other writers on reprisals made it clear that these actions should be rare, used only in case of 'urgent necessity', and that they required formal approval by someone with sufficient authority: 'recourse must first be had to the ordinary remedies, and only if they fail, to this remedy; and this should be ascertained by a judge who is asked to declare reprisals'.[41]

The laws of reprisals came out of the specific historical context of constant warfare between many, small polities in Italy.[42] But these conditions increasingly obtained – de facto if not de jure – in France, and Honorat Bovet's *Arbre des batailles*, the most important French treatise on warfare of the late fourteenth century, closely adapted Giovanni's ideas on these matters.[43] The practice of reprisals was not directly applicable to the case of seigneurial war since reprisals concerned violence by the subjects of one sovereign against those of another. But the theory of warfare carried out by 'non-state actors' in order to protect rights not adequately guaranteed by official justice has obvious relevance for the problems of authority and legitimacy inherent to seigneurial warfare.[44] The key feature of reprisals that made them legal and acceptable, at least in some eyes, is that they required the permission of a superior authority. If any medieval jurist recommended adopting this arrangement to handle the

---

[39] *Tractatus de bello*, ch. 123, ed. Holland, 155–6, trans. 307–8; see also Bartolus, *Tractatus*, prologue, 593.

[40] 'Nam licitum est ob tutelam corporis sui arma movere … et nedum corporis sui privati et individualis, immo et mystici. Nam universitas est unum corpus, cuius partes sunt singuli de universitate … et sic universitati licitum est defendere partes sui corporis' (*Tractatus de bello*, ch. 123, ed. Holland, 155).

[41] *Tractatus de bello*, ch. 124, trans. Holland, 309; see also Bartolus, *Tractatus*, quaest. i ad ii and quaest. ii ad iii–iv; Keen, *Laws of War*, 220.

[42] J. von Elbe, 'The Evolution of the Concept of the Just War in International Law', *American Journal of International Law* 33 (1939): 670–1; see also T. E. Holland, Introduction to Giovanni, *Tractatus de bello*, xii–xiii. Bartolus himself says in the prologue to his treatise that reprisals have become frequent because, after the fall of the Roman empire, 'reges & principes, ac etiam ciuitates, maxime in Italia, saltem de facto in temporalibus dominum non agnoscerent, propter quod de iniustitiis ad superiorem non potest haberi regressus'.

[43] H. Bovet, *L'arbre des batailles*, pt. 4, chs. 79–84, ed. E. Nys (Brussels, 1883), 180–91; *The Tree of Battles of Honoré Bonet*, ed. and trans. G. W. Coopland (Liverpool and Cambridge, MA, 1949), 173–9. See N. A. R. Wright, 'The Tree of Battles of Honoré Bouvet and the Laws of War', in *War, Literature, and Politics in the Late Middle Ages*, ed. C. T. Allmand (Liverpool, 1976), 24–7; G. W. Coopland, 'The Tree of Battles and Some of its Sources', *Tijdschrift voor Rechtsgeschiedenis* 5 (1924): 173–207. Christine de Pisan's *Livre des faits d'armes et de chevalerie* follows Bovet closely on this. See pt. 4, chs. 5–6, *The Book of Deeds of Arms and of Chivalry*, ed. C. C. Willard, trans. S. Willard (University Park, PA, 1999), 192–6. Bovet is the current consensus on the spelling of that author's name. My thanks to Craig Taylor for sending me bibliography on Bovet.

[44] Keen, *Laws of War*, 226–38, mostly for the fifteenth century.

violent, intramural disputes of a kingdom's lords, I am unaware of it. But in practice, as is discussed below, the French crown's inability to resolve or to prevent these disputes seems to have led it to license some lords to wage war in order to pursue disputes for which royal justice and administration could not or would not provide a remedy.[45] Such ideas were far from an endorsement of anarchy; quite to the contrary. But they do suggest how much distance had been travelled from Philip the Fair's 'princes ... divinely deputized for ... the execution of justice'.[46]

A DARKENING MIRROR: SEIGNEURIAL WAR, 1365–1400

For a few years after Charles V's accession, the incidence of seigneurial warfare in the South dropped off considerably. Except for the war fought in Carcassonne in 1364, discussed in Chapter 4, the only large-scale seigneurial conflict that I have located for the second half of the 1360s is a dispute that occurred sometime before August 1366 in the Velay between Guigue de Roussillon and Amédée de la Voulte. In retaliation for Guigue's invasion of Jeanne de Belcastel's castle, Amédée forcibly occupied Guigue's castle, though he also tried to take a castle belonging to the abbey of Le Monastier-sur-Gazeille and did some pillaging in its lands.[47] In addition to this conflict, there was also a 'war or brawl' (*guerra seu rixa*) in the viscounty of Fezensaguet in the Gers between the co-lords of Montbrun, which allegedly involved a cavalcade and pillaging.[48]

The sudden peace is probably due to national and mercenary military movements, which exerted a benign effect on the South. Repression, including the summary execution of known freebooters, began to increase notably from 1364.[49] In combination with the papacy's efforts to send the companies either to the infidels via crusade or to the devil via excommunication, this may have provided a sufficient disincentive for

---

[45] See also ibid., 221–3 for such grants in other contexts.

[46] *Ord.*, I: 390; see also Chapter 2, above.

[47] G. Guigue, *Les tard-venus en Lyonnais, Forez & Beaujolais, 1356–69* (Lyon, 1886), no. 74. For the war fought by the *bourg* of Carcassonne, see above, p. 129.

[48] AD Tarn-et-Garonne 57, fol. 32r, excerpted and translated into French in 'Comptes et mandements des receveurs et maîtres d'hôtel du vicomte de Fézensaguet (1365–1372)', ed. E. Forestié, *Bulletin historique et philologique du Comité des travaux historiques et scientifiques* (1898): 240, where the foliation is given as 86.

[49] P. Contamine, 'Les compagnies d'aventure en France pendant la Guerre de Cent Ans', *Mélanges de l'École française de Rome. Moyen-âge, temps modernes* 87 (1975): 383; Sumption, *Hundred Years War*, II: 530–3.

some men to continue fighting.[50] But the real diversion was a better opportunity in Spain. In 1365, the Constable du Guesclin led the companies out of France ostensibly to crusade against the kingdom of Granada, but really to support Pedro of Aragon and Henry of Trastamara against Pedro the Cruel of Castile. When the Castillian Pedro called upon England for help, Edward III sent the Black Prince and Anglo-Gascon troops – including many freebooters – to his aid, a move that resulted in the destruction of the Trastamarian cause (and many of the mercenaries supporting it) at the Battle of Nájera in 1367.[51]

The respite was short-lived. It is not clear how much the re-establishment of freebooters in France in the 1370s contributed to seigneurial violence (a topic to which I will return below), especially since many mercenaries had remained in their old hunting grounds during the later 1360s.[52] But from around 1370, seigneurial war seems to have become prevalent once more. Some of this had to do with the reignition of the long-standing enmity between the houses of Foix and Armagnac.[53] The death of Pierre-Raymond II, count of Comminges, in late 1375 raised the conflict's stakes considerably as the county essentially lay between Foix and Armagnac lands and had been left to the count's young, unmarried daughter, Marguerite.[54] Pierre-Raymond's will specified that Marguerite was not to be married to either Armagnac or Foix, but the fruit proved too tempting. Despite the provisions of the will, Jean II, count of Armagnac, opened talks with Jeanne, Marguerite's mother and guardian, to arrange the girl's marriage to his younger son, a solution that would have preserved the integrity of Comminges as a separate county though drawing it tightly into Armagnac's orbit.[55]

[50] K. Fowler, *The Great Companies*, vol. I of *Medieval Mercenaries* (Oxford and Malden, MA, 2001), 118–21, 144–6; G. Butaud, 'L'excommunication des agresseurs des terres de l'église (Avignon, Comtat Venaissin) aux XIVe et XVe siècles', in *Prêcher la paix et discipliner la société: Italie, France, Angleterre (XIIIe–XVe siècles)*, ed. R. M. Dessì (Turnhout, 2005), 229–31, 235–42 for excommunication's dissuasive efficacy.

[51] Sumption, *Hundred Years War*, II: 525–30, 543–57; Fowler, *Great Companies*, chs. 6–7.

[52] Fowler, *Great Companies*, 301. A modern history of the freebooters after 1370 has not been written, though Fowler promises to do so. For mercenaries in Auvergne and Languedoc in this period, see *HL*, IX: 859, n. 5, 891, X: 1525–7, 1530–1, 1596–7, 1753, 1792–4, 1816–18, 1823–5. For mercenaries employed by Foix in this period, see the remission issued to the inhabitants of Lautrec and Lauragais, which speaks of 'pluseurs souldoyers & gens d'armes ennemis de nous & de nostre royaume, lesquelz souldoyers ... ont fait guerre ouverte, courses, grevancees, dommages ... telz comme gens d'armes de tele condicion pevent & ont acoustumé à faire' (*HL*, X: 1870–2).

[53] P. Tucoo-Chala, *Gaston Fébus et le vicomté de Béarn (1342–1391)* (Bordeaux, 1959), 302–7.

[54] Accounts of these events in C. Higounet, *Le comté de Comminges de ses origines à son annexion à la couronne*, 2 vols. (Toulouse and Paris, 1949), II: 541–57; Tucoo-Chala, *Gaston Fébus*, 307–16; *HL*, IX: 848–9, 854–8.

[55] BN Doat 199, fols. 183–91, 203–8, 251–6.

Discovering this, Gaston Fébus, the count of Foix, began a war against Comminges, hoping, as the Fuxian chronicler Miguel del Verms reports, to make Marguerite his wife and to unite his disjunctive Pyrenean lands.[56]

Royal mandates prohibiting attacks against the heiress and her mother and the stout defences of the Comminges nobles seem to have discouraged Foix, and an accord was finalized in 1377. But with Foix out of the way, Jeanne refused to fulfil the marriage contract with Armagnac. According to a remission later granted to Jean II, the dowager's refusal to go forward with her daughter's marriage – combined with a rumour that she secretly planned to marry herself to King Charles of Navarre and Marguerite to his son – drove the noblemen of Comminges to revolt against her. Abandoning her cause, the nobles asked Armagnac to force a marriage between Marguerite and Armagnac's eldest son and heir, the future Jean III.[57] Mother and daughter having been sequestered inside the fortress of Muret, Armagnac's troops broke in and seized Marguerite, immediately solemnizing and consummating the marriage.[58] Jeanne was taken prisoner and released only upon the death of Jean III, fourteen years later.[59]

Another long-standing subject of conflict – the role of customary law in the succession of the lands of the Lévis clan – also occasioned new convulsions in the early 1370s. The dispute that had broken out between the old marshal, Jean II, and his oldest son, Roger-Bernard, about the disposition of Mirepoix had been settled for some years.[60] But by 1371, possession of the town of Florensac and neighbouring lands were contested by Jourdain, count of Isle-Jourdain, who claimed them by right of the last holder's testament, and Thibault de Lévis-Montbrun and Bertrand de Lévis-Lautrec, who claimed them by virtue of the custom of Paris. The conflict involved a case in Parlement, as well as the forcible seizure of Florensac and the imprisonment and ransoming of

---

[56] Miguel del Verms, 'Chroniques des comtes de Foix en langue béarnaise', in *Choix de chroniques et mémoires sur l'histoire de France, avec notices biographiques*, ed. J.-A.-C. Buchon (Orleans, 1875), 586.

[57] Higounet, *Le comté de Comminges*, II: no. 9.

[58] Miguel del Verms, 'Chroniques', 587; Higounet, *Le comté de Comminges*, II: no. 9. A different version of events is given in a remission for one of Armagnac's valets, in which the marriage seems to have taken place later (*HL*, x: 1884–5). The marriage contract between Marguerite and Jean III was only drawn up in 1385, about a year after Jean II's death (Higounet, *Le comté de Comminges*, II: 559). See *HL*, IX: 858 regarding the timing of the marriage.

[59] Higounet, *Le comté de Comminges*, II: 564–6. For Jeanne's fate, see *Documents relatifs à la chute de la maison d'Armagnac-Fézensaguet et à la mort du comte de Pardiac*, ed. P. Durrieu (Paris, 1883), 28, n. 1; AN X2a 13, fols. 158, 171.

[60] See above, pp. 99, 125–6.

its inhabitants by the bastard of l'Isle-Jourdain, though the documents are vague about the amount of actual violence involved.[61]

Three years later, this same Thibault suffered Charles d'Espagne's forcible entry into his lands, and Charles's abduction of or elopement with Thibault's daughter, a woman by the name of Cécile de Lévis.[62] Charles returned Thibault's holdings once an accord had been negotiated, but the marriage with Cécile would give rise to further disputes over customs and practices of inheritance in the next generation, when in 1388, their son, Thibault d'Espagne, tried to claim the inheritance left to him by his maternal grandfather.[63] That conflict seems to have been essentially a non-violent, legal problem, but in 1389, Thibault de Lévis-Mirepoix, son of the old marshal Jean II, attacked his brother Roger-Bernard, invading and occupying Mirepoix and taking food and animals because, as he complained, his brother had refused to give him food (*nolebat eidem exponenti fratri suo alimenta sua prestare sive ministrare*), which he was required to do according to the terms of their father's will (*vigore legatorem (sic) dicto exponenti per defunctum Johannem de Levis*).[64]

Elsewhere, Humbert, lord of Villars and Annonay, attacked the castle of Ay, possession of which he disputed with the lord of Vinay at some point before September 1375. This conflict had to do with the recognition of seigneurial rights over the castle during succession and probably relates back to the troubled status of Annonay's holdings, which were passed on to Humbert when he married Aimar de Roussillon's daughter.[65] Feudal discipline was also at issue in 1376, when Jean, count of Astarac, made war (*fist guerre*) against the town of Mirande, which had rebelled against his authority, refusing to provide fiscal or military aid with which to combat mercenary companies.[66] In addition to making war, the count also temporarily took away the town's judicial privileges. Possibly around the same time, the count's cousin, Bertrand d'Astarac, lord of Salveterre and Gangagnez, waged a *guerre* against his subjects in the towns of Simorre and Gimont, who had violently seized a castle from his late parents and had refused to pay the fine adjudicated against them by the lieutenant of

---

[61] P.-C. Timbal, *Un conflit d'annexion au moyen âge: l'application de la coutume de Paris au pays d'Albigeois* (Toulouse and Paris, 1949), 149–51; *HL*, x: 1454–7; AN x2a 8, fols. 234–235r, 287, 306, 322v–323r, 358v; AN x2a 9, fols. 62v–63r, 63r; AN x2a 10, fols. 7r, 21r, 26v. There are also a number of related entries in the civil registers. The brothers were co-lords of Florensac (AN x1a 25, fol. 245r).

[62] 'Vis publica' was said to have been committed, but its extent is unclear (*HL*, x: 1502–3). Cécile and Charles's marriage may have been consensual, and it is possible she was already pregnant (see *HL*, x: 1747–9 for the age of her son, Thibault d'Espagne, in 1388).

[63] *HL*, x: 1747–9.   [64] *HL*, x: 1769–70.

[65] *Titres de la maison ducale de Bourbon*, ed. J.-L.-A. Huillard-Bréholles and L. de la Marche, 2 vols. (Paris, 1867–74), I: no. 3320; AN P 1402(1), no. 1231. For Aimar's troubles, see Chapter 4, above.

[66] *HL*, x: 1816–18; and see *Ord.*, VI: 178 and AN JJ 158, no. 374 (corrected to 353), fols. 206v–208r.

Languedoc.[67] Also in 1376, an inheritance dispute outside Toulouse gave rise to *chevauchées* and 'the violence and terror of arms' when Nicolas de Belfort, lord of Limeuil, seized Bourret and other holdings claimed by the late Bertrand de Terride's widow and minor children.[68] And at some point prior to May 1380, the cardinal of Marmoutier sent troops to assault a number of southern castles and fortresses pertaining to the priory of Langogne.[69]

In 1381 the political and military landscape of Languedoc changed profoundly due to the outbreak of a regional rebellion, known as the Tuchinat.[70] This revolt began as a protest against the appointment of Jean, duke of Berry, as lieutenant of Languedoc, to the exclusion of Gaston Fébus, count of Foix, but as Vincent Challet has shown, it was also an associative movement of self-defence against the freebooters like the Jacquerie, which preceded it.[71] In the city of Narbonne, the Tuchinat was also intertwined with a war (*guerra*) that broke out between Aimery VII, viscount of Narbonne, and the city's consuls and inhabitants.[72] The viscount and the consuls had come down on opposite sides regarding the lieutenancy of Languedoc, but they also disputed many other issues, including the interplay of royal and seigneurial justice in the town, and had brought some of these concerns before Parlement.[73] In October 1381, the consuls attacked the royal castle at Saint-Pierre-des-Clars, and by November, they had begun paying troops recruited from among the Tuchins (*homes d'armas qu s'apelavan tochis*).[74] The viscount soon retaliated, receiving licence from the duke of Berry to wage war against the consuls and townsmen, and on

---

[67] *HL*, x: 1818–20. This took place at some point between 1364, when the castle was seized, and 1391, when the remission documenting the war was issued.

[68] *HL*, x: 1585–7; AN JJ 112, no. 249, fols. 136v–137r.   [69] AN JJ 117, no. 26, fol. 18r.

[70] For what follows, see V. Challet '"Mundare et auferre malas erbas": la révolte des Tuchins en Languedoc (1381–1384)', 4 vols., Ph.D. thesis, Université de Paris–I, 2002; 'La révolte des Tuchins: Banditisme social ou sociabilité villageoise?' *Médiévales* 34 (1998): 101–12; P. Charbonnier, 'Qui furent les Tuchins?', in *Violence et contestation au moyen âge: Actes du 114e Congrès national des sociétés savantes (Paris, 1989)*, (Paris, 1990), 235–47; F. Lehoux, *Jean de France, duc de Berri: sa vie. Son action politique (1340–1416)*, 4 vols. (Paris, 1966–8), II: 47–101; Delachenal, *Histoire de Charles V*, v: 285–340.

[71] See above, pp. 145–7.

[72] See Challet, '"Mundare"', 300–1, 452–6; A. Blanc, Introduction to Jacme Olivier, *Le livre de comptes de Jacme Olivier, marchand narbonnais du XIVe siècle*, ed. A. Blanc (Paris, 1899), lxxxvi–xcix for an account of this war and sources for it.

[73] For the consuls' grievances, see AM Narbonne FF 722, 1462, 1468; *Jacme Olivier*, ed. Blanc, no. 110 (=AM Narbonne FF 1464), 111, 112. For the viscount's: BN Doat 49, fols. 547–66; *Jacme Olivier*, ed. Blanc, no. 116.

[74] *Jacme Olivier*, ed. Blanc, nos. 113, 120; Quote at no. 113. *HL*, IX: 906–8 gives an extensive account of damages inflicted by the men of Narbonne, including the burning of Bougnea and attacks on the castles of Marcorignan, Montredon, and Portel.

1 December, he sent them a letter of formal challenge (*défi*).[75] As the consuls alleged, from 2 December 1381 to the next September, the viscount and his troops publicly and openly made war upon them (*guerram publice et apperte faciendo*), destroying the dam that was vital to the town's commerce and supply lines and forbidding the revictualling of the town on pain of death, as well as raping women, killing people, and confiscating livestock.[76] Although the enemies came to a truce at the end of September 1382, by November the war had resumed.[77] Berry withdrew his support from the viscount in June 1383 and attempted to negotiate an accord the following May, but hostilities continued at least until July 1384.[78]

Similar conflicts related to Berry's lieutenancy and the Tuchinat occurred between Languedocian communities and the local nobility at Béziers, Carcassonne, and Nîmes, though in these cases it is very difficult to differentiate between warfare and rebellion, a problem discussed further below.[79] The civil unrest also seems to have caused or affected a struggle between the lord of 'Aiguesvives' and Nicolas de Lettres, a knight who was also the royal master of water and forests in Carcassonne, over the castle of Campendu, a conflict that broke out into *guerre mortelle* in 1382.[80] Elsewhere another struggle of regional importance – that of French ambitions in Provence – contributed to the *guerre ouverte* that Beaucaire was given licence to wage against its twin-city Tarascon in 1384.[81] Although the documentation for this war does not mention it, the conflict may have been connected to the adventures of Louis d'Anjou and Pope Clement VII in Italy, as Provence was a Neapolitan holding, and to the related affairs of Raymond, viscount of Turenne, who would spend the later 1380s and

---

[75] *Jacme Olivier*, ed. Blanc, no. 116.   [76] AM Narbonne FF 722.

[77] Blanc, Introduction to *Jacme Olivier*, xcii, and *Jacme Olivier*, ed. Blanc, nos. 114, 116.

[78] Blanc, Introduction to *Jacme Olivier*, xcvi–xcix, and *Jacme Olivier*, ed. Blanc, nos. 117, 118 (= BN Doat 54, fols. 110–13). See AM Narbonne AA 111, fols. 22–31, excerpted in *Inventaire des archives communales antérieures à 1790: Ville de Narbonne: Série AA*, ed. G. Mouynès (Narbonne, 1877), 153–4; AM Narbonne FF 1465.

[79] Lehoux, *Jean de France*, II: 47–8. For Nimes, see L. Ménard, *Histoire civile, ecclésiastique, et littéraire de la ville de Nismes avec des notes et les preuves*, 7 vols. (Paris, 1750–8), III: no. 15.

[80] *HL*, x: 1744–7. The lord of Aiguesvives's valet is said to have participated in 'la commocion des communes de nostre pais de Lenguedoc'.

[81] '[D]onnons . . . aux habitans de Beaucaire . . . licence, pouvoir & mandement special resister, faire guerre, prendre, tuer & apprisonner les desssus dits Provençaux' (*HL*, x: 1703–5). Provence was then the object of a struggle between Louis II, *soi-disant* king of Naples, and Jeanne of Naples's protégé, Charles de la Paix. In 1385, France saw an opportunity to seize the territory, and the seneschal of Beaucaire was sent to conquer Provençal fortresses. See A. Venturini, 'La guerre de l'Union d'Aix (1383–1388)', in *1388, la dédition de Nice à la Savoie: Actes du colloque international de Nice (septembre 1988)*, ed. R. Cleyet-Michaud et al. (Paris, 1990), 35–141; *Choix de pièces inédites relatives au règne de Charles VI*, ed. L. Douët-d'Arcq, 2 vols. (Paris, 1863–4), I: nos. 32–3.

1390s waging war first against Clement and then against the kingdom of Sicily on account of Provençal lands that had belonged to his uncle, Pope Gregory XI.[82]

In western Languedoc there were two incidents in 1389 and 1390 that involved the forcible seizure of castles, though neither seems to have involved sufficient violence to be termed a war.[83] There was an alleged war (*guerre*) fought by the bastard of Comminges and Roger de Comminges, lord of Roquefort, against Jean and Géraud de Lantar in the mid-1390s, but the use of the word *guerra* here seems to connote something more like a feud as the conflict arose from interpersonal antipathies, and the violence consisted solely of the murder of three Lantar men.[84] Around the same time, Essieu or Ayssio de Montesquieu made war (*guerre*) against the lord of Autun and the town of Mirande.[85] These conflicts took place under cover of a larger war being waged between the lord of Barbasan and the count of Pardiac, an Armagnac cadet whose holdings also encompassed the viscounty of Fezensaguet in the Gers. Menaud de Barbasan had raised some gibbets in contravention of his lord Pardiac's wishes and he denied that he owed the latter faith and homage, thus setting in motion a war (*guerra*), which, as Pardiac saw it, was a perfectly justified instance of seigneurial correction to vassalic truculence.[86] The seneschal of Toulouse and the lieutenant of Languedoc intervened, but Pardiac refused to accept the terms offered. Both parties were then physically arrested and judged by the lieutenant, whence they appealed to the Parlement in Paris, circumstances which seem to have interrupted the war indefinitely.

However, in 1400, Pardiac was once more engaged in warfare, this time against his own lord, the count of Armagnac. The circumstances of this war grew out of the war fought over Marguerite de Comminges in the 1370s. Following the death of her husband, Count Jean III of Armagnac,

---

[82] For Louis d'Anjou and Clement VII in Italy: Lehoux, *Jean de France*, II: 104–5; Sumption, *Hundred Years War*, III: 346–7, 393–4, 438–41. For Raimond de Turenne: R. Veydarier, '*Una guerra de layrons*: l'occupation de la Provence par les compagnies de Raymonde Turenne (1393–1399)', in *Guerre et violence*, vol. 1 of *La guerre, la violence, et les gens au moyen âge Actes. du 119e Congrès national des sociétés historiques et scientifiques, (Amiens, octobre 1994)*, ed. P. Contamine and O. Guyotjeannin (Paris, 1996), 169–83; *HL*, IX: 955–7, 966, 970, 983–4.

[83] Raimonnet de Péreilles, lord of Caux, for having tried to retake the castle of Saint-Michel-de-Lanes from Pierremont Cur (AN JJ 137, no. 83, p. 83) and Gailhard de la Motte against Perrot de Rives regarding the fortress of Autry (AN x2a 13, fols. 28v–30r).

[84] *Documents . . . Armagnac-Fezensaguet*, ed. Durrieu, nos. 3, 7. The *arrêts* related to the case (AN x2a 15, fols. 115v–116v, 188–189r) speak of the events as isolated murders.

[85] AN JJ 147, n. 56, fol. 28v; AN x2a 12, fols. 407v, 417v; AN x2a 13, fols. 255v–256r, 318; AN JJ 159, no. 294, fols. 171–172r.

[86] The sources for this war include *Documents . . . Armagnac-Fezensaguet*, ed. Durrieu, nos. 3–7; AN x2a 13, fols. 98v, 99, 114v–115, 116; AN x1a 43, fol. 12r. See also the account in *HL*, IX: 967–8.

the heiress married Pardiac's son, Jean d'Armagnac, who was her junior by at least a decade.[87] Marguerite and Jean had different expectations about the marriage. Jean was under the impression that the marriage made him count of Comminges in fact as well as in name. Marguerite seems to have thought that this was a technicality. In September 1400, the bishop of Toulouse negotiated an accord between the couple, but by October the count of Armagnac, Marguerite's former brother-in-law and close ally, had already received assurances that certain mercenary companies were available to succour the countess.[88] Although the seneschal of Toulouse forbade the war in January, Charles VI granted Armagnac the right to defend himself against Pardiac in March.[89] Throughout the winter and spring of 1401, Pardiac and Armagnac's troops ravaged each other's lands, committing 'all the usual crimes of warfare', though the banality of the violence seems to have little comforted the peasants who suffered it.[90] In May, Armagnac managed to capture both Pardiac and his son. According to one story, after interrogating them he cast them into a dungeon, where they were left to die of starvation.[91] Their lands Armagnac claimed for himself.[92]

All told, the last thirty-five years of the fourteenth century saw somewhere between fifteen and twenty wars take place in Languedoc and the Auvergne, an average of about one war every two years. (See Figure 4.) This is more or less in line with the average rate of seigneurial war across the fourteenth century and represents a significant decrease from the rate of warfare in the decade between 1356 and 1365, when more than a dozen wars took place. Partly, the change reflects developments in the overall military picture, particularly regarding the mercenaries. During the dark decade after Poitiers, freebooters seem to have been eager to hire themselves out to fight in seigneurial wars, their availability clearly contributing to a rise in the number of such wars, but from about 1370 onward mercenary participation in these wars was less marked.[93]

---

[87] See *Documents . . . Armagnac-Fezensaguet*, ed. Durrieu, nos. 1, 2.   [88] Ibid., nos. 9, 10.

[89] Ibid., nos. 11, 12; see also AD Tarn-et-Garonne A 39.

[90] *Documents . . . Armagnac-Fezensaguet*, ed. Durrieu, no. 13; accounts of Jean d'Armagnac's actions given by Gersois peasants in AD Tarn-et-Garonne A 38. Pardiac was also accused of using magic against the count (*Documents . . . Armagnac-Fezensaguet*, ed. Durrieu, nos. 14–15). AN x2a 12, fol. 312 also relates to this war (cited in Juchs, 'Vengeance et guerre', I: 212).

[91] The original transcript of the interrogation is at AD Tarn-et-Garonne A 38, and see Higounet, *Le comté de Comminges*, II: 571, n. 93.

[92] *Documents . . . Armagnac-Fezensaguet*, ed. Durrieu, nos. 16–19; AD Tarn-et-Garonne A 39.

[93] Mercenary or 'English' involvement is attested for the seizure of Bourret by Nicolas de Belfort's men (*HL*, x: 1585–7; AN JJ 112, no. 249, fols. 136v–137r); for the Pardiac/Barbasan war (*Documents . . . Fezensaguet-Armagnac*, ed. Durrieu, nos. 3, 4); and for the Pardiac/Comminges/Armagnac war (ibid., no. 11).

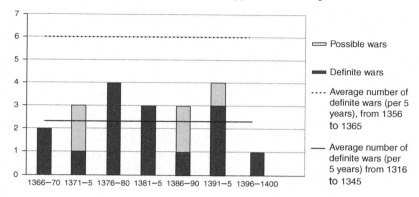

Figure 4   Seigneurial wars, 1366–1400

The absence of mercenaries could possibly be explained if they had begun to seem commonplace and were therefore mentioned less, but it also seems that tactics had changed. Whereas in the 1350s and 1360s freebooting groups went on campaigns whence they could be easily co-opted into local conflicts, from the 1370s their movements seem to have followed one of two patterns. The first was co-optation either by the English cause or into very large campaigns, including the Foix–Armagnac conflict but also extramural wars that took them to Spain or Italy.[94] Unlike mid-century conditions, there were plenty of large-scale conflicts, conceivably offering greater opportunities for booty, with which a man-at-arms could occupy himself. Naturally this circumstance was equally attractive to noblemen, especially penurious ones, who thus would have been less available to fight wars on their own account. The second pattern was for companies to take and hold castles from which they exacted protection money in a quasi-fiscal manner over a long period of time. It seems possible that these 'borrowed lordships', as Nicholas Wright calls them,[95] made their holders into local powers in their own right, whose interests in seigneurial power struggles had less to do with short-term profit than with the stability of their own regimes.

Yet, although factors related to the mercenaries probably had some ameliorative effect, it is possible that the ostensible diminution in seigneurial warfare during the later fourteenth century is more apparent than real. First of all, it is simply harder to identify wars in this period than

---

[94] Sumption, *Hundred Years War*, III: 163–70, 207–11, 243–9, etc.
[95] N. Wright, *Knights and Peasants: The Hundred Years War in the French Countryside* (Woodbridge, 1998), 51. For the southern garrisons, see Sumption, *Hundred Years War*, III: 679–701, 721–2.

previously because their contours are much vaguer than the conflicts of earlier decades. Prior to the 1370s, seigneurial wars were fairly discrete phenomena. They involved a few principal parties supported by groups of allies and clients; they endured a few months to a year at most; and they generally resulted in a reasonably durable settlement that seems to have prevented the outbreak of further violence. Obviously this pattern never held for the Foix–Armagnac war, which essentially lay outside royal judicial purview, but it also began to break down for the conflicts of lesser houses from the last third of the century. From 1370 on, we see many disputes that involve the extended kin-groups of the greatest southern families, that go on for years or decades, often reigniting after a period of dormancy, and that seem irresolvable by either judicial arbitration or mutual compromise. The on-going struggles of the Lévis–Mirepoix–Astarac clan and the interconnected wars of the Armagnac–Comminges houses and related families underline this change most clearly, but even the struggles over the holdings pertaining to the lordship of Annonay or the viscounty of Murat, which continued to generate charges of violence and attempts at settlement well into the fifteenth century, show how seigneurial wars had become less punctual outbursts of violence than quasi-permanent states of enmity.

These bigger, though less frequent wars, could mask a number of lesser conflicts related to or wholly independent of the main dispute, and there are hints that we see fewer wars because smaller powers pursued their own under the cover of these great wars. Certainly, the Tuchinat provided the opportunity, and even the troops, for the pursuit of conflict, as the war in Narbonne illustrates. And the conflicts associated with the Pardiac/Barbasan war show that great lords' followers sometimes saw fit to pursue their own struggles under the cloak of their patron's violence. Indeed, in some cases, the participants welcomed the confusion. For example, during the struggle over the inheritance of Bertrand de Terride, which led to *discursus et cavalgatas* in 1376, its participants shouted 'Guienne, St George!' and also claimed that their actions actually pertained to the war between Foix and Armagnac (who were at that point fighting over Comminges).[96]

But the diminution in the number of visible seigneurial wars is certainly also due to changes in royal enforcement capabilities and interests. It is probably the case that we have sources for fewer wars during this period because fewer wars were being prosecuted. Partly this was because the diplomatic and military situation made getting to court more difficult. As a

---

[96] '[S]ub pretestis (sic) tamen & ficto colore guerre tunc vigentis inter carissimos consanguineos nostros comitem Fuxi ex una parte & comitem Armaniaci [ac comitissam] Convenarum ex altera' (*HL*, x: 1585–7).

number of noblemen from Armagnac argued in the 1390s, they could not be expected to show up for court because 'those who live on the frontiers of the realm' were faced with 'danger to their persons on account of the power of evildoers and enemies of the realm ravaging the country and the wars raging both in this land and in Aragon'.[97]

It is also true, however, that later fourteenth-century officials were primarily focused on military rather than judicial or administrative matters. John II's practice of employing seneschals with military experience – rather than the lawyers habitually appointed by his predecessors – was continued and expanded under his son and grandson,[98] meaning that these men were more focused on maintaining the frontiers and dealing with the mercenaries than on persuading local elites to prefer the *voie de justice* to the *voie de fait*. The seneschal of Beaucaire, for example, spent 1385 conquering castles in Provence, an occupation that could hardly have left him much time for domestic disputes.[99] The count of Pardiac summed up the situation in 1395 when he said that he did not think that war was illegal, 'but even if it was, nobody ever did anything about it' (*s'il n'est loisible, toutesfois on en a ainsi usé au pais sans en estre reprins*).[100]

THE MEMORY OF JUSTICE

If it was true that 'no one ever did anything about it', it was not the case that no one ever wanted anyone to do anything about it. It is obvious that for most of the later fourteenth century royal government was failing to live up to the example of previous decades and the expectations of its subjects. Its twin obligations to execute justice and to provide protection went frequently unfulfilled. As Pardiac's comment suggests, cases were often not pursued. Remissions for seigneurial war from this period frequently speak only of some nervousness about the prospects of future prosecution,[101] and a striking number of such pardons, particularly in the 1390s, were granted for crimes committed years or even decades earlier, suggesting that the recipients had lived unmolested, without even fear of pursuit, for quite some time.[102] While there is less obvious evidence of

---

[97] '[I]psi qui in confinibus seu fronteriis regni nostri morabantur propter periculum personarum suarum attenta potencia suorum malivolorum seu exosorum ac regni nostri inimicorum patriam more predonio discurrencium necnon guerris tam in eadem patria quam in partibus Aragonie vigentibus in eadem nostra curia personaliter comparere nequibant' (AN x2a 13, fol. 171).

[98] Sumption, *Hundred Years War*, II: 385.   [99] See n. 81, above.

[100] *Documents . . . Armagnac-Fezensaguet*, ed. Durrieu, no. 3.

[101] *HL*, x: 1502–3, 1744–7, 1816–18, 1818–20; Higounet, *Le comté de Comminges*, II: no. 9; AN JJ 117, no. 26, fol. 18r.

[102] E.g. 15, 26, 12, 10, and 24 years ago: *HL*, x: 1816–18, 1818–20, 1823–5, 1849–51, 1876–8.

official corruption during this period than in the decade immediately preceding it, there are indications that royal representatives were casually accustomed to use their offices for their personal purposes. The seneschal of Carcassonne, for example, used his office to procure a remission in 1374 for his nephew, Charles d'Espagne, and the viguier of Toulouse and his lieutenant were both implicated in the conflict between Thibault and Bernard de Lévis and the count of Isle-Jourdain over Florensac.[103] And although communal assemblies continued to grant taxes 'so that [the crown] ... will hold the frontiers with armed men in such a way that it might resist thieves and other armed men ... so that the communities can be secure',[104] the duke of Berry's lackadaisical lieutenancy and military distractions elsewhere meant that insecurity was often just as great as it had been under John II.

Inevitably, this led to violence as individuals and communities took it upon themselves to defend themselves and their rights (as they perceived them). This was the context that led many Tuchins to take up arms against the mercenaries, as well as against local lords and the representatives of the duke of Berry.[105] It also seems to have meant that there was more occasion than usual for lords to go to war against their vassals. Of the fifteen definite wars from this period, six took place as a result of disputes over what might be considered 'feudal discipline',[106] that is, conflicts over submission to justice, the duty to do faith and homage, and fiscal obligations. These sorts of disputes had taken place in earlier periods, but they had not done so with this preponderance. It seems that the weakening of coercive royal justice, which had served to arbitrate many of these disputes in the past, played some part in their apparent increase during these decades. As Bernard d'Astarac explained in 1391, he had successfully won a court case before the lieutenant of Languedoc (then Louis d'Anjou) against the towns of Simorre and Gimont for their rebellion against his parents, but he had had no success in having the sentence carried out and thus, 'seeing that

---

[103] For the seneschal of Carcassonne, see *HL*, x: 1502–3. For the viguier of Toulouse see *HL*, x: 1454–7 and n. 58, above.

[104] '[U]t nos, mediante dicta offra, dictas fronterias garnitas gentium armatarum tenebimus & tenere promittimus, taliter quod latrunculis seu aliis hominibus armatis, dictas senescallias seu aliquam earum invadere cupientibus, si qui essent, resistemus & per easdem gentes armadas resistere faciemus, ut dicte communitates sub securitate possint remanere' (*HL*, x: 1512–22, art. 10 from a 1375 grant following the assemblies of the three seneschalsies).

[105] Challet, '"Mundare"'; Challet, 'La révolte'.

[106] Humbert, lord of Villars and Annonay vs. the lord of Vinay (1375); Jean, count of Astarac vs. town of Mirande (1376); Aimery VII, viscount of Narbonne vs. inhabitants of Narbonne (1381–4); Bertrand d'Astarac, lord of Salveterre and Gangagnez vs. Gimont and Simorre (between 1364 and 1391); Gérard de Armagnac, count of Pardiac and viscount of Fezensaguet vs. Menaud de Barbasan (1394); Viscount of Fezensaguet and Jean d'Armagnac vs. Bernard VII, count of Armagnac and Marguerite, countess of Comminges (1400–1).

satisfaction could not be had by justice' (*voyant que satisfacion n'en povoit avoir par justice*), he made war against them.[107]

The added impetus to address one's quarrels through self-help did not necessarily mean that seigneurial war had become less illicit, however. In the 1390s, the count of Pardiac claimed that when he complained of Barbasan's misdeeds, royal officers told him that they did not know whether the truce with England still held and that he could provide his own remedy (*ilz ne savoient se les treves estoient faillies entre les deux Roys, et que le conte se pourveust d'autre remede*), but the argument does not seem to have swayed the court, which also ruled against this argument in a contemporaneous case.[108] In any case, the prosecution's habitual assertion that war had been *per ordinationes nostras Regias . . . notorie prohibite* (notoriously prohibited by our royal edicts) was employed with frequency throughout these decades, appearing at least thirty times in thirty-five years.[109]

The claim to wage war by custom also continued to be rejected, often in strong terms. For example, the count of Pardiac and Menaud de Barbasan, who both claimed that Gascon nobles were allowed to wage war on their own authority,[110] were sharply rebuked by the court. In Barbasan's case, the *arrêt*'s disposition explicitly stated that 'the propositions asserted above to proceed by force or war without our permission . . . were condemnable and inadmissible, and were to be rejected or deleted from Menaud's articles', and the decision regarding Pardiac was similarly worded, two rare examples of the court communicating the rationale on which it based its decision.[111] Similarly, in a case relating to a war in Picardy, the court pronounced the claim that war was licit by custom an

---

[107] '[A]près certaine complainte . . . iceulz communes & populaires furent condempnez . . . laquelle amende lesdiz populaires ne vouldrent puis paier . . . Et pour ce ledit exposant . . . voyant que satisfacion n'en povoit avoir par justice . . . commença guerre contre les diz populaires & communs de Gimont & de Simorra' (*HL*, x: 1818–20). It is worth noting that Bernard characterized these actions as 'vengence' (see pp. 139–40, above).

[108] *Documents . . . Armagnac-Fezensaguet*, ed. Durrieu, no. 3. The other case, between Robert Daine and Jean Jeumont, is discussed by L. de Carbonnières, 'Le pouvoir royal face aux mécanismes de la guerre privée à la fin du moyen âge. L'exemple du Parlement de Paris', *Droits. Revue française de théorie, de philosophie et de culture juridiques* 46 (2007): 14–15.

[109] In addition to citations at nn. 17 and 18 above, see AN x2a 8, fols. 191v–193; AN x2a 9, fols. 2v–3r; AN x2a 13, fols. 267v–269r; *Documents . . . Armagnac-Fezensaguet*, ed. Durrieu, no. 3.

[110] '[I]nter nobiles patrie Vasconie & Ducatus Acquitanie . . . fuerat & erat licitum & permissum tam per privilegia quam ex consuetudine & observancia notoriis & a tempore de cuius contrario memoria non extitabat observatis guerram inire seu facere ac per viam guerre sive facti precedere nostra vel alterius cuiuscumque superioris licencia super hoc non obtenta' (AN x2a 13, fol. 116; see also 114v–115; These documents are based on the *procès-verbal* published in *Documents . . . Armagnac-Fezensaguet*, ed. Durrieu, no. 3).

[111] 'Prefata curia nostra proposita superius declarata de procedendo via facti sive guerre absque nostra licencia . . . dampnabilia seu non admissibilia et ab eisdem articulis ipsius Menaldi reicienda seu

'unjust abuse and corruption', language that may well have been chosen in conscious imitation of the custom/corruption and use/abuse equivalences made in late Capetian ordinances against warfare.[112] Both of these rulings were collected by the *parlementaire* Jean le Coq in his *quaestiones*, a compilation of notable decisions, presumably because he thought them to be of relevance for other cases.[113]

As this suggests, Parlement may have begun to employ some case law or at least to consider precedent in a more systematic fashion during this period. Indeed, in 1387 the crown's proctor not only argued that war was illegal on account of the *ordonnances* against it, but also reminded the court of a previous case (*un example*) that took place under Charles V, when a suit against the lord of 'Virines' had led the king to reiterate that 'no one of whatever status or region should proceed by force or war under penalty of losing body and goods'.[114] At least some *gens de justice* maintained the position that war was legislatively prohibited and perhaps even attempted to strengthen that position through reference to past judgments.

... *ALA HOBEDIENSA DEL REY DE FRANSSA*: LEGITIMACY AND LICENCE

Yet despite these developments, there still seems to have been no sense that every case against seigneurial war-makers involved the transgression of royal *ordonnances*; of the fifteen definite southern wars during these decades, only three of them have an associated document that mentions the *ordonnances*.[115] Indeed, at least as regards the South, the documents suggest a growing realization that it was now more than ever impossible to reserve the exercise of violence to the crown alone. Nevertheless, through the granting of licence for self-defence or even for punitive reprisals, the crown maintained its claim to authority over violence, a claim that effectively preserved its superior position and one that subjects were

---

delenda per arrestum pronunciavit & declaravit, ac pronunciat & declarat' (AN x2a 13, fols. 114v–115). For Pardiac, see AN x2a 13, fol. 116. On rationales for judgments, see T. Sauvel, 'Histoire du jugement motivé', *Revue du droit public et de la science politique* 51 (1955): 5–53.

[112] '[P]refata curia nostra dictam consuetudinem de procedendo via facti seu vindicte abusiam injustam et corruptelam pronunciavit et declaravit ac pronunciat et declarat' (AN x2a 13, fols. 21–23r). For the custom/corruption equivalence, see Chapter 2, above.

[113] *Questiones Johannis Galliani*, ed. M. Boulet (Paris, 1944), 389–90, 430–1.

[114] '[L]es queles choses sont directement contre les ordonnances . . . et allegne un example de la prise du seigneur de Virines (?) dont la cause fu plaide devant la Roy Charles dernierement trepasse, et a dont le Roy defendy . . . que aucun de quelques estat ou pays quil feust ne procedast par voye de fait ou de guerre sur peine de perdre corps & biens' (AN x2a 10, fols. 246v–247).

[115] The Narbonnais war (AM Narbonne FF 722, pc. 2), Pardiac/Barbasan, for which only the *procès-verbal* mentions the prohibitions (*Documents . . . Armagnac-Fezensaguet*, ed. Durrieu, no. 3), and Armagnac/Pardiac (ibid., no. 11).

often keen to recognize, not least because it could be employed to their own advantage.

Each of the three southern cases that make reference to royal *ordonnances* demonstrates a belief that war was not illicit by virtue of the act itself, but rather could be regularized by the king's permission. In the case of Narbonne, the town and its clerical allies cited John II's 1352 prohibition of seigneurial war as part of their complaint against the viscount.[116] But the arguments about the war's legality turned on the issue of authority for the violence. Some of this was the by now familiar argument that the viscount was merely exercising his rights as lord over rebellious subjects, and that his violence was committed 'as the immediate lord of the said inhabitants' (*tanquam dominus inmediatus dictorum habitatorum*), an argument which his opponents countered by noting that he held the viscounty from the bishop of Narbonne and that some of his actions were directed at people and places outside his remit, where he had no (legal) power (*predicta fecit sua propria auctoritate et absque eo quod ad id aliquam haberet potestatem*).[117]

In addition, however, the viscount argued that the authority for some of the violence might not inhere in his own, seigneurial prerogative, but might rather have arisen from a delegation of royal right. When the viscount sent a letter of *défi* to the town, he did so having received permission (*congie et licence*) from the duke of Berry, who was serving as the royal lieutenant of Languedoc, 'to make open war for and in the name of the king' (*de fere guerre ouverte pour et au nom de monsiengeur le roi et de nous*).[118] The viscount thus presented (and perhaps even thought of) this war not only as a seigneurial war against his own subjects but also as a royal war against people rebelling against the king.[119] In the complaint of the Narbonnois against their viscount, the citation of the 1352 *ordonnance* and the account of the viscount's licence and *défi* follow one after another, as if the redactors wished to contrast two different forms of royal power: on one hand, the king's legal authority expressed (and perhaps restrained) through legislation, and on the other, his autocratic, arbitrary power expressed through special privilege.

---

[116] AM Narbonne FF 722, pc. 2.

[117] *Jacme Olivier*, ed. Blanc, no. 118; AM Narbonne FF 722 (second quote from pc. 2).

[118] *Jacme Olivier*, ed. Blanc, no. 116.

[119] As his opponents pointed out, there were considerable inconsistencies in the viscomital position. For example, if he had actually been fighting on behalf of the crown, then he would have had no authority with which to make an accord with the Narbonnois: 'se nomine regio dumtaxat guerram faceret nunquam acordum fecisset . . . cum dictis de Narbone sans voluntate et licentia regia' (AM Narbonne FF 1468).

173

In two other cases, though, the possibility of royal permission for seigneurial warfare seems not to stand in contrast to the *ordonnances*, but rather to be a corollary of them. In the case stemming from the Pardiac/ Barbasan war, both the crown's proctor and the lord of Barbasan asserted that royal *ordonnances* trumped the nobles' alleged right to war by custom and that 'it is not at all licit to make war without the king's permission' (*sans congié du Roy*).[120] The court's *arrêts* regarding this case also gestured towards the principle of seigneurial war with royal authorization, ruling that it was not admissible to argue that one could wage war *absque nostra licencia*.[121] Six years after this, when Armagnac was faced with Pardiac's rebellion, he summoned his vassals, subjects, and allies, but (as he claimed) some of them refused to appear because of the prohibition against warfare (*pour doubte de certaines deffences faites de par nous ou dit pays par lesquelles a este defendu a tous nos subjects que ils ne procedassent aucunement l'un contre l'autre par voie de fait*).[122] Consequently, he petitioned the crown for permission (*congie et licence*) to defend himself, a request granted *de grace speciale*, that signal marker of exceptional royal privilege.[123] That this war was fought with royal permission was important not only during the war – because it restrained royal officers from intervening – but also afterwards, as it was used to demonstrate that the count had fought the war legally and therefore had the right to claim Pardiac's lands for himself.[124]

The principle that one could licitly wage a seigneurial war on behalf of the crown (in the Narbonnais case) or with its permission (in the cases regarding Pardiac) seems to have been new in the last decades of the fourteenth century.[125] This was a principle that arose from a more general practice of granting royal permission for the violent actions of private individuals and groups, often in situations where the crown had a stake in the outcome. Both the war of Beaucaire against Tarascon and the violence of the citizens of Nîmes against the region's nobles, for example, took

---

[120] *Documents . . . Armagnac-Fezensaguet*, ed. Durrieu, no. 3.

[121] AN x2a 13, fols. 114v–115, 116.

[122] *Documents . . . Armagnac-Fezensaguet*, ed. Durrieu, no. 12; see also AD Tarn-et-Garonne A 39.

[123] '[N]ous audit suppliant nostre cousin avons donné et occtroié, donnons et octroions de grace speciale, par ces presentes, congié et licence de deffendre soi, sa terre et subjects' (*Documents . . . Armagnac-Fezensaguet*, ed. Durrieu, no. 12). And see ibid., no. 11, where the seneschal notes that no one may go to war 'absque licentia et authoritate ejusdem domini nostri Regis, seu alterius ab eodem potestatem habentis'.

[124] AD Tarn-et-Garonne A 39; *HL*, x: 1903–5; *Documents . . . Armagnac-Fezensaguet*, ed. Durrieu, nos. 25–30, no. 28 of particular interest for references to canon law.

[125] The one possible precedent that I know of comes from a 1339 remission for a Bigordian nobleman accused of warfare, the *narratio* of which notes a failure to obtain permission of a superior (*superioris licencia non obtenta*), but it looks as though this comment primarily applied to his calling an assembly of noblemen, not to the war (AN x1a 8, fols. 17–18r). The war was that of Raymond Almeric, lord of Bazillac, and Bernard de Castelbajac, for which see above Chapter 3, p. 95.

place with the crown's permission (*license/licentia*).[126] The importance of permission in legalizing military actions comes out especially clearly in complaints about those committed in the absence of such approval. For example, the Tuchins were described as having acted 'without having asked licence of us or our representatives', while an illicit redemption of prisoners from the English in the Auvergne was said to have taken place *sine nostri licencia vel congedio*.[127] This development was not restricted to the South; Pierre de Craon, for example, was accused by the royal proctor in 1396 of *faisant guerre ou royaume sanz licence du roy*.[128]

The idea of licence was closely connected to that of sufficient authority; it was thus a question not just of obtaining permission, but of obtaining permission from someone competent to give it. So in the Velay in the 1370s the reconstruction and fortification of a castle was described as illicit not only because the possessor had not asked for *license & congié* from the royal bailiff, but also because the viscount of Polignac – from whom he *had* obtained permission – 'did not have the power to give him leave' (*n'avoit pas la puissance de lui en donner congié*).[129] And in 1392 a squire of the seneschalsy of Toulouse admitted to pillaging livestock 'without any licence or permission from anyone having power to give it' (*senz aucune licence ou congié d'aucun ayant povoir à ce*).[130]

This emphasis on sufficient authority and its delegation owes much to normative developments discussed earlier in this chapter: the new military regulations set out a hierarchy of command, stipulating that letters of authorization be given to captains and that these captains grant *congé* for their soldiers' movements. And the system for granting reprisals that was laid out by jurists like Bartolus de Saxoferrato and Giovanni de Legnano bears resemblance to the practice of granting licence for war. But it is also reflective of the same pervasive political and military insecurity that led to those normative developments. The crown was failing to protect its subjects, just as it had in the 1350s and early 1360s. Indeed, by systematically allowing the English to spend their forces in fruitless raids on the denuded countryside, it had now made a policy of doing so.

It was this abdication of responsibility that led to the necessity of licensing violence. In addressing the hostilities between Beaucaire and

---

[126] Beaucaire: *HL*, x: 1703–5 (see n. 81, above). Nîmes, faced with unremitting reprisals from Beaucaire's nobles on account of the Tuchinat, 'habuerunt & obtinuerunt licentiam resistendi discursibus predictis & se deffendendi' (Menard, *Histoire civile*, III: no. 15).

[127] '[N]ostrorum vel suorum officiariorum & gencium licencia minime petita seu obtenta' (*HL*, x: 1716–18); *HL*, x: 1685–6.

[128] AN X2a 12, 322v–324, quoted in Juchs, 'Vengeance et guerre', I: 183.

[129] *HL*, x: 1628–30, and see similar at *HL*, x: 1651–2.   [130] *HL*, x: 1836–7.

Tarascon, the duke of Berry acknowledged that 'the king's subjects and lands . . . should not be harmed, but maintained, guarded and defended' (*les subjets & pays de mondit seigneur & nostres ne soient grevés, mais tenus, gardés & deffendus*), but he nevertheless proposed that they do this for themselves by way of licence to go to war.[131] Similarly, during a 1375 meeting of the Estates of the southern seneschalsies, although it was agreed that taxes would be paid so that the king could maintain the frontiers with armed garrisons 'in order that these communities could live in safety' (*ut dicte communitates sub securitate possint remanere*), necessity also required that the communities be granted licence to defend themselves (*communitatibus . . . licentiam concedimus . . . hominibus depredatoribus resistere valeant impune*).[132]

The licensing of war, self-defence, or other sorts of violence thus arose from the crown's inability and unwillingness to implement justice and to provide for public safety, a sign of its significantly weakened position in the latter half of the century. As was already observable at the end of the reign of Philip VI, the protection of 'public' right was increasingly carried out by 'private' individuals. But just as occurred during mid-century, individuals' and communities' actions were frequently made in concert with royal judicial and administrative decisions and acknowledged royal authority. These grants of licence should also certainly be read as a sign of the strength and durability of the *idea* of royal power, albeit in the absence of its reality. By granting licence the crown asserted (and the grantees recognized) that violence could only be licit when committed under royal authority. As Maurice Keen noted, 'the principle. . . that any sort of hostile act requires sovereign authority, was an important one . . . The redress of wrong is no longer to be regarded as a matter of private enterprise; it is the business of the public authority which represents the members of the community. . .'[133] It is certain that we are here observing a watershed moment in the move away from self-help towards a system of state-dominated conflict resolution, even if in the short term that actually meant more violence carried out by individuals. But, in fact, those accused of making seigneurial war or other kinds of violence sometimes did assert the justice of their cause. The difference was that it was no longer always phrased in terms of an individual's particular rights or even the sort of absolute moral good associated with the peace-keeping efforts of the thirteenth and the early fourteenth century, but rather presented as integral to the welfare of the kingdom.

---

[131] *HL*, x: 1703–5.   [132] *HL*, x: 1512–22, arts. 10, 15.   [133] *Laws of War*, 237.

This attention to the political community was part of the broader concern to represent one's own violence as sublimated to the crown's interests. Warring parties tried hard to describe their actions in the idiom of obedience to the crown. Narbonne began its list of complaints against the viscount by stating that the consuls and inhabitants were 'good, faithful and obedient subjects to our lord king . . . and to his officers and to the commissioners and justiciars deputized by them'.[134] By the 1390s the count of Foix promised to ask royal permission before going to war with Armagnac and to submit to punishment if he did otherwise.[135] It is even possible that lords may really have thought that their actions were fully consonant with obedience to the crown. When the count of Armagnac interrogated the captured Jean d'Armagnac (son of the count of Pardiac) about the war Pardiac had waged against him, for example, Jean not only affirmed that he was subject to the king of France (*home in subiectli del Rey de Franssa*), but elaborated that since he had given faith and homage to the seneschal of Toulouse, he was in the crown's obedience (*es ala hobediensa del Rey de Franssa*).[136]

It would be easy to dismiss these displays of obedience as cynical manipulations of rhetorical convention. Certainly, the *bonum commune* was a flexible concept whose meaning was contingent on the particular interests of individuals and groups, much as 'democracy' or the 'free market' may be attributed to wildly different objectives in our own society.[137] There is no doubt that parties had become increasingly sophisticated in using not only the language but also the infrastructure of royal justice to pursue their own conflicts in the century's final decades, as is particularly well demonstrated by the wars of Narbonne and Armagnac–Pardiac. This instrumentalization of royal authority obviously served individual ends. Some of Armagnac's vassals probably saw the *ordonnances* not as a binding law, but rather as a convenient excuse to avoid going to war against the county's second strongest lord, and both the viscount of Narbonne and the count of Armagnac seem to have

---

[134] '[B]oni subjecti et fideles obedientes domino nostro regi . . . et quibuscumque officiariis commissariisque et justiciaris ab eisdem deputatis' (AM Narbonne FF 722, pc. 1).

[135] '[A]vant que nous li encommensons guerre, nous le ferons savoir au Roy nostredit seigneur, pour en prendre droit par davant lui, & nous soubzmetons au Roy en toutes poines qu'il voudra ordenner sur nous, ou cas que nous allissions au contrayre' (*HL*, x: 1789–90). Auguste Molinier reported that the count of Armagnac made a similar promise at the same time (*HL*, ix: 948, n. 6), but I have not been able to locate the document from his citation (AN J 293, Armagnac, no. 32).

[136] AD Tarn-et-Garonne A 38.

[137] E.g. essays in E. Lecuppre-Desjardin and A.-L. van Bruaene, eds., *De Bono Communi: the Discourse and Practice of the Common Good in the European City (13th–16th c.)* (Turnhout, 2010); J. Watts, *The Making of Polities: Europe, 1300–1500* (Cambridge, 2009), 384–6; G. Naegle, 'Bien commun et chose publique: Traités et procès à la fin du moyen âge', *Histoire et archives* 19 (2006): 87–111.

understood their grants of licence not as limited exceptions, but rather as *cartes blanches*. Still, by waging their wars under the banner of royal authority, or at least with reference to it, lords incorporated both the ideas and the administrative structures of royal governance into these local power struggles. Though grants of licence were born of royal weakness, they were also one more way by which royal authority could penetrate and complicate seigneurial relationships. Seigneurial violence and royal government could thus work together to maintain rights and to restore order.

CONCLUSION

In comparison with the years immediately preceding, the latter decades of the fourteenth century are most remarkable for their placidity. With the mercenaries otherwise occupied and the Anglo-French war in a state of uneasy truce, some semblance of peace may have returned to Languedoc. This may be partly a trick of the sources, and the wars that did take place were bigger and longer lasting than those of earlier times. But there also seems to have been little movement during this period in either the normative or the judicial sphere. The crown seems to have stopped issuing *ordonnances* against seigneurial war. And while the royal courts and officers remained somewhat concerned to enforce earlier prohibitions, they appear no more so than their predecessors had been, nor did they seek novel ways of coercively enforcing peace. The areas of development which had been most important over the previous century lost momentum and direction in these decades, a drift that seems to have set in well before Charles VI took the throne. Indeed it may have been a by-product of Charles V's policy of conserving his resources and cutting his losses. With so much else to do on so many fronts, peace-keeping within the realm – beyond the bare fact of controlling the freebooters as much as possible – may have been an unaffordable luxury.

The developments that did take place in the last thirty or forty years of the century occurred mainly outside the traditional royal/seigneurial dialogue. Continuing a trend first visible in the 1350s, violence of non-seigneurial provenance provoked the greatest impetus for change. The need to regulate an increasingly professionalized and non-noble army and to establish a hierarchy of authority derived from the crown fostered the development of ideas about licence and delegation that had broad applicability to a range of other situations, including but not limited to seigneurial war. By the same token, the weakening of the crown's ability to enforce justice coercively meant that other expedients had to be found, including that of granting permission to individuals to protect their own rights by violence. These developments are notable for the manner in which they combined a frank admission of royal limitations with the assertion that, none the less, authority over violence remained in the crown's possession. The idea of royal authority remained robust, even as actual royal power became less so. While royal officials and courts may have had less active involvement in the arbitration of conflict than before, there was a widely held assumption that the crown would play some sort of role, even if it was only to invoke its authority as a legal strategy. The crown does not seem to have been any closer to supressing warfare successfully at the end of the century than it had been at the beginning, but it had moved closer to monopolizing legitimate authority for large-scale violence, a victory ironically owing as much to royal weaknesses as to strengths.

CONCLUSION

The phenomenon of seigneurial war highlights the complexity of the relationship between the crown and the lords in France at the end of the Middle Ages. It was not a relationship that was becoming progressively more favourable to autocratic monarchy at the expense of violent seigneurial power. It is true that later Capetian kings and their early Valois successors did assert the crown's theoretical supremacy over justice and violence in the *ordonnances* against warfare, but not only were there prevarications and the occasional wholesale retreat, the crown eventually abandoned the project altogether. More importantly, in terms of putting such grand ambitions into action royal dominion was in fact very limited, much more limited than is admitted by the popular narrative of a crown destined for absolute power. Despite royal prohibitions and the development of royal courts and administration, lords continued to pursue their disputes violently with regularity. The crown could not prevent them from doing so, and its ability to impose punitive sanctions seems to have been subject to significant restraints. Nevertheless, the perdurance of governmental institutions and their professional staffs meant that the crown remained actively involved with seigneurial war, even during periods of disorder and relative royal weakness. Much of this involvement occurred through conciliation and negotiation rather than coercive sanctions, but this engagement allowed the crown to maintain a durable and important role in the violent disputes through which local power was adjudicated.

The multi-faceted way that the crown dealt with seigneurial warfare continued into the fifteenth century and proved a lasting legacy. Circumstances were, if anything, less favourable to the coercive exercise of royal power in the increasingly confused and anxious years after 1400, and legal compulsion does not seem to have been an option that the crown used very often. There are no known royal *ordonnances* on warfare in the early fifteenth century, though, again, royal proctors did continue to bring up violation of *ordonnances* in prosecutions against war-makers.[1] But prosecution, at least in the South, was sparse. Although the *capitouls* (councillors) of Toulouse complained in 1407 that 'in Gascony and around Toulouse ... the nobles and people of these counties and lands are used to having wars, conflicts, and divisions and to making *chevauchées* with great groups of men at arms',[2] Parlement's criminal registers record only two seigneurial wars in the South in the decade and a half before Agincourt: in 1402, the conflict over the viscounty of Murat broke out once more into *guerra publica*,[3] and in 1408, Jean de Beaufort, lord of Limeuil, and his numerous accomplices seized and burned the castles of Rives and Puy, whose lord had had the temerity to cite Jean before Parlement.[4] This small number of cases may reflect the limitations placed on the crown by a major renegotiation of the relationship between royal and seigneurial jurisdiction in 1408, the near entirety of which is given over to jurisdiction and judicial precedence:[5] among other provisions, it forbade officers to interfere in seigneurial jurisdiction and promised strict limitations on the granting of safeguards to seigneurial subjects.

Yet, while it is tempting to conclude that the disasters of the early fifteenth century temporarily destroyed the administrative and judicial legacy of the thirteenth and fourteenth centuries, there is evidence that even in these troubled years at least some people continued to use the courts and to use royal opposition to seigneurial warfare in a strategic way.[6] For instance, although an accord made in 1414 about the barony of Solignac, a conflict that dated back to the 1350s, evinces the crown's inability or unwillingness to bring enmities to a conclusion, the document's allusion to and incorporation of Parlementary decisions, and its assertion that the aggressors had 'lost all right to the disputed barony' by waging war, suggests

[1] E.g. AN x2a 15, fols. 41v–46, 169–171r, 199–201.

[2] 'Item que es parties de Gascoigne et environs laditte Cite de Thoulouse a pluseurs grans comez & nobles terres ... Item que les nobles & gens desdis contez & terres ont accostume, davoir entre eulx guerre, debaz & divesions et de faire chevauchees, a grans asemblees de gens darmes dont le pays soeffre moult de dommaiges pertes & inconveniens' (AM Toulouse FF 80, fol. 8).

[3] AN x2a 15, fols. 116v–118, 119–120. See above, Chapter 4, pp. 128–9 for earlier episodes in this conflict. In 1415 Armagnac confiscated this viscounty from Reginald de Murat on account of his support for Burgundy: T. R. Pollack-Lagushenko, 'The Armagnac Faction: New Patterns of Political Violence in Late Medieval France', Ph.D. thesis, The Johns Hopkins University, 2003, 11, 270; *Documents historiques relatifs à la vicomté de Carlat* ..., ed. G. Saige and le comte de Dienne, 2 vols. (Monaco, 1900), I: 437; *Documents historiques et généalogiques du Rouergue*, ed. H. de Barrau, 4 vols. (Rodez, 1853–60), IV: 30.

[4] AN x2a 15, fols. 232v–233r.

[5] *HL*, X: 1931–42. The importance of this measure is evidenced by the multiple manuscript copies, which include AD Hérault A 8, art. 22, fols. 48–59; A 9, art. 116, fols. 326–42; A 16, art. 112, pp. 360–79.

[6] In addition to nn. 1–4, above, for seigneurial war see AN x2a 15, fols. 290v–292; AN x2a 16, fols. 39–41, 51–5.

that the legal implications of local war remained at least potentially serious, even on the eve of military and political disaster.[7] Moreover, the military *ordonnances* issued under royal aegis in the early fifteenth century demonstrate a continuance of the practice of granting licence to resist forcibly the violent tendencies of the *gens d'armes*.[8] Recognizing that the king's officers were not always *assez fors pour ce faire*, a promulgation of 1405, for example, authorized 'all nobles . . . to protect and defend their lands and people [from the pillaging of the king's troops], and to resist the evils done by these men at arms'.[9]

Indeed, if we can go so far as to speak of a 'popular consciousness' about the control of violence, evidence for its conservation is to be found in the so-called *ordonnance Cabochienne*, promulgated in May 1413, which adopts the same approach and even the same language as the *ordonnance* of the Estates General of 1357, allowing pillaging to be 'resisted by force (*voye de fait*) as we commanded at an earlier time'.[10] This measure also contains the only explicit prohibition of warfare in fifty years, forbidding *guerre ou defiance particulière*, and, eloquently testifying to the influence of royal precedent, it specified that the prohibition held good 'regardless of any privileges, usages, customs, or regional observances whatsoever' (*nonobstant quelzconques privileges, usaiges, coustumes ou observances de lieu ou de pays*).[11] A legacy that valorized public order over particular privilege thus lived on, all the more powerful because the cause could be adopted by the crown's critics as well as its advocates.

In fact, it was just this moulding of expectations that was the most important and durable impact of royal peace-keeping. In the thirteenth and fourteenth centuries, many people, including lords themselves,

---

[7] '[Q]uia avus dictorum fratrum per guerram et viam facti processerat. . .propter quod idem dominus vicecomes dicebat ipsos dominos de Rota jus suum, si quod haberent in dicta baronia, perdidisse' (*Preuves de la maison de Polignac. Recueil de documents pour servir à l'histoire des anciennes provinces de Velay, Auvergne, Gévaudan, Vivarais, Forez, etc., IXe–XVIIIe siècle*, ed. A. Jacotin, 5 vols. (Paris, 1898–1906), IV: no. 712). See also p. 174, above, for similar circumstances regarding the disposition of Pardiac's property following his war with Armagnac.

[8] L. Cazaux, 'Réglementation militaire royale et usage de la force dans le royaume de France (XIVe–XVI siècles)', *Inflexions. Civils et militaires: pouvoir dire* 13 (2010): 103. Cazaux lists *Ord.*, IX: 96–7, 203–4, 292, 515–17, 530–1, 531–4, 573–5, 652–3, X: 159–60, XII: 222–3, to which one should also add *Ord.*, X: 146–7, 147–50. After 1410 (*Ord.*, IX: 515–17 onward), it should be noted that these are not really regulations for the army, but rather efforts by the Burgundian faction to undercut that of the Armagnacs. Cazaux also cites AN Y 6(I), fol. 55, which I have not been able to consult.

[9] '[C]ommandons & commettons à tous Nobles . . . que chascun endroit soy puist garder & deffendre ses terres & hommes, & résister tellement que aucuns maulx ou dommages ne leur soient faiz par icelles Gens d'armes' (*Ord.*, IX: 96–7; see also *Ord.*, IX: 203–4).

[10] '[R]esisté par voye de fait comme l'en pourra, ainsi comme autres foiz l'avons ordonné' (*L'ordonnance cabochienne (26–27 mai 1413)*, ed. A. Coville (Paris, 1891), art. 250; See also arts. 251–5. This *ordonnance* was previously published in *Ord.*, X: 70–140).

[11] *L'ordonnance cabochienne*, ed. Coville, art. 255.

learned to expect royal involvement in large-scale seigneurial conflicts. It is true that this involvement was not always punitive or coercive, nor was it invariably enacted through institutional avenues. Official royal influence was felt as much, or perhaps even more, through the extra- and quasi-judicial actions of administrators negotiating settlements both between war-makers through accords and between war-makers and the crown through *rémissions* and *compositions*. It was as much or more this accommodating authority as it was coercive compulsion that enabled royal authority to embed itself within local seigneurial society and to remain important to it, even as the crown's ability to execute justice and force obedience was debilitated by circumstances. Rather than the aggrandize-ment of absolute royal power through the suppression of violent seigneurial privileges, there was instead the growth of collaborative practices that would tend to limit, but certainly not obviate, seigneurial violence.

This conclusion fits in neatly with recent Anglophone work on the early modern French state, which rejects the old historiography of 'absolutism' in favour of an understanding of government as a cooperative project shared between the crown and local elites, including the nobi-lity.[12] This understanding of royal/seigneurial (or royal/elite) relations comes out of a closer focus on the actual mechanisms of rule, rather than its normative and (theoretically) constitutive principles. For example, as David Parker has argued, seventeenth-century jurists were much more concerned with conserving patrimonial jurisdiction and administering the law than they were with upholding 'abstract principles' of royal legislative sovereignty.[13] And Zoë Schneider's work on justice in Normandy emphasizes the extensive autonomy that local officials had in the admin-istration of government well into the mid-eighteenth century.[14] Most appositely, Stuart Carroll's work on feud and duel in the sixteenth and seventeenth centuries demonstrates the endurance of private vengeance among French nobles and argues that such violence, in concert or in competition with legal processes, was a normal and functional element of early modern political economy in France, one primarily dealt with through the negotiation of accords.[15] There have, of course, been efforts to re-emphasize the centralizing agenda of the early modern crown, but

---

[12] In addition to work cited below, see J. B. Collins, *The State in Early Modern France*, 2nd edn (Cambridge, 2009).

[13] 'Sovereignty, Absolutism, and the Function of the Law in Seventeenth-Century France', *Past & Present* 122 (1989): 36–74.

[14] Z. Schneider, *The King's Bench: Bailiwick Magistrates and Local Governance in Normandy, 1670–1740* (Rochester, NY, 2008).

[15] *Blood and Violence in Early Modern France* (Oxford, 2006); S. Carroll, 'The Peace in the Feud in Sixteenth- and Seventeenth-Century France', *Past & Present* 178 (2003): 74–115.

the basic picture, at least at the provincial level, remains one of cooperation and mutual benefit rather than of suppression and exclusion.[16] In short, early modern royal power bears a family resemblance to the picture presented throughout this book of a crown whose power – despite elaborate ideological justifications – was maintained by being cooperatively interwoven with local political society.

Thus, even if we think about the thirteenth and fourteenth centuries as a transitional moment between the fragmented society that was the legacy of the Carolingian breakdown and the monarchical state of the *ancien régime*, it is not necessarily useful to look for the roots of 'absolutism' in the courts of Louis IX or Charles V. What it is possible to see are patterns of engagement, accommodation, negotiation, clemency, and arbitration that were perhaps basic to French political society and would endure, albeit in very altered form, through the centuries. Certainly, by the turn of the fifteenth century, ideas and methods of royal peace-keeping had undergone significant changes, and it is not this book's intention to minimize that development. There is a story to be told about the progressive expansion of royal authority over violence entailing the promulgation of legislation and its enforcement through governmental apparatus. But legislation had no apparent link to most of the action that royal agents took against war-makers, and there was frequently no clear relationship between royal judgments and their execution. This was not just an administrative problem, but reflected two key assumptions: first, that the royal/seigneurial relationship was primarily one of mutual accommodation and even benefit, and second, that justice was an open-ended process intended for pursuit and eventual resolution of the conflict, not for the protection of abstract principles. If the French polity of the later Middle Ages had some features that prefigured those of the modern state, this should not distract from its historical particularism. Through its varied reactions to seigneurial violence, the monarchical French state found many avenues for the expansion of its power, but this was not inevitable or even wholly intentional, and it occurred as much through cooperation as through compulsion.

---

[16] See W. Beik, 'The Absolutism of Louis XIV as Social Collaboration', *Past & Present* 188 (2005): 195–224.

ROYAL *ORDONNANCES* REGARDING
SEIGNEURIAL WAR

The following list comprises those royal acts touching on seigneurial war that exist or are attested to have once existed, information on publication, and the manuscript copies that I have consulted. Further discussion is to be found in the first section of the relevant chapters.

November 1229
Council of Toulouse prohibits peace-breaking.
Mansi, XXIII: 191–204.

October 1246
Louis IX issues the *quarantaine du roi?*
Non-extant. Although published at *Ord.*, I: 56–8, the text was taken from an act of John II dating from 9 April 1353/4.

January 1258
Louis IX prohibits wars, arson, and attacks on peasants.
Ord., I: 84.
BN Latin 4651, fol. 74v.

29 November 1270
Alphonse de Poitiers prohibits the barons of the counties of Toulouse and Albi from maintaining those who engaged in cavalcade and *portatio armorum*.
Enquêtes administratives d'Alfonse de Poitiers, arrêts de son Parlement tenu à Toulouse, et textes annexes, 1249–1271, ed. P.-F. Fournier and P. Guébin (Paris, 1959), no. 135; *HL*, VIII: 1715–23.

17 October 1274[1]
Philip III defines the offence of peace-breaking as including wars.
HL, X: 131–2; also published in *Ord.*, I: 344–5 note b.
BN Latin 9988, fol. 117v; BN Latin 9989, p. 239; AN P 2529, fol. 27.

Between 1 November 1296 and 15 March 1297
Philip IV prohibits wars, duels, and tournament during his own wars

---

[1] On the dating of this document, see *Essai de restitution des plus anciens mémoriaux de la Chambre des comptes de Paris*, ed. M. J. Petit *et al.* (Paris, 1899), no. 161 and p. 28, n. 18, above.

Olim, II: 405; *Ord.*, I: 328–9.
AN XIa 2, fol. 114v; AD Tarn-et-Garonne A 297, fols. 931–932r.

13 May 1302
Philip IV defines the offence of peace-breaking as including wars.
Ord., I: 344–5.

18 January 1304
Philip IV prohibits wars, homicides, arson of dwellings, and aggression against
    peasants.
Ord., I: 390.
AM Toulouse AA 4, no. 37, fol. 46.

1 June 1306
Philip IV issues instructions for judicial duel, observing that he had generally prohib-
    ited war to all his subjects.
Ord., I: 435–41.
AN U 446, fol. 4r; AM Toulouse AA 4, fol. 41.

30 December 1311
Philip IV prohibits war.
Ord., I: 492–3, XI: 426–7.
AN P 2290, pp. 89–90, 91–2.

29 July 1314
Philip IV prohibits all wars for the duration of his own
Ord., I: 538–9.
Reported to have been in the destroyed register A of the Chambres de comptes de
    Paris at fol. 60, but is not found in the reconstruction of this register at AN P 2290.

Prior to April 1315
Louis X prohibits warfare in the Vermandois and Amiens?
Non-extant. Referred to in *Ord.*, I: 557–60, and see note at *Ord.*, II: vi.

April 1315
Louis X grants the demands of the nobles of Burgundy, Langres, Autun, and Forez,
    including the right to war, if it is found that they possess the right by custom.
Ord., I: 557–60, arts. 3, 6, 7.
AN JJ 41, no. 210, fols. 116–117r; AN JJ 52, no. 59, fols. 31–32r.

15 May 1315
Louis X grants the demands of the nobles of Amiens and Vermandois, including the
    right to war, if it is discovered in the 'registers of Saint Louis' that they possess this
    right.
Ord., I: 561–7, art. 6.
AN JJ 41, no. 212, fols. 119–121v; AN JJ 52, no. 81, fols. 40–1.

17 May 1315
Louis X grants the demands of the nobles of Burgundy, Forez, Langres, Autun,
    and Chalons the right to war, if it is found that they possessed the right by
    custom.

Royal ordonnances regarding seigneurial war

Ord., I: 567–73, art. I.
AN JJ 41, no. 211, fols. 117–119r; AN JJ 52, no. 110, fols. 58v–6or.

January 1316
Louis X grants the demands of the nobles of Toulouse, Carcassonne, Périgueux, Rodez, Beaucaire, and Lyon, and concedes by *speciali gratia* the right to war, provided that the *défi* had been accepted, that fire was not set to any buildings except fortifications, that neither the king nor overlord had a war in progress, and that the war was not directed against a minor or a widow with children.
HL, X: 547–55, arts. 22–3; *Ord.*, XII: 411–15, arts. 22–4.
BN Latin 5138, fols. 74–78r; BN Latin 3359, fol. 148r.

May 1316
Louis IX grants the demands of the nobles of Nevers and Donzy, including the right to war, if it is found that they possess this right by custom.
Ord., XI: 441–4, art. I.

Before 29 April 1318
Philip V prohibits war for the duration of his own
Non-extant. Referred to in AN x2a 2, fol. 7v and *Ord.*, I: 655–6.

29 April 1318
Philip V reissues the 1306 *ordonnance* of Philip IV in which is mentioned the problems caused by his prohibition against wars.
Unpublished.
AN x2a 2, fol. 7v.

1 June 1318
Philip V orders the bailiff of Vermandois to enforce the prohibition of warfare during the king's war, which the inhabitants of the bailliage had flouted.
Ord., I: 655–6.

June 1319
Philip V grants the demands of the inhabitants of the bailliage of Auvergne, including an article recognizing the right to cavalcade.
Ord., I: 688–91, art. 14.
AN JJ 59, no. 115, fol. 49.

June 1319
Philip V grants the demands of the inhabitants of the bailliage of the Mountains of Auvergne, including an article recognizing the right to cavalcade.
Unpublished.
AN JJ 59, no. 113, fol. 48.

11 November 1319
Philip V prohibits arson, destruction of vines or trees, taking animals, peasants, or instruments related to agriculture, and the overturning of houses on account of war, vengeance, or enmity in the county of Burgundy.
Ord., I: 701–2.
AN JJ 59, no. 172, fol. 72v; AN JJ 59, no. 373, fol. 211r.

Appendix A

c.1320
Philip V prohibits armed congregations and war to everyone of whatever status everywhere in the realm.
Non-extant. Referred to in AN x1a 5, fols. 97v–98r.

February 1323
Charles IV confirms the grant made to the inhabitants of the bailliage of the Auvergne in 1319, which included a clause recognizing the cavalcade.
Ord., i: 780–1.

Before 9 April 1335
Philip VI prohibits bearing arms and wars in the realm of France.
Non-extant. Referred to in AN x2a 3, fol. 9 (9 April 1335); AN x2a 3, fol. 71; AN x2a 3, fols. 79v–80r; AN x2a 2bis, fol. 2; AN x1a 8, fol. 143.

February 1339
Philip VI grants the petition of the nobles of Gascony, including the right to war, if the *défi* is accepted, and provided that such wars cease if he or his successor kings have a war.
Ord., ii: 61–3.

Before April 1343
Philip VI prohibits non-royal wars for the duration of the king's war.
Non-extant. Referred to in AN x1a 9, fols. 492v–494r (8 April 1343); AN x2a 5, fol. 186; *Ord.*, ii: 511–12.

30 March 1351
John II grants privileges to the bailliage of Vermandois, including the nobles' right to wars, provided that the accustomed delays after the *défi* are respected and damages are specifically limited.
Ord., ii: 391–6, arts. 16–18.

5 April 1351
John II prohibits war in Normandy.
Ord., ii: 400–10, art. 27.

19 September 1351
John II decreases the accustomed delay after the *défi* for principal parties at war in the Vermandois and Beauvais.
Ord., ii: 447–8.

August 1352
John II issues privileges to the bailliage of Vermandois, including the nobles' right to war, provided that the accustomed delays after the *défi* are respected and damages are specifically limited.
Ord., ii: 505–8, arts. 13–15.

17 December 1352
John II renews the prohibition of wars during royal war.
Ord., ii: 511–12.
AN Y 4, fols. 5–6r; AN x2a 6, fols. 5v–6r; AM Narbonne FF 722, pc. 2.

Royal ordonnances *regarding seigneurial war*

August 1353
John II issues privileges to the bailliage of Vermandois, including the nobles' right to war, provided that the accustomed delays after the *défi* are respected and damages are specifically limited.
Ord., II: 529–32, arts. 13–15.

9 April 1353/4
John II renews the *quarantaine du roi*, with the stipulation that it does not indicate that wars are allowed during royal wars.
Ord., II: 552–3.
AM Amiens AA 1, fols. 175 (Latin) and 176 (French), and AA 5, fol. 93r.

December 1354
John II issues privileges to the bailliage of Vermandois, including the nobles' right to war, provided that the accustomed delays after the *défi* are respected and damages are specifically limited.
Ord., II: 567–70, arts. 13–15.

December 1355
Following the Estates General of Languedoïl, John II issues an ordinance including instructions to resist pillagers by force.
Ord., III: 19–37, arts. 30–2.
AN Y 2, fols. 11–15r; AN JJ 84, no. 400, fols. 210–13 and no. 401, fols. 213v–214r; AN P 2293, pp. 277–317.

March 1357
Following the Estates of Languedoïl, the Dauphin Charles, acting as regent for John II, prohibits war during his own wars and aggression against bourgeois, and authorizes resistance by force.
Ord., III: 121–46, arts. 34, 57.
AN Y 2, fols. 15v–23r (cancelled act); AN P 2293, pp. 351–416.

5 October 1361
John II prohibits war.
Ord., III: 525–7.
AN U 446, fols. 47–48r.

5 December 1363
Following the Estates General at Amiens, John II issues instructions, including the prohibition of war and vengeance for as long as the enemy and evildoers should be in the country.
Ord., III: 646–9, art. 8.

Before 30 May 1365
Charles V prohibits local war, *défis*, and *voies de fait* during royal wars.
Non-extant. Referred to in AN x2a 7, fols. 178v–179 (30 May 1365) and AN x2a 9, fol. 199 (published in J. Monicat, *Les grandes compagnies en Velay, 1358–1392*, 2nd edn, (Paris, 1928), no. 16).

Appendix A

20 July 1367

Following the Estates General at Sens, Charles V issues instructions, including that both parties must agree to have a war, and that warring parties should not damage or take the goods of the *bonnes gens*.

Ord., v: 19–22, art. 10.

August 1367

Charles V confirms a grant made in 1349 by Humbert II to the nobles of the Dauphiné, including the right to war, provided that the war had not been previously forbidden and that damage was not done to the Dauphiné.

Ord., v: 34–56, art. 14.

23 May 1383

Confirmation of an agreement with the bishop and chapter of Viviers, including the right to wage war outside the realm unimpeded by the crown.

Ord., VII: 7–14, art. 19.

June 1394

Confirmation of privileges granted to Beauvais in 1182, including the right to undertake *vindicta* against the goods and inhabitants of a fortress where a wrong-doer was sheltering.

Ord., VII: 621–5.

Appendix B

SEIGNEURIAL WARS IN SOUTHERN FRANCE

The following list comprises wars fought in the seneschalsies of Toulouse, Carcassonne, and Beaucaire and the bailliages of the Auvergne and Mountains of Auvergne. Unless other information allows a more precise date, the date usually given is that of the first source that mentions the war.

An asterisk (*) indicates conflicts whose status as a war is open to doubt (i.e. 'possible wars').

For the characteristics and definition of war, see the Introduction, pp. 17–20. Note that the relatively large number of starred items in the early period may partly stem from less complete documentation. Discussion and sources for each conflict can be found in the second section of the relevant chapter.

December 1250 to spring 1251	Guillaume de Vendat vs. Chatard and Pierre de Saint-Germain
*1251	Uldin Cholet vs. Chatard, lord of Thiers
*1251	Count of Foix vs. King James of Aragon
1252	Bishop and town of Albi vs. seneschal of Carcassonne
*Before November 1254	G. de Niort and B. Semon vs. G. de Canet
1255–8	King James of Aragon vs. Montpellier, the viscount of Narbonne, and King Louis of France
*1255–58	Viscount of Lautrec and viscount of Narbonne vs. Philipe II de Montfort, lord of Castres
*1256	Count of Foix vs. count of Urgel
March–September 1256	Viscount of Béarn vs. Esquivat de Chabanais, count of Bigorre
Before January 1257	Montpellier vs. Marseilles
July 1259	Bishop and town of Albi and Isarn and Almaric, viscounts of Lautrec vs. the abbot of Gaillac, Bertrand, viscount of Lautrec, and Bertrand, viscount of Bruniquel
c. summer 1262	Viscount of Béarn, count and countess-dowager of Armagnac vs. count of Comminges and lord of Isle-Jourdain

★*c.*1264	Son of the count of Rodez vs. sons of Lord Dieudonné de Canillac, brother of Lord Guy de Séverac
1265–9	Jourdain de l'Isle vs. Isarn de l'Isle
★Before April 1267	Count of Comminges vs. count of Foix
★Before August 1267	Philippe de Montfort vs. Sicard Alaman
★Before March 1268	Géraud, count of Armagnac vs. people of Condom
★1268–9	Gaja-la-Selve, Barsa, Saint-Estèphe, Cazalrenoux, and Plaigne vs. Gui de Lévis, lord of Mirepoix
★Before June 1269	Count of Foix vs. castle of Montégut (and possibly the abbey of Lézat)
★Before April/May 1270	Anglise de Marestang/Ros vs. counts of Armagnac, Astarac, and Comminges
Summer 1272	Count of Foix and count of Armagnac vs. Géraud de Causabon, seneschal of Toulouse, and king of France
★Before 1287	Viscount of Narbonne vs. Narbonne's cathedral chapter
Before 31 March 1294	Roger d'Anduze, lord of la Voulte vs. bishop of Valences
★*c.*1295	Géraud d'Ami, lord of Castelnau vs. Raymond Gaucelin, lord of Uzès, over the barony of Lunel
★*c.*1295	Viscount of Béarn's cavalcades
★Before 9 April 1302	Inhabitants of Foix and Andorra vs. lord of Mirepoix
★Before 28 July 1304	Viscount of Narbonne vs. Bernard de Durban, knight
★Before August 1304	Jean de Chanlayo, knight vs. Guillaume Buisard
★Before 8 June 1306	Bertrand de Roquefort vs. priory of Moulinpessin
Before 16 March 1309	Castelnaudary vs. Gaillac
★Before 26 April 1309	Eudes de Roquefort vs. Raymond Unaud
★Before 16 September 1311	Pierre d'Avène vs. Raimond de Sanséchelle
Before 26 May 1312	Viscount of Polignac vs. church of Brioude
Before 26 May 1312	Viscount of Polignac vs. Bertrand de Saint-Nectaire
Before 17 October 1312 to November 1313	Bishop of Albi vs. Amblard de Pullan, knight, lord of la Bastide and Puygozon
Before 20 February 1313	Pierre de Maumont, knight vs. lord of Beaufort
Before 6 April 1314	Town of 'Helizona,' Eauze, and Bretagne-d'Armagnac vs. Othon de Cazeneuve and consuls of Gondrin
*c.*1316 to 1332	Bernard, count of Comminges, Pierre-Raymond and Gui de Comminges vs. Eleanor de Montfort, countess of Vendôme, and sons
Before 18 February 1317	Othon de 'Temda' vs. abbot and convent of Belleperche
Before 1318/19	Les Bordes-sur-Arize and its co-lords vs. the men and monks of Mas-d'Azil and Severac
Before 16 May 1321	Lord and inhabitants of Florensac vs. town of Méjan
Before 18 December 1322	Lord of Pierrefort vs. Guillaume, lord of 'Bresons'

Before September 1326	Arnaud-Guillaume de Monlezun, count of Pardiac, and others vs. Genses de Montesquiou
Before September 1326	Loup de Foix, lord of Crampagna vs. Fortanier de Durban
Before 21 November 1332	Aymar, lord of Roussillon vs. Briend de Lagnieu, lord of the castle of Thorrenc
★Before 13 February 1338	Pierre de Maumont vs. priory of Saint-Hilaire la Croix
Before 16 January 1339	Othon de Pardeillan, damoiseau, lord of la Motte and the bastide of Pardeillan, Bernard of Lavardac, lord of Campagne, and others vs. 'Avisantius' de Caumont and the communities of 'Helizona'
Before 16 January 1339	Raymond-Almeric, lord of Bazillac in Bigorre vs. Bernard de Castelbajac
c.1339	Bertrand-Jourdain de l'Isle vs. Pierre-Raymond and Gui de Comminges
c.1342	Guillaume-Bernard d'Asnave, Jean de Castelgaillard, and others vs. Loup de Foix, lord of Crampagna, Roger de Crampagna, and others
Before 5 March 1343	Aicard, Béraud de Miremont, Aimeri and Estieu de Roquefort, Roumens, and others vs. Sicard de Paulin
★Before 8 April 1346	Gibert, lord of Pierrefort vs. Pierre de Turlande
c.1347	Géraud, lord of Crussol, Briand, lord of Belcastel, and Gerenton, lord of Solignac vs. Jauserans, lord of Saint-Didier
Before 20 December 1347	Viscount of Carlat vs. priory of Saint-Michel-de-Laussac and some nobles of Rouergue and the Auvergne
c.spring 1348	Géraud de la Barthe, lord of Aure vs. Hugues of Arpajon, lord
Before 28 June 1348	Jean de Lévis, marshal and lord of Mirepoix vs. François de Lévis of la Garde
1350	Lord of Mirambel vs. lord of Herment
★c.1351–62	Roger-Bernard de Lévis vs. Jean de Lévis, marshal and lord of Mirepoix
★Before January 1352	Aimieri de Thuri, lord of Puichéric vs. Guillaume and Pierre de Voisines
Before August 1352	Aimar de Roussillon, lord of Peyraud vs. city of Lyon
Before 6 December 1352	Hugues Adhémar, lord of Garde-Adhémar vs. bishop of Viviers
Before March 1355	Gui de Comminges vs. count of Isle-Jourdain
c.1359	Garin and Pierre de Pouzols vs. the family of a girl whom they had kidnapped
c.spring 1359/60	Guillaume de Jagonas vs. the lord of Faugerolles
c.1359–61	Armand de la Roüe and Robert Dauphin, lord of Saint-Ilpize vs. viscount of Polignac

From March 1360	Stephen de Vissac vs. Bertrand Bertrandi, lord of Saint-Roman
Before February 1361	Arnaud d'Allègre vs. Guillaume de Chalençon
March 1361/2	Pierre, viscount of Lautrec, and others vs. Sicard Hébert, lord of a castle in Aigrefeuille (Albigeois)
November 1361	Aimar, lord of Roussillon and Annonay vs. Celestine monks holding the castle of Colombiers
Before 24 March 1362	Gui de Lévis, viscount of Lautrec vs. bishop of Albi
★Before June 1362	Mura and Guillaume Causit vs. Johannes Columberii and son, holders of the castle of Savignac
Before August 1362	Guillaume de Cardillac, soi-disant viscount of Murat vs. Pierre and Reginald de Murat, soi-disant viscounts of Murat, town of Murat, and the bishop of Saint-Flour
16 February–May 1363	Sicard de Lescure vs. bishop and inhabitants of Albi
July 1363–4	Viscount of Montclar vs. Guillaume Agasse, co-lord of Saint-Urcisse
June 1364	*Bourg* of Carcassonne vs. castle of Trèbes and *cité* of Carcassonne
Before August 1366	Guigue and Géraud de Roussillon vs. Jeanne de Belcastel and Amédée de la Voulte
Before May 1369	Géraud and Ermessende de Montbrun, co-lords of Montbrun vs. Pierre de Montbrun, co-lord of Montbrun
★Before August 1371	Jourdain, count of l'Isle-Jourdain vs. Thibault de Lévis-Montbrun and Bertrand de Lévis-Lautrec, soi-disant co-lords of Florensac
★April 1374	Charles d'Espagne vs. Thibault de Lévis-Montbrun
Before September 1375	Humbert, lord of Villars and Annonay vs. lord of Vinay
c.1376	Jean, count of Astarac, vs. town of Mirande
c.1376	Nicolas de Beaufort, lord of Limeuil and Caumont, vs. Maragda, widow of Bertrand de Terride, and the other guardians of their children
1376–7	Count of Foix and count of Armagnac vs. Jeanne, dowager-countess of Comminges, and Marguerite, countess of Comminges
Before May 1380	Cardinal of Marmoutier vs. occupiers of the forts of the priory of Langogne
1381–84	Aimery VII, viscount of Narbonne vs. the inhabitants of Narbonne
1382	Lord of 'Aiguesvives' vs. Nicole de Lettres
1384	Beaucaire vs. Tarascon
★Before July 1389	Raimonnet de Péreilles vs. Perremont Cur
1389	Thibault de Lévis-Mirepoix vs. Roger-Bernard, marshal of Mirepoix
★c.1390	Gailhard de Motte vs. Perrot de Rives

Seigneurial wars in southern France

Between 1364 and 1391	Bertrand d'Astarac, lord of Salveterre and Gangagnez vs. Gimont and Simorre
c.1394	Essieu/Ayssio de Montesquieu vs. lord of Autun and town of Mirande
c.1394	Gérard de Armagnac, count of Pardiac and viscount of Fezensaguet vs. Menaud de Barbasan
*Before December 1395	The bastard of Comminges and Roger de Comminges, lord of Roquefort vs. Jean and Géraud de Lantar
Winter and spring 1400–1	Viscount of Fezensaguet and Jean d'Armagnac vs. Bernard VII, count of Armagnac and Marguerite, countess of Comminges
c.1402	Pons de Cardillac and sons vs. Reginald II, viscount of Murat
c.1408	Pierre and Bernard 'Coteti', heirs of the late Adhémar, lord of Rives and Puy vs. Jean de Beaufort, lord of Limeuil and numerous accomplices

BIBLIOGRAPHY

MANUSCRIPT SOURCES

ARCHIVES DÉPARTEMENTALES DE L'HÉRAULT (MONTPELLIER)

A 1–16 (registres des sénéchaux), 231, 238, 242
1E 1379

ARCHIVES DÉPARTEMENTALES DU TARN (ALBI)

Edt 4 FF 41
Edt 4 CC 151

ARCHIVES DÉPARTEMENTALES DE TARN-ET-GARONNE (MONTAUBAN)

A (*fonds d'Armagnac*) 38, 39, 297

ARCHIVES MUNICIPALES DE NARBONNE

AA 111
FF 722, 1462, 1464–5, 1468, 1700

ARCHIVES MUNICIPALES DE TOULOUSE

Series AA
Series FF

ARCHIVES NATIONALES DE FRANCE (PARIS)

Series J – Royal chancery
Series JJ – Registers, royal chancery
Series P 1420, 2288–97 – Records and Memorials of the Chambres des comptes de Paris
Series U 446 – Register of royal ordinances
Series X1a 1–47, 1469–77, 4784, 8300, 8844–9 – Registers, Parlement de Paris, civil
Series X1c – Accords, Parlement de Paris

Bibliography

Series x2a 1–16[1] – Registers, Parlement de Paris, criminal
Series Y 1–6 – Registers, Châtelet

CENTRE D'ÉTUDE D'HISTOIRE JURIDIQUE

Catalogues and database indexes at the Archives nationales, including 'Indexation des matières de XIA 12 (1347–1348)–XIA 31 à 38 (1381–1391)' and 'Indexation des matières des Olim ou registres des arrêts rendus par la cour du roi sous les règnes de Saint Louis à Philippe Le Long [1254–1319]' (both online at http://194.167.97.145/ihd/article.php3?id_article=35 [most recently accessed January 2013]), a keyword database of x2a 6–9 (Parlement criminel, December 1352–August 1382) (available on site), and card catalogues of names of parties to Parlement suits from 1350–1400 and of parties to accords (both available on site).

BIBLIOTHÈQUE NATIONALE DE FRANCE (PARIS)

Doat 49, 54, 110, 130, 191, 199, 249–57
Français 20692
Latin 4651, 3359, 5138, 9988, 9989, 9990, 11017
Nouvelles Acquisitions Françaises 7365

PRINTED SOURCES AND WORKS USED MAINLY FOR EDITIONS OF SOURCES

Actes du Parlement de Paris, ed. E. Boutaric, 2 vols. Paris, 1863–7 [repr. 1975].
Actes du Parlement de Paris, deuxième série – de l'an 1328 à l'an 1350: Jugés, ed. H. Furgeot, 3 vols. Paris, 1920.
Actes du Parlement de Paris: Parlement criminel: Règne de Philippe VI de Valois: Inventaire analytique des registres x2a 2 à 5, ed. B. Labat-Poussin, M. Langlois, and Y. Lanhers. Paris, 1987.
Alberico de Rosate, '*Commentarium de Statutis, libri quator*', *Tractatus de statutis diversorum autorum et Jc. in Europa praestantissimorum* ... Frankfurt, 1606.
Archives administratives de la ville de Reims, ed. P. Varin, 3 vols. in 5, DI. Paris, 1839–48.
Les archives de la cour des comptes aides et finances de Montpellier avec un essai de restitution des premiers registres de sénéchaussée, ed. E. Martin-Chabot, Bibliothèque de la Faculté des lettres de l'Université de Paris 22. Paris, 1907.
Bartolus of Saxoferrato, *Interpretum iuris civilis coryphaei*, in *Institutiones et Authenticas, commentaria. eiusdem tractatus XXXIX* ... Basel, 1562.
Bovet, H., *L'arbre des batailles*, ed. E. Nys. Brussels, 1883.
  The Tree of Battles of Honoré Bonet, ed. and trans. G. W. Coopland. Liverpool and Cambridge, MA, 1949.
Le cartulaire de Bigorre (XIe–XIIIe siècle), ed. X. Ravier and B. Cursente, DI, ser. in octavo 36. Paris, 2005.

---

[1] The first eleven folios of x2a are a later addition, containing letters from the session of 1338–9. Because the foliation starts over, I refer to documents from these first eleven folios as coming from x2abis and those from the rest of the register as x2a.

Bibliography

Cartulaire de Mirepoix, ed. F. Pasquier, 2 vols. Toulouse, 1921.

Choix de pièces inédites relatives au règne de Charles VI, ed. L. Douët-d'Arcq, 2 vol., SHF. Paris, 1863–4.

Christine de Pisan, *The Book of Deeds of Arms and of Chivalry*, ed. C. C. Willard, trans. S. Willard. University Park, PA, 1999.

Collections manuscrites sur l'histoire des provinces de France. Inventaire, ed. P. Lauer, 2 vols. Paris, 1905–11.

'Compte en dialecte lyonnais du XIVe siècle', ed. E. Philipon, *Revue de philologie française et de littérature* 19 (1905): 249–65.

'Comptes et mandements des receveurs et maîtres d'hôtel du vicomte de Fézensaguet (1365–1372)', ed. E. Forestié, *Bulletin historique et philologique du Comité des travaux historiques et scientifiques* (1898): 229–42.

Confessions et jugements de criminels au Parlement de Paris (1319–1350), ed. M. Langlois and Y. Lanhers. Paris, 1971.

Construire l'armée française. Textes fondateurs des institutions militaires, ed. V. Bessey, P. Bonin, and A. Crépin, 3 vols. Turnhout, 2006.

Le conventum (vers 1030). Un précurseur aquitain des premières épopées, ed. G. Beech, Y. Chauvin, and G. Pon, Publications romanes et françaises 212. Geneva, 1995.

Corpus iuris civilis, 5 vols. Lyon, 1612 (with *Glossa ordinaria*).

Corpus iuris civilis, ed. T. Mommsen, P. Krueger, and W. Kroll, 3 vols. Berlin, 1872–95 [repr. 1970–3].

Corpus iuris canonici, ed. E. Friedburg, 2 vols. Leipzig, 1879–81 [repr. 1959].

Correspondance administrative d'Alfonse de Poitiers, ed. A. Molinier, 2 vols., DI, ser. in quarto. Paris, 1894–1900.

Documentos de Jaime I de Aragón, ed. M. Desamparados Cabanes Pecourt and A. Huici Miranda, 5 vols., Textos medievales 49–51, 55, 77. Valencia and Zaragoza, 1976–88.

Documents historiques et généalogiques du Rouergue, ed. H. de Barrau, 4 vols. Rodez, 1853–60 [repr. 1972].

Documents historiques sur le Gévaudan. Mémoire relatif au paréage de 1307 conclu entre l'évêque Guillaume Durand II et le roi Philippe le Bel, ed. A. Maisonobe. Mende, 1896.

Documents historiques relatifs à la vicomté de Carlat..., ed. G. Saige, and le comte de Dienne, 2 vols., Collection de documents historiques. Monaco, 1900.

Documents nouveaux sur les moeurs populaires et le droit de vengeance dans les Pays-Bas au XVe siècle, ed. C. Petit-Dutaillis, Bibliothèque de XVe siècle 9. Paris, 1908.

Documents relatifs à la chute de la maison d'Armagnac-Fézensaguet et à la mort du comte de Pardiac, ed. P. Durrieu, Archives historique de la Gascogne, 2nd ser., 2. Paris, 1883.

du Breuil, Guillaume, *Stilus curie Parlamenti*, ed. Félix Aubert, CTSEEH. Paris, 1909.

du Cange, C. du Fresne, *Glossarium mediae et infimae latinitatis*, new edn, 10 vols. in 5. Niort, 1883–7 [repr. 1954].

Enquêtes administratives d'Alfonse de Poitiers, arrêts de son Parlement tenu à Toulouse, et textes annexes, 1249–1271, ed. P.-F. Fournier and P. Guébin, DI, ser. in quarto. Paris, 1959.

Essai de restitution des plus anciens mémoriaux de la Chambre des comptes de Paris, ed. M. J. Petit *et al.*, Bibliothèque de la Faculté des lettres de l'Université de Paris 7. Paris, 1899.

Bibliography

Études historiques et documents inédits sur l'Albigeois, le Castrais et l'ancien diocèse de Lavaur, ed. C. Compayré. Albi, 1841.

Étude sur les relations politiques du pape Urbain V avec les rois de France Jean II et Charles V (1362–1370), ed. M. Prou, Bibliothèque de l'École des hautes études, Sciences philologiques et historiques 76. Paris, 1887.

Étude sur la vie d'Arnoul d'Audrehem, maréchal de France, 1302–1370, ed. E. Molinier, Mémoires présentés par divers Savants à l'Académie des inscriptions et belles-lettres, 2nd ser., 6. Paris, 1883.

Extraits et procédures judiciaires (ancien régime et Révolution). Répertoire de la série U, ed. F. Hildesheimer. Paris, 2003.

Froissart, Jean. *Chroniques*, ed. K. de Lettenhove, 25 vols. Brussels, 1870–7.

Chroniques, ed. S. Luce *et al.* 15 vols. to date, SHF. Paris, 1869–present.

La Gascogne dans les registres du Trésor des Chartes, ed. C. Samaran, DI, ser. in octavo 4. Paris, 1966.

Giovanni da Legnano, *Tractatus de bello, de represaliis, et de duello*, ed. and trans. T. E. Holland, Classics of International Law 8. Oxford, 1917.

Les grandes chroniques de France. Chronique des règnes de Jean II et de Charles V, ed. R. Delachenal, 4 vols., SHF. Paris, 1910–20.

Gregory XI, *Lettres secrètes et curiales du pape Grégoire XI (1370–1378) rélatives à la France extraites des registres du Vatican*, ed. L. Mirot et al., 5 vols., Bibliothèque des Écoles françaises d'Athènes et de Rome, 3rd ser., 7. Paris, 1935–57.

La Guerre de Cent Ans vue à travers les registres du Parlement (1337–1369), ed. P.-C. Timbal et al. Paris, 1961.

Guide des recherches dans la fonds judiciaires de l'ancien régime, ed. M. Antoine et al. Paris, 1958.

Guillaume de Nangis, 'Chronicon', *HF*, xx: 543–82.

'Gesta Philippi regis Franciae, filii sanctae memoriae regis Ludovici', *HF*, xx: 466–539.

Guillaume de Puylaurens, *The Chronicle of William of Puylaurens: the Albigensian Crusade and its Aftermath*, ed. and trans. W. A. Sibly and M. D. Sibly. Woodbridge, 2003.

Chronique (1145–1275): Chronica magistri Guillelmi de Podio Laurentii, ed. and trans. (into French) J. Duvernoy, Sources d'histoire médiévale. Paris, 1976.

Inventaire analytique des livres de couleur et bannières du Châtelet de Paris, ed. A. Tuetey, 2 vols. in 1. Paris, 1899–1907.

Inventaire analytique des ordonnances enregistrées au Parlement de Paris jusqu'à la mort de Louis XII, ed. H. Stein. Paris, 1908.

Inventaire des archives communales antérieures à 1790: Ville de Narbonne: Série AA, ed. G. Mouynès. Narbonne, 1877.

Inventaire des archives communales antérieures à 1790: Ville de Toulouse, ed. E. Roschach, 2 vols. Toulouse, 1891.

Inventaires sommaires des archives communales antérieures à 1790: Nord, archives civiles, série B, ed. l'Abbé Dehaisnes and J. Finot, 2 vols. Lille, 1899.

Inventaire sommaire des archives communales antérieures à 1790: Somme, ville d'Amiens, série AA, ed. G. Durand. Amiens, 1891.

Inventaire sommaire des archives communales antérieures à 1790: Tarn, ville d'Albi, ed. E. Jolibois. Paris, 1869.

Bibliography

Inventaires sommaires des archives communales antérieures à 1790: Tarn-et-Garonne, archives civiles, série A, fonds d'Armagnac, ed. M. Maisonobe, C. Samaran, and M. Imbert. Montauban, 1910.

Inventaire sommaire des archives départementales antérieures à 1790: Aveyron, archives civiles, séries B, C et D, ed. H. Affre. Paris, 1866.

Inventaire sommaire des archives départementales antérieures à 1790: Basses-Pyrénées, archives civiles, série E, ed. P. Raymond, 2 vols. Paris, 1867–70.

Itinéraire de Philippe IV le Bel (1285–1314), ed. E. Lalou, 2 vols., Mémoires de l'Académie des inscriptions et belles-lettres 37. Paris, 2007.

Jean le Bel, *Chronique*, ed. J. Viard and E. Déprez, 2 vols. Librairie de la Société de l'histoire de France 317 and 324. Paris, 1904–5.

Jean de Joinville, *Vie de Saint Louis*, ed. J. Monfrin, Classiques Garnier. Paris, 1995.

le Coq, Jean, *Questiones Johannis Galli*, ed. M. Boulet, Bibliothèque des Écoles françaises d'Athènes et de Rome 156. Paris, 1944.

Le Languedoc et le Rouergue dans le Trésor des Chartes, ed. Y. Dossat, A.-M. LeMasson, and P. Wolff, DI, ser. in octavo 16. Paris, 1983.

Lettres closes, Lettres 'de par le roy' de Philippe de Valois, ed. R. Cazelles, SHF. Paris, 1958.

Lettres inédites de Philippe le Bel, ed. A. Baudouin. Paris, 1887.

Lettres de Philippe le Bel relatives au pays de Gévaudan, ed. J. Roucaute and M. Saché. Mende, 1896.

'Majus chronicon Lemovicense' and continuations, *HF*, XXI: 761–800.

'Mandements inédits d'Alphonse de Poitiers, comte de Toulouse (1262–70)', ed. A. Molinier, *Annales du Midi* 12 (1900): 289–328.

Ménard, L., *Histoire civile, ecclésiastique, et littéraire de la ville de Nismes avec des notes et les preuves*, 7 vols. Paris, 1750–8.

Miguel del Verms, 'Chroniques des comtes de Foix en langue béarnaise', in *Choix de chroniques et mémoires sur l'histoire de France, avec notices biographiques, XIVe siècle*, ed. J.-A.-C. Buchon. Orléans, 1875.

Olivier, Jacme, *Le livre de comptes de Jacme Olivier, marchand narbonnais du XIVe siècle*, ed. A. Blanc. Paris, 1899.

L'ordonnance cabochienne (26–27 mai 1413), ed. A. Coville, CTSEEH 8. Paris, 1891.

Périgueux et les deux derniers comtes de Périgord, ou Histoire des querelles de cette ville avec Archambaud V et Archambaud VI, ed. L. Dessalles. Paris, 1847.

Philippe de Beaumanoir, *Coutumes de Beauvaisis*, ed. A. Salmon, 2 vols., CTSEEH. Paris, 1899–1900.

Preuves de la maison de Polignac. Recueil de documents pour servir à l'histoire des anciennes provinces de Velay, Auvergne, Gévaudan, Vivarais, Forez, etc. (IXe–XVIIIe siècle), ed. A. Jacotin, 5 vols. Paris, 1898–1906.

'Procès de Bigorre, Pièces justificatives', ed. G. Balancie, *Bulletin de la Société académique des Hautes-Pyrénées* 77 (1930): 1–128.

'Procès de Bigorre, Pièces justificatives', ed. G. Balancie, *Revue des Hautes Pyrénées* 3 (1908): 44–48, 122–29, 276–282, 416–424; 4 (1909): 40–49, 169–80, 321–332; and 5 (1910): 5–15.

Recueil général des anciennes lois françaises, depuis l'an 420 jusqu'à la révolution de 1789 . . . , ed. F. A. Isambert *et al.*, 29 vols. Paris, 1821–33.

Registre criminel du Châtelet de Paris du 6 septembre 1389 au 18 mai 1392, ed. H. Duplès-Aiger, 2 vols. Paris, 1861–4.

Bibliography

Registres de la Jurade. 2 vols. Archives municipales de Bordeaux 3 and 4. Bordeaux, 1873–83.

Registres du trésor des chartes: Inventaire analytique établi par les archivistes aux Archives nationales, ed. R. Fawtier *et al.,* 3 vols. in 6. Paris, 1958–99.

Relations politiques des comtes de Foix avec la Catalogne jusqu'au commencement du XIVe siècle: Pièces justificatives, ed. C. Baudon de Mony. Paris, 1896.

Répertoire critique des anciens inventaires d'archives: Archives nationales, ed. L. le Grand *et al.,* 5 vols. Paris, 1929–38.

Répertoire numérique des Archives de la Chambre des comptes de Paris, série P, ed. A. Bruel. Paris, 1896 [repr. 1977].

Répertoire numérique des Archives du Parlement de Paris, série X, ed. E. Campardon. Paris, 1889 [repr. 1977].

Saisimentum comitatus Tholosani, ed. Y. Dossat, DI, ser. in octavo 1. Paris, 1966.

Sceaux gascons du moyen âge (gravures et notices), ed. P. Laplagne-Barris, 3 vols., Archives historiques de la Gascogne 15, 17, and 22. Paris and Auch, 1888–92.

'Sentence d'arbitrage entre Jourdain et Isarn de l'Isle (30 avril 1265)', ed. F. Galabert, *Annales du Midi* 9 (1897): 97–106.

'Some Documents Regarding the Fulfillment and Interpretation of the Treaty of Brétigny (1361–1369)', ed. P. Chaplais, *Camden Miscellany* 19, Camden 3rd ser., 80 (1952): 5–50.

Textes relatifs à l'histoire du Parlement depuis les origines jusqu'en 1314, ed. C.-V. Langlois, CTSEEH. Paris, 1888.

Titres de la maison ducale de Bourbon, ed. J.-L.-A. Huillard-Bréholles and L. de la Marche, 2 vols. Paris, 1867–74.

Urban V, *Lettres secrètes et curiales du pape Urbain V (1362–1369) se rapportant à la France publiées ou analysées d'après les registres du Vatican,* ed. P. Lecacheux and G. Mollat, 4 vols., Bibliothèque des Écoles françaises d'Athènes et de Rome, 3rd ser., 5. Paris, 1902–55.

The War of Saint-Sardos (1323–1325): Gascon Correspondence and Diplomatic Documents, ed. P. Chaplais, Camden, 3rd ser. 87. London, 1954.

SECONDARY WORKS

Aiton, D., '"Shame on Him who Allows Them to Live": the Jacquerie of 1358', Ph.D. thesis, University of Glasgow, 2011.

Algazi, G., *Herrengewalt und Gewalt der Herren im späten Mittelalter: Herrschaft, Gegenseitigkeit und Sprachgebrauch,* Historische Studien 17. Frankfurt am Main, 1996.

'The Social Use of Private War: Some Late Medieval Views Reviewed', *Tel Aviver Jahrbuch für deutsche Geschichte* 22 (1993): 253–73.

Althoff, G., 'Ira Regis: Prolegomena to a History of Royal Anger', in *Anger's Past: the Social Uses of an Emotion in the Middle Ages,* ed. B. Rosenwein. Ithaca, NY, 1998, pp. 59–74.

'Satisfaction: Peculiarities of the Amicable Settlement of Conflicts in the Middle Ages', in *Ordering Medieval Society: Perspectives on Intellectual and Practical Modes of Shaping Social Relations,* ed. B. Jussen, trans. P. Selwyn, The Middle Ages Series. Philadelphia, 2001, pp. 270–84.

Artonne, A., *Le mouvement de 1314 et les chartes provinciales de 1315.* Bibliothèque de la Faculté des lettres de l'Université de Paris 29. Paris, 1912.

Bibliography

Aston, T. H. and C. H. E. Philpin, eds., *The Brenner Debate: Agrarian Class Structure and Economic Development in Pre-Industrial Europe*, Past & Present Publications. Cambridge, 1985.

Aubert, F., *Histoire du Parlement de Paris de l'origine à François Ier (1250–1515)*, 2 vols. in 1. Geneva, 1970 [1894].

Autrand, F., *Charles VI: la folie du roi*. Paris, 1986.

Naissance d'un grand corps de l'état: les gens du Parlement de Paris, 1345–1454, Publications de la Sorbonne, NS Recherche 46. Paris, 1981.

Baldwin, J. W., *The Government of Philip Augustus: Foundations of French Royal Power in the Middle Ages*. Berkeley, 1986.

Balencie, G. 'Procès de Bigorre, pièces justificatives', *Bulletin de la Société académique des Hautes-Pyrénées* 77 (1930): 1–128.

Barnabé, P., 'Guerre et mortalité au début de la Guerre de Cent Ans: l'exemple des combattants Gascons (1337–1367)', *Annales du Midi* 113 (2001): 273–305.

Barstow, A. L., ed., *War's Dirty Secret: Rape, Prostitution, and Other Crimes against Women*. Cleveland, 2000.

Barthélemy, D., *L'an mil et la paix de Dieu: la France chrétienne et féodale, 980–1060* (Paris, 1999).

La mutation de l'an mil a-t-elle eu lieu? Servage et chevalerie dans la France des Xe et XIe siècles. Paris, 1997.

The Serf, the Knight, and the Historian, trans. G. R. Edwards. Ithaca, NY, 2009.

Bartlett, R., '"Mortal Enmities": the Legal Aspect of Hostility in the Middle Ages', in *Feud, Violence, and Practice: Essays in Medieval Studies in Honor of Stephen D. White*, ed. B. S. Tuten and T. L. Billado. Farnham, 2010, pp. 197–212.

Barton, R. E., '"Zealous Anger" and the Renegotiation of Aristocratic Relationships in Eleventh- and Twelfth-Century France', *Anger's Past: the Social Uses of an Emotion in the Middle Ages*, ed. B. Rosenwein. Ithaca, NY, 1998, pp. 153–70.

Beaune, C., *The Birth of an Ideology: Myths and Symbols of Nation in Late-Medieval France*, trans. S. R. Huston, ed. F. L. Cheyette. Berkeley, 1991.

Beik, W., 'The Absolutism of Louis XIV as Social Collaboration', *Past & Present* 188 (2005): 195–224.

Bellamy, J. G., *Bastard Feudalism and the Law*. London, 1989.

Bennett, M., 'The Development of Battle Tactics in the Hundred Years War', in *Arms, Armies and Fortifications in the Hundred Years War*, ed. A. Curry and M. Hughes. Woodbridge, 1994, pp. 1–20.

Berger, É., *Histoire de Blanche de Castille: reine de France*, Bibliothèque des Écoles françaises d'Athènes et de Rome 70. Paris, 1895.

Bériac-Lainé, F. and C. Given-Wilson, *Les prisonniers de la bataille de Poitiers*, Études d'histoire médiévale 6. Paris, 2002.

Bessen, D. M., 'The Jacquerie: Class War or Co-opted Rebellion?', *Journal of Medieval History* 11 (1985): 43–59.

Biget, J.-L., 'Un procès d'inquisition à Albi en 1300', in *Le credo, la morale et l'Inquisition*, Cahiers de Fanjeaux 6. Toulouse, 1971, pp. 273–341.

Biraben, J.-N., *Les hommes et la peste en France et dans les pays européens et méditerranéens*, 2 vols., Civilisations et sociétés 35–6. Paris, 1975–6.

Bibliography

Bisson, T. N., *Assemblies and Representation in Languedoc in the Thirteenth Century.* Princeton, 1964.

'Consultative Functions in the King's Parlements (1250–1314)', *Speculum* 44 (1969): 353–73 [repr. 1989].

The Crisis of the Twelfth Century: Power, Lordship, and the Origins of European Government. Princeton and Oxford, 2009.

'The "Feudal Revolution"', *Past & Present* 142 (1994): 6–42.

The Medieval Crown of Aragon: a Short History. Oxford, 1986.

Medieval France and her Pyrenean Neighbors: Studies in Early Institutional History, Studies presented to the International Commission for the History of Representative and Parliamentary Institutions/Études présentées à la Commission internationale pour l'histoire des assemblées d'états 70. London, 1989.

'The Organized Peace in Southern France and Catalonia (*c.* 1140–*c.* 1233)', *AHR* 82 (1977): 290–311 [repr. 1989].

Bloch, C. and J. M. Carbasse, 'Aux origines de la série criminelle du Parlement: le registre x2a 1', *Histoire et archives* 12 (2002): 7–26.

Bloch, M., *Feudal Society*, trans. L. A. Manyon, 2 vols. Chicago, 1961.

Bois, G., *The Crisis of Feudalism: Economy and Society in Eastern Normandy, c. 1300–1550*, Past & Present Publications. Cambridge, 1984.

Bommersbach, B. 'Gewalt in der Jacquerie von 1358', in *Gewalt im politischen Raum. Fallanalysen vom Spätmittelalter bis ins 20. Jahrhundert*, ed. N. Bulst, I. Gilcher-Holtey, and H.-G. Haupt, Historische Politikforschung 15. Frankfurt, 2008, pp. 46–81.

Bongert, Y., 'Rétribution et réparation dans l'ancien droit français', *Mémoires de la Société pour l'histoire du droit et des institutions des anciens pays bourguignons, comtois et romands* 45 (1988): 59–107.

Bonnaud-Delamare, R., 'Fondement des institutions de paix au XI siècle', in *Mélanges d'histoire du moyen âge dédiés à la mémoire de Louis Halphen.* Paris, 1951, pp. 19–26.

'La légende des associations de la paix en Rouergue et en Languedoc au début du XIIIe siècle (1170–1229)', in *Bulletin philologique et historique, Comité des travaux historiques et scientifiques, année 1938.* Paris, 1938, pp. 47–78.

Boudet, M., *Thomas de la Marche, bâtard de France et ses aventures (1318–1361).* Riom, 1900.

Boutaric, É., *Saint Louis et Alfonse de Poitiers. Étude sur la réunion des provinces du Midi et de l'ouest à la couronne.* Paris, 1870.

Boutruche, R., *La crise d'une société. Seigneurs et paysans du Bordelais pendant la Guerre de Cent Ans*, Publications de la Faculté des lettres de l'Université de Strasbourg 110. Paris, 1947.

'The Devastation of Rural Areas during the Hundred Years War and the Agricultural Recovery of France', in *The Recovery of France in the Fifteenth Century*, ed. P. S. Lewis, trans. G. F. Martin, Stratum Series. London, 1971, pp. 23–59.

Braun, P., 'La valeur documentaire des lettres de rémission', *La faute, la répression et le pardon*, vol. I of *Actes du 107ème Congrès national des sociétés savantes (Brest, 1982).* Paris, 1984, pp. 207–21.

Brissaud, Y.-B., 'Le droit de grâce à la fin du moyen-âge (XIVe–XVe siècles): Contribution a l'étude de la restauration de la souveraineté monarchique', Ph.D. thesis, Faculté de droit et des sciences sociales, Université de Poitiers, 1971.

Bibliography

Brown, E. A. R., 'Cessante Causa and the Taxes of the Last Capetians: the Political Applications of a Philosophical Maxim', in *Post Scripta: Essays on Medieval Law and the Emergence of the European State in Honor of Gaines Post*, ed. J. R. Strayer and D. E. Queller, Studia Gratiana 15. Rome, 1972, pp. 565–87.

'Charters and Leagues in Early Fourteenth-Century France: the Movement of 1314 and 1315', Ph.D. thesis, Harvard University and Radcliffe College, 1961.

The Monarchy of Capetian France and Royal Ceremonial, Collected Studies 345. Aldershot, 1991.

'Moral Imperatives and Conundrums of Conscience: Reflections on Philip the Fair of France', *Speculum* 87 (2012): 1–36.

'Persona et Gesta: the Image and Deeds of the Thirteenth-Century Capetians, the Case of Philip the Fair', *Viator* 19 (1988): 219–46.

'Philippe le Bel and the Remains of Saint Louis', *Gazette des beaux-arts* 95 (1980): 175–82.

Politics and Institutions in Capetian France, Collected Studies 350. Aldershot, 1991.

'The Prince is Father of the King: the Character and Childhood of Philip the Fair of France', *Mediaeval Studies* 49 (1987): 282–334.

'Reform and Resistance to Royal Authority in Fourteenth-Century France: the Leagues of 1314–1315', *Parliaments, Estates, and Representation* 1 (1981): 109–37.

'Royal Commissioners and Grants of Privilege in Philip the Fair's France: Pierre de Latilli, Raoul de Breuilli, and the Ordonnance for the Seneschalsy of Toulouse and Albi of 1299', *Francia* 13 (1985/6): 151–90.

Brown, W. C., *Violence in Medieval Europe*. Harlow, 2011.

Brownmiller, S., *Against our Will: Men, Women, and Rape*. New York, 1975.

Brundage, J. A., 'The Limits of the War-Making Power: the Contribution of the Medieval Canonists', in *The Crusades, Holy War, and Canon Law*, Variorum Collected Studies 338. Aldershot, 1991 [1986], pp. 69–85.

Brunel, C., 'Les juges de la paix en Gévaudan au milieu du XIe siècle', *BEC* 109 (1951): 32–41.

Brunner, O., *Land und Herrschaft: Grundfragen der territorialen Verfassungsgeschichte Südostdeutschlands im Mittelalter*. Veröffentlichungen des Instituts für Österreichische Geschichtsforschung 1. Baden bei Wien, 1939.

Land and Lordship: Structures of Governance in Medieval Austria, trans. H. Kaminsky and J. Van Horn Melton, The Middle Ages Series. Philadelphia, 1992.

Buisson, L., *König Ludwig IX., der Heilige, und das Recht: Studie zur Gestaltung der Lebensordnung Frankreichs im hohen Mittelalter*. Freiburg, 1954.

Butaud, G., 'L'excommunication des agresseurs des terres de l'église (Avignon, Comtat Venaissin) aux XIVe et XVe siècles', in *Prêcher la paix et discipliner la société: Italie, France, Angleterre (XIIIe–XVe siècles)*, ed. R. M. Dessì, Collection d'études médiévales de Nice 5. Turnhout, 2005, pp. 225–42.

Buylaert, F., W. de Clercq, and J. Dumolyn, 'Sumptuary Legislation, Material Culture, and the Semiotics of 'Vivre Noblement' in the County of Flanders (14th–16th Centuries)', *Social History* 36 (2011): 393–417.

Campbell, B., 'The Agrarian Problem in the Early Fourteenth Century', *Past & Present* 188 (2005): 3–70.

Bibliography

Carbonnières, L. de, 'Le pouvoir royal face aux mécanismes de la guerre privée à la fin du moyen âge. L'exemple du Parlement de Paris', *Droits. Revue française de théorie, de philosophie et de culture juridiques* 46 (2007): 3–17.

La procédure devant la chambre criminelle du Parlement de Paris au XIVe siècle, Histoire et archives, hors-série, 4. Paris, 2004.

'La vanité de dire le droit ou l'inexécution des arrêts: l'affaire de la succession à la vicomté de Murat (vers 1360–vers 1470)', in *Dire le droit: Normes, juges, jurisconsultes*, ed. B. Anagnostou-Canas. Paris, 2006, pp. 191–221.

Carolus-Barré, L., 'La grande ordonnance de 1254 sur la réforme de l'administration et la police du royaume', in *Septième centenaire de la mort de Saint Louis: Actes des colloques de Royaumont et de Paris (21–27 mai 1970)*, Paris, 1976, pp. 85–96.

Carpenter, C., *The War of the Roses: Politics and the Constitution in England, c. 1437–1509*, Cambridge Medieval Textbooks. Cambridge, 1997.

Carroll, S., *Blood and Violence in Early Modern France.* Oxford, 2006.

'The Peace in the Feud in Sixteenth- and Seventeenth-Century France', *Past & Present* 178 (2003): 74–115.

Cazaux, L., 'Réglementation militaire royale et usage de la force dans le royaume de France (XIVe–XVIe siècles)', *Inflexions. Civils et militaires: pouvoir dire* 13 (2010): 93–104.

Cazelles, R., 'La Jacquerie fut-elle un mouvement paysan?' *Académie des inscriptions et belles lettres. Comptes rendus* 122 (1978): 654–66.

'La peste de 1348–1349 en langue d'oïl: Épidémie prolétarienne et enfantine', in *Bulletin philologique et historique (jusqu'à 1610) du comité des travaux historiques et scientifiques, année 1962.* Paris, 1965, pp. 293–305.

'La réglementation royale de la guerre privée de Saint Louis à Charles V et la précarité des ordonnances', *RHDFE*, 4th ser., 38 (1960): 530–48.

La société politique et la crise de la royauté sous Philippe de Valois, Bibliothèque Elzévirienne, new ser., études et documents. Paris, 1958.

Société politique, noblesse et couronne sous Jean le Bon et Charles V, Société de l'École des chartes, mémoires et documents 28. Geneva, 1982.

'Une exigence de l'opinion depuis Saint Louis: la réformation du royaume', *Annuaire-bulletin de la Société de l'histoire de France* (1962–3): 91–9.

Challet, V., '"Mundare et auferre malas erbas": la révolte des Tuchins en Languedoc (1381–1384)', 4 vols., Ph.D. thesis, Université de Paris–I, 2002.

'La révolte des Tuchins: Banditisme social ou sociabilité villageoise?' *Médiévales* 34 (1998): 101–12.

Chanson, M., *Les grandes compagnies en Auvergne au XIVe siècle: Seguin de Badefol à Brioude et à Lyon.* Brioude, 1887.

Chaplais, P., 'La souveraineté du roi de France et le pouvoir législatif en Guyenne au début du XIVe siècle', *Le moyen âge* 18 (1963): 449–69.

Charbonnier, P., *Une autre France: la seigneurie rurale en Basse Auvergne du XIVe au XVIe siècle*, 2 vols., Publications de l'Institut d'études du Massif central 20. Clermont-Ferrand, 1980.

'Qui furent les Tuchins?', in *Violence et contestation au moyen âge: Actes du 114e Congrès national des sociétés savantes (Paris, 1989).* Paris, 1990, pp. 235–47.

Cheyette, F. L., '"Feudalism": a Memoir and an Assessment', in *Feud, Violence, and Practice: Essays in Medieval Studies in Honor of Stephen D. White*, ed. B. S. Tuten and T. L. Billado. Farnham, 2010, pp. 119–33.

Bibliography

'The Royal Safeguard in Medieval France', in *Post Scripta: Essays on Medieval Law and the Emergence of the European State in Honor of Gaines Post*, ed. J. R. Strayer and D. E. Queller, Studia Gratiana 15. Rome, 1972, pp. 631–52.

'Some Reflections on Violence, Reconciliation, and the "Feudal Revolution"', in *Conflict in Medieval Europe: Changing Perspectives on Society and Culture*, ed. W. C. Brown and P. Górecki. Aldershot, 2003, pp. 243–64.

'Suum cuique tribuere', *French Historical Studies* 6 (1970): 287–99.

Cohn, S. K., *The Black Death Transformed: Disease and Culture in Early Renaissance Europe*. Oxford, 2002.

Lust for Liberty: the Politics of Social Revolt in Medieval Europe, 1200–1425: Italy, France, and Flanders. Cambridge, MA, 2006.

Collins, J. B., *The State in Early Modern France*, 2nd edn, New Approaches to European History. Cambridge, 2009.

Contamine, P., 'Les compagnies d'aventure en France pendant la Guerre de Cent Ans', *Mélanges de l'École français de Rome. Moyen-âge, temps modernes* 87 (1975): 365–96.

'The French Nobility and the War', in *The Hundred Years War*, ed. K. Fowler. London, 1971, pp. 135–62.

Guerre, état, et société à la fin du moyen âge: Études sur les armées des rois de France, 1337–1494, Civilisations et sociétés 24. Paris, 1972 [repr. 2004].

Coopland, G. W., '*The Tree of Battles* and Some of its Sources', *Tijdschrift voor Rechtsgeschiedenis* 5 (1924): 173–207.

Coss, P. R., 'Bastard Feudalism Revised', *Past & Present* 125 (1989): 27–64.

Cowdrey, H. E. J., 'The Peace and Truce of God in the Eleventh Century', *Past & Present* 46 (1970): 42–67.

Curry, A., *The Hundred Years War, 1337–1453*, 2nd edn. London, 2003.

Cuttler, S. H., *The Law of Treason and Treason Trials in Later Medieval France*, Cambridge Studies in Medieval Life and Thought, 3rd ser., 16. Cambridge, 1981.

Davis, N. Z., *Fiction in the Archives: Pardon Tales and their Tellers in Sixteenth-Century France*. Stanford, 1987.

Society and Culture in Early Modern France: Eight Essays. Stanford, 1975.

Delachenal, R., *Histoire de Charles V*, 5 vols. Paris, 1909–31.

Denifle, H., *La désolation des églises, monastères et hôpitaux en France pendant la Guerre de Cent Ans*, 2 vols. Paris, 1897–9 [repr. 1965].

Desazars, M.-L., 'Les évêques d'Albi aux XIIe et XIIIe siècles: Origines et progrès de leur puissance temporelle et de leurs revenus ecclésiastiques', *Mémoires de la Société archéologique du midi de la France* 12 (1880–2): 305–88.

DeVries, K., *Infantry Warfare in the Early Fourteenth Century: Discipline, Tactics, and Technology*, Warfare in History 2. Woodbridge, 1996.

Dillay, M., 'Instruments de recherche du fonds du Parlement de Paris, dressés au greffe de la juridiction', *Archives et bibliothèques* 3 (1937–8): 13–30, 82–92, 190–9.

Dognon, P., *Les institutions politiques et administratives du pays de Languedoc du XIIe siècle aux guerres de religion*, Bibliothèque méridionale, 2nd ser., 4. Toulouse, 1895.

Donahue, C., 'The Emergence of Crime–Tort Distinction in England', in *Conflict in Medieval Europe: Changing Perspectives on Society and Culture*, ed. W. C. Brown and P. Górecki. Aldershot, 2003, pp. 219–28.

Dossat, Y., 'Alfonse de Poitiers et les clercs', in *Les évêques, les clercs et le roi (1250–1300)*, Cahiers de Fanjeaux 7. Toulouse, 1972, pp. 361–91.

Bibliography

Les crises de l'Inquisition toulousaine au XIIIe siècle (1233–1273). Bordeaux, 1959.

'Gui Foucois, enquêteur–réformateur, archevêque et pape (Clément IV)', in *Les évêques, les clercs et le roi (1250–1300)*, Cahiers de Fanjeaux 7. Toulouse, 1972, pp. 23–57.

'Patriotisme méridional du clergé au XIIIe siècle', in *Les évêques, les clercs et le roi (1250–1300)*, Cahiers de Fanjeaux 7. Toulouse, 1972, pp. 419–52.

Duby, G., *Le dimanche de Bouvines, 27 juillet 1214*, Trente journées qui ont fait la France. Paris, 1973.

La société aux XIe et XIIe siècles dans la région mâconnaise, Bibliothèque générale de l'École pratique des hautes études 6. Paris, 1953.

Dumolyn, J., 'Justice, Equity, and the Common Good: the State Ideology of the Councilors of the Burgundian Dukes', in *The Ideology of Burgundy: the Promotion of National Consciousness, 1365–1565*, ed. D. J. D. Boulton and J. R. Veenstra, Brill's Studies in Intellectual History 145. Leiden, 2006, pp. 1–20.

'Nobles, Patricians, and Officers: the Making of a Regional Political Elite in Late Medieval Flanders', *Journal of Social History* 40 (2006): 431–52.

Dupont-Ferrier, G., *Les officiers royaux des bailliages et sénéchaussées et les institutions monarchiques locales en France à la fin du moyen âge*, Bibliothèque de l'École des hautes études: Sciences historiques et philologiques 145. Paris, 1902 [repr. 1974].

Durvin, P., 'Les origines de la Jacquerie à Saint-Leu-d'Esserent en 1358', in *Actes du 101e Congrès national des sociétés savantes (Lille, 1976)*. Paris, 1978, pp. 365–74.

Elías, N., *The Civilizing Process: Sociogenetic and Psychogenetic Investigations*, rev. edn, ed. E. Dunning, J. Goudsblom, and S. Mennell, trans. E. Jephcott. Oxford, 2000.

Emery, R. W., 'The Black Death of 1348 in Perpignan', *Speculum* 42 (1967): 611–23.

Famiglietti, R. C., *Royal Intrigue: Crisis at the Court of Charles VI, 1392–1420*, AMS Studies in the Middle Ages 9. New York, 1986.

Favier, J., *Philippe le Bel*. Paris, 1978.

Firnhaber-Baker, J., 'Formulating Opposition to Seigneurial War in the Parlement de Paris', in *La formule au moyen âge*, ed. E. Louviot, ARTEM 15. Turnhout, 2013, pp. 209–18.

'From God's Peace to the King's Order: Late Medieval Limitations on Non-Royal Warfare', *Essays in Medieval Studies* 23 (2006): 19–30.

'*Guerram Palam et Publice Faciendo:* Local War and Royal Authority in Late Medieval Southern France', Ph.D. thesis, Harvard University, 2007.

'*Jura in medio:* the Settlement of Seigneurial Disputes in Later Medieval Languedoc', *French History* 26 (2012): 441–59.

'Seigneurial War and Royal Power in Later Medieval Southern France', *Past & Present* 208 (2010): 37–76.

'*À son de cloche:* the Interpretation of Public Order and Legitimate Authority in Northern France, 1355–58', in *Espacio público, opinión y comunicación política a fines de la Edad Media*, ed. H. R. Oliva Herrer. Seville, forthcoming.

'Techniques of Seigneurial War in the Fourteenth Century', *Journal of Medieval History* 36 (2010): 90–103.

Flammermont, J., 'La Jacquerie en Beauvaisis', *RH* 9 (1879): 123–43.

Fourquin, G., *The Anatomy of Popular Rebellion in the Middle Ages*, trans. A. Chesters Europe in the Middle Ages 9. New York, 1978.

Bibliography

Fowler, K., *The Great Companies,* vol. 1 of *Medieval Mercenaries.* Oxford and Malden, MA, 2001.

François, M., 'Note sur les lettres de rémission transcrites dans les registres du Trésor des chartes', *BEC* 103 (1942): 317–24.

Funck-Brentano, F., *Les origines de la Guerre de Cent Ans. Philippe le Bel en Flandre.* Paris, 1897.

Gaposchkin, M. C., 'Boniface VIII, Philip the Fair, and the Sanctity of Louis IX', *Journal of Medieval History* 29 (2003): 1–26.

The Making of Saint Louis: Kingship, Sanctity, and Crusade in the Later Middle Ages. Ithaca, NY, 2008.

Gauvard, C., *'De grace especial': Crime, état et société en France à la fin du moyen âge,* 2 vols., Histoire ancienne et médiéval 24. Paris, 1991.

'Grâce et exécution capitale: les deux visages de la justice royale française à la fin du moyen âge', *BEC* 153 (1995): 275–90.

'L'image du roi justicier en France à la fin du moyen âge, d'après les lettres de rémission', in *La faute, la répression et le pardon,* vol. 1 of *Actes du 107ème Congrès national des sociétés savantes (Brest, 1982).* Paris, 1984, pp. 165–96.

Violence et ordre public au moyen âge, Les médiévistes français 5. Paris, 2005.

Geary, P., 'Living with Conflicts in Stateless France: a Typology of Conflict Management Mechanisms, 1050–1200', in *Living with the Dead in the Middle Ages.* Ithaca, 1994 [1986], pp. 125–60.

Gluckman, M., 'The Peace in the Feud', in *Custom and Conflict in Africa.* Oxford, 1956, pp. 1–26.

Goetz, H.-W., 'Protection of the Church, Defense of the Law, and Reform: On the Purposes and Character of the Peace of God, 989–1038', in *The Peace of God: Social Violence and Religious Response in France around the Year 1000,* ed. T. Head and R. Landes. Ithaca, NY, 1992, pp. 259–79.

Gouron, A. and A. Rigaudière, eds., *Renaissance du pouvoir législatif et genèse de l'état modern,* Publications de la Société d'histoire du droit et des institutions des anciens pays de droit écrit 3. Montpellier, 1988.

Grabher O'Brien, J., 'In Defense of the Mystical Body: Giovanni de Legnano's Theory of Reprisals', *Roman Legal Tradition* 1 (2002): 25–55.

Graboïs, A., 'De la trêve de Dieu à la paix du roi: Étude sur les transformations du mouvement de la paix au XIIe siècle', in *Mélanges offerts à René Crozet,* ed. P. Gallais and Y.-J. Riou, 2 vols., Cahiers de civilisation médiévale. Poitiers, 1966, 1: 585–96.

Grün, A., 'Notice sur les archives du Parlement de Paris', in *Actes du Parlement de Paris,* ed. E. Boutaric, 2 vols. Paris, 1863–7, 1: I–CCCXXX.

Guenée, B., *States and Rulers in Later Medieval Europe,* trans. J. Vale. Oxford, 1985.

Tribunaux et gens de justice dans le bailliage de Senlis à la fin du moyen âge (vers 1380–vers 1550), Publications de la Faculté des lettres de l'Université de Strasbourg 144. Strasbourg, 1963.

Guigue, G., *Les tard-venus en Lyonnais, Forez et Beaujolais, 1356–1369.* Lyon, 1886.

Guilhiermoz, P., *Enquêtes et procès. Étude sur la procédure et le fonctionnement du Parlement au XIVe siècle.* Paris, 1892.

Guillot, O., A. Rigaudière, and Y. Sassier, *Pouvoirs et institutions dans la France médiévale,* 2nd edn, 2 vols. Paris, 1994.

Bibliography

Halsall, G., 'Violence and Society in the Early Medieval West: an Introductory Survey', in *Violence and Society in the Early Medieval West*, ed. G. Halsall. Woodbridge, 1998, pp. 1–45.

Hanawalt, B. A., 'Fur-Collar Crime: the Pattern of Crime among the Fourteenth-Century English Nobility', *Journal of Social History* 8 (1975): 1–17.

Harding, A., *Medieval Law and the Foundations of the State*. Oxford, 2002.

Harriss, G., 'Political Society and the Growth of Government in Late Medieval England', *Past & Present* 138 (1993): 28–57.

Shaping the Nation: England, 1360–1461, New Oxford History of England. Oxford, 2005.

Head, T., 'Peace and Power in France around the Year 1000', *Essays in Medieval Studies* 23 (2006): 1–17.

Henneman, J. B., *Olivier de Clisson and Political Society in France under Charles V and Charles VI*, The Middle Ages Series. Philadelphia, 1996.

Royal Taxation in Fourteenth-Century France: the Captivity and Ransom of John II, 1356–1370, Memoirs of the American Philosophical Society 116. Philadelphia, 1976.

Royal Taxation in Fourteenth-Century France: the Development of War Financing, 1322–1356. Princeton, 1971.

'Who were the Marmousets?', *Medieval Prosopography* 5 (1984): 19–63.

Henry, A., 'Guillaume de Plaisians, ministre de Philippe le Bel', *Le moyen âge* 5 (1892): 32–8.

Hewitt, H. J., *The Black Prince's Expedition of 1355–1357*. Manchester, 1958.

Higounet, C., *Le comté de Comminges de ses origines à son annexion à la couronne*, 2 vols., Bibliothèque méridionale, 2nd ser., 32. Toulouse and Paris, 1949.

Hildesheimer, F., 'Les deux premiers registres des "ordonnances" ou la logique floue de l'enregistrement', *Histoire et archives* 12 (2002): 79–114.

Hoffmann, H., *Gottesfriede und Treuga Dei*, MGH, Schriften 20. Stuttgart, 1964.

Hyams, P. R., 'Does it Matter When the English Began to Distinguish between Crime and Tort?', in *Violence in Medieval Society*, ed. R. W. Kaeuper. Woodbridge, 2000, pp. 107–28.

'Nastiness and Wrong, Rancor and Reconciliation', in *Conflict in Medieval Europe: Changing Perspectives on Society and Culture*, ed. W. C. Brown and P. Górecki. Aldershot, 2003, pp. 195–218.

Rancor and Reconciliation in Medieval England, Conjunctions of Religion and Power in the Medieval Past. Ithaca, NY, 2003.

'Was There Really Such a Thing as Feud in the High Middle Ages?', in *Vengeance in the Middle Ages: Emotion, Religion, and Feud*, ed. S. A. Throop and P. R. Hyams (Farnham, 2010), 151–75.

Jordan, W. C., 'Anti-corruption Campaigns in Thirteenth-Century Europe', *Journal of Medieval History* 35 (2009): 204–19.

The Great Famine: Northern Europe in the Early Fourteenth Century. Princeton, 1996.

Louis IX and the Challenge of the Crusade: a Study in Rulership. Princeton, 1979.

Unceasing Strife, Unending Fear: Jacques de Thérines and the Freedom of the Church in the Age of the Last Capetians. Princeton, 2005.

Juchs, J.-P., 'Enjeux de l'identité au Parlement criminel: l'exemple des actes relatifs à la faide (début du XIVe siècle)', in *Hypothèses 2006, Travaux de l'école doctorale d'histoire de l'Université Paris 1 Panthéon–Sorbonne*. Paris, 2007, pp. 179–90.

Bibliography

'"Et par vertu aussi du general commandement que nous aviens fais faire pour cause de nos guerres c'est assavoir que aucun ne guerroyast ne fist aucun contrevangement nos dictes guerres durans" la faide entre normes juridiques et pratiques judiciaires en France dans la première moitié du XVe siècle', in *Normes juridiques et pratiques judiciaires du moyen âge à l'époque contemporaine*, ed. B. Garnot. Dijon, 2007, pp. 51–9.

'Vengeance et guerre seigneuriale au XIVe siècle (royaume de France–principauté de Liège)', Ph.D. thesis, 2 vols., Université Paris I Panthéon–Sorbonne, 2012.

Kaeuper, R. W., 'Chivalry and the "Civilizing Process"', in *Violence in Medieval Society*, ed R.W. Kaeuper. Woodbridge, 2000, pp. 21–35.

Chivalry and Violence in Medieval Europe. Oxford, 1999.

War, Justice, and Public Order: England and France in the Later Middle Ages. Oxford, 1988.

Kaminsky, H., 'The Noble Feud in the Later Middle Ages', *Past & Present* 177 (2002): 55–83.

Kämpf, H., *Pierre Dubois und die geistigen Grundlagen des französischen Nationalbewusstseins um 1300*, Beiträge zur Kulturgeschichte des Mittelalters und der Renaissance 54. Leipzig and Berlin, 1935.

Keen, M. H., *The Laws of War in the Late Middle Ages*, Studies in Political History. London, 1965.

'Treason Trials under the Law of Arms: the Alexander Prize Essay', *Transactions of the Royal Historical Society*, 5th ser., 12 (1962): 85–103.

Kicklighter, J., 'English Bordeaux in Conflict: the Execution of Pierre Vigier de la Rouselle and its Aftermath, 1312–24', *Journal of Medieval History* 9 (1983): 1–14.

'The Nobility of English Gascony: the Case of Jourdain de l'Isle', *Journal of Medieval History* 13 (1987): 327–42.

Koziol, G., *Begging Pardon and Favor: Ritual and Political Order in Early Medieval France*. Ithaca, NY, 1992.

Krynen, J., *L'empire du roi: Idées et croyances politiques en France, XIIIe–XVe siècle*, Bibliothèque des histoires. Paris, 1993.

Langlois, C.-V., 'Les origines du Parlement de Paris', *RH* 42 (1890): 74–114.

'Les papiers de Guillaume de Nogaret et de Guillaume de Plaisians au Trésor des Chartes', *Notices et extraits des manuscrits de la Bibliothèque nationale et autres bibliothèques* 39, pt. I (1909): 211–54.

Le règne de Philippe III le Hardi. Paris, 1887.

Langlois, M., 'Les archives criminelles du Parlement de Paris', in *La faute, la répression et le pardon*, vol. I of *Actes du 107ème Congrès national des sociétés savantes (Brest, 1982)*. Paris, 1984, pp. 7–14.

Langmuir, G. I., '"Judei Nostri" and the Beginning of Capetian Legislation', *Traditio* 16 (1960): 203–39.

Lecuppre-Desjardin, E. and A.-L. van Bruaene, eds., De Bono Communi: *the Discourse and Practice of the Common Good in the European City (13th–16th c.)*, Studies in European Urban History (1100–1800) 22. Turnhout, 2010.

le Goff, J., *Saint Louis*, Bibliothèque des histoires. Paris, 1996.

Lehoux, F., *Jean de France, duc de Berri: sa vie. Son action politique (1340–1416)*, 4 vols. Paris, 1966–8.

Lehugeur, P., *Histoire de Philippe le Long, roi de France (1316–1322)*, 2 vols. Paris, 1897–1931 [repr. 1975].

Bibliography

Lexicon des Mittlealters, ed. R. Auty *et al.*, 10 vols. Munich, 1977–99.

Lot, F. and R. Fawtier, *Histoire des institutions françaises au moyen âge,* 3 vols. Paris, 1957–62.

Lucas, H. S., 'The Great European Famine of 1315, 1316, and 1317', *Speculum* 5 (1930): 343–77.

Luce, S., *Histoire de la Jacquerie d'âpres des documents inédits,* new edn. Paris, 1895.

McFarlane, K. B., '"Bastard Feudalism"', *Bulletin of the Institute of Historical Research* 20 (1943–5): 161–80.

The Nobility of Later Medieval England: the Ford Lectures for 1953 and Related Studies. Oxford, 1973.

McNamara, J., *Giles Aycelin: the Servant of Two Masters.* Syracuse, NY, 1973.

Maddern, P. C., *Violence and Social Order: East Anglia, 1422–1442,* Oxford Historical Monographs. Oxford, 1992.

Maddicott, J. R., *Simon de Montfort.* Cambridge, 1994.

Magee, J., 'Crusading at the Court of Charles VI, 1388–1396', *French History* 12 (1998): 367–83.

Maillard, F., 'À propos d'un ouvrage récent. Notes sur quelques officiers royaux du Languedoc vers 1280–1335', in *France du Nord et France du Midi: Contacts et influences réciproques,* vol. 1 of *Actes du 96e Congrès national des sociétés savantes (Toulouse, 1971).* Paris, 1978, pp. 325–58.

Malegam, J. Y., *The Sleep of Behemoth: Disputing Peace and Violence in Medieval Europe, 1000–1200.* Ithaca, NY and London, 2013.

Marca, P. de, *Histoire de Béarn,* 2 vols. Paris, 1640 [repr. 2000].

Mas-Latrie, R. de, 'Du droit de marque ou droit de représailles au moyen âge', *BEC* 27 (1866): 529–77; 29 (1868): 294–317.

Mathieu, I., *Les justices seigneuriales en Anjou et dans le Maine à la fin du moyen âge.* Rennes, 2011.

Mazon, A., *Essai historique sur le Vivarais pendant la Guerre de Cent Ans.* Tournon, 1890 [repr. 1992].

Medeiros, M.-T. de, *Jacques et chroniqueurs. Une étude comparée des récits contemporains relatant la Jacquerie de 1358* (Paris, 1979).

Michel, R., *L'administration royale dans la sénéchaussée de Beaucaire au temps de Saint Louis,* Mémoires et documents publiés par la société de l'École des chartes 9. Paris, 1910.

Miller, W. I., *Bloodtaking and Peacemaking: Feud, Law, and Society in Saga Iceland.* Chicago, 1990.

Mirot, L., *Les insurrections urbaines au début du règne de Charles VI (1380–1383), leurs causes, leurs conséquences.* Paris, 1905.

Miskimin, A., 'The Last Act of Charles V: the Background of the Revolts of 1382', *Speculum* 38 (1963): 433–42.

Mollat, M. and P. Wolff, *The Popular Revolutions of the Late Middle Ages,* trans. A. L. Lytton-Selis, The Great Revolutions Series 6. London, 1973.

Monicat, J., *Les grandes compagnies en Velay, 1358–1392,* 2nd edn, Publications de la Société des études locales dans l'enseignement public, Section de la Haute-Loire 8. Paris, 1928.

Mousnier, M., *La Gascogne toulousaine aux XIIe–XIIIe siècles: une dynamique sociale et spatiale,* Tempus. Toulouse, 1997.

Bibliography

Mundy, J. H., *Society and Government at Toulouse in the Age of the Cathars*, Studies and Texts 129. Toronto, 1997.

Studies in the Ecclesiastical and Social History of Toulouse in the Age of the Cathars, Church, Faith, and Culture in the Medieval West. Aldershot, 2006.

Naegle, G., 'Bien commun et chose publique: Traités et procès à la fin du moyen âge', *Histoire et archives* 19 (2006): 87–111.

Nelson, J. L., 'Violence in the Carolingian World and the Ritualization of Ninth-Century Warfare', in *Violence and Society in the Early Medieval West*, ed. G. Halsall. Woodbridge, 1998, pp. 90–107.

Netterstrøm, J. B., 'Introduction: the Study of Feud in Medieval and Early Modern History', in *Feud in Medieval and Early Modern Europe*, ed. J. B. Netterstrøm and B. Poulsen. Aarhus, 2007, pp. 9–67.

Nortier, M., 'Le sort des archives dispersées de la Chambre des comptes de Paris', *BEC* 123 (1965): 460–537.

Offenstadt, N., *Faire la paix au moyen âge: Discours et gestes de paix pendant la Guerre de Cent Ans*. Paris, 2007.

Oman, C., *A History of the Art of War in the Middle Ages*, 2 vols. London, 1924.

Pailhès, C., *Le comté de Foix, un pays et des hommes: Regards sur un comté pyrénéen au moyen âge*. Cahors, 2006.

Parker, D., 'Sovereignty, Absolutism, and the Function of the Law in Seventeenth-Century France', *Past & Present* 122 (1989): 36–74.

Patchovsky, A., 'Fehde im Recht: Eine Problemskizze', in *Recht und Reich im Zeitalter der Reformation. Festschrift für Horst Rabe*, ed. C. Roll. Frankfurt am Main, 1996, pp. 145–78.

Paxton, F. S., 'History, Historians, and the Peace of God', in *The Peace of God: Social Violence and Religious Response in France around the Year 1000*, ed. T. Head and R. Landes. Ithaca, NY, 1992. pp. 21–40.

Payling, S. J., 'Murder, Motive, and Punishment in Fifteenth-Century England: Two Gentry Case Studies', *EHR* 113 (1998): 1–17.

Pegues, F. J., *The Lawyers of the Last Capetians*. Princeton, 1962.

Perrot, E., *Les cas royaux: Origine et développement de la théorie aux XIIIe et XIVe siècles*. Paris, 1910 [repr. 1975].

Perroy, E., *The Hundred Years War*, trans. W. B. Wells. London, 1951.

Phalip, B., *Seigneurs et bâtisseurs. Le château et l'habitat seigneurial en Haute-Auvergne et Brivadois entre le XIe et le XVe siècles*, Publications de l'Institut d'études du Massif central, Collection Prestige 3. Clermont-Ferrand, 1993.

Pollack-Lagushenko, T., 'The Armagnac Faction: New Patterns of Political Violence in Late Medieval France', Ph.D. thesis, The Johns Hopkins University, 2003.

Potter, J. M., 'The Development and Significance of the Salic Law of the French', *EHR* 52 (1937): 235–53.

Powell, E., 'The Settlement of Disputes by Arbitration in Fifteenth-Century England', *Law and History Review* 2 (1984): 21–43.

Prat, G., 'Albi et la peste noire', *Annales du Midi* 64 (1952): 15–25.

Reinle, C., *Bauernfehden. Studien zur Fehdeführung Nichtadliger im spätmittelalterlichen römisch-deutschen Reich, besonders in den bayerischen Herzogtümern*, Vierteljahrschrift für Sozial- und Wirtschaftsgeschichte 170. Stuttgart, 2003.

Bibliography

Reyerson, K. L., *The Art of the Deal: Intermediaries of Trade in Medieval Montpellier*, The Medieval Mediterranean 37. Leiden, 2002.

Richard, J., *Saint Louis: Roi d'une France féodale, soutien de la Terre sainte*. Paris, 1983.

Riches, T., 'The Peace of God, the "Weakness" of Robert the Pious, and the Struggle for the German Throne', *Early Medieval Europe* 18 (2010): 202–22.

Rigaudière, A., *Penser et construire l'état dans la France du moyen âge (XIIIe–XVe siècle)*. Paris, 2003.

Rogers, C. J., 'The Military Revolutions of the Hundred Years' War', *Journal of Military History* 57 (1993): 241–78.

War Cruel and Sharp: English Strategy under Edward III, 1327–1360, Warfare in History. Woodbridge, 2000.

Rogozinski, J., *Power, Caste, and Law: Social Conflict in Fourteenth-Century Montpellier*, Medieval Academy Books 91. Cambridge, MA, 1982.

Rossignol, E.-A., *Monographies communales; ou, Étude statistique, historique et monumentale du département du Tarn*, 4 vols. Toulouse, 1864–6.

Russell, F. H., *The Just War in the Middle Ages*, Cambridge Studies in Medieval Life and Thought, 3rd ser., 8. Cambridge, 1975.

Sanders, I. J., 'The Texts of the Peace of Paris, 1259', *EHR* 66 (1951): 81–97.

Sassier, Y., 'Louis VII et la pénétration de la paix royale en Nivernais et Auxerrois', *Bulletin de la Société des sciences historiques et naturelles de l'Yonne* 113 (1981): 53–72.

'Les progrès de la paix et de la justice du roi sous le règne de Louis VII', in *Structures du pouvoir, royauté, et res publica (France, IX–XIIe siècle)*. Rouen, 2004, pp. 177–90.

Sauvel, T., 'Histoire du jugement motivé', *Revue du droit public et de la science politique* 71 (1955): 5–53.

Schneider, Z. A., *The King's Bench: Bailiwick Magistrates and Local Governance in Normandy, 1670–1740*, Changing Perspectives on Early Modern Europe. Rochester, NY, 2008.

Sheehan, J. J., 'The Problem of Sovereignty in European History', *AHR* 111 (2006): 1–15.

Shennan, J. H., *The Parlement of Paris*, rev. edn. Gloucester, 1998.

Sivéry, G., *Philippe III le Hardi*. Paris, 2003.

Smail, D. L., *The Consumption of Justice: Emotions, Publicity, and Legal Culture in Marseille, 1264–1423*, Conjunctions of Power and Religion in the Medieval Past. Ithaca, NY, 2003.

'Hatred as a Social Institution in Late Medieval Society', *Speculum* 76 (2001): 90–126.

Small, G., *Late Medieval France*, European History in Perspective. Basingstoke, 2009.

Solon, P., 'Private War and the Renaissance Monarchy: Case Studies from Southwestern France', unpublished paper.

Soman, A., 'Deviance and Criminal Justice in Western Europe, 1300–1800: an Essay in Structure', *Criminal Justice History* 1 (1980): 3–28.

'La justice criminelle: vitrine de la monarchie française', *BEC* 153 (1995): 291–304.

Strayer, J. R., *The Albigensian Crusades*. New York, 1971 [repr. 1992].

Les gens de justice du Languedoc sous Philippe le Bel, Cahiers de l'Association Marc Bloch de Toulouse, Études d'Histoire méridionale 5. Toulouse, 1970.

Medieval Statecraft and the Perspectives of History. Princeton, 1971.

On the Medieval Origins of the Modern State. Princeton, 1970.

Bibliography

The Reign of Philip the Fair. Princeton, 1980.

'Viscounts and Viguiers under Philip the Fair', *Speculum* 38 (1963): 242–55.

Sumption, J., *The Albigensian Crusade*. London, 1999.

The Hundred Years War, 3 vols. to date, The Middle Ages Series. Philadelphia, 1990–2009.

Takayama, H., 'The Local Administrative System of France under Philip IV (1285–1314) – *Baillis* and Seneschals', *Journal of Medieval History* 21 (1995): 167–93.

Taylor, C., 'The Salic Law and the Valois Succession to the French Crown', *French History* 15 (2001): 358–77.

Terharn, C., *Die Herforder Fehden im späten Mittelalter: Ein Beitrag zum Fehderecht*, Quellen und Forschungen zur Strafrechtsgeschichte 6. Berlin, 1994.

Texier, P., 'La rémission au XIVème siècle: significations et fonctions', in *La faute, la répression et le pardon*, vol. 1 of *Actes du 107ème Congrès national des sociétés savantes (Brest, 1982)*. Paris, 1984, pp. 193–205.

Timbal, P.-C., *Un conflit d'annexion au moyen âge: l'application de la coutume de Paris au pays d'Albigeois*, Bibliothèque méridionale, 2nd ser., 33. Toulouse and Paris, 1949.

Toulet, M., 'L'incrimination de port d'armes au bas moyen-âge', *Mémoires de la Société pour l'histoire du droit et des institutions des anciens pays bourguignons, comtois, et romands* 45 (1988): 435–48.

Tucoo-Chala, P., *Gaston Fébus et la vicomté de Béarn (1343–1391)*. Bordeaux, 1959.

La vicomté de Béarn et le problème de sa souveraineté, des origines à 1620. Bordeaux, 1961.

Ullmann, W., *Principles of Government and Politics in the Middle Ages*. New York, 1961.

Vale, M., *The Angevin Legacy and the Hundred Years War, 1250–1340*. Oxford, 1990.

'Seigneurial Fortification and Private War in Later Medieval Gascony', in *Gentry and Lesser Nobility in Late Medieval Europe*, ed. M. Jones. Gloucester, 1986, pp. 133–48.

Vaughan, R., *Philip the Bold: the Formation of the Burgundian State*, new edn, The Dukes of Burgundy. Woodbridge, 2002.

Venturini, A. 'La guerre de l'Union d'Aix (1383–1388)', in *1388, la dédition de Nice à la Savoie: Actes du colloque international de Nice (septembre 1988)*, ed. R. Cleyet-Michaud *et al.*, Histoire ancienne et médiévale 22. Paris, 1990, pp. 35–141.

Verbruggen, J. F., *The Art of Warfare in Western Europe during the Middle Ages*, 2nd edn, trans. S. Willard and R. W. Southern, Warfare in History 3. Woodbridge, 1997.

The Battle of the Golden Spurs (Courtrai, 11 July 1302), ed. K. DeVries, trans. D. R. Ferguson, Warfare in History. Woodbridge, 2002.

Veydarier, R., 'Una guerra de layrons: l'occupation de la Provence par les compagnies de Raymonde Turenne (1393–1399)', in *Guerre et violence*, vol. I of *La guerre, la violence, et les gens au moyen âge, Actes du 119e Congrès national des sociétés historiques et scientifiques (Amiens, octobre 1994)*, ed. P. Contamine and O. Guyotjeannin. Paris, 1996, pp. 169–83.

Viader, R., *L'Andorre du IXe au XIVe siècle: Montagne, féodalité, et communautés*. Toulouse, 2003.

Vicaire, M.-H., '"L'affaire de paix et de foi" du Midi de la France (1203–15)', in *Paix de Dieu et guerre sainte en Languedoc au XIIIe siècle*, Cahiers de Fanjeaux 4. Toulouse, 1969, pp. 102–27.

Bibliography

von Elbe, J., 'The Evolution of the Concept of the Just War in International Law', *American Journal of International Law* 33 (1939): 655–88.

Wakefield, W. L., *Heresy, Crusade, and Inquisition in Southern France, 1100–1250*. Berkeley, 1974.

Wallace-Hadrill, J. M., 'The Bloodfeud of the Franks', in *The Long–Haired Kings and Other Studies in Frankish History*. New York, 1962, pp. 121–47.

'War and Peace in the Earlier Middle Ages: the Prothero Lecture', *Transactions of the Royal Historical Association*, 5th ser., 25 (1975): 157–74.

Watts, J., *The Making of Polities: Europe, 1300–1500*, Cambridge Medieval Textbooks. Cambridge, 2009.

Weber, M., *The Theory of Social and Economic Organization*, ed. and trans. A. M. Henderson, and T. Parsons. New York, 1947.

Wenk, K., *Philipp der Schöne von Frankreich, seine Persönlichkeit und das Urteil der Zeitgenossen*. Marburg, 1905.

White, S. D., 'Feuding and Peace-Making in the Touraine around the Year 1100', *Traditio* 42 (1986): 195–263.

'"Pactum . . . Legem Vincit et Amor Judicium": the Settlement of Disputes by Compromise in Eleventh-Century Western France', *American Journal of Legal History* 22 (1978): 281–308.

'The Politics of Anger', in *Anger's Past: the Social Uses of an Emotion in the Middle Ages*, ed. B. Rosenwein. Ithaca, NY, 1998, pp. 127–52.

Wieruszowski, H., *Vom Imperium zum Nationalem Königtum: Vergleichende Studien über die publizistischen Kämpfe Kaiser Friedrichs II. und König Philipps des Schönen mit der Kurie*. Beihefte der Historischen Zeitschrift 30. Munich and Berlin, 1933.

Wolfe, M., 'Siege Warfare and the Bonnes Villes of France during the Hundred Years War', in *The Medieval City under Siege*, ed. I. A. Corfis and M. Wolfe. Woodbridge, 1995, pp. 49–66.

Wolff, P., *Commerces et marchands de Toulouse (vers 1350–vers 1450)*. Paris, 1954.

Wood, C. T., 'The Mise of Amiens and Saint-Louis' Theory of Kingship', *French Historical Studies* 6 (1970): 300–10.

'Regnum Francie: a Problem in Capetian Administrative Usage', *Traditio* 23 (1967): 117–47.

Wright, N., *Knights and Peasants: the Hundred Years War in the French Countryside*, Warfare in History 4. Woodbridge, 1998.

'"Pillagers" and "Brigands" in the Hundred Years War', *Journal of Medieval History* 9 (1983): 15–24.

'*The Tree of Battles* of Honoré Bouvet and the Laws of War', in *War, Literature, and Politics in the Late Middle Ages*, ed. C. T. Allmand. Liverpool, 1976, pp. 12–31.

Zerner, M., 'Le *negotium pacis et fidei* ou l'affaire de paix et de foi, une désignation de la croisade albigeoise à revoir', in *Prêcher la paix et discipliner la société: Italie, France, Angleterre (xiiie–xve siècle)*, ed. R. M. Dessì, Collection d'études médiévales de Nice 5. Turnhout, 2005, pp. 63–102.

Zmora, H., *State and Nobility in Early Modern Germany: the Knightly Feud in Franconia, 1440–1567*, Cambridge Studies in Early Modern History. Cambridge, 1997.

INDEX

Index

Index

Made in United States
Orlando, FL
09 January 2022

13224426R00134